# THE
# AMERICAN INDIAN
## IN THE
## UNITED STATES

PERIOD 1850-1914

BY

WARREN K. MOOREHEAD, A.M.,

AUTHOR, "THE STONE AGE IN NORTH AMERICA," CURATOR
OF THE DEPARTMENT OF AMERICAN ARCHAEOLOGY,
PHILLIPS ACADEMY, ANDOVER, MASS.; MEMBER OF
THE UNITED STATES BOARD OF INDIAN
COMMISSIONERS; FELLOW, AMERICAN
ASSOCIATION FOR THE
ADVANCEMENT OF
SCIENCE, ETC.

THE PRESENT CONDITION OF THE AMERICAN INDIAN;
HIS POLITICAL HISTORY AND OTHER TOPICS

A PLEA FOR JUSTICE

1914
THE ANDOVER PRESS
ANDOVER, MASS.

Copyright 1914
Warren K. Moorehead

**RED CLOUD (MAKH-PIYA-LUTA)**
War Chief of all the Sioux

# TABLE OF CONTENTS

# TABLE OF CONTENTS

# LIST OF ILLUSTRATIONS

# INTRODUCTION

## ADDITIONAL COMMENTS

With some diffidence I present a history of the American Indian during the transition period.

Excepting two or three bulletins, and some public addresses, all my publications have dealt with archaeological subjects, and the Indian of the past.* A study of the Indian of this country, during recent years, seems to indicate that at no time in his history has he faced a more critical situation than that which confronts him today.

A helpful understanding of him and his needs is vastly more important than further scientific study.

In writing this book it has been difficult to select that which should be published. A wealth of material relating to the complex life of modern Indians and their affairs was offered. The comparisons between tribes of today and a century ago present an absorbing field for study. I have frequently with difficulty checked myself, as it was more easy and pleasant to speak of the past rather than of modern days.

It is comparatively simple to record existing Indian customs still surviving in out-of-the-way corners of the United States. But such do not represent the present cultural state of the Indian as a whole. As my book aimed at a correct perspective of the Indians today, the inclusion of such matter and the exclusion of the widespread Indian activities in other directions, might result in a distorted perspective — certainly the picture (while more pleasing) would not be true to life. It will be observed by readers, that while I have generally described the activities of modern Indians, that the real purpose of the book is to bring before the American public the acuteness of the Indian problem, and to suggest certain recommendations.

A perusal of the following chapters will acquaint readers with all the facts — how that the Indian has been hurried into citizenship. We have changed his entire life within the space of a few generations and forced upon him serious problems. In fact, we have brought about so stupendous a change in his life, that his very existence is threatened. As will be in-

---

* A bibliography of these will be found in "The Stone Age in North America."  Vol. II, pages 408-410.

dicated, much of the old life obtains in spite of all our civilizing influences. While this is true, the preponderance of evidence indicates that the greater majority of our Indians have passed into the transitional state. Whether they shall become upright, self-supporting, intelligent American citizens, depends upon our attitude rather than upon them.

Since we have brought about the extinction of tribal and communistic life among the Indians, absolute responsibility for the future of the Indian rests with us   In the olden days, under the general tribal life, the Indians were able to band together and protect themselves. Now that most of our reservations have been cut up, and the Indians placed upon individual farms, it is impossible for them to join in any movement for self-protection. They are now citizens, rather than members of a tribe. Hence, it is quite easy for unscrupulous white persons to take advantage of them. While we thought we were acting in the best interests of the Indian, what we really did, was to destroy natural barriers which formerly kept out the enemy.

One should not object to, or find fault with an established policy, unless one offered a constructive policy in the place of that which he sought to destroy. I have, therefore, pointed out in my Conclusions what, in my opinion, must be done would we save the Indian.

### Indian Art and Old Industries

The arts and industries of the Indians (barring a few exceptions) have been modified by contact with the Whites. As an illustration, the bead-work of the Ojibwa, Malecite, Penobscot, Iroquois and others is very different from the art of two centuries ago. Basketry still obtains, but except on the Pacific coast and in the Southwest, much of the textile work is influenced by European culture, and I have therefore omitted a consideration of Indian art in general.

In the chapter on the Navaho there was reference to the extensive blanket industry of that people. There is no danger of the blanket industry becoming extinct, although it may deteriorate because certain well-meaning, but misguided persons desire to superintend the Navaho art.

The basketry is threatened with extinction. The manufacture of beadwork, moccasins and Indian garments continues in various sections of the country, but has become modernized in design and manufacture. With the scarcity of deer, elk and buffalo, substitutes are now employed.

This is observed in so common an article as moccasins — which are far inferior to those in use fifty years ago.

When Honorable R. G. Valentine was Commissioner, I made a somewhat lengthy report on the possibilities of aboriginal art, or manufacture, as a commercial asset to the Indians. I recommended that the old basket and blanket weavers, and the few remaining Indians who are skilled in making bead designs, moccasins, and other articles, be encouraged in their native arts. I recommended to the Commissioner that he establish a Bureau of Arts and Industries somewhat different from that one maintained at the present time. That the older men and women should be encouraged to make their baskets and blankets as in olden days, and that these should be marketed through certain agencies and the profits accrue to the Indians. I took the position that it was useless to attempt to instruct young Indians in the arts of their parents. That these persons were properly instructed in the great Indian schools, but that the true expression of aboriginal art was found among the few, old, self-taught persons. Art cannot be superintended, and if we continue such a course we will destroy what remains and have in its place that which is the opposite of true art. Our attempt to "teach" the Indians music ended in failure.

The Indian Office should encourage the old art-workers to make their products in their own way with absolutely no supervision upon our part.

## A Prophecy Verified

Events have moved rapidly of late, and as the Introduction proofs come back from my publishers, the press dispatches from Washington announce the appointment of Honorable Gabe E. Parker as Commissioner to the Five Civilized Tribes in Oklahoma. Mr. Parker is one of the brightest of our educated Indians. Miss Barnard has just informed me that her successor in the Department of Charities and Corrections has been named. With these changes, Mr. Mott's remarkable prophecy of last February (*See p. 163*) is with one exception, completely verified.

# ACKNOWLEDGMENTS

There are many persons, and a number of governmental Departments, to whom I am especially indebted. When I began the preparation of this manuscript nearly a year ago, I explained to officials in the United States Indian Office, Department of Justice, Smithsonian Institution, Indian Rights Association, and other organizations that I intended to prepare a history of the Indian of the transition period. It was made clear that a history must contain both the good and the bad; that a mere description of school activities and progress in arts and industries, would result in confirming the public in the present erroneous, but widespread opinion, that all our Indians are properly cared for, protected, and really becoming self-supporting.

Great credit must be given to various officials and private citizens for their earnest cooperation. The subject was a delicate one for them to handle. Taking everything into consideration, I have clearly indicated that the present unsatisfactory condition of our Indians grew up through a gradual process of evolution. We must not select the administration of Mr. Morgan, or that of Messrs. Leupp and Valentine, or the present one, under Mr. Sells, and state —"It was under this regime that the Indian began to lose his property." Beginning fifty years ago, the evolution proceeded regularly, but irresistibly, until it terminated in the bureaucracy of present times. No particular administration, and no group of men are to blame.

Honorable Cato Sells, Commissioner of Indian Affairs, and Honorable E. B. Meritt, Assistant Commissioner, both instructed under-officials to afford me every possible courtesy in the preparation of this book, and I am greatly indebted to both of them.

To Mr. Rodman Wannamaker and Dr. Joseph K. Dixon, I express thanks for the permission to reproduce photogravure plates illustrating the Indian of fifty years ago. Messrs. Doubleday Page & Co., publishers of Dr. Dixon's book, "The Vanishing Race", were good enough to make the impressions.

Mr. George Wharton James and his publishers, A. C. McClurg & Co., permitted me to reproduce a fine, colored Navaho blanket and an illustration of a weaver, from "Indian Blankets and Their Makers". Mr.

J. Weston Allen of Boston also rendered me valuable assistance. The Carlisle School, Haskell Institute, and the United States Indian School, Chilocco, furnished information regarding their work, loaned me several plates and sent photographs. I have thanked the Superintendents in the list on this and the next page.

Mr. C. E. Kelsey of California; Mr. Grant Foreman of Oklahoma; Capt. G. W. Grayson of Oklahoma, and L. V. McWhorter of Washington, have my special thanks for contributing pages to this book. I also am indebted to Hon. F. H. Abbott, Secretary of the Board of Indian Commissioners, for information; Mr. M. K. Sniffen for Alaskan notes, and Miss Kate Barnard, Mr. M. L. Mott and H. C. Phillips for suggestions.

In addition to the above I am indebted to many other persons, all of whom contributed more or less information. The list of these follows:

Miss Caroline W. Andrus of Hampton, Va.; Mr. Marshall C. Allaben of New York City; Mr. Edgar A. Allen of Chilocco, Oklahoma; Mr. Benjamin W. Arnold of Albany, N. Y.; Hon. Edward E. Ayer of Chicago; Mr. S. L. Bacon; Mr. A. F. Beard of New York City; Dr. Carl B. Boyd; Major John R. Brennan of Pine Ridge, So. Dak.; Hon. John B. Brown of Muskogee, Okla.; Dr. Charles M. Buchanan of Tulalip, Wash.; Rev. Eugene Buechel, S. J.; Miss Gertrude A. Campbell; Mr. W. S. Campbell; Rev. Aaron B. Clark; Rev. John W. Clark of New York City; Hon. P. P. Claxton of Washington, D. C.; Miss Mary C. Collins; Mr. Charles E. Dagenett of Washington, D. C.; Mr. Ira C. Deaver; Rev. P. Flor Digman, S. J.; Dr. Fred Dillon; Rev. George D. Doyle; Dr. Charles A. Eastman of Amherst, Mass.; Mr. J. R. Eddy; Mr. F. E. Farrell; Mr. E. R. Forrest of Washington, Pa.; Hon. A. N. Frost of Lawrence, Mass.: Mrs. Bella McCallum Gibbons; Mr. H. V. Hailman; Hon. C. F. Hauke of Washington, D. C.; Rev. Aloysius Hermanutz, O. S. B.; Dr. F. W. Hodge of Washington, D. C.; Rev. Roman Homar, O.S.B.; Rev. Alexander Hood; Rev. Ebenezer Hotchkin; Major John R. Howard of White Earth, Minn.; Mr. Seth K. Humphrey of Boston; Mr. H. Huson of Oklahoma City, Okla.; Rev. Julius Jette, S. J., of Tanana, Alaska; Hon. Dana H. Kelsey of Muskogee, Okla.; Rev. William H. Ketcham; Rev. Bruce Kinney, D. D., of Topeka, Kan.; Mr. Wm. C. Kohlenberg; Mr. J. T. Lafferty of Winfield, Kas.; Dr. A. D. Lake; Rev. Simon Lampel, O. S. B.; Hon. Franklin K. Lane of Washington, D. C.; Hon. E. B. Linnen of Washington, D. C.; Mr. G. Elmer E. Lindquist of Lawrence, Kas.; Hon. O. H. Lipps of Washington, D. C.; Rt. Rev. Arthur S.

Lloyd, D. D., of New York City; Colonel J. S. Lockwood of Boston, Mass.; Mr. Charles F. Lummis of Los Angeles; Mr. Arthur E. McFatridge; Mr. David L. Maxwell; Mr. A. P. Miller; Mr. John M. Moore of Nashville, Tenn.; Rev. S. L. Morris, D. D., of Atlanta, Ga.; Rev. George de la Motte, S. J.; Dr. Joseph A. Murphy of Washington, D. C.; Rev. J. S. Murrow; Mr. A. F. Nicholson; Mr. A. S. Nichelson; Mr. E. C. O'Brien of Washington, D. C.; Mr. Arthur C. Parker of Albany, N. Y.; Mr. Henry W. Parker of Boston; Rev. Herman F. Parshall; Dr. Charles Peabody of Cambridge, Mass.; Mr. H. B. Peairs of Washington, D. C.; Mr. Charles E. Pierce of Flandreau, So. Dak.; Rev. W. A. Petzoldt; Rev. W. B. Pinkerton; Mr. J. Harvey Randall; Mr. G. W. Reed; Rev. John Robinson; Rev. Fridolin Schuster, O. F. M.; Rev. Simon Schwarz; Rev. Paul de Schweinitz of Bethlehem, Pa.; Mr. W. W. Scott; Mr. John H. Seger of Clinton, Okla.; Mr. Theodore Sharp; Miss Frances C. Sparhawk of Hyde Park, Mass.; Mr. Ernest Stecker; Rev. W. E. Stevenson; Rev. Bernard Strassmaier; Mr. Edward L. Swartzlander; The Editors of the *North American Review;* Miss Eliza W. Thackara; Mr. Frank A. Thackery of Sacaton, Ariz.; Mr. Harry H. Treat; Rev. Edward F. Van Waerbergh; Hon. George Vaux, Jr., of Philadelphia; Rev. Chrystom Vermyst, O. F. M.; Dr. W. W. Wallace of Farmington, N. M.; Rev. Anselm Weber, O. F. M.; Mr. William H. Weinland; Mr. M. M. Welch of Atlanta, Ga.; Rev. Charles L. White, D. D., of New York City; Mr. H. C. Wilson; Mr. John R. Wise of Lawrence, Kan.; Mr. E. M. Wistar of Philadelphia, Pa.; Rev. C. A. Woody, D. D.; Hon. J. George Wright of Muskogee, Okla.; Mr. Robert M. Wright of Dodge City, Kas.

## A GENERAL BIBLIOGRAPHY OMITTED

It is difficult, if not almost impossible, to compile a satisfactory bibliography relating to Indians and Indian affairs between the years 1850 and 1914. Aside from reports emanating from officials and Departments, the largest body of literature is that dealing with the ethnology of existing tribes. Under the term ethnology would be included several divisions of the science. Most of the ethnologic works, reports and papers fall within no specified dates. Hence, a paper may cover one or two centuries, or it might be confined to some aboriginal activity in modern times. To compile a bibliography restricted to governmental reports, books by individuals, addresses, special articles, etc., concerning the administration of Indian affairs, and omitting scientific books and papers, is unsatisfactory and quite incomplete. I therefore omitted a general bibliography, although I cite some 150 books, reports and addresses. To readers who may desire to pursue the subject further, I would suggest that in addition to the Handbook of American Indians, there are the publications of the Smithsonian Institution and Bureau of Ethnology, Washington. A large number of reports have been issued by these scientific institutions the past forty years, and they cover practically all activities of many of our Indian tribes. The American Anthropologist (1888-1914) will be found to contain valuable papers upon the language, folk-lore, religion, philology and general ethnology of modern tribes. The Handbook of American Indians contains a bibliography of more than forty-two pages in length.

Indian songs and music are presented in a large volume in a most attractive manner by Miss Nathalie Curtis. Basketry and blankets are described by Professor Mason and Mr. G. W. James. Dr. Charles A. Eastman's books of Indian life are excellent — and there are many others. These in addition to the Smithsonian, Bureau of Ethnology, Handbook, and Anthropologist cited, will afford readers an abundance of material.

## Corrections

After Chapters I–XXX had been printed, Commissioner Sells notified me that through a typographical error on page 27, the 600,000 acres of irrigable lands had become 6,000,000! It would be exceedingly gratifying could we claim that the Indians had under cultivation 6,000,000 acres, but as the sum total is but 600,000, I cite the correction.

On page 25, last paragraph, fourth line, "under the Chiefs of Divisions"; should be, "in the various Divisions".

Page 112, second paragraph from bottom, fifth line: "witnessed many of these dances", should be "witnessed many different dances".

Page 217. It was necessary to omit a special chapter devoted to agriculture for the reason that in various places in the book the industries of modern Indians were commented on at length. In Chapter XXXIII, Farming and Stock Raising, it was thought best to omit the bibliography. Therefore, the last sentence in the paragraph should read, "These cover, in a general way, all phases of education."

Page 247. Last paragraph. "John T. Shelton" should be, "William T. Shelton".

Page 252, center of page: Parquette, should be Paquette.

# CHAPTER I.  TWO POINTS OF VIEW

The American Indian may be regarded from two wide and divergent points of view; that of the scientist, and that of the humanitarian.  Under the former should be grouped all study of the Indian, past and present, falling under the general science of anthropology, and its various divisions and sub-divisions.  This includes the study of the Indian as a primitive man belonging to the Red Race, and different from all other races on the face of the earth.  This view comprises archaeology, physical anthropology, ethnology, folklore, religion, etc.

The second, under the general title of humanitarianism, includes all progress, education, missionary endeavor, and that which may be summed up under the title Civilization, or as the modernists have it, "Social Service."

After much thought, it occurs to me that we must view the Indian from these two and quite opposed angles — the scientific, the philanthropic.

The average man or woman is not interested in the Indian from the point of view of the scientist.  This is quite natural.  But, persons of intelligence are interested in the Indian as a strange and peculiar individual.  He appeals to their imagination.  The public has had presented to it during past years, great numbers of books, pamphlets and articles all dealing with the Indian, and most of them regard him from what is known as "the popular point of view."  Having read, or glanced through scores of these, it is my firm conviction that, after all, we have not properly understood the Indian.

The scientists have made him the subject of technical study, beginning with the generalities of two centuries ago and continuing down to the minutest of detail of modern investigations.  Through our records of wars, and our sensational articles, we have been given the impression that his days were spent in fighting, and his nights in war dances.  To the scientist he has appeared, not as a man, but as a bit of life to be dissected and preserved; or a specimen duly catalogued, described, and placed in an exhibition case.  To the average man or woman, influenced by sensational books, and degrading wild-west shows, and that modern invention, the motion picture, he presents a figure as unreal as it is unhuman.

The Indian of today, with few exceptions, having lost his aboriginal characteristics, the faith of his fathers and his whole life changed, is indeed, a fit subject for the educator, the philanthropist, and the social reformer.

Would one desire to understand this very peculiar race of red men, one should begin his study by observing the Indian of today. And his observation should cover the character, activities and condition of this Indian of modern times. He should regard him not merely through the cold, unsympathetic eyes of the scientist, who looks for survival of savage or primitive customs, but in a larger and broader sense. To begin with, everyone should realize that the survivors of the American race* are more in need today of protection and help than of scientific study. From a purely scientific point of view, the Indian has been pretty thoroughly studied the past fifty years. This statement of mine does not necessarily imply that there should be no technical study of the American Indian in these present days. But as between the work of the scientist and that of the humanitarian the Indian is vastly more in need of the latter than of the former.

In the belief that our studies of the American Indian have so progressed that one may now consider the race in its entirety, I have set myself the rather ambitious task of preparing a number of volumes treating of the American Indian of the present and past. After much deliberation it has occurred to me that the Indian of today should be first considered — hence this volume. At the outset, we find that generally speaking the Indian throughout the United States although maintaining much of his original speech, and in places some of his aboriginal characteristics, yet, as a whole, he is in the transition period.

Our native Americans are, and have been, a remarkable people. Their very manner of life, their striking and picturesque costumes, their peculiar color and their diversified languages seem to have challenged the attention of explorers, travelers, priests and scientists. It is to be doubted if there is another aboriginal race, on the face of the earth, concerning which more books, articles and reports have been published. In Europe, as well as in America, the Indian is celebrated in song and story, yet since the discovery of America his domination has gradually diminished, and the period of his greatest activity (since the advent of the white race) is very short lived compared with that of other tribes of men. From 1500 to 1700, he may be said to have controlled a sufficient extent of the United States and Canada, to dominate it. His power after the year 1700 rapidly diminished, and in 1800 we find that he did not control any large areas save west of the Mississippi and west of Lake Superior. Up to the year 1865, he dominated a large portion of the West, South West and North West. From 1880 down to the present time, his sun has rapidly declined and he

* We are Americans by adoption.   The real American race is the Indian.

**ARTHUR C. PARKER**

Iroquois.   State Archaeologist of  New York; Secretary Society
American Indians

may be said today to have passed out of the tribal estate, to have ceased to be a factor in national life as a separate race. He is rapidly becoming merged into our larger body of citizens, and while some thousands of Indians (perhaps 45,000) live and think in the past, the great majority of Indians, like the great majority of foreign immigrants, belong to the body politic.

So, we consider the majority in this study of the Indian, rather than the minority; leaving that fraction to the scientist.

If we are consistent in the statement that we shall begin with the present and work backward into the past, we must consider in this volume the activities and the life of the modern Indian, and the modern Indian being in the transition period presents us very little in the way of folklore and traditions. A careful study of the recent reports of ethnological investigators emphasizes this truth. The writers have invariably sought out the *older* Indians, for the very good reason that they knew much concerning the past. The greater number of Indians — the middle-aged and young, and the thousands of educated Indians — are not able to furnish material such as scientific investigators seek. A confirmation of my statement will be found in that excellent memoir, "Chippewa Music," by Miss Frances Densmore. This was published by the Bureau of Ethnology in 1913. In this worthy publication, denoting much research, Miss Densmore is dependent on the older people for her information. Even these older persons, as they appear in the photographs accompanying the book, are dressed in garments such as are worn by white persons. Many of these Indians (as in the case of other tribes) keep a few old war bonnets, buckskin coats, moccasins, leggings, embroidered belts, etc., with which they adorn themselves on state-occasions, but their natural dress today, is European in character. Not only in Miss Densmore's book but in the reports of other investigators in the United States, where a group of Indians are assembled, one observes more evidence of European than native American costumes. It is frequently (if not usually) necessary to ask the Indians to put on their tribal costumes, and sometimes they are compelled to borrow a garment here and there among their friends in order to make up properly. There naturally arises the pertinent question — are not modern Indians so saturated with civilization that their opinions of tribal customs of past decades should be accepted with due reserve? This important question should be considered by some one of our numerous writers on Indian topics.

The two maps presented opposite pages 25 and 35, will bring home to readers the tremendous shrinkage of Indian lands during the short space of thirty-five years.

The map, presented by Commissioner Sells in his report for 1913, as contrasted to the map of 1879, shows that the Indian reservations have been cut down to at least one-third. The population in the year 1881 will be found in small figures on each area given on the map. It will be seen by comparing the period of 1879 with 1913, that the Navaho have greatly increased, and also the tribes now living in Oklahoma (formerly Indian Territory). Others have either diminished, or show slight increases.

The increases are due to growth of the mixed-blood elements, to white men marrying Indian women.* The allotment plan, the accumulation of tribal funds, the increase in property values — all these factors

INDIAN HOME, ONONDAGA RESERVATION, NEW YORK

induced many persons to "get on the Indian rolls" and thus swell the numbers; while the pure-blood Navahos are increasing, I doubt if other tribes show growth — save in the mixed-blood element referred to above.

Certainly these two maps present us with facts for serious study. They indicate the rapidity with which the Red Race's property is being legislated away. Many reservations have been abolished, and the Indians allotted land in severalty. If the Indians held such lands as white men hold their farms, the whole Indian area today would be as large as formerly, even though reservation lines are abolished. Some do hold their

* Excepting the Navaho.

lands. But most of them sell, lease, or mortgage; the maps, after all, tell the sad truth, and the erasure of governmental lines usually means the blotting out of Indian titles.

TABLE 1.— INDIAN POPULATION OF THE UNITED STATES FROM 1850 TO 1913

| Year | Authority | |
|------|-----------|--------|
| 1850 | Report of H. R. Schoolcraft | 388,229 |
| 1853 | Report of United States Census, 1850 | 400,764 |
| 1855 | Report of Indian Office | 314,622 |
| 1857 | Report of H. R. Schoolcraft | 379,264 |
| 1860 | Report of Indian Office | 254,300 |
| 1865 | do | 294,574 |
| 1870 | Report of United States Census | 313,712 |
| 1875 | do | 305,068 |
| 1876 | do | 291,882 |
| 1877 | do | 276,540 |
| 1878 | do | 276,595 |
| 1879 | do | 278,628 |
| 1880 | do | 322,534 |
| 1881 | do | 328,258 |
| 1882 | Report of Indian Office | 326,039 |
| 1883 | do | 331,972 |
| 1884 | do | 330,776 |
| 1885 | do | 344,064 |
| 1886 | do | 334,735 |
| 1887 | do | 243,299 |
| 1888 | do | 246,036 |
| 1889 | do | 250,483 |
| 1890 | Report of United States Census | 248,253 |
| 1891 | Report of Indian Office | 246,834 |
| 1892 | do | 248,340 |
| 1893 | do | 249,366 |
| 1894 | do | 251,907 |
| 1895 | do | 248,340 |
| 1896 | do | 248,354 |
| 1897 | do | 248,813 |
| 1898 | do | 262,965 |
| 1899 | do | 267,905 |
| 1900 | do | 270,544 |
| 1901 | do | 269,388 |
| 1902 | do | 270,238 |
| 1903 | do | 263,233 |
| 1904 | do | 274,206 |
| 1905 | do | 284,079 |
| 1906 | do | 291,581 |
| 1907 | do | 298,472 |
| 1908 | do | 300,412 |
| 1909 | do | 300,545 |
| 1910 | do | 304,950 |
| 1911 | do | 322,715 |
| 1912 | do | 327,425 |
| 1913 | do | 330,639 |

TABLE 2.— INDIAN POPULATION OF THE UNITED STATES, EXCLUSIVE OF
ALASKA, JUNE 30, 1913

(Figures compiled from reports of Indian School superintendents, supplemented by information from 1910 census for localities in which no Indian Office representative is located.)

| | | |
|---|---:|---:|
| Grand total | | 330,639 |
| Five Civilized Tribes, including freedmen and intermarried whites | | 101,216 |
| By blood | 75,253 | |
| By Intermarriage | 2,582 | |
| Freedmen | 23,381 | |
| Exclusive of Five Civilized Tribes | | 229,423 |
| Grand total | | 330,639 |

INDIAN POPULATION BY STATES AND TERRITORIES, 1913

| State | Pop. | State | Pop. |
|---|---:|---|---:|
| Alabama | 909 | Montana | 11,331 |
| Arizona | 41,505 | Nebraska | 3,890 |
| Arkansas | 460 | Nevada | 7,756 |
| California | 16,513 | New Hampshire | 34 |
| Colorado | 870 | New Jersey | 168 |
| Connecticut | 152 | New York | 6,029 |
| Delaware | 5 | New Mexico | 21,725 |
| District of Columbia | 68 | North Carolina | 7,945 |
| Florida | 600 | North Dakota | 8,538 |
| Georgia | 95 | Ohio | 127 |
| Idaho | 4,089 | Oklahoma | 117,274* |
| Illinois | 188 | Oregon | 6,414 |
| Indiana | 279 | Rhode Island | 284 |
| Iowa | 365 | South Carolina | 20,555 |
| Kansas | 1,345 | South Dakota | 20,555 |
| Kentucky | 234 | Tennessee | 216 |
| Louisiana | 780 | Texas | 702 |
| Maine | 892 | Utah | 3,231 |
| Maryland | 55 | Vermont | 26 |
| Massachusetts | 688 | Virginia | 539 |
| Michigan | 7,512 | Washington | 11,335 |
| Minnesota | 11,338 | West Virginia | 36 |
| Mississippi | 1,253 | Wisconsin | 9,930 |
| Missouri | 313 | Wyoming | 1,715 |

It will be observed that between 1850 and 1887 there is wide difference of opinion as to the number of Indians. In 1886 there were 334,000 Indians, whereas in '87 the number is given as 243,000. This must be due to faulty enumeration, or to estimating rather than counting. The gradual increase from 1898 to 1913 is for the reason assigned, page 21.

In the table presented by Commissioner Sells it will be observed that the Indians have made some progress along various industrial directions.

* Includes 23,381 freedmen and 2,582 intermarried whites.

As he has grouped under a total valuation of $22,238,242, all the horses, cattle, hogs and sheep raised by the Indians, it is difficult to compare this table with those of 1879–1881. I present tables of those years prepared long ago by the Board of Indian Commissioners and published by them February 1st, 1882. It will be seen that the number of acres under cultivation are about the same thirty-two years ago as at the present time. In 1881 there were over 2,000,000 head of stock owned by Indians. The value of sheep would reduce an average of $10 per head, horses and cattle would raise it. Some horses might be worth as high as $50, most of them would average $15. Cattle would range from $15 to $25 per head at that time. Mules would be higher, while hogs might be averaged at $8 per head, and sheep, $2. We might strike an average of $10 per head, which would amount to $20,000,000. In view of the present increased value of livestock, the $22,000,000 worth of property and livestock at the present time cannot amount to more than 2,000,000 head. (*See page 29*)

I think the slight increase noted in the 1912 table is due to the progress of certain Indian tribes (notably the Navaho) and the increased money value per head of stock. It does not mean that the Indians own more "live" property today than they did in 1881.

All of this, it is understood, is no reflection on the Honorable Commissioner or his able assistants. It merely indicates that the Indians, as a body, have not progressed to the extent that we would desire.

| | Acreage agricultural lands cultivated by Indians | Crops Raised by Indians | | | | Stock Owned by Indians | | | |
| | | Hay Tons | Corn Bu. | Wheat Bu. | Oats and Barley Bu. | Horses | Cattle | Swine | Sheep |
|---|---|---|---|---|---|---|---|---|---|
| 1912 | 558,503 | 158,478 | 1,525,334 | 1,343,213 | 1,001,504 | *$22,238,242 | | | |
| 1904 | 365,469 | 405,629 | 949,815 | 750,788 | 1,246,460 | 295,466 | 297,611 | 40,898 | 792,620 |
| 1898 | 352,217 | 215,163 | 1,339,444 | 664,930 | 599,665 | 328,866 | 214,474 | 37,359 | 1,041,315 |

*Commissioner Sells gives in his 1912 report only the value of the stock owned, whereas in 1904 and 1898 the number is given.

## CHAPTER II—THE U. S. INDIAN OFFICE IN 1913

The Bureau of Indian Affairs was organized in 1824, and was under the War Department. On March 3, 1849, the Interior Department took over the management of the Indians. Since 1832, there have been 31 Commissioners of Indian Affairs. The longest tenure of office was that held by Honorable Wm. A. Jones.

The present Commissioner is Honorable Cato Sells of Texas, who took charge June 4, 1913. Mr. Sells has already inaugurated a new and progressive policy and his work is highly commended by every person having the welfare of the Indians at heart. (1) A splendid tribute has been paid him by M. K. Sniffen, Esq., Corresponding Secretary of the Indian Rights Association. Honorable Edgar B. Meritt, who has served faithfully for many years, is Assistant Commissioner.

There are in addition to these high officers, Second Assistant Commissioner, Honorable C. F. Hauke; and Honorable E. B. Linnen, Chief of the Inspection Service. I have always considered the Inspection Service the most important of all. It is therefore very satisfactory that we have as Chief of the Division, a man who has had twenty-five years' experience as Inspector and former Secret Service official. And right here, I wish to state that if the Inspection Service had been efficient in past years, the horrible scandals in Minnesota, Oklahoma and elsewhere never would have occurred.

There are Chiefs of Divisions in education, land and finance; Chief Supervisors of schools, health, industries, irrigation, forestry and construction. There are ten Supervisors and eight Special Agents serving under the Chiefs of Divisions. The roster of officers for this year contains the names of hundreds of conscientious and competent men and women scattered throughout the entire West and in Washington, whose sole purpose is to make of these Indians good American citizens. No one who has investigated the Indian situation as it presents itself today can do other than accord to all these persons the full meed of praise. They labor under great disadvantages. If they are radical, they call down upon their heads the wrath of those who covet Indian lands; if they are conservative, the officials of various benevolent organizations accuse them of aiding and abetting the grafters in their nefarious work. If a single mistake is made — though unintentional — it is pointed out by some disgruntled person living in the Indian country. The complications, the situation,

(1) Cato Sells—An Appreciation. Pamphlet; Philadelphia, 1914.

and the opposition which they are called upon to face might well cause many of their critics to timidly decline to exchange places with them.

I am entirely sincere in the above statement. Because it has been my unpleasant duty to point out needed reforms — not to use a stronger term — a few good people have imagined that I criticised the personnel of the Indian Service. That would be not only unkind, but also unjust, and in all that I have published, written or spoken, I have never thought to criticize any man or woman save those who were engaged in defrauding Indians.

As will be presented in the final chapter of this book, the Indian Office machinery is efficient, and the personnel competent. The only question — and it is a great question — is whether our manufactured product is what it should be. Our machines are perfect, but do we run them properly?

The Commissioner of Indian Affairs, Mr. Sells, issued a valuable report December 8, 1913. It covers the period from July 1, 1912, to June 30, 1913. In order that we may grasp the full significance of the work being done by the Indian Office, and the magnitude of the problems confronting us, it is necessary to present some statistics, taken from this report.

There are some 6,000 employees in the Indian Service, and 330,639 Indians. Among the Indians are included a great many mixed bloods and persons who have married Indian women. This swells the total, as I have pointed out on Page 21.

The property of these Indians is estimated by the Commissioner to be worth nearly $900,000,000. As competent observers in the State of Oklahoma claim the Indians have property there rising $500,000,000 in value, it is my candid opinion, after considering the Navaho, Crow, Sioux, Yakima, Apache and all other lands, minerals, timber, etc., in the United States, that the sum is probably nearer $1,200,000,000. There is also in the United States Treasury some $48,848,744 in cash.

There has been appropriated since the year 1881, and including the year 1914, this generous sum for the education, allotting, protection of Indians and the maintenance of the thousands of employees in the Indian Service, viz: — $263,623,004.01. This enormous sum properly and wisely expended from the year 1881 to the present time would have solved the Indian problem in the United States. But two great obstacles stood in the way — the politician in the East and the grafter in the West. The Honorable Commissioner cannot state in his report that it is due to these two influences that our Indian history is, beyond question, the darkest page in the general American history, but such a statement is absolutely correct.

Of these 330,000 Indians, 180,000 have received farms, or as the Indian Office calls them, allotments. 34,000,000 acres have been used for this purpose and there remain 39,000,000 acres. The Commissioner states that the timber held by Indians is worth $80,000,000.

Since 1876 the Government has spent $80,000,000 for schools and education, and there are now 223 Indian day schools on or near Indian communities; 76 boarding-schools on reservations and 35 non-reservation schools. There are 65,000 Indian children, and all go to school save 17,500 who are either defectives or unprovided for.

There are 25,000 Indians suffering from tuberculosis; yet there are but 300 beds in all the Indian hospitals. This is a condition that would not be tolerated outside of an Indian community in the United States, for twenty-four hours. Thirty-two per cent of the Indian deaths are due to pulmonary tuberculosis as against 12.02 per cent among the white people of the United States. 60,000 Indians suffer from trachoma. This eye disease was introduced by the lower class of European immigrants and it spread throughout nearly every Indian community.

"I find that the Indians have more than 6,000,000 acres of irrigable land, approximately 9,000,000 acres of other agricultural lands, more than 50,000,000 acres grazing lands, and that the Government has expended approximately $10,000,000 in connection with Indian irrigation projects.

"Many able-bodied Indians who have valuable lands are wholly or partially without seeds, teams, implements, and other equipment to utilize properly such lands. This is particularly true in several reservations where large sums of public or tribal funds have been used in constructing irrigation systems, and is in part the reason why such large areas of irrigable and other agricultural lands are not under cultivation.

"The valuable grazing lands of the Indians offer unusual opportunities for increasing the meat supply of the country, at the same time furnishing a profitable employment for the Indians as well as ulitizing their valuable grazing lands. During the last year the Indians cultivated less than 600,000 acres of their vast area of agricultural lands.

"It shall be my purpose to attempt to procure reimbursable appropriations so as to advance to the Indians needed agricultural equipment in order that they may make beneficial use of their resources and become self-supporting and progressive citizens. These reimbursable appropriations, if procured and properly used, will result in ultimately decreasing the gratuity appropriations for Indians."[*]

* Sells' Report, 1913.

Commissioner Sells very wisely emphasizes agricultural work, stock-raising and cooperation with the United States Department of Agriculture. He calls attention to the enormous number of lands leased by the Indians to white men, for agricultural purposes.

One of the most interesting and illuminating sections in the report is, to my mind, the table number 7: "General data for each Indian reservation, under what agency or school, tribes occupying or belonging to it, area not allotted or specially reserved, and authority for its establishment, to Nov. 3, 1913."

A study of this table indicates that tracts of these lands have been sold under various acts of Congress. The statements appear: "Open to settlement 1,449,268 acres" or, "1,061,500 acres were open to settlement." All this indicates that enormous tracts have been sold to settlers, or disposed of by the Government after the Indians had been allotted. This policy has been persistently carried on in the State of Oklahoma, although I have repeatedly urged not only the Commissioner of Indian Affairs, but also the Commissioner of the Five Civilized Tribes to conserve some of these lands. I have contended, also, that the Indians are not properly protected in their property rights, and many of them are becoming paupers; that large tracts of land should be reserved by the Government in order that each dispossessed or pauperized Indian should be entitled to a small home at some future time. The policy of disposing of enormous tracts of grazing and agricultural land is extremely short-sighted.

I have been told, when calling attention of Commissioner Wright, or the Indian Office, to the fact that some of these surplus lands should be conserved, that under the law, this cannot be done. The land is tribal property, or by act of Congress on such and such a date the lands were ordered sold. There is always authority for these sales, and no one can question it. But the policy continues, and to me appears very pernicious. Certain Indians on some of our reservations have either disposed of their holdings, or been swindled out of them. If none of the surplus lands are retained, there will be nothing available for these Indians, and they will soon become homeless paupers. We have an illustration of that in California. There we permitted the Indians to lose their property, or to be evicted. In recent years we have spent large sums of money purchasing tracts of irrigated land to provide homes for the very Indians we permitted to lose their homesteads. Certainly this is a very short-sighted and unbusiness-like policy.

The progress of the Indian the past year in arts and industries has been fairly satisfactory. Most of the Superintendents report increased industry on the part of their wards. The Commissioner presents nearly 200 pages of tabulated statistics covering progress and values. The Indians have not worked in the same proportion as have white people for various reasons. I shall set forth these in detail in a subsequent Chapter.

### RESULTS OF INDIAN LABOR

#### INDIANS EXCLUSIVE OF FIVE CIVILIZED TRIBES

|  | 1879 | 1880 | 1881 |
|---|---|---|---|
| Number of acres broken by Indians | 24,270 | 27,105 | 29,558 |
| Number of acres cultivated | 157,056 | 168,340 | 205,367 |
| Number of bushels of wheat raised | 328,637 | 408,812 | 451,479 |
| Number of bushels of corn raised | 643,286 | 604,103 | 517,642 |
| Number of bushels of oats and barley raised | 189,054 | 224,899 | 343,444 |
| Number of bushels of vegetables raised | 390,698 | 375,843 | 488,792 |
| Number of tons of hay cut | 48,333 | 75,745 | 76,763 |
| Number of horses owned | 199,732 | 211,981 | 188,402 |
| Number of cattle owned | 68,894 | 78,939 | 80,684 |
| Number of swine owned | 32,537 | 40,381 | 43,913 |
| Number of sheep owned | 863,525 | 864,216 | 977,017 |
| Number of houses occupied | 11,634 | 12,507 | 12,893 |
| Number of Indian houses built during the year | 1,211 | 1,639 | 1,409 |
| Number of Indian apprentices who have been learning trades | 185 | 358 | 436 |
| **FIVE CIVILIZED TRIBES** | | | |
| Number of acres cultivated | 273,000 | 314,396 | 348,000 |
| Number of bushels of wheat raised | 565,400 | 336,424 | 105,000 |
| Number of bushels of corn raised | 2,015,000 | 2,346,042 | 616,000 |
| Number of bushels of oats and barley raised | 200,000 | 124,568 | 74,300 |
| Number of bushels of vegetables raised | 336,700 | 595,000 | 305,000 |
| Number of tons of hay cut | 176,500 | 125,500 | 161,500 |
| Number of bales of cotton raised | 10,530 | 16,800 | |
| Number of horses owned | 45,500 | 51,453 | 64,600 |
| Number of mules owned | 5,500 | 5,138 | 6,150 |
| Number of cattle owned | 272,000 | 297,040 | 370,000 |
| Number of swine owned | 190,000 | 400,282 | 455,000 |
| Number of sheep owned | 32,400 | 34,034 | 33,400 |

At the conclusion of Chapters upon health, education, irrigation, etc., I have presented bibliographies. Readers will obtain a good idea of the progress made along various directions if they will consult some of the writers' reports, speeches, etc.

*The Red Man*, published at Carlisle Indian School; the *Chilocco School Journal*, and papers printed at Haskell, Pine Ridge, and Hampton all contain many practical articles upon arts and industries and kindred topics. For these journals the Indian Service officials frequently write articles, and in them speeches and addresses upon Indian topics by prominent men are often reproduced.

These journals are creditable publications and do much toward enlightening the boys and girls as to progress in other schools — thus acting as an incentive to further effort. It is unfortunate that the public at large is not familiar with them. Were they generally circulated, much ignorance of Indian education would disappear.

MODERN INDIAN HOUSE
Although on the Allegheny reservation, N. Y., this is the common type
of house occupied by better-class Indians in many States

## CHAPTER III.  THE INDIANS TODAY AND
## HON. E. E. AYER'S REPORT

We have seen in the preceding chapter that the Commissioner of Indian Affairs, his assistants, Supervisors, Inspectors and Special Agents stand at the head of a very great Bureau; and that under them are thousands of employees.  The diagram on the following page is an outline plan of the entire Indian Service, beginning with that great body, the Congress of the United States, and passing through its various ramifications down to the amalgamation of the educated, competent Indian into the body of American citizens.

This comprehensive table was published by Honorable F. E. Farrell, Superintendent of the Cheyenne and Arapaho Agency, in the school publication *The Carrier Pigeon*, in December, 1912.

We should first realize the tremendous difference between the Indians of 1850 and those of 1914.  A comparison of the Indian reservation map of 1879 and the map of 1913 will give readers some idea of the tremendous changes in Indian life in this country.  In the short space of fifty years, the entire West has been transformed from an Indian country to a white man's country.  The problem of these Indians is today, not so much an ethnologic study, as it is a citizenship and humanitarian problem.

Although there are a few scattered bands of Indians on the public domain (notably Papago and Navaho, and a few other bands) more than nine-tenths of these people are under direct Federal or State supervision.  As I have remarked elsewhere, a great many of the Navaho and certain other Indians still keep up tribal customs and continue in the faith of their ancestors, but for the greater part, the Indians are, and should be, considered a part of our body politic.  Before discussing some of the larger tribes, and certain phases of Indian history in the broad sense, we should review the Indian situation as it presents itself generally in the United States.

Beginning with the far East, we should glance at the thousand or more native Americans living in Maine and New Brunswick.

Several hundred Penobscot and Passamaquoddy Indians are located at Oldtown, Maine, and on the St. Croix River above Princeton, Maine. These are of superior intelligence, and all are self-supporting.  There is some drunkenness, but it is not prevalent, as among some of our western tribes.

DIAGRAM OF THE INDIAN SERVICE

| Congress of United States |
| Statutes, United States |
| The President |
| Secretary of Interior |
| Regulations, Indian Service |
| Commissioner of Indian Affairs / District Supervisors |

| Non-reservation Schools |
| Reservation Agencies |
| Agent, Superintendent |

| AGENCY OFFICE WORK | AGENCY FIELD WORK | BOARDING SCHOOL |
|---|---|---|
| Inheritance:<br>  Family history<br>  Hearings, reports, findings, etc.<br>Land Patents:<br>  Sales — P.<br>  Leasing<br>  Negotiations, bonds, rentals, reports, authorities, etc.<br>Individual Indian Money:<br>  Banking, bonds of bank, authorities, disbursements, reports, etc.<br>Industrial reports, statistics, agricultural fairs, etc.<br>Finance:<br>  Agency and School funds, apportionments, disbursements, reports, etc.<br>Purchases:<br>  Advertisements,<br>  Vouchers, etc.<br>Property:<br>Employees:<br>  Records, reports<br>Tribal Funds, Interest | Individual Indian Money:<br>  Purchases — Animals' feed, implements, buildings<br>Industries:<br>  Care of farm, stock, implements, methods, seed selection, meetings, etc.<br>Health and Sanitation:<br>  Care of home, premises, Matron, Farmer and Physician<br>Law and Order:<br>  Suppression liquor traffic, dances, peyote feasts, customs, care of minors, etc.<br>Forestry:<br>  Sale of timber, permits, fires, etc.<br>Irrigation:<br>Leasing:<br>  Negotiations, improvements, collection rentals, appraisement, etc.<br>Land:<br>  Sales, appraisements, allotments<br>Construction:<br>  Specifications, superintending construction, repairs, insuring | Education<br>Health<br>Academic and<br>  industrial training<br>Recreation<br>Religious and<br>  moral instruction<br>Employees — social<br>  relations<br>Property<br>Supplies<br>Outing system |
| | | Day School |
| | | Public School |
| | | Amalgamation |

The Indians are under the jurisdiction of the State of Maine. The Penobscots own all the islands in the Penobscot River between Oldtown and Millinockett. They are, for the most part, guides, farmers, carpenters, clerks and lumbermen. Many of them earn excellent wages — from $2 to $5 per day. I saw no evidences of poverty. The people are intelligent and of good character. Consumption is not common, and trachoma cases are rare.

The reason for the splendid condition of the Penobscot and Passamaquoddy Indians should not be lost upon our officials and Indian Committees in authority in Congress.

They have been surrounded by a high class of white people, and have been left alone to develop and progress. While they have been protected by the State of Maine, no discrimination has been made against them, as in the case of Indians in Oklahoma, Minnesota, California and elsewhere. They enjoy the same citizenship as is conferred upon Whites, and it does not consist of "paper promises," but is real and effective. Theirs is no story of dishonesty and disease.

The past summer, while on an archaeological expedition on the St. John River, I visited three villages occupied by Malecite Indians, in New Brunswick, Canada. All of them are well situated, one at the mouth of the Tobique River; another at Edmunston; and a third near Woodstock. While these Indians are poor, there is no general pauperism, and their general health is better than among the Indians I have visited in our United States (exclusive of Maine).

In one respect the plans followed by the Canadian officials are superior to ours, and evince more ability (or rather stability) in the handling of the Indians. Instead of allotting these Indians, giving them deeds to valuable property, permitting them to be swindled by unscrupulous white persons, and then spending years in profitless litigation, in an attempt to make grafters return property taken from the Indians, these Canadians have continued the reservation system under a modified form. The Indians own their tracts of land, as with us, but do not hold deeds, or trust patents to same, therefore the lands cannot be sold or mortgaged; thus the incentive to fraud is removed.

The Indians serve as farmers, guides, carpenters and fishermen. Most of them are Catholics, and there is a priest located at the Tobique village. He lives among them and encourages them in various arts.

The census gives a few Indians as residing in our eastern states, but they are white people in every way, save color.

To discover the next body of Indians exceeding more than three or four hundred, we must go down South where we find a few bands of Cherokees in Swain and Jackson Counties, North Carolina; and scattered throughout Tennessee, Georgia, and Alabama there are 1100 or 1200 residing on what was originally a part of the habitat of this great nation.

Some of the Iroquois still reside in western New York, notably in settlements not far from Buffalo. These Indians, as in the case of the North Carolina Cherokees, are chiefly mixed-bloods, have adopted our

GOVERNMENT SAWMILL, FT. BELKNAP RESERVATION, MONTANA

Lumber cut by Indians

customs, live in fairly comfortable houses and are in no need of Government supervision. Among the Iroquois of New York, the percentage of tuberculosis and other diseases was so low as to be practically nil. In one of the recent Government reports it is given as but a fraction over one per cent.

There has recently developed agitation seeking to break up their reservation. This is most unfortunate, as the tracts are small; the Indians are doing well and desire to be let alone. They deserve to remain in peaceful possession of their old-time homes.

All of the remaining Indians east of the Mississippi, and south of the Great Lakes need not enter into our discussion. Save for a noticeable Indian color in the case of some individuals, the bulk of them have ceased to be real Indians. The New York Iroquois, in recent times, have made creditable progress in arts, and have produced a number of prominent men and women. A large number of them serve in responsible positions and so far as they are concerned there is no Indian problem. We may, therefore, eliminate the eastern half of the United States, with the exception of Wisconsin, Michigan and Florida.

In Florida we have the descendants of the Seminoles, estimated at 600, and are an offshoot of the Creeks, or Muskokis. These still cling to their ancient homes in the Everglades, and have withstood all attempts to make of them either educated Indians or agency Indians. During Mr. Leupp's administration, he proposed to me that I go to Florida and spend a winter cultivating the friendship of these Indians and see if it were not possible to persuade them to send their children to school. I was unable to carry this mission into effect, but I understand that recently the Government sent a Special Agent there, who has compelled a number of the children to attend school. The draining of the Everglades is now well under way, and soon the hunting and fishing-grounds of these people will be very much restricted. They have always been self-supporting and they merit consideration, and should have our help. It is to be hoped that before the ditching of the Everglades is completed, these Indians will be properly provided for. This is a subject I would commend to the attention of the Federal authorities.

In Wisconsin we have quite a large number of Indians at the present time, located on reservations, or clustered about schools. These number 9,930, and Wisconsin ranks ninth in the entire country in point of Indian population. Wisconsin is the first State, on our inspection tour from the East to the West, wherein we find a large body of Indians still in the transition period. They belong to the following bands: — the Ojibwa (Chippewa), Menominee, Potawatomi, Oneida, Winnebago and a few others.

The Ojibwa are by far the most numerous, amounting to, approximately, two-thirds of the entire number. Whether all of these five tribes originally belonged in Wisconsin, is a question which may be deferred to the ethnologist. We are treating of the State in recent times, as I have previously remarked in this book. Therefore that great question — the origin of these Indians and their presence in the State of Wisconsin — is not our concern. They are here located at the present time, and, in general, are making fair progress.

Honorable Edward E. Ayer, of the Board of Indian Commissioners, last year, made an extended investigation of the timber problem confronting the Menominee Indians. Mr. Ayer has kindly furnished me with an advance copy of his report in order that I might present a synopsis. Seldom has an investigation been conducted under more auspicious circumstances. Mr. Ayer took with him a number of persons, including a practical lumberman of wide experience. As the Menominee problem is one concerned with timber, rather than land values, it was very important that the work be thoroughly done. Mr. Ayer covered the entire reservation in his report.

"The Menominee Indians originally occupied the greater part of the State of Wisconsin. They ranged from what is now the site of Milwaukee north along the west shores of Lake Michigan to Menominee, North Michigan, and west to the Wisconsin River and Black River. Along Green Bay and the Fox River Valley were their principal settlements, and on the shores of Green Bay they first met the white man, when Father Marquette, La Salle and the first French descended the Great Lakes from the Canada settlement on exploration voyages of early days. On the reservation at Keshena is now the successor of the first French Mission established by Marquette at Green Bay.

"A woods Indian, the Menominee was a striking figure, of generally six feet and over in height, a giant in strength. Few in numbers when compared with other great tribes, his bravery and fighting qualities enabled him to hold his own with surrounding tribes, Potawatomies on the south, Sauk and Fox and Winnebago on southwest, the great Dakota or Sioux natives to west and Chippewa on the shore of Superior to the north, and the Hurons to the east of them. Their word once given could be relied upon. The French, English and American nations, each in turn, made treaties with them and all were faithfully kept. The Menominee was a peaceful nation, seldom the aggressor, but mighty in wrath, once justified in taking the warpath. From early times these Indians have been the white man's friend. In our Civil War many soldiers were recruited from their band, and today here exists the only Indian G. A. R. Post in America.

Their pursuits are farming, lumbering and manufacture of lumber products. At Neopit is the seat of a large milling-plant industry, capitalized for one million dollars. It has a sawmill with an output of forty million feet yearly, a planing-mill of twenty million capacity and carries a stock on hand of forty million feet of lumber, also laths, shingles, etc. The town numbers about one thousand men, women and children, and here may be seen the advanced Indian living in his modern cottage surrounded with

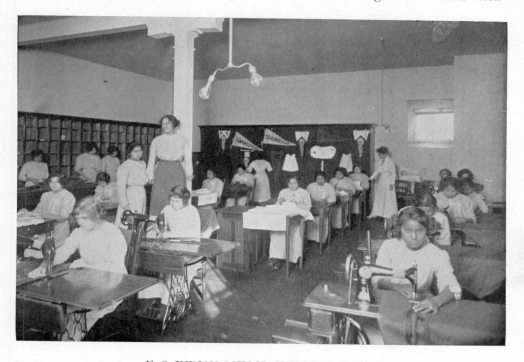

U. S. INDIAN SCHOOL CHILOCCO, OKLA.
A glimpse in one of the rooms of the Department of Domestic Art. Students making Uniforms and other dresses for school use

all the home comforts of modern life and partaking of the same social enjoyments as his white brother. A modern day school and a mission day school furnish education to his children, as does town life social instruction to his home, and the mill industrial education to himself and sons.

"At Keshena is the seat of the Agency, head of administrative affairs, and two large boarding-schools, Government and mission, with combined capacity for 300 children. Scattered out from Keshena for a radius of

**LEWIS TEWANIMA**

In the 10,000-meter run at the Olympic Games in Stockholm Tewanima
won second place. He is a full-blood Hopi Indian and is
considered America's greatest long-distant runner
Educated at Carlisle

**JAMES THORPE**

World's Champion All-Round Athlete, Winner of the Pentathlon and
the Decathlon, Stockholm, 1912
Educated at Carlisle

twelve miles is a scene of agricultural progress, Indian farmers whose efforts vary from farms of 5 to 80 acres, cleared, fenced and in various stages of improvement.

"The tribal funds on deposit in the Treasury of the United States are approximately $2,000,000, gathered from fruits of their own toil and in the sale of their timber products.

"The tribe numbers about 1700 souls. Statistics show about 575 able-bodied males, aged 18 years and over. Labor figures for the reserve show of this number an average of 264 adult Indians continuously employed the year round, earning in wages $91,630.47, not including subsistence. The greatest value of the Neopit operations is as a school of industry. Its value educationally, morally and civilly cannot be measured in dollars and cents."

Mr. Ayer found that the Government had erected a sawmill at Neopit. This mill sawed Indian timber exclusively.

Some years ago the mill's operations were not satisfactory, there being extravagance in management. Since Mr. Nicholson was appointed, all of this has been remedied, and after liberal deductions for all expenses, the mill shows a profit of $443,176.17 to the Menominee Indians (from July, 1910 to September 30, 1913). He found the mill employed a large number of Indian men, while other Indians found employment working with the logging crews in the woods. The mill served a double purpose. Not only were the Indians employed and earned good wages, but they also received the benefits of the mill's earnings.

There is practically no poverty on the reservation, and little sickness. The houses are clean and well kept.

Mr. Ayer's exhaustive study of conditions led him to make several recommendations, one or two of which I append herewith: —

"I recommend that two, four or six of the brightest young Indians on the Reservation be sent to Wisconsin State College of Agriculture at Madison to take a full course in forestry and scientific farming, that they may come back to the reservation equipped to teach the Indians who have elected to make farms.

"I would also recommend that there be a company or tribal store at Neopit and a branch one at Keshena and that the goods shall be sold say on a basis of 12½ or 15 per cent, which would make the stores absolutely self-sustaining and the Indians would get the necessities of life much cheaper. These stores should also carry a stock of the ordinary agricultural tools that might be used and there should also be a bank, say with forty or fifty thousand dollars capital connected with the Neopit store, where the employees of the mill could get checks cashed.

"Now, if they want to buy anything extraordinary, an agricultural tool or any other thing, or cash their check, they have got to go twenty miles away to Shawano for the purpose, and they are subjected to all the temptations of the outside towns. I think everything ought to be supplied to the Indians on the reservation so that they would have as little necessity of leaving it as possible."

A complaint had gained circulation to the effect that the mill was losing money and had been extravagantly managed. There were some grounds for this five years ago, but not during the past three years. A certain attorney, wishing to take over the management of tribal affairs, visited the Indians and, calling their attention to a few logs here and there, which had not been properly handled, persuaded the Indians to raise a sum of money to pay his expenses to Washington. Here he made complaints to the Commissioner and others. His presence on the reservation caused dissatisfaction. Ayer's investigation proved that the loss was nothing compared with the great financial benefits accruing to the Indians, through the mill's operation.

I mention this at some length for the reason that Mr. Ayer's report was unjustly criticised by one or two persons who lent willing ears to the self-seeking attorney.

His report covers all questions relating to farming, education, health, and the sale of timber to better advantage. The mill is a model of efficiency, conserves the Indians' timber to the tribe's best interest, and similar mills should be conducted on other reservations.

The amount of timber remaining to be cut is variously estimated at from 1,500,000,000 to 2,000,000,000 feet. It will thus be observed that the Menominee Indians are possessed of a very valuable property. The authorities should heed Mr. Ayer's suggestions, coming as they do, from a practical timber man of many years' experience.

The greatest tracts of timber (aside from Menominee) are on Chippewa lands at Bad River and La Pointe. Some are exceedingly valuable. I addressed the Department and received assurance that the Commissioner was aware of the dangers of a "second White Earth." The following official communication (in part) is evidence that these Indians will be protected: —

"Under the treaty of September 30, 1854 (10 Stats. L., 1109), 1063 Indians within the La Pointe or Bad River Reservation, Wisconsin, have been allotted a total area of 8,387,068 acres. Approximately 45,000 acres of surplus tribal land remain, authority for the allotment of which exists in the Act of February 11, 1901 (31 Stats. L., 766), as amended by the Act of March 2, 1907 (34 Stats. L., 1217). Nothing is said in these acts about the allotment of timber lands and the remaining tribal lands within this reservation are very valuable for timber purposes, some of the eighty-acre tracts being estimated to yield approximately $30,000 for the timber alone. Other tracts containing but little timber are not desirable and an equitable division of the lands in allotment cannot be made under existing conditions.

"Two factions exist in the tribe, one in favor of allotting under existing laws and the other in favor of selling the timber, distributing the proceeds per capita and thereafter allotting the lands to the unallotted Indians belonging on this reservation.

"Appended hereto is the part of the Office file relating to this allotment correspondence, particularly the submission to the Department of the request for authority to procure agreements from the Indians to allot the lands under the existing laws with the understanding that the timber should be cut and sold for the benefit of the tribe at large." (File omitted in this book.)

For several years there have been extensive cuttings of pine timber on the reservations at Bad River, Lac du Flambeau, Lac Courte Oreille, and Fond du Lac. The total amount cut on each of these reservations was as follows: Bad River, 57,183,770 feet; Lac du Flambeau, 23,049,110 feet; Lac Courte Oreille, 4,268,050 feet; Fond du Lac, 13,128,775 feet. All of this timber was cut on allotments except 12,068,620 feet cut from unpatented lands of the Lac du Flambeau Reservation, claimed by the State of Wisconsin as swamp lands, and 56,955 feet cut from tribal lands of the Bad River Reservation.

A number of circular letters were addressed by me to persons living in Wisconsin, requesting information as to the condition of the Indians. It is known that not only is there vocational training in the schools, but also more or less higher educational training. One of my correspondents, a missionary, takes the view that there has been too much higher education of Indian children in his State, and it would be far better to confine the work to the teaching of trades and give no book instruction beyond the fundamentals. He thinks that the average Indian when educated beyond this point, is not willing to take his place as an ordinary workman. Another gentleman, while expressing satisfaction with much that has been done, sums up the situation in the particular Indian community in which he resides as follows: "Too much red tape."

The progress of these Indians while slow, is satisfactory. They do not present a sufficiently interesting problem for our study at the present time. It is safe to predict that within a generation, a full-blood Indian in Wisconsin will be a rarity. They may continue to live an indefinite length of time in various communities where they are now settled, but Government supervision (save possibly on the Menominee reservation) may be safely withdrawn in the near future.

In Michigan the larger number of Indians are Chippewa (Ojibwa), with a sprinkling of Ottawa and Potawatomi. Schools care for a majority of their children, and the adults are, for the most part, quite self-supporting. They may be dismissed from our pages.

Proceeding westward to the headquarters of the Mississippi, we have the great Minnesota region which is generally covered in my four chapters upon White Earth reservation. West of the Mississippi River, there are very few Indians in that great area of Texas (but 702), and in Iowa, Missouri, Arkansas and Louisiana; the numbers range from 313 to 780. These areas may be set aside as containing such a preponderance of white population as to render those of Indian blood an extreme minority. Of the mountain states, Colorado contains but 870 Indians, Wyoming 1715, and the others 4,000 to 11,000. The great Indian populations are, therefore, confined to nine states. Ten states contain from 800 to 8,000. The remaining twenty-nine contain but a fraction of the entire Indian body, and they are now more white than Indian.

Texas, in spite of its enormous size, is interesting in that but a handful of Indians are in evidence. In 1850 the Indian population was considerable. Nelson Lee's book of captivity among the Comanches(1) gives an idea of the extent of the roving bands of Comanches and Apaches infesting the State in early days. The hostility of the Texas people was such that through the organization of the famous Texas Rangers those Indians were either driven out of the State or exterminated. Very little consideration was shown them, and I can find no evidence of any general effort being put forward to protect these Indians in their rights or place them upon reservations or establish schools among them. Our troops were frequently sent into Texas, and as late as 1875, roving bands of Indians infested the western part of the State and carried on raids into old Mexico, or stole stock from Texas ranches. As to the number of Indians in the State of Texas just prior to the Civil War, there seems to be no reliable statistics.

The Texas tribes were of the general Caddoan stock, of which the Comanche appear to have been the largest and strongest branch. These

(1)  Three Years Among the Comanches; Albany, 1859.

Indians ranged through the valleys of the Brazos and Colorado and extended their conquests to the land of the Apache, along the Rio Grande, to the west. They were essentially buffalo Indians and were not agriculturalists, but presented the purest nomadic type found in the southwest. This must not be misunderstood. The Navaho are nomadic to a certain extent, but their range has been limited. Moreover they possess flocks and herds. There is no evidence that the Comanche ever domesticated sheep, goats, and cattle, although they frequently obtained stock in their raids against the Texans. As they were continually on the move following the buffalo in its migrations, or planning war parties against the white people and Mexicans alike, they were pure nomads, as stated above.

Years ago, during the height of Indian troubles in Texas, a law was passed expelling red men from that State. Indians entering the State were subjected to fine, imprisonment or expulsion. The feeling against the race was very bitter, and Indians in Texas never received just treatment.

A few of them were, in later years, taken to Indian Territory, but most of the Comanches, it is safe to affirm, were killed in action. Although the Texas rangers were superiorly armed and better mounted, the Apaches continued their warfare from the earliest times down to about 1870, when their power was permanently broken. They were very cruel and vindictive. Nelson Lee's narrative, to which I have referred, is one of the most interesting Indian captivities ever brought to my attention. It presents a vivid picture of the Comanche as they were during the period preceding our war with Mexico.

# CHAPTER IV.   THE OJIBWA OF MINNESOTA

The Ojibwa commonly known as Chippewa, constitute one of the great divisions of the Algonkin stock.   We shall have much to say concerning their ethnology, in a subsequent volume.   But following the scope accepted for this book, we shall treat of the Ojibwa as one of the great Indian tribes (numerically), at the present time and one much "advanced" along the white man's trail.

The year 1850 found the Ojibwa, or Chippewa, Indians located as they are at the present time, with some exceptions.   A few in Wisconsin and on the shores of Lake Superior; some at Turtle Mountain in North Dakota, but most of them living in the State of Minnesota at Leech Lake, White Earth, Red Lake and Cass Lake.   The number of these Indians in the year 1851 was about 28,000.   In 1884 the entire number is given as 16,000.   In 1905,   the "Handbook of American Indians" estimates that there are 15,000 in British America and 17,144 in the United States.

Those who wish to trace the migrations, and study the interesting customs and folklore of these people would do well to consult an interesting book written by an Ojibwa, Mr. William W. Warren.   The manuscript of this work was prepared between 1850 and 1853.   Warren's mother was three-fourths Ojibwa and his father a white man.   He died of tuberculosis June 1, 1853, and the Minnesota Historical Society did not publish his history of the nation until 1885.   Clearly, Warren was the most prominent of later-day Ojibwa; he had served in the Minnesota Legislature, and he was possessed of a brilliant mind and would doubtless have made his mark in the world had he lived.

In the early '50's and '60's a few of the fur companies still did business in northern Minnesota.   It was no uncommon sight to see the "Red River ox carts" bringing supplies into northern Minnesota, or carrying loads of furs to the nearest Hudson Bay post, in the Red River valley to the north.   The Ojibwa came in contact with the French-Canadian element during the activities of the fur trade, and had little in common with, or met few Americans, until white settlers from the East increased in numbers in the State of Minnesota.

While this and the succeeding chapter are confined chiefly to White Earth, a description of Leech Lake and Red Lake reservations should not be omitted.

The Ojibwa Indians living on Red Lake have not been allotted, but hold their land in common.   The pine timber possessed by them is valued

HONORABLE GABE E. PARKER, CHOCTAW
Registrar of the United States Treasury

at several million dollars. Most of the cabins are grouped about the shores of Red Lake, and the Indians while not well-to-do, are far from pauperism. It has not been necessary to ration them as in the case of White Earth, where the Superintendent, Major John R. Howard, last winter fed 762 Indians. The reasons for this are set forth in succeeding pages.

The Ojibwa at Leech Lake have valuable white pine, but this has been cut under Government supervision and the dreadful scandals occurring at White Earth have been avoided. At Leech Lake, Red Lake, and Cass Lake, the Indians live by working in the lumber camps, agriculture, fishing, and some serve in other branches of industry. They have, however, depended entirely too much upon interest payments made by the Government. Much of the educating, training and support of these Indians is paid for by the interest accruing to the Indian on a fund of several million dollars in the United States Treasury and belonging to the Ojibwa of Minnesota. It has been pointed out by other observers, and emphasized in addresses at Lake Mohonk and elsewhere, that this fund is a curse rather than a blessing. The mixed-blood element, controlled by a few shrewd French-Canadians, wish to secure possession of it; attorneys are attracted by its presence; the young men and women, in some cases, will not work since they expect to be supported out of the fund. It should be divided up per capita among the Indians. The Government should control, or supervise, the portions belonging to Indians known to be incompetent or drunkards, and instead of paying them money, give them groceries and clothing until their portion of the fund is exhausted. Councils should be called on all reservations, or at central points, on allotment groups, and the Indians made to understand that with the payment of this money, responsibility on the part of the United States ceases,— excepting in the case of incompetents, referred to above.

With the dreadful lesson of White Earth, staring everyone in the face, it is incomprehensible that Red Lake should be allotted, and the timber issued to the Indians. Yet there was a determined effort to bring about such a result, and it was only through opposition of the Indian Office, and Inspector E. B. Linnen and others that the steal was prevented.

The Indians live in frame and log dwellings. The birch-bark wigwam is rare — save for summer residence. Ordinary "store clothes" are worn by all persons. The birch-bark canoe still persists, and there are some survivals of ancient customs. Such a majority of the people speak English and live like the lower classes of Caucasians, that the bands may be considered less Indian than the Sioux, and much less primitive than the Navaho. The photographs prove this statement.

Let us look backward and compare conditions of the '80's and of 1905-'12.

Rev. Joseph A. Gilfillan was a missionary in northern Minnesota for twenty-five years. He became entirely familiar with the Ojibwa language and spoke it fluently. He is a quiet, modest man. The Indians told me of numbers of heroic actions on his part during the twenty-five years he labored in and about White Earth reservation. During the spring of one year, when the ice on the lake was breaking up, two white men were

BUILDINGS PINE POINT, WHITE EARTH, MINNESOTA
Built and formerly occupied by Rev. James Gilfillan as a school. Now used as Government School

in a most perilous situation, and although there were larger and stronger men standing about, no one would venture out to save the lives of the unfortunates. Gilfillan went out — although he frequently broke through the ice — and managed to bring both men ashore.

On another occasion, he was held up by several armed men, sent out by the mixed-blood and French-Canadian element, who opposed his missionary labors. In fact, one of the men presented a gun and threatened to shoot him if he continued in his determination to preach to the Indians that Sunday. The above incidents (and more could be related) give an idea of the character of this worthy man.  He has never been engaged in any of the disputes regarding the deplorable situation among the Minnesota Ojibwa, and it required considerable urging on my part to persuade him to testify before the Congressional Investigation Committee of which Honorable James Graham was Chairman.

Rev. Gilfillan, largely at his own expense, built splendid schoolhouses, missions and chapels at Pine Point, White Earth and Twin Lakes. His mission was successful and he had at one time several hundred Indians in attendance in both school and church, and a corps of efficient workers. I think it is correct to state that there were more church members on White Earth reservation during Gilfillan's administration than at the present time.  Certainly the moral tone was far above that which obtains today.  It is sad to relate that Gilfillan's missions were discontinued, and the buildings where he devoted so many years of unselfish labor were taken over by the United States Government at far less than their actual value.

Rev. Gilfillan's statement made to me, and accepted by the Congressional Committee* and published in their report is as follows: —

WASHINGTON, D. C., DEC. 9, 1910

"Hon. Warren K. Moorehead,
     Andover, Mass.

"My dear Sir:  Your favor of 8th instant has just reached me, and it gives me pleasure to answer your inquiries.  The first is, 'While there was much suffering when you were missionary at White Earth, Pine Point, Twin Lakes, etc., is it not your opinion that there was less swindling than at the present time?'

"In answer I would say that I do not consider there was any suffering at all to speak of from June, 1873, when I went there, till along toward 1898, when I left.  The Indians raised garden produce; many had fine fields of wheat.  They could gather all the wild rice they wanted to; fish were abundant.  Some of the men made two or three hundred dollars by the muskrat hunt each spring.  They made a good deal by furs.  Some hunters killed as many as forty deer in a winter.  They made maple sugar. They had all the berries they could gather.  From all these varied sources they made a good living.  They had unlimited fuel at their doors.  They were rent free.  I have heard people say, and I believe it, that there was not nearly so much poverty or suffering as in a white city, where the poor

* Hearings before a subcommittee of the Committee on Expenditures in the Interior Department, House of Representatives.  House Resolutions, 103, March 6, 1912.

have only one resource — wages. If they had wished to raise a little more vegetables, as potatoes, corn, etc., they could have lived on the fat of the land. They were in those days happy, peaceful, and contented communities. To the above-enumerated sources of income of theirs I omitted to mention that there passed through my hands for them, given by the Episcopal mission, more than $130,000 in money for all imaginable purposes — from spectacles to building churches for them and supporting their children in schools. There were several thousand dollars' worth of clothing sent me for them by charitable people. There was no crime during the twenty-five years I was there, although for many years there was not even Indian police. There was no instance of holdup or robbery, not to speak of greater offenses. Life and property were absolutely safe — far safer than in any white community I know. None of them would ever have thought of molesting anyone. They were in those days happy, peaceful, harmless people. As to how the present state contrasts with that, you have been out there lately and know better than I.

"As to your second question, whether there was less swindling than at the present time, I would say that then there was none at all. The Indians had no lands to sell; no property of any kind except their little patches of gardens, their little furs, wild rice, etc. There was nothing to tempt the cupidity of the white man. As to how that contrasts with the present, you have been out there and know better than I.

"But I ought to qualify this by saying that for some years in the nineties there was a great deal of swindling from them unwittingly perpetrated by the Government, for an account of which I refer you to my inclosed printed statement made to Mohonk Conference in 1898, which you will find on Page 13 of the inclosed pamphlet. And that you may know that the statements made therein are true, I may inform you that the then Commissioner of Indian Affairs, Hon. William Jones, who went to the ground and personally investigated, endorsed upon that statement: 'I find that the statements herein made by Mr. Gilfillan are in the main correct.' This indorsement does not appear on the copy I send you, but is on other copies. To briefly specify the heads under which this swindling was done: it was; First, by billeting upon them three Chippewa commissioners at $39 a day for the three, making with their clerks, etc., $88 a day, the Indians said; said commissioners being mostly politicians out of a job, and their positions almost sinecures. Secondly, by repeated farcial 'estimating' of their pine; three several 'estimations' (pretended), covering a period of perhaps nine years; two of said estimations costing $360,000, and then done dishonestly in the interests of those who bought the pine, whereas the real worth of the work, done honestly, was only $6,000. Thirdly, by cutting green pine, but paying for it as 'dead and down' pine, so getting for it seventy-five cents a thousand instead of five dollars a thousand. But most destructive of all was the swindling done by fire; the timber being fired to allow of its being cut as 'dead and down' and paid for at seventy-five cents a thousand instead of five dollars. It was a pitiful sight to see those magnificent pine forests, where I used to ride for seventy miles on a stretch through great pine woods, shapely and tall, the trees reaching up, it seemed, 100 feet, that, like the buffalo, could never be replaced, now all blackened and scarred, killed and dead. The glory of the State of Minnesota was gone when in the nineties her magnificent pine forests that covered so large an area of her northern part were fired to get the Indians' pine for seventy-five cents a thousand.

"Now, as to your next question, whether there was more drinking among the Indians then than now. I am glad to say that for many years after 1873, when I first knew them, there was, one may say, no drinking among the Indians. The mixed-bloods, who were mostly French-Canadian mixed bloods, always drank a little, but the Indians were remarkably free from it. The White Earth Indians lived twenty-two miles from the railroad, the nearest place where they could get liquor; they were almost that distance from the nearest white men. The Red Lake Indians were one hundred miles from the railroad, the Cass Lake one hundred, the Leech Lake seventy miles. They were almost as far from any white men, except the Government employees and the missionaries. So they were secluded from the white man and his vices. But the great reason of their immunity was the missions. The influence of the Gospel and the church in their secluded position kept them safe. It is no reflection on the White Earth Indians to say that in the place from which they had been removed in 1868 — Crow Wing — they had fallen most dreadfully under the dominion of the 'firewater,' both men and women. They were in a most dreadful state of degradation from that cause. But never was the power of the Gospel more signally shown than in their cleansing and renovation on the White Earth reservation. I never saw a drunken Indian nor even one that I thought had tasted liquor. They had become communicants of the church, had their family prayers, their weekly prayer meetings from house to house, where they exhorted each other to steadfastness in the Christian life. What had such a people to do with liquor? Some of them, who at Crow Wing had been in the lowest depths, told me that they had not tasted liquor in twenty years, others for other periods; and I know they told the truth. Among all the chiefs, numbering perhaps

OJIBWA, BLIND, FROM TRACHOMA, PINE POINT,
WHITE EARTH RESERVATION, MINNESOTA

twenty, on White Earth Reservation, there was just one who drank, and he, I am informed, had the liquor supplied to him by a mixed-blood, who, in payment, got him to swing the Indians to his schemes.

"But into this fair garden of temperance Satan drew his shining trail and toward the last years of my residence there sadly marred it. It was found that much money could be made out of Indians drinking, and it soon grew up into a most profitable industry. It came about in this way: Congress, as everybody knows, passed a law that liquor should not be sold or given to Indians. A set of men arose who saw the money there was in that; they arrested Indians who had taken a drink, or as witnesses, took them to St. Paul or Duluth, fiddled with them a little, and then presented a bill of $400, I believe, to the Government for each Indian, which money was paid, and they divided it up among them. The Indians had all the whisky they wanted while under the care of these deputy marshals, as they were called; they kept drunk while with them, and they brought plenty of liquor home with them to the reservations when they returned. They did not want to stop the Indians drinking; they encouraged it; the more drinking the more cases and the more money for them. This was found so profitable that it grew to a monstrous height. Once they had, it was said, every adult male Indian on the White Earth Reservation in St. Paul in whisky cases, a distance of, say 240 miles, and for every one of these men they got perhaps $400. The most of the deputy marshals who made the arrests were French-Canadian mixed-bloods of the lowest character, nearly all of whom openly and frankly drank themselves, though in the eyes of the law Indians like the Indians they arrested; and a high official of the United States Government told the writer that one of those halfbreeds made $5,000 a year out of it, as much, perhaps, as the salaries of the members of the Cabinet of the United States Government. How many hundreds of thousands of dollars or how many millions they got out of the Government by this swindle under the form of law it would be interesting to know. Some of those mixed-bloods worked that gold mine for eighteen years. The loss of so much money to the Government was pitiful, but not half so pitiful as the terrible demoralization of the Indians by the operations of those men. Here again the good intentions of the Government in passing that law, that liquor must not be given or sold to Indians, was turned into death and destruction to them, and became most bitter gall in its carrying out by the agents of the Government to enrich themselves.

"So the answer to your question as to whether the Indians drank more then or now must be that in the early years after 1873, when there was just one honest white deputy marshal named Nichols, they drank practically none at all, most of them never tasting it for years; but that later, after the swarm of mixed-blood deputy marshals arose, there was much drinking under the manipulation of those men, restrained, however, by their very great lack of money, for at that time none of them had got any.

"As to your other question, namely, the relative healthfulness of the Indians then and now, I would say that there was always much tuberculosis among them, owing to their crowding into one-room cabins, heated very hot in the winter, without ventilation; and if there was one tubercular patient, that one was spitting over everything, so that if there was one sick in a family he or she almost necessarily communicated the infection to everyone who was infectible. They say that formerly, when they lived practically in the open air, winter and summer, in their birchbark wigwams, though in a 40-degrees-below-zero temperature in winter, and lived on a flesh diet, that consumption was unknown among them; but in the transition state, when shut up in the one-room cabin, living on salt pork and heavy bread, and in many other unsanitary ways, the ravages of consumption have been serious. Whether worse now than in the days from 1873 to 1898 I do not know. I only remember a few who had sore eyes, which I suppose was trachoma, in those days.

"Believe me, very respectfully yours,

"J. A. GILFILLAN"

There has always been a conflict between the full-bloods and mixed-bloods of Minnesota, and especially at White Earth reservation. This dates from the migration of a number of mixed-blood Indians (chiefly French-Canadian) from Canada. They have caused no end of trouble, and by clever manoeuvering dominated the councils.

The favorite chief of the entire Ojibwa nation was Hole-in-the-Day. He became war chief in 1846. The Indians talk of him even at the present day, and the story of Ojibwa, presented towards the end of this book, will be found of interest in this connection.

The Indians told me, during the investigation of 1909, who were responsible for the murder of this fine old chief, but they were unwilling to testify, fearing the vengeance of the French-Canadian element. The following interesting communication, from one in authority, clears up the murder of Hole-in-the-Day, and explains the hostility between the scheming mixed-bloods, and the honest, although ignorant full-bloods.

"During the summer of 1912 Mr. James T. Shearman was detailed by the Honorable Secretary of the Interior to secure testimony concerning the eighty-six mixed-blood Indians suspended from the White Earth rolls. At this hearing certain testimony was given that may be of interest to you, as it explains the assassination of the then head chief of all the Chippewas, Hole-in-the-Day, who was killed at Crow Wing by a party of Leech Lake Indians in 1886. At this hearing an old, blind Indian testified that Clement Beaulieu, father of Gus. Beaulieu, Albert Fairbanks, uncle of Ben Fairbanks, and certain other mixed-bloods employed him and other Indians then living at Leech Lake to go to Crow Wing and

INDIAN SCHOOL CHILDREN IN UNIFORM, PINE POINT
WHITE EARTH, MINNESOTA

kill Chief Hole-in-the-Day, agreeing to pay the Indians $2000 for the deed. They went to Crow Wing and killed him according to agreement. Later, when the mixed-bloods refused to pay the price agreed upon, they organized another party and came to White Earth, intending to kill Beaulieu and certain other mixed-blood families. Upon their arrival here they were induced by the present Head Chief, Me-zhuck-ke-ge-shig, who was related to one of the party, to return to Leech Lake. After this old, blind Indian finished his story, Me-zhuck-ke-ge-shig, now about ninety years of age, went upon the stand and confirmed the testimony of the former witness. Mr. Shearman's report is probably on file in the Secretary's office, and I am informed that a brief of the testimony was made by Mr. E. C. O'Brien of the Department of Justice, and you can probably obtain a copy of the same.

"Since Mr. Shearman was here on the matter referred to, I have been furnished additional testimony concerning the killing of Hole-in-the-Day. It appears that the party left Leech Lake under the pretext of going hunting, there being nine in the party, and that only four of them were in the plot to kill Hole-in-the-Day. When they got to the Crow Wing country May-dway-we-mind said: "Hole-in-the-Day dies today." Later, they met him about a mile and a half from the Crow Wing Agency at a branch of the two roads, where he was killed. After the deed was done, one of the party named Ay-nah-me-ay-gah-bow asked why he had been killed. The answer was that they were told to do it and that there was a reward for killing him, that each one of the party was to get a thousand dollars and a nice house built for him, and the one who shot first was to take Hole-in-the-Day's place as Head Chief. The man who asked the first question also asked who offered the reward and he was told that Clement Beaulieu (father of Gus. H. Beaulieu), Albert Fairbanks (uncle of Ben L. Fairbanks), ————————————* with others, were the men.

"Me-zhuck-ke-gwon-abe or Jim Bassett also stated that about four years after the killing he came with May-dway-we-mind, Num-ay-we-ne-nee, Way-zow-e-ko-nah-yay, O-didh-quay-ge-shig and Day-dah-tub-aun-gay to White earth for the money that had been offered as a reward and which they did not obtain.

"It is a matter of history that Hole-in-the-Day was opposed to the admission of the mixed-bloods to this reservation and that he was killed at their instigation, and there has been irrepressible friction between these Indians ever since."

---

* Name omitted.

# CHAPTER V. THE LEGAL COMPLICATIONS AT WHITE EARTH—THE DEPARTMENT OF JUSTICE

Judge Marsden C. Burch, representing the Attorney General of the United States (Department of Justice) before the Committee on Expenditures in the Interior Department, House of Representatives, went into modern Ojibwa history at great length. The hearings began July 25, 1911, and continued through March 27, 1912. The testimony lies before me, and it fills 2,759 pages. It would be well nigh impossible for readers to consult this enormous bulk of evidence submitted by several hundred witnesses. He found, as have others, that they moved into Minnesota from the head of Lake Superior some seventy years ago. About 1868 the White Earth reservation was established, and the following bands were located at White Earth, Leech Lake, Red Lake, and Cass Lake in Minnesota: the Mississippi; the Otter Tails; the Pillagers; and a few Indians still claiming they belonged to the Lake Superior band and the Fond du Lac band. The White Earth reservation consisted of thirty-six townships, or 829,440 acres. The population in 1909 was 5,300; about 700 full-bloods and 4,600 mixed-bloods. Those who have traveled over it will agree with Judge Burch's statement.

"I have never seen a more beautiful stretch of territory than that embraced in the present White Earth reservation. It contained lakes and streams, prairies and forests, timber enough of white pine originally there to build all the elegant buildings that might have been needed for centuries to come, of the most valuable character — timber which now converted into lumber would be worth in the open market, ranging by various grades, from $35 to $110 per thousand feet, board measure. It is hard wood, ample for fuel and all kinds of purposes. There were marshes and lakes wherein they could fish, and whereon they could hunt and gather wild rice for their sustenance; and the richest of prairie lands imaginable, high, rolling, healthy — everything that could be desired for the last stand of a great race."

On January 8, 1912, Judge Burch made a longer speech which reviews the entire political and Departmental history of White Earth.* Some readers may wish to know a little concerning the legal procedures by which Indians are dispossessed. We will, therefore, take White Earth as an

---

* Hearings before the Committee on Expenditures in the Interior Department of the House of Representatives, H. R., 103, pp. 244-261.

JAMES BASSETT, FULL-BLOOD OJIBWA IN TRIBAL COSTUME

example, and omit the discussion of similar troubles elsewhere. I present about a fourth of his address.

In 1869, the Nelson Act was passed. This provided for the collecting of scattered Ojibwa from ten localities and concentrating them at White Earth, Red Lake and Leech Lake. Judge Burch enters into a lengthy discussion of how the Nelson Act was followed by a bill introduced by Senator Clapp, and that in January, 1904, Representative Steenerson of Minnesota introduced another bill. Of this the Judge says: —

"Under the terms of this Steenerson Act each Indian who had received an allotment on the White Earth Reservation or was entitled thereto should have an additional allotment sufficient to make the original and additional total 160 acres, provided that if there should not be enough land for 160 acres each, the additional allotments should contain only so much land as could be allotted by dividing the total remaining allotable land by the number of eligible allottees.

"We expect to show that of this White Earth Reservation there was an area of lake surface aggregating 59,731.24 acres; also that there is claimed as swamp land going to the State as part of its quota under the organic law of Congress 26,658.15 acres. The allotments additional under the Steenerson Act were made by one Simon Michelet, the White Earth Indian Superintendent, or Agent, at that time. By omitting the two items of lake land and State swamp land from consideration, he figured that there was sufficient territory practically to furnish each allottee the full 160 acres of land, and thus he proceeded to allot to those who first came to be served the total of 160 acres; of course, including all the valuable pine upon the reservation.

"We expect to show that those who were thus favored by these complete additional allotments were largely composed of persons who could be handled in the matter of purchase of the timber by the representatives of the lumber companies that had procured the greater portion of the timber in the four townships. Large numbers of persons eligible to additional allotments, but who came later, were denied the same because there was no land left for them, there being 31,516.88 acres lacking. It will thus be seen that the so-called additional allotment under Michelet was a fraud upon the rights of from 400 to 500 Indians who were absolutely left out in the cold. In addition to this, it would seem that the allotments made included the 59,000 odd acres of lake land, thus increasing the fraud upon those who were not favored with pine in these additional allotments. The allotment was, of course, in direct violation of the Steenerson Act itself. It is a matter of question whether those who had knowledge of and participated in the benefits arising from these illegal allotments can not be yet reached by a court of equity and they compelled to account for their misdeeds.

\* \* \* \* \* \*

"No machinery for carrying into effect the Clapp amendment was provided therein, and thus it remained to be determined who were and who were not adults of the mixed-blood and freed from restraint as to alienation. The result was that designing persons rushed in and obtained deeds and mortgages indiscriminately; that is, from children of the mixed-blood and adults of the full-blood the same as adults of the mixed-blood. In all of these they were accustomed to recite the competency of the Indian, and attached to the deed in each case they usually secured what purported to be the affidavit of two persons that the allottee was an adult Indian of the mixed blood, which affidavits were ordinarily passed with the deed in making mesne conveyances or in recording in the proper county record-ing office. In connection with these transactions we shall be able to demon-strate to the committee that every variety of fraudulent schemes and devices which would occur naturally to acute minds was resorted to to defraud the Indians. The taking of these deeds in violation of law from minors of the mixed-blood and from full-bloods eventuated in the action of the Government in requiring the Department of Justice to file about 1,200 bills in equity to remove the clouds from the titles to lands thus unlawfully obtained.

"Following upon the sudden acquirement of money by persons in some respects less fitted to handle the same and make proper use of it than white children of tender years, there came a condition of affairs which we expect to demonstrate to the committee as most deplorable and shame-ful, a stain upon the fair fame of a great and enlightened State. Saloons ran wide open. Cheap and tawdry articles were sold at extravagant prices. The Indians were overreached, and the money they had obtained from selling or mortgaging their lands or timber was coaxed from them in exchange for objects of little or no value, but of supposed utility — such as decrepit horses, defective vehicles, unmanageable sewing machines, and even pianos of little worth. A perfect frenzy of drunkenness charac-terized many who took their way to the neighboring town of Detroit, and encamped in its vicinity, and practically the same conditions occurred in the hamlets along the Soo Road. The land-shark, passing under the more dignified title of real-estate agent, was everywhere in evidence, and the money-loaning shark, posing under the more dignified business appellation of banker, was engaged in over-reaching the Indian right and left.

\* \* \* \* \* \*

"From the close of 1906 or 1907, when isolated transactions were going on, the fiercest of the fraud and debauchery had subsided, till the summer of 1909 a condition like that of the quiet which succeeds a prolonged intoxication occurred. The Indians had mainly, in one form or another, parted with their heritage and in most instances, had suffered severely from the result. Poverty, sickness, a sense of mortification and loss at the hands of the white men pervaded their minds and depressed their spirits. The pine again, as in the case of the four townships, by clean-cut lines of apparent division had shown up in the ownership and possession as to certain territory (and this the largest and most valuable part) of the Nichols-Chisolm Lumber Co.— pine reputed in extent to be of the amount of 150,000,000 feet.

DISPOSSESSED OJIBWA AT REAR OF AGENCY BUILDINGS
Rice River, White Earth, Minn., 1909.

"Pine in another clean-cut and well-defined territory, reputed to amount to about 50,000,000 feet, was found to be in the possession and under the control of the Park Rapids Lumber Co.; and in still another section, equally well defined in its boundary line, a reputed 50,000,000 feet was controlled by the Wild Rice Lumber Co. Likewise the best of the agricultural lands had fallen into the hands of, or under the control of, the so-called bankers at the hamlets before mentioned, and certain men of great wealth and influence resident in the city of Duluth, as well as in St. Paul and Minneapolis.

*     *     *     *     *     *

"The first result of the treaties of 1889 was the saddling upon the Chippewas of an allotting commission of three members and a large retinue of subordinates. The expense of this commission was $88 a day, and the work that the commission and its subordinates accomplished could doubtless have easily been done by an allotting clerk at $1,000 a year. Besides this commission many other white officials were sent to the reservations, ostensibly to supervise the cutting of the timber and on many other pretexts, for all of which the Indians had to pay. A corps of estimators, each drawing $6 a day of the Indians' money, was appointed to estimate the pine on the Red Lake Reservation. Fraud having been discovered in making this estimate, a new corps of estimators, numbering about twenty-six, was appointed to do the work over again. Each of the new corps also received $6 per day of the Indians' money.

"The new corps proved to be grossly incompetent. They were always well supplied with whiskey and drank heavily. They spent most of their time in towns fifteen or twenty miles distant from the pine they were sent to estimate. Some of the interlopers were members of this corps of examiners, and, though they absented themselves for long periods of time, they still drew their pay. It has been asserted that the total cost to the Indians of these two corps of estimators was $350,000 and that the real value of their work was about $6,000; that in many cases the pine had been underestimated in the interest of the purchasers. The second corps of estimators were likewise discharged and a third corps appointed to go over the work previously done. Like the celebrated case of Jarndice v. Jarndice, it seems that after all the proceedings were over, although the pine alone on the reservations, exclusive of that on the White Earth Reservation, was supposed to be worth from $25,000,000 to $50,000,000, there would be little or nothing left but heirs. Although an Indian entitled to a share of the immense value of these lands and forests might be starving to death, he could not procure two cents from his great wealth to buy a pound of flour.

"While the proceeds from the sale of the pine was thus being squandered, the Indians were also being defrauded by the loggers and lumbermen who were purchasing the timber. By the conspiracy at the Crookston sale in 1900, the Indians doubtless lost several thousand dollars, and by the fraudulent operations under the so-called 'dead and down' act, they lost even a greater sum.

"Another source of complaint on the part of the real Indians of Minnesota is the payment of annuities to persons whom the Indians contend are not members of their tribe, and whose names are not properly upon the tribal rolls, and who consequently had no rights thereto.

"Another grievance of which the real Indians bitterly complain and which was the immediate cause of the outbreak of the Pillagers in 1898, resulting in the killing of a major and six soldiers of the United States Army, and the wounding of many others, was the conduct of certain mixed-blood deputy marshals, several of whom it is claimed by the Indians were persons who had improperly been placed upon their tribal rolls. These deputy marshals originated and developed, as we shall expect to show, a system of arresting and transporting to St. Paul, Duluth, and Detroit various members of the tribe, charging them either with bringing whiskey upon the reservation or with some other like offense. We expect to show that the purpose of these mixed-blood deputy marshals was to secure fees for making such arrests and for bringing other Indians to the said cities as witnesses against the Indians accused. The practice continued for some years, until finally, as we expect to show, a member of the Pillager Band was arrested in this manner and taken to Duluth. He was left at Duluth without money to buy food or to buy transportation home, and compelled to walk back to the reservation, a distance of more than 200 miles. When he arrived at the reservation he was nearly dead from exposure and starvation.

*   *   *   *   *   *

"An instance of the manner in which the Minnesota Indians have been made the instruments or causes for defrauding the Government through Congress, in the interests of attorneys, and these same parties who have been so often suggested, is the Mille Lac Indian case. An appropriation of $40,000 was secured through an act of Congress ostensibly for the relief of the Mille Lac Indians as a payment for certain alleged improvements made by them upon the Mille Lac Reservation. The matter came up this way:

"In 1854 the Mille Lac Band ceded their reservation to the Government. In 1862, when Chief Hole-in-the-Day advised a combination with the Sioux for an uprising against the Government, these Indians refused to participate on account of their ancient enmity with the Sioux. To reward them for their loyalty the President promised them they might still remain on their reservation as long as they did not interfere with the Whites.

"Under the Nelson Act, in the treaty of 1889, they ceded this privilege of occupancy to the Government, but some portions of them refused to remove to White Earth, claiming that they had never really ceded anything to the Government.  As an inducement for these parties to leave, Congress was persuaded to appropriate $40,000, or so much thereof as might be necessary for the purpose, to pay these parties for the improvements they had made during their occupancy of the reservation. (32 Stat. L. 268.)   Michelet and this same———————*went over for the Govern-

GROUP OF THIRTY PERSONS CONSTITUTING LINNEN-MOOREHEAD FORCE
WHITE EARTH INVESTIGATION, 1909

ment to investigate and appraise the improvements, and found practically none — nothing but the charred remains of some Indian tipis; but to eat up, that is, to cover the entire $40,000, these charred remains were appraised at the original cost of the tipis, and items were inserted in the list of improvements, such as the profit an Indian would make gathering wild rice for a year, for gathering wild honey for a like period, and other like items.   Now, the real disposition of the money seems to have been as follows:

_____
* Name omitted.

"First, $4,000 was paid to Gus H. Beaulieu for attorney's fees, $2,500 was paid to D. B. Henderson as attorney's fees, and $1,500 to D. B. Henderson for expenses. Four chiefs received $1,000 each. About $17,000 was then prorated among the Indians; $10,020 then remained in the hands of Gus. H. Beaulieu.

"It then became necessary for the Mille Lac Indians to employ another set of attorneys to sue Beaulieu for the $10,020. After considerable expensive litigation, Beaulieu deposited $5,600 to the credit of the Mille Lac Band in the Merchants National Bank of St. Cloud, Minn., and paid $1,000 to the Indians' attorneys.

"The traders in the vicinity of the Mille Lac Reservation then commenced suit for the money so deposited, claiming that the individual members of the band owed them money for goods. Again a compromise was effected with the result that a portion of the $5,600 was turned over to Agent Michelet for distribution. There is now about $208 waiting for the claimants.

"We think this is indicative of the way in which Congress has contributed innocently from the public funds to the support and enrichment of a few persons of little or no merit, by a species of pretense of recompensing the Indians who, in the end, have slight participation in the generous provisions so by Congress made."

# CHAPTER VI.  THE WHITE EARTH SCANDAL

Judge Burch's research led him to conclude that the Indians were in vastly better shape forty years ago than at the present time.  The reading of Warren's book, Gilfillan's testimony, and other evidence establishes it beyond question that the Indian does not seem to have suffered to any great extent in either health or morals prior to 1880.  The older men of the tribe, who were keen mentally in spite of great age, when I visited those Indians in 1909, told me much regarding their past.  I visited them under most auspicious circumstances, being empowered by the Indian Office to conduct investigations of affairs at White Earth, and having at my command numerous interpreters and assistants.  The old shaman, Bay-bah-dwun-gay-aush,  Me-zhuck-ke-ge-shig,  Ojibwa,*  Mah-een-gonce, and others with whom I talked a great deal, laid the blame for their present deplorable condition on the unscrupulous French-Canadians, mixed-blood element, as well as covetous white men who sought timber and land.  Gilfillan has pointed out in his letter the increase of drunkenness due to large financial rewards offered by the Government in pursuing a mistaken policy.

Father Aloysius Hermanutz has been at White Earth since 1878.  In his testimony before the Graham Investigating Committee, he stated that the full-blood Indians at that time were in good condition.  Nearly everyone owned a team of oxen, a cow, and cultivated fields.  Many of them raised vegetables and there was much weaving of rugs and small carpets.  They had an Agent, Mr. Charles Ruffey, who was kind to them but very strict.  The farmer was a competent man and knew how to make Indians work.

"I met him one day on the road on horseback.  He went to that Indian — to that farm — I met him there and asked him where he was going, and he said: 'There are two Indians, Father, up beyond that church.  They didn't plow their field in order to put the seeds in, and the Agent ordered me to tell them if they don't plow their fields now (it was in April) that the team will be taken away from them.'  And of course they were old-timers.  That was Saturday when I saw them, and on Sunday morning they started to plow.  They were scared and they plowed their fields.  At the time the Indians were in very good condition, and then afterwards it changed and they went down again."

---

* According to Miss Densmore's spelling: "Odjibwe"; "Maingans"; "Meja-kigi-jig".  I have spelled the names as pronounced.

The illustrations accompanying these chapters were taken during the investigation of 1909 and give some idea of conditions obtaining at that time. So much has been said and written regarding the situation of the Minnesota Ojibwa, that the Government adopted heroic measures, and conditions are to a great extent ameliorated, but they are still far from satisfactory.

Omitting the racial traits of the people the past sixty years, let us consider their present condition and the causes leading up to it.

The 1889 bill (Congress) was known officially: "For the Relief and Civilization of the Chippewa Indians." There is both sarcasm and irony in that phrase, which only those of us who know what kind of "relief and civilization" the Chippewas have received since the bill was passed, can appreciate.

At the time White Earth reservation was created, a treaty was made with the Ojibwa bands, March 19th, 1867. It was the Government's intention at the time this solemn treaty was signed, to encourage progress in industry, and to permanently locate the Ojibwa upon farms. With so laudable a purpose in view, one of the provisions of this treaty was as follows: Any Indian who brought under cultivation ten acres of land, was entitled to a fee simple patent, or deed, for forty acres additional, and so on up to 160 acres. This encouraged many Indians to become industrious and they brought under cultivation many tracts of land. In 1887, under the Dawes Act, the holdings of agricultural land were limited to eighty acres. After the "Relief and Civilization" act of 1889, Gus Beaulieu, a French-Canadian-Indian politician, and others became very active in and about White Earth reservation. A Mr. Darwin S. Hall was appointed Chippewa Commissioner and became interested in Mr. Beaulieu's projects.

Whatever the original purpose of this act, it was used by venal white men to get hold of the Indians' land. Previously the land had all been in a reservation and could not be touched. Now it was coming under the control of individual Indians and might be sold.

The Indians could not be thrown neck-and-heels off their reservation, although I suppose certain interested persons of northern Minnesota would have adopted that happy expedient were it possible. Some kind of legislation must be enacted whereby the wolves could enter the flock, if not entirely disguised, at least so covered that the shepherd of the flock might have some difficulty in differentiating between the sheep and the wolves. So it came about that the "Clapp Amendment" was passed as a rider to the general Indian appropriation bill. The Clapp amendment in substance, provided that any mixed-blood Indian could dispose of his property, but full-bloods and minors could not.

If either Senator Clapp or Congressman Steenerson ever endeavored to put an end to the abuses resulting from the passage of this legislation their efforts have failed to accomplish results. I never heard that anyone in Congress tried to remedy the evils following the passage of these bills. Two of the missionaries, Rev. Felix Nelles of Pine Point and Rev. Aloysius Hermanutz of White Earth, wrote to the Indian Office, protesting that the Indians were being swindled out of their property. But Father Felix reports to me by letter that so far as he is aware neither the protest of himself nor his superior, Father Aloysius, had any effect.

When the Act of 1867, establishing White Earth reservation, and which Judge Burch has discussed, was put into effect, a great number of Indians by hard work, notably the chief of the entire five living bands of Chippewa, a grand old man, whose name is Me-zhuck-ke-ge-shig, took advantage of this and earned many acres of land. This chief was looked up to by the Indians, was a good man himself, and many of his friends followed his example, worked hard and earned forty, eighty or one hundred and sixty acres. Imagine the surprise of these Indians when, at the time the pine lumber was allotted, some one in Washington announced that the Indians who had received farm lands could not participate in the pine allotting. In other words, the French-Canadians, the mixed-bloods and such full-bloods as had not worked and were not industrious, received pine tracts valued from few to many thousands of dollars, and those who had obeyed the wishes of the Indian Office, had advanced by hard work along the "road to civilization," were debarred from participation. It was precisely as if a college passed its drones and conditioned its honor-roll men. No wonder these White Earth Indians do not care to work, and say they "cannot understand Washington." If whoever was responsible for such a ruling had sat down and deliberately tried to figure out the most certain way of injuring the Ojibwa Indians, he could not have conceived a better plan.

Immediately after I was appointed on the Board of Indian Commissioners, a correspondent wrote me from Wisconsin that the Ojibwa Indians at White Earth were in bad condition. The Indian Rights Association had made a similar complaint. Rev. Charles Wright, Episcopal missionary at Cass Lake, shortly after the scandals began to develop, on his own responsibility borrowed money and in spite of the opposition of the Indian Agent, Simon Michelet, he went to Washington to lay the grievances of the Indians before the President. He bore letters of introduction from Governor John A. Johnson and United States Senator Knute Nelson. The lumber companies, it was supposed, wired the Indian Commissioner of Wright's mission. He did not find favor at Washington, never succeeded in seeing the President, and sorrowing and sick at heart he was compelled to return to Minnesota.

The Board of Indian Commissioners having no funds, I asked the Indian Office to appoint me as Special Agent with full powers, and send me to White Earth. This was done about March 1st. I spent five weeks investigating conditions in the southern part of the reservation, Pine Point, and returned to Washington the latter part of April, 1909. The first of July, Inspector E. B. Linnen and myself were sent to White Earth with full authority. We employed a total force of thirty-seven persons and made a complete investigation.

During the first five weeks at White Earth, save for local employees, I was entirely alone. The investigation soon developed that millions of dollars' worth of pine timber and farm lands had been stolen from the Indians. As soon as it was ascertained that I was working in the interests of the Indian, the lumber companies and the mixed-blood and French-Canadians attempted in every possible way to end the investigation. They first tried bribery, and later intimidation. They lured away several of my witnesses, and even some of the Government employees informed me that it was hopeless to fight the great land and timber interests back of the despoliation of 5,300 Indians. Matters went from bad to worse. Some idea of the physical strain may be had from the statement that I lost fifteen pounds weight in five weeks. As the other Inspectors and Special Agents had not reported on White Earth conditions, the Indian Office could not, at first, believe my story. At last, I received a telegram asking me to come to Washington. I had at that time one hundred and three affidavits representing more than a million dollars worth of property, and involving county officials, lumbermen and presidents of national banks. Ill feeling had developed in the local towns. The nearest railway station, Park Rapids, was distant eighteen miles. Ogema, on the "Soo Line," lay forty-five miles to the north. Knowing that the enemy would attempt to prevent the affidavits going East, I started Doctor Isaac Stahlberg, Government physician, for Park Rapids at noon. He arrived there about half-past three o'clock and volunteered the information that I would probably take the 5 o'clock train East.

Meanwhile, at 7 o'clock that same morning, in three vehicles, nine of us, including five armed Indian policemen, started for Ogema to the north. We reached our destination without incident, and I delivered the affidavits to Commissioner Valentine in Washington two days later.

Honorable Robert G. Valentine, then Commissioner, took great interest in the White Earth affair, supported my contentions, and at his suggestion a very experienced man, Inspector Linnen, returned with me to the scene of action, as has been stated. We had the hearty cooperation of Superintendent John R. Howard, who was appointed early in 1908 and succeeded Simon Michelet. Major Howard has filled one of the most difficult positions in the entire Indian Service. He has been bitterly opposed by the mixed-blood element through Beaulieu's newspaper. Neighboring towns have organized Boards of Trade, and these have appealed by committee and through the press to Congress, alleging that the Interior Department and Department of Justice have interfered with business.

Howard's position has been no sinecure, and in addition to his other troubles, he was given a chief clerk who happened to be a disputatious person, who had caused trouble in California, and on arrival at White Earth became friendly with some of those who were opposing him. This tense situation was not brought to an end until vigorous protests were lodged by a number of us at Washington.

The beginning of the great scandal at White Earth is interesting as well as dramatic. What I have to say in succeeding pages is not in the official language of the report made by Linnen and myself, but is drawn from departmental sources.

I make this explanation, for I am well aware that what follows will sound to some readers as a page from Russian, or Turkish, history, rather than a leaf from the history of one of our own states in our own great and free country!

The 24th of April, 1905, was set as the date on which the white, Norway and other valuable pine tracts would be allotted to the Indians of White Earth. The word was passed throughout the reservation, and the French-Canadians, who are there in considerable numbers and most of whom show very slight trace of Indian blood, were the first to appear. Educated mixed-blood Indians also arrived some days previous. A line was formed near the United States Government building door some time Saturday afternoon. The allotting was to begin Monday morning. It is interesting to note that first in the line was Margaret Lynch, a young white girl, whose father and mother were white people, and who, the Indians properly maintained, had no right to an allotment. The girl received allotment number one, for which her father refused $22,000 cash the next day.

The Agent at this time was Simon Michelet. He was possessed of a violent temper, according to the sworn testimony of a policeman employed at the White Earth Agency for nearly ten years. Michelet was friendly with Gus H. Beaulieu, the Nichols-Chisolm Lumber Company and others who were equally interested in obtaining timber from the White Earth Indians. It was bad form, to say the least, for the United States Agent to use his office at this time to hold long conferences with the representatives of the lumber companies.

What was said behind the closed doors no one knows, but what occurred at the time of the allotting sheds a little light on the situation. The chief clerk of agent Michelet was one J. T. Van Metre. As he resigned his position after the timber was allotted and entered the real estate business, this added another complication to the already confused affairs at White Earth.

During the allotting of the pine timber there was such confusion, the line became broken and many people lost their places. My two investigations on the reservation, covering nearly seventeen weeks, lead me to believe that the most valuable tracts were selected in advance, and that the names of those who were to have them were entered on a list for use at the allotment.

In support of this contention is the affidavit of Robert Henry, sworn to September 24th, 1909, who came early to White Earth at the time of the allotment and passed into the agent's office shortly after the allotting began. He held in his hand descriptions of forty or fifty different pine tracts, and yet was told that all had been selected and he could not have a good pine allotment. Not enough people preceded Henry to have drawn each of these allotments. The same is true of a woman who had in her hand fifty descriptions, and she was told that all of these had been selected. It early in the day became evident that the full-bloods were, if possible, to be kept from getting any land, for by the Clapp amendment only the mixed-bloods could sell their land.

Early in the day when the full-blood Indians were clamoring for recognition and insisting that the French-Canadians and white people be kept back, John St. Luke, the policeman, testifying under oath, September 24th, 1909, says: "Agent Simon Michelet came out of his office in an excited manner, and told me to keep the Indians out and let the mixed-bloods in. There seemed to be confusion in the line. Michelet pushed some of these Indians back, swearing at them, and told me to club them if necessary, to keep them from crowding in." St. Luke refused to do this.

At last the full-bloods registered a protest, some of the Indians sent for their guns, and things took on a serious aspect. Presently by way of compromise it was agreed that for every mixed-blood that received a pine allotment a full-blood should also obtain one. This continued until

OJIBWA CHIEF, KE-WAY-DIN, PINE POINT, WHITE EARTH
RESERVATION, MINNESOTA, 1909

all of the twenty or more miles of pine timber had been allotted in tracts of eighty acres each to the Indians.

The pine timber allotted these Indians ranged all the way from tracts worth $2,000 or $3,000 to those valued as high as $25,000. Since the lands were allotted, iron ore has been found in quantities under certain parts of the reservation. How extensive are these bodies, no man may know, and the value might be a few millions, or many hundreds of millions.

EVICTED INDIANS, TWIN LAKES, WHITE EARTH RESERVATION, MINNESOTA, 1909

The effect of the allotment on the Whites near White Earth was immediate. Mushroom banks sprang up in the surrounding small towns. The Indians in their affidavits (of which Linnen and myself took 505) testified that lawyers, banks, county officials, and business men of prominence in Detroit, Ogema, Mahnomen, and other towns, joined in the scramble to secure their pine lands and farm tracts.

As few of these men spoke the language, it was necessary to have interpreters, and the educated Indians were soon divided into two camps, those who were willing for pay to interpret for the land-sharks and timber thieves, and those who would not help in defrauding their own people.

It is sad to note that in a hundred or more instances the Indians were purposely made drunk and their lands taken away from them while under the influence of liquor. Many of the Indians do not remember what kind of papers they signed, whether deeds or mortgages, or whether any papers were signed at all.

While our investigation was in progress, and we had moved over to Rice River, Mr. J. Weston Allen visited us for three weeks. He came as a representative of the Boston Indian Citizenship Committee, and because of his high standing in the legal profession, rendered valuable assistance in the investigation.

The key to the whole situation lay in the question of blood. As has been shown before, the mixed-bloods only could sell their land. The full-bloods could not. Consequently we assembled the old record-keepers, medicine men, chiefs, and Indians of prominence who knew their own people. Some of these were more than eighty-five years of age and none of them under seventy. When an Indian appeared before us to give his testimony, we first asked him whether he was a full-blood or a mixed-blood, and the names of his parents and grandparents. The old witnesses, probably twelve or fifteen, might not all know the parents or grandparents of the Indian testifying. But three, four, six, and sometimes eight of them would know the family history, and would be able to swear whether the Indian was a full-blood. If he was a mixed-blood, we told him with regret that we could do nothing for him.

One affidavit of the Indian himself as to his blood relationship and parents was taken, another signed by the old witnesses to the same effect. A third affidavit related to the property possessed by the Indian, with number and description of allotments, and by careful questioning we ascertained when and where he had disposed of his land. The fourth affidavit was by the interpreters in which they solemnly declared that they had correctly interpreted our statements to the Indian and his answers to us, and that he understood the nature of the papers that he had signed. The interpreters also made further affidavit that they had carefully interpreted to the old Indian witnesses the papers that they signed. In addition to all of the above, we frequently took affidavits of Indians who were present during the swindling operations. Thus it will be seen that the evidence was very complete, positive and exact. So far as I know, no investigating force on a reservation had ever done more work in the same length of time. We labored from eight o'clock to twelve, one to six, and frequently from seven until eleven at night.

The Indians took great interest in the investigation, and as we moved from one portion of the reservation to another we were accompanied by large numbers of these poor people. On one occasion over eighty Indians were present, and we were compelled to turn two large school buildings into dormitories.

These Indians had lost their property almost without exception. Whether the term "swindle" is used or not is immaterial. They lost their property through many and devious ways. The affidavits indicated that in many instances Indians appeared before the buyers either drunk or somewhat under the influence of liquor. Not only did the interpreters give the Indians liquor, but frequently the Indians drank of their own accord. Of course the bankers, lawyers, county officials and real estate men knew that the ordinary code of business ethics would not countenance their dealings with drunken persons. But these land-owners being Indians, and the sentiment of the thirty-seven individuals and firms who in the affidavits are shown to be responsible for the conditions at White Earth being against Indians as land-owners, no discrimination was made and Indians were permitted to "do business" whether drunk or sober. Next to drunkenness as a means of separating the Indian from his land, the deliberate deceit practised by the buyers stands out conspicuously. Scores of affidavits and statements were taken of Indians who owned two, three, five, or even seven or eight trust patents. The trust patent was preliminary paper, but as trust patents would in the process of time become deeds, the white people did not differentiate and trust patents were in most cases accepted the same as deeds. In order to be within the law it was necessary to prove the Indians mixed-bloods. Most of the Indians were therefore sworn as mixed-bloods. They frequently protested, stating that they were full-bloods, but were described in the papers as mixed-bloods just the same. Therefore few of the papers signed by these Indians were read or interpreted to them, and in the majority of cases, as the Indian could neither write nor read, he did not know whether he was signing receipts, mortgages, deeds or releases. The favorite form of expression used by the interpreter, according to affidavits, was "the buyer says this is a legal document which you would not understand if read to you, and all you have to do is to sign your name and receive the money." Very few Indians appear to have sworn to the papers they signed.

When an Indian appeared with more than one trust patent he was usually told that one of these would be purchased or mortgaged and the others would be held for him and he could sign papers for all of them. Many of the buyers were accustomed to say to the Indian, "You have no safe in your cabin, and if these papers burn up you would lose your land. You had better let me keep them in my safe." Then the Indian signed and parted with the papers and we can imagine the result.

Allotments acquired by inheritance are called by the Indians "dead allotments." Such estates must be probated. In other communities the fee is anywhere from a few dollars to fifteen dollars or more, but in Detroit, Mahnomen, Ogema and Wauban, the usual charge varied from $50 to as high as $150, according to the credulity of the victim — and there were other charges. When the Indians reported to us that they had signed over "dead allotments" to be probated, we frequently discovered that it was not clear in the Indian's mind how so much money was necessary in order to settle these estates, but having surrendered the trust patent, he was without anything to show for his inheritance. Frequently little or nothing accrued to the Indian after the benevolent attorney or banker had been paid for his efforts in directing the Indian's footsteps along the broad highway of civilization.

Instances are not wanting where deceased Indians were actually resurrected long enough to dispose of land which they had neglected to convey during life, and affidavits are not lacking which recite that so-and-so was an adult mixed-blood and competent to handle his affairs. I have in mind one case of a boy resting in his grave at Pine Point. Certain individuals made affidavit that this boy was alive, and was of age, and thereby they secured control of his valuable pine allotment.

The affidavits bristled with forgery and perjury.

Men employed in the livery stables of Detroit and elsewhere told me that as soon as the lands were allotted all the available teams and drivers were engaged by the buyers, and that night and day for many months these men scoured the reservation and pursued the Indian men, women and children until they had secured the best farms and timber tracts available. There is one man in particular whose history is interesting. He walked into Detroit a tramp ten years ago and began washing dishes in a hotel. Just how he got his start is under dispute, one man claiming that a stranded theatrical company left several trunks of gaudy paraphernalia in Detroit, which this man traded to some drunken Indians for a tract of land. Whether this is true or not, he was successful in Indian land speculation, and at present he is now a leading citizens of the region. Some of the Indians call him, "the white wolf, with the gold teeth."

Where was the United States Indian Bureau, while this disgraceful scene was being enacted? Where was the Indian Agent, sworn to protect these people? Where were the Inspectors and Special Agents? How was it that the testimony of missionaries and others, and their warnings, produced no effect in Washington? These are questions I have repeatedly asked, and nobody has ever answered them.

# CHAPTER VII. SOME INDIAN TESTIMONY AND AFFIDAVITS. SICKNESS.

During the height of the pine and land purchases, crowds of Indians at White Earth were persuaded to visit Detroit and Park Rapids and Ogema. Contrary to the law, whiskey was frequently sold them. They tell how at Park Rapids, in the little square in the centre of the village, drunken Indians were lying on the grass in numbers, and at Ogema a saloon keeper was passing liquor in a bucket, and handing it out by the dipperful to Indians.

After the buyers had used persuasion to get the Indians to give up their allotments, they resorted to stronger measures in dealing with those who would not sell. A wife of a policeman at Pine Point, Mrs. John Rock, was awakened at eleven o'clock in the night by Detroit buyers, who forcibly entered her cabin, and stayed until two o'clock in the morning until they obtained one of her tracts of land.

When Indians visited Detroit and partook of liquor they were arrested. On being brought before the authorities and fined, they were told by the attorney who was supposed to defend them, or by the kind-hearted land buyer, that they must sell or deed over a tract of land in order to pay the fine. Sworn testimony in several cases is to this effect.

When Indians were brought into the offices of the buyers and hesitated about selling or mortgaging, more persuasive arguments were used. In the case of Grace Rock, who visited E. G. Holmes' bank, the testimony now in the hands of the Government is to the effect that as she did not wish to sell at the price offered, and started into the hall, one of those present cried to Interpreter Morrison, "Go and fetch her back, and if she will not sell, we will throw her into the lake."

Me-zhuck-ke-gway-abe in affidavit No. 268, July 29, 1909, states that one Fred Saunders got him to drink and then bought his land. A minor son, Willy Bassett, was told to sign papers, or he would be put in jail.

In the case of Mrs. Lawrence Roberts, her affidavit recites that she appeared before banker Anundensen with Interpreter Robert Morrison — "Anundensen asked if I was a mixed-blood and I said my parents are full-bloods. He said that is all right. We signed papers."

I quote this case because it is typical of nearly one hundred others. The papers which she signed were not explained to this woman and may well have recited that she was a mixed-blood Indian.

ROSE ELLIS

One of the interpreters serving during the investigation of 1909.
Carlisle graduate.  Full-blood Ojibwa

A number of Indians have stated that "If you are related to mixed-bloods, it is all right." I make particular mention of this mixed-blood question because, before the Congressional Investigation Committee Gus Beaulieu claimed that I endeavored to prove all Indians full-bloods, and that these Indians, having previously sworn before the land buyers that they were mixed-bloods, should now be indicted for perjury. We were especially careful in all our evidence, and we discriminated against those who appeared to be mixed-bloods — if there was any discrimination at all. Only Indians who were undoubtedly full-bloods were entered as such.

The fact that many Indians may have previously sworn that they were mixed-bloods does not prove them to be such. They were made to sign these papers, the papers were not explained to them, and if there is any perjury, the white people are responsible, rather than the Indians who have been duped.

When the business of dealing in Indian lands was at its height, car-loads of wild bronchos from South Dakota, and broken-down horses from St. Paul were shipped up to the Indian country. The business was apparently conducted on a large scale, for several hundred Indians testified to having traded their allotments for a little cash and teams of horses, buggies, harnesses and sleighs, not to mention old pianos, graphophones and other useless articles in the struggle of the aborigines for existence. As the Ojibwa are woods or canoe Indians, and not "Horse Indians" as are the Sioux, very few of them understood the management of horses. Even if the horses had been strong and active, it is doubtful if they would have been of any considerable value to these Indians. Some of the horses lived but a few weeks. Many of them were so old that their teeth were worn down. The broncho would run away and smash the old buggy or sleigh.

Five interpreters, who confessed as to their part in these proceedings in order to escape prosecution, told how the bankers and real estate men often stood in their office doors and laughed heartily as the poor Indians drove away after conducting their business.

One young lady, who is a Carlisle graduate, told me that she and her sister, believing that the man who paid the Indians money for their land was cheating, put on Indian costumes, painted up and passed before him. Each girl was to receive $750. He said, "Do you speak English?" She replied, "kawin," which is emphatic "no." He then proceeded to count ones and twos aloud until he had reached what would appear to an ignorant Indian to be $750, but was in reality about $130. This girl stood aside and her sister then appeared. The man asked the same question, and she, waiting until he had counted the money, then said in English, "Don't you think you had better count that over?" He flushed and stammered and made good the full amount to each sister. A woman sold a million feet of pine timber for $10,000 and came home with a thousand one-dollar bills stuffed in a long stocking.

One of our old Indian witnesses at Pine Point, sold seventy thousand feet of pine timber valued at nearly a thousand dollars, and all he received was ten dollars.

In the case of the old woman O-mo-du-yea-quay, she testified she was visited by interpreter Joe Flammand, who told her that Lawyer Beum would pay her $500 for her eighty acres. "When I got there, they gave me a little less than forty dollars and bought me a house alongside the railroad, containing one bedstead, two chairs, a small table and a little cook-stove. After that Flammand would come to my house and give me a dollar or a quarter. After a little while he told me that my money was all gone."

One of the saddest stories told me at White Earth will be found in Official Affidavit 359, that of O-nah-yah-wah-be-tung. This man had valuable pine timber which, he states, he sold for $7000. The Indian having received the money, the grafters immediately got busy. One William Lufkins, a mixed-blood, persuaded him to pay $1800 for a ranch building. This was moved from some distance on the prairie to Ogema. A large sum was charged for moving the building. I heard that $400 was charged for moving it across the railroad tracks, which procedure occupied less than an hour. After the house was established on a lot fronting on the main street of Ogema, the Indian was told that he should go into business as do white people. It was suggested that he start a feed store. He trusted one or two men to visit St. Paul and buy flour and feed in order to stock his store. These men squandered a thousand dollars in dissipation. He sent them three hundred more and they returned with a small quantity of feed stock. Thus the man's money dwindled until he was defrauded out of his entire $7000, and is today a pauper.

In the following cases I have stated the facts briefly, without giving the Indian's name.

In the testimony on file in case numbered 382, it appears that a certain attorney and prominent man, had brought before him an Indian woman who did not wish to sign papers, and the attorney said if she did not do so he would have her arrested and put in jail. The proprietor of a lodging house at Detroit, according to this sworn statement, gave these Indians liquor.

State of Minnesota   )
                     )SS
County of Becker     )

          On this 8th day of September, A.D. 1909, before
me, E. B. Linnen, U. S. Inspector, Dept. of Interior, personally came
Gah-bay-yah-nah-quod-doke, who being first duly sworn by me according
to law, deposes and says:
          I am a full blood Indian of the Otter Tail Pillager
band of Chippewa Indians belonging to and residing upon the White
Earth Indian reservation in Minnesota; my father's name was Be-wash and
my mother's name was Mah-ge-moze-o-quay; the names of my grandfather
and grandmother on my father's side were Con-duh-wah-we-zoo and
_____ ; the names of my grand-
father and grandmother on my mother's side were Wah-be-gay-cake and
Ah-go-mo; and each of said persons was a full blood Indian.

                                                      Her mark.

Witness to mark.        Gah-bay-yah-nah-quod-doke        X

*E. B. Linnen*

          We, the undersigned being first duly sworn according to law,
each for himself and not one for the other, all depose and say:
          That we are Chippewa Indians belonging to and residing upon
the White Earth Indian reservation in Minnesota; that we are personally
acquainted with the above mentioned deponent and know her to be a full
blood Chippewa Indian; that the names of her parents and grandparents
are as set forth above, and that each of said persons was a full blood
Indian.

Witness *Georgia Lacy*        His mark        Witness *John Leecy*        His mark.

May-zhuck-ke-ge-shig                          Gay-bay-yah-mah-ge-wabe

Witness                       His mark        Witness *Wm Dailey*        His mark
*L. R. Tarts*

Day-cah-me-ge-shig                            Ah-yah-baince

Witness                       His mark        Witness                    His mark
*Warren K Moorhead*                           *Susie McDougall*

Gay-me-wah-nah-na-quoit                       Bay-bah-dwung-way-aush

          Subscribed and sworn to before me this 8th  day of
September, A.D. 1909.

                        *E. B. Linnen*
                 U. S. Inspector, Dept. of Interior.

Copy of Official Affidavit with thumb-print signatures, used by
Linnen-Moorehead Investigators

According to affidavit numbered eleven, banker M. J. Kolb at Ogema sent for one of the Indians and stated that he wished to buy the pine on the minor son's allotment. The minor was aged fourteen. The Indian went to Kolb's bank and found another man there, who stated that, although the child was a minor, yet he would buy the timber and stand the risk. Kolb paid the Indian $100 and ten dollars of this was given to Jim Bunker, the interpreter. A month later the banker sent for the Indian and stated, "You better bring your trust patent of your original allotment to me or you will probably be arrested." Thus Kolb obtained the Indian's original allotment in addition to the minor child's pine. I might continue repeating similar instances.

Two important and shocking statements I reproduce here. Government official numbers, 247 and 92. They are self-explanatory.

STATE OF MINNESOTA  
COUNTY OF MAHNOMEN } SS

On this 23d day of August, A.D. 1909, before me, W. K. Moorehead, Spec. U. S. Indian Agent, personally came Mayn-way-way-be-nace, who being first duly sworn by me according to law, on oath deposes and says:

Two years ago Mr. Waller of Waubun, Minn., came to my house for the trust patent of my original allotment No. 2321 for E2NE—Sec. 8, 144-40. This was hardwood timber. He gave me $20 cash. When he came he made this statement, "I have already arranged at the Court House to have you arrested, and have come over here to get your trust patent to take care of your land for you." My wife, Ah-be-dah-sah-mo-quay, and my children, Antoine and Maggie (Mah-geed) were witnesses. Andrew Vanoss came with Mr. Waller as interpreter. Vanoss gave me whiskey and also presented me with a pint bottle of whiskey. Mr. Waller took the trust patent and handed me $20 in cash. As near as I can judge, my giving up the trust patent cancelled the obligations incurred in the mortgage referred to in the affidavit signed by my wife, Ah-be-dah-sah-mo-quay.

In the fall of 1908 I went to Mahnomen with the Trust Patent of my additional allotment No. 1702 for N2SW—Sec.36—145–38. This may be timber land. I saw L. O. Johnson, of the Prairie Land Company. I sold the land to Johnson for $364. He did not ask any questions as to my blood relationship. I signed papers, my wife was present. Willie Brunette was interpreter. I was drinking at the time.

Three years ago Fargo and Peake of Ogema, Minn., came to my house and asked if I had any dead allotments to sell. I told them I had three: Naysh-kah-we-gah-bow, age 36 yrs.; Mah-co-day-we-gwaince, and Zo-zed, age about 4 yrs. Fargo and Peake said that they would take these three trust patents of the dead allotments to be probated. They also stated that when my grandchildren (who were also heirs) come of age they would pay the value of these allotments. This summer they paid me $130. This is all I have ever received. My wife and I signed papers. Willie Lufkin, was interpreter. I paid him one dollar ($1.00).

About the middle of June, 1909, I took the trust patent of my deceased grandchild, Simon Smith, to J. T. Van Metre of Mahnomen, Minn., to be probated. I have received no money. This was allotment No.—— for ——————————————

The allotment of Naysh-kah-we-gah-bow was No. 2323 for S2SE—Sec. 2—144–41; of Mah-co-day-we-gwaince was No.—— for ——————————————————; of Zo-zed was No. 2326 for E2SE—Sec. 5—144–40. *His mark*

MAYN-WAY-WAY-BE-NACE.

Witness to mark
    GEORGIA LACY

Subscribed and sworn to before me this 23d day of August, A.D. 1909.

WARREN K. MOOREHEAD<br>*Spec. U. S. Indian Agent*

STATE OF MINNESOTA } SS
COUNTY OF BECKER

Margaret Coburn, or<br>Margaret Colburne    Age 45.<br>Allottee Orig. 2951, Lots 1-2- &9,<br>Sec. 6, Twp 142, R 42.

On this 6th day of September, A.D. 1909, before me, W. K. Moorehead, Spec. U. S. Indian Agent, personally came Margaret Colburne, who being first duly sworn by me according to law, deposes and says:

That about two years ago, in August, 1907, a man named Ephraim Budrow came to my house at Cloquet, Minn., and finding me there alone and observing my crippled condition, said, "I am surprised to see you in this condition. Why don't you sell some of your land?" He asked me how much land I had. This man seemed to know about my land. He asked for the two trust patents of my deceased husband, Joe Colburne, No. 2950 for SW|4 of SW|4, Sec. 32 & SE|4 of SE|4, Sec. 31, T 143–42, for my own trust patent, as above, and for that of my child Joseph, No. 2953 for Lots 4 and 12, Sec. 30, Twp 143, R 42. Said Budrow walked back and forth in the room in an excited and nervous manner, and presently he went out before I could stop him, taking the three trust patents with him. Because of my crippled condition I could not run after him but managed to crawl to the window and called to him to stop. He paid no attention to me.

My son-in-law came home about noon. His name is Frank Houle. He asked me what I was crying about and I told him that said Budrow had run off with the three trust patents belonging to my husband (dec'd), myself and the boy. My son-in-law started at once for town to hunt for Budrow but could not find him. That same evening, however, my son-in-law caught hold of this Ephraim Budrow as Budrow was boarding the train and told Budrow to give up the trust patents he had taken from me. Budrow reached into a pocket and handed out some papers to my son-in-law, which my son-in-law thought were the three trust patents but which proved to be only the trust patent of my child Joseph. Three days after, when we managed to get enough money, my son-in-law went to Ephraim Budrow's house at Fish Lake, White Earth reservation and said Budrow promised to give up the other two trust patents the next morning, but during the night Budrow went away. My son-in-law waited for Budrow two days but Budrow failed to turn up.

About two months ago, when I was in Waubun, I was taken sick and needing some money, the lawyers were very insistent that I touch a pen, and after I did so I received $400 for myself and $100 for my son. They asked me if I was a mixed-blood and I told them no, that I was a full-blood. I was not sworn to these papers. There was no interpreter and I did not understand the papers.

Her mark
MARGARET COLBURNE.

Witness to mark

C. E. DENNIS.

Subscribed and sworn to before me this 6th day of September, A.D. 1909, at White Earth, Minn.

WARREN K. MOOREHEAD,
*Spec. U. S. Indian Agent.*

It should be clear to all persons that those in authority should have informed these Indians that a trust patent lost did not mean the loss of property. By sending a small fee to Washington a duplicate trust patent would be issued to any Indian who could prove that he had lost his. Indians were allowed to remain in ignorance of this, and were led to believe that the trust patent was everything. Therefore, when they lost a trust patent they supposed they had lost their allotment.

The entire space assigned to this chapter could be devoted to a discussion of health conditions but it is too heart-rending to take up in detail. The Chippewa Indians are suffering from tuberculosis, scrofula, trachoma and other diseases. Thirty-two per cent of the children in the Government schools on examination by Government physician, Dr. Edwards, were found to have trachoma; fifty per cent of the Indians living at Pine Point have tuberculosis. Unless drastic remedies are adopted the Ojibwa will soon be a thing of the past. The Indian Office has built a hospital, and has rented of the Episcopal church a small one, yet these care for but a fraction of the sick.

The Catholic priest, Father Roman Homar, in charge of the Mission at Rice River, reported to me under date of April 29, 1910, that there was more suffering than ever before in his territory; that Indians died that winter, that many of the Indians were compelled to hunt rabbits, not for pleasure, but from necessity, and that practically all the rabbits on the reservation were killed. He exhausted his little fund and much of his own salary in caring for the unfortunate. Early in April he had utilized all the lumber at his disposal for the making of coffins, and for the last Indian that he buried, just previous to writing the letter, he made the coffin out of the church wood-box.

Rev. Father Felix, Catholic Missionary at Pine Point, and Rev. Wilkins Smith, Episcopal missionary at Twin Lakes, both wrote to me of the great suffering and poverty, sickness and death, and how their resources were taxed beyond their ability to meet the same, in order to relieve even such Indians as were connected with their various missions. The large orphan school near White Earth village is crowded.

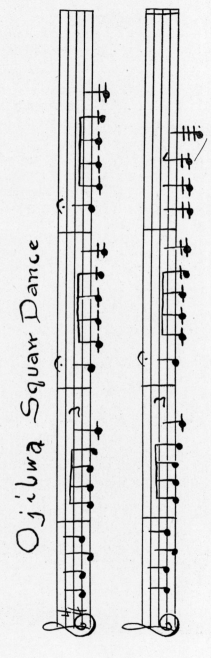

# Ojibwa Squaw Dance

Sung during the dance at Rice River, August, 1909. Recorded by W. K. Moorehead.

This is the favorite song of the squaw dance. During five evenings, when I listened to the music, and observed the ceremony of the dance, this song was rendered more frequently than any of those reproduced in Miss Densmore's book. There are no words. The musicians, five to eight in number, sat around a large drum, beating time thereon and singing at the top of their voices. The repetition of the song continues for nearly an hour. After a short intermission the singers change to another air, but soon return to the favorite.

Gifts or favors are bestowed by dancers on their partners, and according to Indian etiquette the full value must be returned when one asks a person who has "favored him" to dance. The Indians never slight each other or return trinkets for valuables. That "right" is reserved to the white participants who once in a while take part.

The Government boarding school is now attended by about 300 pupils and does excellent work. At the time of our investigation, however, it was in a most unsatisfactory condition, and immediate reforms had to be inaugurated.

Prior to the Linnen-Moorehead investigation there was entirely too much swindling of school children. One would imagine that pupils in a Government school, and under the protection of the American flag, would be safer than pupils in ordinary institutions not governmental in character. Yet there are many cases on record where children, little and big, have lost their allotments while attending school. For this the Indian Office does not seem so much to blame as the teachers and superintendents who should have refused admission to persons who came to transact business with minors. It is gratifying to learn that the Commissioner has issued strict orders, and now it is impossible for strangers, land sharks, or others to enter Government boarding schools and swindle minors out of their property. My only regret is that the strong, right arm of the Government did not protect these poor people and their children prior to my arrival at White Earth.

Miss Phillomea Donnell was a pupil in the school at Flandreau, South Dakota, where many Indian children are assembled each year for instruction. She lived as do the others, in large dormitories. She testifies that while she was there, a prominent, educated Indian appeared and entered the music room without opposition on the part of any teacher or person in authority, and sent for Miss Donnell. She came down from her room, and the man produced a folded paper and a fountain pen. He said that there was a dispute as to how her name was spelled on the Government roll. There was some discussion about it, and he secured her signature on each side of this paper in order, as he assured her, to correct any error in the record. So she signed the paper in both places, and he gave her a folded piece of paper, or an envelope, and told her it was a present for her. Indians frequently make each other presents when visiting, and so she did not look at this paper until she had been in her room some time, as he told her it was a surprise. When she looked at the paper she found it was a check for $500. Then, realizing that her allotment of eighty acres, near the town of Mahnomen, was a valuable allotment, she concluded that probably he had made her sign a paper the result of which would be the loss of her land. She immediately sought the superintendent of that school and he referred the matter to Inspector Linnen and myself. The Indian had come to the school in an automobile to hasten matters. There were no witnesses to the signature, and he had no power of attorney in

South Dakota, but only in Minnesota. Yet in a few days the deed was recorded with the signature of witnesses.

In our capacity as Government officials we reported this outrageous proceeding to the Department, prepared carefully-drawn affidavits covering the entire circumstances, and rushed them to Washington to enable the Commissioner to take immediate action. Up to the last that I heard from Miss Donnell, she had obtained no relief from the Government, but has been compelled to pay $57 out of her own funds (which were limited) to obtain her own land. The buyer would not have given it up but for the fact that he knew we were ready to proceed against him. I cite the case of this girl in detail, although there are others which could be mentioned where frauds were practised on minor children in the Government schools.

When the Graham Committee hearings were published, the affidavits and correspondence were made public. The Indian is supposed to have persuaded Miss Donnell to speak in his favor. One of the Department of Justice officials told me that the case against him was dropped.

We learned that certain educated Indians made a practice of going to these Government schools, calling the pupils into the parlor or the music-room or parade-ground, and transacting business with them.

## CHAPTER VIII.  THE ROLL.  STORIES.  RESPONSIBILITY
## FOR WHITE EARTH

Many years ago the employees at White Earth Agency made a roll of the Chippewa Indians.  One would suppose that so important a document as a register of all the Indians would be accurate.  But the original roll, as on file at the White Earth office, in 1909, bristled with inaccuracies.  For instance, the name Mah-geed is the Ojibwa pronunciation of Maggie.  Many of the Indian girls were named Mah-geed by the priests and missionaries.  Those who made the Government roll apparently thought that Mah-geed was a distinguished Indian name, so they had entered up quite a number of Mah-geeds.  No other name is added.

The Ojibwa name for old woman is Min-de-moi-yen.  To the clerks who made the roll this sounded like the name of an Indian, so they solemnly set down many such names.  "Young girl" is E-quay-zince.  There are a large number of E-quay-zinces in the roll.  Yet, mind you, this is the official roll, to which I objected, and to which the Indian Office employees replied that if it was so entered on the roll it must be correct!  When Indians are assembled together, if one would call for E-quay-zince or Mah-geed, it would be precisely as if, in an audience of two or three hundred white persons, the speaker should ask for a "young girl" named Mary to come forward, or request that "the lady" come to the platform.

By whom, aside from old Joe Pereault, an illiterate and troublesome French-Canadian, who was employed for some time in the Agent's office at White Earth, this roll was made, I do not know.

As the roll we found in the Agent's office in 1909 had been there for years, I have often wondered how the authorities could differentiate between the various Mah-geeds.  If annuity money is to be paid an Indian woman, E-quay-zince; what E-quay-zince would receive said payment?  And the same is true with reference to Min-de-moi-yen.  If on an occasion of great moment all the women of these names should appear at the agency simultaneously, how would the employees be able to deal with them?  The spectacle would be amusing, and complicated, to say the least.

Inspector Linnen and myself made an accurate roll of the full-blood Indians.  We did not trouble ourselves concerning the mixed-bloods, who were citizens, and under the law can dispose of their property.  We were sent to Minnesota to make an investigation as to the full-blood Indians, and our work was confined to these Indians.  If I remember correctly, we entered five hundred and fifteen names.

The oldest and most reliable men of the tribe were assembled at the various points where we investigated. These men knew all of the Indians living in certain parts of the reservation, and their parents. In many instances, they knew the grandparents and whether they were full-blood or mixed-blood Indians. Through the assistance of two or three interpreters, we carefully examined the witnesses in the presence of those old men. An affidavit was drawn, in accordance with the facts, and each witness attached his thumb-print thereto. On page 81 I present a photographic copy of an affidavit taken by Mr. Linnen. It will be observed by study of this that the testimony was exact in detail, and the Indian proved to be a full-blood. If this plan were followed on all the reservations in the United States, accurate lists of Indian population would result. The list was made on ethnological lines. The trouble has been, that men who were not acquainted with Indian customs or descent, and who did not assemble together a sufficient number of the older Indians, have attempted to make these rolls.

At the conclusion of our work at White Earth, the affidavits, the rolls, and other papers were given to the Indian Office, and submitted by them to the Department of Justice. The Department accepted our affidavits and put them in legal form and began prosecutions, which have extended down to the present time.

When Hon. Marsden C. Burch had charge of the White Earth cases for the Attorney General, Mr. E. C. O'Brien served as his assistant. Hon. C. C. Daniels succeeded Judge Burch, and Mr. O'Brien is associated with him in the prosecutions. Mr. O'Brien kindly read proofs of my White Earth chapters and offered suggestions. Mr. O'Brien says:—

"All suits are based on the Linnen-Moorehead roll, except a few suggested by Mr. Hinton. The Hinton roll includes all Indians on the reservation, and was prepared to determine who were entitled to fee simple patents."[*]

\* \* \* \* \* \*

Mr. John H. Hinton was appointed Special Agent and sent to White Earth to make a new roll of the Ojibwa. I was informed he added many names, but Mr. O'Brien's recent letter indicates that this is not correct. The "interests" responsible for the White Earth scandal, petitioned Congress a year ago to make a new roll of the Ojibwa. This bill nearly passed. A Commission of two is now making a roll of allotments, which Mr. O'Brien assures me are not included in the suits.

All lovers of justice may pray that no new roll be attempted. The Linnen-Moorehead list is accurate and has stood the test.

---

[*] Letter of Dec. 2nd, 1914. Federal Building, Minneapolis.

Having assembled as our witnesses the most reliable old Indians, we were able to check up the many errors in the Government roll. Frequently there would be as many as forty or fifty Ojibwa assembled in the schoolroom where our hearings were held. When the interpreter called out such a name as Min-de-moi-yen, or E-quay-zince, or Mah-geed, the other Indians would shout with laughter, and when they had recovered sufficiently they would state they did not know what individual Indian was named as there were a score who might respond to that appellation.

The Ojibwa Indians have had a number of attorneys in the past twenty, or twenty-five years. None of these men seem to have concerned themselves with the prevention of the wholesale thefts of land and timber. The gentleman who acted as attorney at the time of our arrival, became active toward the end of our investigation, and did what he could to secure justice for the Indians. But he had done nothing previously along such lines, and his activities savored of a death-bed repentance. The Secretary of the Interior did not approve his re-election. The full-blood Indians were against the employment of the attorney, and the mixed-blood Indians, headed by Gus Beaulieu, were very insistent that the attorney be retained. During the three years prior to 1909, the attorney had received in salary and expenses about $20,000.

A large council was called in July by the Indians to talk over the attorneyship. Mr. Linnen and myself were spectators, and while we could have helped the poor, ignorant full-bloods, because of our official position, we were compelled to sit in silence and see Gus Beaulieu and John Carl, Rev. Clement Beaulieu and others manipulate the meeting. The first morning, there were sufficient full-bloods to have outvoted the Beaulieu element, two to one. But Gus Beaulieu and his brother, Rev. Clement Beaulieu, consumed the time in speech-making, while Ben Fairbanks sent mixed-bloods in teams all over the reservation to bring in those who would vote according to Gus Beaulieu's desires. At the afternoon session the full-blood Indians might have carried their point, but they spent their time answering the arguments of the two Beaulieus and others, being cleverly heckled into making long speeches.

The next morning, the council adjourned to a larger hall, in the center of White Earth village. By this time the mixed-blood element predominated and a very motley crowd was assembled, including a number of saloon-keepers of Ogema and other towns, and several interpreters who were mentioned in the affidavits as having acted as go-betweens in land and timber deals. To shorten my story, the poor full-blood Indians were outvoted, they were asked to write out ballots (which they did not under-

**OJIBWA GRAVEYARD, WHITE EARTH MINNESOTA**
Nearly all of these burials are those of consumptives
the past few years

stand and most of them could not write) and the attorney was re-elected. We made a report against the council, and the Secretary of the Interior sustained our objections.

In addition to the Chippewa attorney, there was also a Chippewa Commissioner. The Graham Investigating Committee considered him at some length.

Senator Clapp asked that Darwin H. Hall be appointed Chippewa Commissioner. The history of this appointment is interesting, but must not (at present) be related. Previous to that, Hall had been employed at various intervals until his employment totaled eight years and cost $31,845. In this connection it is well to remark that the investigation made by Linnen and myself, including the employment of thirty-seven persons, and lasting all summer and part of the fall, cost for my part $3,066.64. Mr. Linnen's expenses could not have been more than a third of that sum.

Hall came to White Earth while Linnen and I were investigating, and was of no value to us. He helped us in no way. He was detailed to move some 200 or 300 Mille Lac Indians about one hundred miles (more or less). I had offered to move these same Indians in sixty days, but my offer met with no cordial response. During the twenty months that Hall was in office he moved fifty Indians, according to my information, and fifty-one according to the Indian Office report. At that rate, his job would have lasted nearly seven years! It cost him $167.50 per head to move an Indian one hundred miles. It would have cost $33,500 to move 200 Indians to White Earth!

I met Hall at the Hiawatha Hotel, White Earth, prior to the arrival of Mr. Linnen. We stepped out into the street in order not to be over-heard and I told him of the dreadful situation of the Chippewa Indians and how that he could help us right their wrongs. He informed me that he had no sympathy with the investigation, and I could see his attitude was hostile.

The Secretary of the Bureau of Catholic Missions, Charles S. Lusk, wrote to the Commissioner of Indian Affairs in August, 1910, calling attention to the sad condition of these Indians, that the removal of a portion of them to White Earth had brought them under the influence of one Gus Beaulieu and other politicians. They were promised houses, lands and farming implements. In Washington three years ago I met a delegation of the Ojibwa. Three of the members of this body were personally known to me, and the Chief Ah-bow-we-ge-shig well known. They told me that the last thing that Darwin Hall did was to summon the Mille

Lacs and persuade them to move a considerable distance from their homes. He left them in camp, promising to return shortly and move them to White Earth. These Indians waited two weeks. They had little food. Mr. Hall did not move them, and they suffered privations, and at last returned to their former homes. The story of the Mille Lacs reads as a page from Helen Hunt Jackson's "Century of Dishonor," yet this scandal did not occur in the old days, but is recent history. Who is responsible?

Almost any other body of men and women in the world would be utterly discouraged if they had passed through the same experience that fell to the lot of the Ojibwa Indians of White Earth, Minnesota, during twenty-five years. I am acquainted with no community in the East where, in the minds and hearts of the citizens, there would remain even a particle of respect, or regard, or confidence, in any government, or culture, or civilization, responsible for such a condition. The sole saving grace is the natural cheerfulness and optimism of the Ojibwa people, as a whole. Many of them are discouraged, and most of them will not farm or work, for the reason that the farming and working in the past resulted in those who were industrious being disciplined, (see page 68) and those who were indolent being rewarded. No white man or woman would work under similar circumstances. Yet, contrary to all precedents, they are cheerful and optimistic. They have a keen sense of humor, they laugh and joke among themselves. I desire to vary the monotony of this recital of wrongs and sufferings, by illustrating a few incidents.

The old witnesses and the interpreters, after dinner one noon hour, were having an animated discussion. A number of us were lolling about on the ground, smoking, and one of the officials happened at this moment to stretch and yawn. One of the old Indians immediately laughed and said something which caused the other Indians to shout with merriment. The interpreter turned to me and said, "Mah-een-gonce says, that that is the first white man he has seen to open his mouth and a lie did not hop out."

When the Indians were assembled in council on one occasion, a long letter from Washington arrived which was read by the clerk, and interpreted by John Lufkins, a Carlisle graduate. At the conclusion of a tedious interpretation requiring an hour, a prominent Indian, whom we called "Shorty," but whose correct name was Ah-bow-we-ge-shig, arose and uttered a few words not requiring more than fifteen or twenty seconds in utterance. His reply to the long, well-worded, indefinite Washington letter is worthy of preservation. "That letter is like the food that we Indians have today, all soup and no meat."

When some of the preliminary trials were heard at White Earth, previous to action by the Department of Justice, the old Indian Bay-gah-dwun-gay-aush, eighty-two years of age, and who was possessed of remarkable memory, was on the witness stand. This Indian knew the family history of several hundred persons and was entirely familiar with all parts of the reservation. The lawyers, however, would ask him where was located a piece of land described as Township 4, Section 15, Range 142, and who owned it, instead of asking the Indian, "Who owns the land at the head of Otter Creek?" or "Who used to live at the head of Otter Creek?" The attorneys purposely asked the Indian in a way to confuse him, in order to substantiate their contention that Indian testimony was not reliable.

Having stood this annoying and unfair grilling for a long time, old Bay-bah-dwun-gay-aush said something to the interpreter which caused the other Indians to laugh. His remark was, "Why does the lawyer ask me where the Indian land is? The white lawyers know better than I, because they now own most of the lands." I believe that he added that they had stolen them, or words to that effect.

Inspector Linnen, Mr. Allen and myself were criticised by those who sought, unsuccessfully, to discredit our work; for the reason that we looked on during a squaw dance. One reverend gentleman contended that we were encouraging "pagan ceremonies". In fact, he reproached one of the Government officials rather severely. The Government official denied having taken part in a pagan dance, whereupon the reverend gentleman asked him, "Have you seen many pagan dances?" "I can truthfully say," replied the official, "that I never observed but one dance which might truly be called pagan." The reverend gentleman seemed shocked, but made bold to inquire: "On what reservation?" "It was on no reservation. The only real pagan dance I ever witnessed was the inaugural ball in Washington during Harrison's administration."

On another occasion, toward the end of the investigation, we were visited by a reverend gentleman much concerned as to the welfare of the Indians, a most worthy person, but who seemed to concern himself with details, rather than the great important questions and problems of White Earth. There was a good deal of drinking among the Indians, and the police made frequent arrests. The day following an arrest, when the Indians had become sober, they were brought into Major Howard's office where a sort of "fatherly court" was held. These hearings might be roughly compared to police court affairs in other communities. Mr. Linnen and myself occasionally went in, but usually we were in the schoolroom taking testimony. Because we did not assume charge of all those multitudinous details, the worthy gentleman from the East seemed to think that we were neglecting our duties. He thought we did not seem appalled by the laxity of morals, etc. Such was not the case, for we had already made a lengthy report to the Secretary of the Interior and Commissioner of Indian Affairs on the whiskey curse and on immorality. However, he spoke to an educated Indian, and rather reprimanded us. The Indian's answer was one of the best I have ever heard. He said, "Doctor, I will give you an Indian illustration. The shed, the stable and the house are all on fire. Linnen and Moorehead are trying to save the house first, and the stable next, but the shed is doomed. You want them to abandon work on the house and begin on the shed."

Today the Department of Justice has before it something like sixteen hundred cases involving lands at White Earth. Several times have I written the Honorable Attorney General for information. While some lands have been returned, and some reforms instituted, it must be admitted that there has not been the prompt, efficient "clean-up" for which we hoped. This has had a bad effect elsewhere on both Whites and Indians. It is my firm conviction that white people are encouraged to defraud Indians, for the reason that they are willing to "take a chance." That is, they know that the Indian property can be obtained in a short time, whereas the procedure of recovery will drag through months, (and usually years) and that the Government stands more than an even chance of being defeated. It was defeated in the first White Earth cases.

The Indians take the point of view that the grafters are more powerful than the Great Father at Washington. While this seems entirely illogical, nevertheless it is entirely true — from the Indians' point of view. The Indian loses his property under such conditions as occurred at White Earth, by the removal of restrictions, in a few days, or a few weeks, elsewhere in a few months, or not more than a few years. He knows that this is true and that it occurs all over the United States. The Government does not spend a few weeks, or a few months in recovering the property, save in very rare instances. Usually, the Government cases drag on for years. The Indians write letters to the men who began the investigation, or the attorneys who tried the cases, and they receive just such replies as fill the files in my office: "I have the honor to advise you that the Department is doing all it can to bring the cases to trial. There was much testimony to be taken before they could be tried on their merits.* Some are now almost ready for trial, and we hope to submit them before

---

* Letter of Aug. 29th, 1914.

the close of the calendar year;" or, "The Department is doing all possible;" or, "The delays are due to the activity of the attorneys on the other side;" or, "It has been found that according to Act 462, 57th Congress, that these white persons are empowered", etc.; or, "The information contained in your communication of the 13th has been submitted to our legal department," etc., etc. From the Indian point of view, there is anything and everything under the sun except the return of the property or the punishment of the guilty. This is strong language, but it is absolutely true. So long as we permit Indians to lose their property without let or hindrance from us, our Indian citizens will lose their property; and so long as we administer our justice in such a manner that the burden of the proof seems to rest on the poor Indian rather than upon the white grafter, just so long will the bulk of the Indians care neither for industry nor education, neither for civilization nor Christianity. The Indian must have the same standing and the same justice in court as the white man. Furthermore, there must be a swift administration of justice, and some means devised whereby the tricks of grafters' lawyers may be overcome.

The Inspection Service, under the supervision of Honorable E. B. Linnen, is now what it should have been ten years ago. I went into this phase of the White Earth situation in 1909, very thoroughly. There had been Special Agents and Inspectors at White Earth time and again.

One who had done real work was Mrs. Elsie E. Newton, one of the most able and conscientious women in the Indian Service. She had visited the sick and the suffering, had made recommendations, had done her part toward remedying intolerable conditions.

How the others could have visited such a place as White Earth and not reported on actual conditions is incomprehensible, unless we accept Mr. Valentine's address at Lake Mohonk, in October, 1909, in which he stated that too many of his Inspectors were blind and deaf! I talked with one or two men now out of the Service, who used to be Special Agents, and they did not even know the names of all the places on the reservation! I don't know of one of them who went into the cabins and sat down and talked to the Indians and heard their troubles. Most of them drove from the railroad station at Ogema, over to the Agent's office and talked with Mr. Michelet, the agent preceding Howard.

I would close this chapter on White Earth with an incident which occurred at Pine Point during the first investigation, March-April, 1909.

The Chief of the Otter Tail Pilligers lives at Pine Point. One of the most dramatic instances which occurred during the investigation happened in the latter part of March before the large party, employed during the summer, had begun their labors. It was cold and we were compelled to hold our examinations indoors. Just opposite the office was a schoolroom in which some sixty Indian children were assembled under the charge of three or four white teachers. The chief had lost a number of children and other relatives, and thus he and his wife were heirs to about eleven allotments. These were easily worth $45,000 or $50,000, being mostly pine timber. With the exception of one or two others, this man had been robbed of more property than anyone else, and it was pathetic to hear him state how certain men in whom he trusted, had taken advantage of his ignorance. When he had finished his long recital of wrongs, I remarked, "You must have lost entire faith in the white people and in the Government at Washington." "Oh, no," he replied, "I think that Washington would give me justice if only the men there could hear my story." Just as he completed this statement, the school session came to an end, and we heard through the thin partition the childish voices singing in unison "My Country, 'Tis of Thee, Sweet Land of Liberty"— and this was the first time in my life that the words sounded in my ears like a hollow mockery and a sham.

### BIBLIOGRAPHY OF WHITE EARTH

Omitting ethnological reports and Warren's book (*see page 45*) those who desire to study conditions at White Earth, Leech Lake, Red Lake, and Cass Lake, are referred to the reports of the Secretary of the Interior, Commissioner of Indian Affairs, and the Board of Indian Commissioners the past twenty years. These contain all administrative details.

The legal aspect of the prosecution will be found in pamphlets issued by the Department of Justice, and the U. S. Court of Claims.

White Earth has been the subject of much investigation on the part of Committees of the Senate and House of Representatives. The most lengthy and exhaustive investigation, covering every phase of the subject, is the report of the Committee on Expenditure in the Interior Department, Honorable James M. Graham of Illinois, Chairman. House Resolution No. 103; July 25, 1911 – April, 1912; 2759 pp. Those who care to follow the subject further, will find in this lengthy report an enormous amount of material.

A synopsis entitled "The Lesson of White Earth" will be found in the report of the 30th Conference of Friends of the Indian and Other Dependent Peoples held at Lake Mohonk, N. Y., October, 1912.

# CHAPTER IX.  THE SIOUX AND THE MESSIAH CRAZE

The Sioux is one of our most famous Indian nations.  As the Iroquois activities two centuries ago placed them in the forerank of American aborigines, so the Sioux from the days of Lewis and Clark down to the present have been much in evidence.  They are primarily a strong, hearty race possessed of dominant spirit.  Their reservations at Standing Rock, Rosebud, Pine Ridge, etc., contain most of the 28,000 natives of this stock.  Reference to Major Powell's linguistic map will acquaint readers with the enormous extent of territory they once occupied.  The Commissioner's map of 1913 shows that these people today own a small fraction of their original holdings.

The general progress of the Sioux, the famous men that they have produced, I have covered in the chapters treating of Education, Red Cloud, Sitting Bull, etc.

They were known to the army officers as Horse Indians, and to many others as Plains Indians.  The horse was to the Sioux what the birch bark canoe was to the Ojibwa or the Penobscot.  In early days their habitat was almost entirely confined to the Great Plains, the foothills of the Black Hills and the Missouri River.  They were in Minnesota at an early period, but were driven westward and southward by the Ojibwa.  The older Ojibwa claim that the Sioux frequently surprised hunting parties of these woods Indians, and that whenever the Ojibwa were caught out on the plain by the Sioux, they were invariably defeated with great loss.  The Ojibwa therefore resorted to the strategy of luring the Sioux into the woods.  Where this was possible, the expert woodcraft of the Ojibwa came into play and they generally defeated their enemies with heavy slaughter.

1850 to 1868 found the Sioux supremacy on the Great Plains unquestioned.  With the coming of the railroad, and steamboat navigation on the Missouri, and the great influx of white traders, their powers declined as I have indicated in some detail on other pages.

The story of the Brulé, Miniconjou, Oglala, Teton and other divisions, so far as history is concerned, is pretty much the same.  The buffalo was their chief support, in fact their very life was bound up in this animal.  The wild horse was a later acquisition.  In order to understand them thoroughly, the past fifty years, we should study in detail the life of Red Cloud, that of Sitting Bull, and in addition the Messiah craze, as previously mentioned.

The contrast between the Pine Ridge of today and that of 1890 is almost beyond belief. In 1890, one of the strangest ceremonies imaginable was in full swing. In 1909, when I visited Pine Ridge, exactly nineteen years later, I found the Sioux working upon their allotments, farming, digging irrigation ditches, and doing their best toward "taking the white man's road." On the plains where once clustered the tipis of the Ghost dancers were the large, modern brick buildings of the Oglala school, a most successful institution where young men and women are trained in the arts. Certainly the progress of these Indians is more than surprising — it is remarkable. And it is chiefly due to the fact that they have had as their Superintendent or Agent a man who is in sympathy with them and who has not been replaced through political influence. Major John R. Brennan has supervised the famous old fighting Oglala Sioux for more than fifteen years.

The progress of these Indians is, as I have said, creditable, but they are still poor, there is much suffering, and the increase in stock has not been as large as desired. Farming operations continue on a large scale, but the soil is more suited to grazing than farming, although the Indians do the best they can under the circumstances.

All of the Sioux have so far progressed, that it is unthinkable that any fanaticism such as the Ghost dance will again overtake them. It is quite safe to predict that since all of their children have been educated and nearly all of the Sioux of every reservation have been allotted land in severalty, they will continue to progress, and if the ravages of tuberculosis are stayed, a large number of the descendants of the full-bloods will survive and become useful citizens.

These Indians, after the surrender of Sitting Bull, were not much in the public eye until occurred the famous Ghost dance, or Messiah craze, and that being the chief event since the Custer fight we must needs devote considerable space to it.

On several occasions during the past two centuries, in this country, Indian shamans, or priests, have prophesied the coming of an Indian Messiah. We shall at some future time consider this interesting subject in detail, but within the period embraced in this book, that peculiar craze which swept throughout the West and the South during the year 1890, and known as the Ghost Dance, is the chief religious event.

Mr. James Mooney of the Bureau of Ethnology, published a very comprehensive monograph, in 1896, entitled "The Ghost Dance Religion", in the Fourteenth Annual Report of the Bureau of Ethnology. I shall draw the information presented in this chapter partly from Mr. Mooney's account, but more especially from my own investigation made in the winter of 1890 at Pine Ridge reservation, South Dakota, where among the Oglala Sioux the Messiah craze reached its culmination.

The music of the Oglala dances was taken down at the time by Mr. George E. Bartlett (Husté) and myself. Our work was not copyrighted, and soon found its way into various publications, and after being harmonized, our music was soon in general use. It is no more than fair to say that as I lay no claim to special skill as an ethnologist, Mr. Mooney, having more training and experience in such studies, was able to present the songs and their translations more accurately. I believe, in my original articles published in the *Illustrated American* of New York in January and February, 1891, some of the Sioux word-syllables were not properly spaced, a number of accent marks omitted, and there were a few minor errors. But in the main the account as published was correct, although it was a "popular", rather than a technical paper.

I did not investigate the Messiah in the West, although the new religion was inaugurated by him. The Sioux told me a great deal concerning him. He was known to them as Johnson, whereas Mooney gives as his proper name, Wovoka. In November, 1891, a year after the trouble at Pine Ridge, Mr. Mooney set out for Pine Ridge, where he spent considerable time, and then visited Walker Lake reservation in Nevada, where Wovoka (Johnson) lived. Here he obtained at first hand the information concerning the origin of the Messiah religion, and has presented us with a very valuable and interesting account.

As in the case of all Messiahs or prophets, Wovoka was a dreamer. He inherited the spirit of prophecy, for his father before him was known as a prophet. The young man at the time of Mooney's visit, had never wandered beyond the valley wherein he resided — a small area, some thirty miles in length. Wovoka belonged to the Paiute, and his religion may be summed up in this statement which Mooney records.

"When the sun died, I went up to heaven and saw God and all the people who had died a long time ago. God told me to come back and tell my people they must be good and love one another, and not fight, or steal, or lie. He gave me this dance to give to my people."

If the missionaries and Government employees had seized upon the beautiful sentiment uttered in this remarkable paragraph, the new religion might have been turned to good account. Instead of that, as we shall see presently, an Agent utterly ignorant of Indians, saw in this sacred ceremony nothing beyond a "war dance" and he sent for troops — the very worst possible thing he could have done.

Mooney spent many days conversing with this interesting person, Wovoka, who told him that he had given to his people this dance about two years previously.  He seems to have talked very freely with Mr. Mooney, permitting him to take his photograph, and when Mooney left, the prophet gave him as souvenirs to exhibit to his friends, a blanket of rabbit skins, sacred paint endowed with miraculous powers and which plays an important part in the ritual of the Ghost dance religion, and other trinkets.

In Oklahoma Mooney met with the Cheyennes and Arapahoes and they gave him a written statement of the doctrine of Wovoka, which he was permitted to take to Washington to convince the authorities, "that there was nothing bad or hostile in the new religion."

Mooney traveled many months West and South and his excellent report is evidence that he studied every phase of the dance.  My work was confined to Pine Ridge where I studied the dance while it was in progress.  There it appeared in all its purity;  there the white people made of it a "warlike" demonstration;  there stupidity and ignorance transformed a peaceful, religious ceremony into a bloody tragedy — Wounded Knee.

I employed three interpreters:  the Weasel (Itonkasan,) George Bartlett (Husté), and a Frenchman, whose name I do not recall.

Doctor Charles A. Eastman, the Sioux, some years after my account was published, informed me that it was correct, and he was present before, during and after the trouble at Pine Ridge, and knew all the actors intimately.

Summing up Mr. Mooney's conclusions in a few words, the Messiah craze of 1890 was a mixture of Christianity and Indian religion.

In a nutshell, the Messiah craze conformed to the sentiments of Jesus Christ.  It was not expressed in His language, but the frequent repetitions of such sentiments as "you must not fight", and, "do injury to no one"; "give up the bad white man's ways"; "live as brothers as you did before the Whites came"; "Dance faithfully to the Great Spirit"; "Father and Mother are talking"; etc., indicate a belief in the better things of life and of the hereafter.  Instead of hostility, peace was proclaimed;  instead of avarice, the communistic life was advocated.

There was only one discontented element, or discordant note, and that was the stand taken by Sitting Bull and a few other Indians, who seized upon this craze to further their own personal aims.  Major Mc-Laughlin has commented in full on Sitting Bull's attitude in his book, pages 183-220.  And while I do not entirely agree with him, it is beyond question that Sitting Bull sought to gain through the Messiah craze.  To a certain extent he advocated armed resistance, but the dominating desire in his mind, a careful review of events would indicate, was that Sitting Bull desired above all things to see the Indians restored to their old-time domination.  Like the others, he prayed for the return of the buffalo, without which "the good old days" would be impossible.  He probably believed that volcanic action ("wave of mud", as the Oglala called it) would sweep across the country, destroy the Whites and leave the red men happy possessors of the Plains and countless herds of bison, elk and deer. That was the belief of many of the Indians, and so expressed by them during the Ghost dance.

The Ghost dance, or Messiah craze, was seized upon by all these Sioux as a means of salvation out of their troubles.  We must remember that these Indians had lived but a few years on the reservation at Pine Ridge.  In 1876, only fourteen years before, they killed Custer and wiped out several companies of the Seventh Cavalry.  They had made some progress, but they were still ration Indians, and the cutting down of the supply of beef, etc., hundreds of thousands pounds, before the Indians had become self-supporting, caused widespread suffering.

It is not necessary to repeat the troubles of the Sioux here.  I have referred to some of the treaties, Indian cause for dissatisfaction, in other pages of this book.  In the spring of 1889, so I was informed at Pine Ridge, Congress passed an act authorizing the purchase of a large tract of land from these people.  Honorable Charles Foster, ex-Governor of Ohio, and several other gentlemen were appointed a committee to negotiate with the Indians.  According to the Indians' version, many councils were held and a great deal of discussion ensued.  Sometimes the debates were rather strenuous and they all related to purchase of lands — to the further curtailing of the Sioux reservation — the same old story.  An intelligent educated Indian summed up their cause as follows: —

"The lands secured by the treaty were divided into three classes.  All tracts selected for farming or grazing purposes within a period of three years from February 15, 1890, were to be sold at $1.25 per acre.  Those purchased during the two years following were valued at seventy-five cents per acre.  The portions remaining unsold after the expiration of five years could be bought for fifty cents per acre.  The money received from the sale of the land was to be placed in the United States Treasury, subject to interest, which was to be paid to the Indians at regular intervals.

"Any Sioux whom his Agent considered qualified for supporting himself was to be allowed to select for his own use a tract of land, the area of which was determined by the number of members in his family.  Farming implements and utensils, oxen or horses, seed, etc., and fifty dollars in cash were also to be given him. Notices to acquaint the Sioux with this proposition were posted in conspicuous places in the agency buildings, and every inducement was offered the people to take the land in severalty. So far, about one hundred at Rosebud, a smaller number at Standing Rock, and some two hundred at Pine Ridge have made applications to the Agents for allotments.

MODERN SIOUX CABIN AND SUMMER TENT. PINE RIDGE, 1909

"Inquiries were made of many of the leading men on the reservation as to why more persons did not avail themselves of the Government's liberal offer and become self-supporting. The Indians' answers and their reasons for not taking up land in severalty convinced all questioners not already prejudiced that under the present condition of affairs it would be impossible to interest more than a small percentage of the nation in agriculture."*

Some of the Indians' statements may be denied in Washington. The Indians have always maintained that many things are told them by Commissioners which are never carried into effect. I am quite aware that

* Written in 1890, at Pine Ridge.

only the written recommendations are acted upon. That is, the report of a Commission may be quite different from the Indians' ideas or understandings of the councils and the debates. Politicians will cultivate the good will of Indians just as they cultivate voters. The politician frankly admits: "a platform is made to get in on." The failure to keep these promises, and the difference between the actual performance and the words so freely uttered in the presence of the Indians, caused much dissatisfaction and paved the way for the Messiah craze.

Another serious cause for complaint occurred after the Messiah craze started. Doctor Royer sent out the Indian police and brought in all the friendly Indians, in order to differentiate them from the "hostiles." That is, he compelled all Indians who were not dancing, and those who were lukewarm toward the Messiah doctrine, to move to the agency and live in tents and canvas tipis under his direct supervision. When I reached Pine Ridge, these tents extended in little groups, here and there, for two miles. As most of the Indians lived in log cabins, this foolish order worked great hardship. Many of them lost stock, their cabins were broken into, and they were compelled to seek support from the Government. Royer was forced to issue a great quantity of rations. As the younger children, for the most part, were accustomed to living in the log houses referred to, this change in winter to life in the open was responsible for a heavy increase of diphtheria and other diseases.

The Indians bitterly complained and began to say they thought the Government had deliberately set about destroying the Pine Ridge Sioux.

As a result of the mismanagement, the ignorance, the suffering, and the presence of the troops, the progress of the Pine Ridge Sioux was delayed many years, and much of the advancement of the previous ten years was forever lost. The only redeeming feature at Pine Ridge, in my opinion, was the appointment of Major John R. Brennan as Agent. He took charge shortly after the military domination ended and after years of labor managed to inspire confidence in the Oglalas.

The succeeding pages describe the dance ceremonies as related to me at Pine Ridge in November and December, 1890. I have left much of the narrative in the present tense, as written then.

The Indians located in the Dakotas have been in the habit of visiting the Utes and Arapahoes every summer for the purpose of trading. They also hunted game en route. While the Sioux are unable to converse with these tribes, means of communication is possible through the medium of the sign-language, which was well understood by all Plains Indians. Most of the older Oglala, Miniconjou, and Brulé are able to use it at present.

GOVERNMENT SCHOOL BUILDINGS ; ON SITE OF "HOSTILES' CAMP" OF 1890.  PINE RIDGE, 1909

Keeps-the-Battle (Kicizapi Tawa) told me a few days ago that it was during the visit of the Pine Ridge Sioux last July that he first heard of the coming of the new Messiah. He related the following story:

"Scarcely had my people reached the Ute village when we heard of a white preacher whom the Utes held in the highest esteem, who told a beautiful dream or vision of the coming of a great and good red man. This strange person was to set aright the wrongs of my people; he could restore to us our game and hunting grounds, was so powerful that every wish or word he gave utterance to became fulfilled.

"His teaching had a strange effect upon the Utes, and, in obedience to the commands of this man, they began a Messiah dance."

Keeps-the-Battle further said that, immediately upon the arrival of the hunting-party at Pine Ridge, a small dance was held in imitation of the ones they had seen while among the Utes, but that until the medicine men began to superintend the ceremonies nothing unusual occurred. The dances were held every few days until the middle of August. Then, with scarcely any warning, a wild and general desire took possession of a large part of the nation to welcome the expected Messiah the moment he set foot upon earth. Mr. H. G. Galagher was then Agent, and, fearing that the enthusiasm of the Sioux under his charge might terminate in an outbreak, he visited White Bird's camp accompanied by fourteen Indian police. As he approached the village, twenty warriors sprang out of the brush and, drawing their Winchesters, called upon him to halt. They would not permit him to advance, and compelled the party to turn about and retrace its footsteps to the agency.

The news of this bold action spread like wildfire through the country, and being heralded and exaggerated by the daily press, caused many an uneasy and timid settler to prepare to remove to the nearest point upon the railroad.

The news of the failure of the agent to stop the Messiah dance was carried by couriers to the Indians at Rosebud and Standing Rock reservations, and the more susceptible persons became infatuated with the new craze. Meetings and dances were arranged at points distant from the agency posts, in order that no employee might interfere. Of course, both the Sioux and the Whites were much excited. The former were ready and willing to throw off forever the odious yoke of oppression; the latter, fearful for the safety of their homes and families.

The white people became frantic from fear, houses were barricaded and all Indians viewed with suspicion. A sensational press magnified events, and settlers accused many friendly Indians, who had joined the dance for no other purpose than worship, of hostile intentions. This accusation, coupled with the arrival of some four or five times as many troops as were necessary to subdue the small number of lodgers which later fled into the borders of the Bad Lands, had the effect of turning the more timid toward the agency, while the braver middle-aged and young men fled to the northward.

But to return to the mission of Agent Galagher last summer. It is quite natural to suppose that the Agent was not a little frightened at his reception near "White Bird's" camp, and, as subsequent events would

SIOUX FARMING. WHITE CLAY CREEK, PINE RIDGE, 1909

seem to indicate, he feared to assert his authority and compel the Sioux to discontinue their dance. He hoped that in time the craze would die out without interference on his part. But instead of ceasing, the number participating increased, and really things began to assume a very threatening aspect. Then came the change of Agents and Dr. D. F. Royer, of Alpina, South Dakota, succeeded Mr. Galagher. Royer was not the man for so trying a post, and as both the Agents were political appointees, trouble was certain to follow. And no sooner did Indians begin to dance than Royer bombarded Washington with requests for troops. He sent a letter or telegram every day.

The dancers were not slow to take advantage of Galagher's or Royer's non-interference, and a report gained wide circulation to the effect that their Agent was afraid to command the police to arrest the principals in the dance. The medicine men and Indians of the same stamp as the late Sitting Bull, addressed the young men somewhat after the following manner:

"Do you not see that the Whites on the reservation are afraid of you? Why do you pray to great Wakantanka to send the Saviour on earth when the remedy lies in your own hands? Be men, not children. You have a perfect right to dance upon your own reservation as much as you please, and you should exercise the rights, even if you find it necessary to use your guns. Be brave, and the good and great Wakantanka will aid your arms. Be cowards, and he will be ashamed of you."

Now let us consider the Messiah craze as it appeared in its purity.

In nearly all religious beliefs the candidate for admission to the church or body of worshippers is compelled to pass through certain ceremonies. In our own day we maintain certain practices which have nothing whatever to do with one's salvation, but which have been handed down both by tradition and historical record, and on this account are sacredly preserved.

There do not appear to have been any special preparations on the part of the candidates. The sweat-lodge was in frequent use, and many Indians purified themselves. The sweat-bath was common among the Sioux in 1889-1890. But during the Messiah craze its use became widespread, and the dancers thought it prepared them, or purified them, for the dance. The pipe is also smoked during the sweat. When the young men issue from their bath the perspiration is fairly streaming from every pore. If it is not cold weather they plunge into a pool in the creek nearby, but if it is chilly they wrap blankets about their bodies. None of the Whites and half-breeds who have witnessed these things ever saw a Sioux rub himself after issuing from the bath.

The largest camp of the dancers prior to the departure for the North was located upon Wounded Knee creek. Other camps of considerable extent existed upon White Clay creek, four miles from the agency headquarters, upon Porcupine and Medicine Root streams. No Water's camp became, later, the general rendezvous.

The shamans took the dance under their charge. One of them seemed to be "high priest," or at least controlled the affair. Three or four assistants served, and had power to stop or start the dance.

NO WATER'S CAMP OF GHOST DANCERS, 1890

A. Council Lodge. B. No Water's Tipi

Sketch by Husté, Pine Ridge

# CHAPTER X.  THE DANCE

Several sweat-houses are erected in order to prepare the young men for the dance.  When a good number of young men, say fifty or sixty, have taken the sweat-bath, and prepared themselves, the high priest and his assistants come forward.  The high priest wears eagle-feathers in his hair, and a shirt reaching nearly to his knees.  The assistants are dressed in similar manner, but wear no ornaments other than the eagle-feathers.  The dancers wear no ornaments whatsoever, and enter the circle without their blankets.

That Indians should lay aside all ornaments and finery and dance without the trappings which they so dearly love proves conclusively that some powerful religious influence is at work.  In their other dances, (the Omaha, the Old Woman, the Sun) feathers and bangles; weapons, herbs or painted and plaited grasses; porcupine quills, horses' tails and bits of fur-skins; necklaces, bells, silver discs, etc., are worn in great profusion.

At Pine Ridge few candidates for "conversion" fasted.  After they have come forth from the sweat-house they are ready to enter the sacred circle.  The high priest runs quickly from the village to the open space of ground, five or six hundred yards distant, and, stationing himself near the sacred tree, begins his chant as follows:

"Hear, hear, all you persons!

"Come, hurry up and dance, and when you have finished running in the circle, tell these people what you have seen in the spirit land.

"I myself have been in the spirit land and have seen many strange and beautiful things, all of which my eyes tell me are good and true."

As the speaker proceeds, the men and women crowd to the dance-ground.  They form two or three circles, according to the number of persons who wish to participate, and, grasping hands with fingers interlocked ("Indian grip"), the circles begin to move around toward the left.*

In the center, at No Water's camp, stands the sacred tree.  It is a nearly straight sapling thirty or forty feet high, trimmed of branches to a height of several feet.  To the topmost twigs is attached a small white flag or canvas strip, supposed to be an emblem of purity, together with some colored strips.  The base of the tree is wrapped with rushes and flags to a thickness of some feet.  Between the reeds the dancers from time to time thrust little gifts or peace-offerings.  These offerings are supposed to allay the anger of the Great Spirit, and are given in perfectly good faith by the poor natives.  They consist of small pieces of calico, bags of tobacco, or

---

* This Chapter was written at Pine Ridge, December, 1890.

pipes.  During the height of excitement, those worshippers most deeply affected cut small particles of flesh from their arms, and thrust these, also, between the rushes of the holy tree.

Henry Hunter (the Weasel, "Itonkasan") informs me that after the dance had been running some days, the rushes covering the base of the tree were literally besmeared with human blood!

As the circle moves toward the left, the priest and his assistants cry out loudly for the dancers to stop a moment.  As they pause he raises his hands toward the west, and upon all the people acting similarly, begins the following remarkable prayer:

"Great Spirit, look at us now.  Grandfather and Grandmother have come.  All these good people are going to see Wakantanka, but they will be brought safely back to earth.  Everything that is good you will see there, and you can have these things by going there.  All things that you hear there will be holy and true, and when you return you can tell your friends how spiritual it is."

As he prays, the dancers cry aloud with all the fervor of religious fanatics.  They moan and sob, many of them exclaiming:  "Great Father, I want you to have pity upon me."

One can scarcely imagine the terrible earnestness of these people. George E. Bartlett, and Mr. Sweeney, one of the agency school-teachers, the chief herder, Mr. John Darr, and others, have informed me that during their extended experience at the agency, of many years' duration, they have witnessed many of these dances.  They describe the scene of the dance, especially at night, as most weird and ghostlike.  The fires are very large, and shed a bright reflection all around; the breasts of the worshippers heave with emotion; they groan and cry as if they were suffering great agony, and the priest begs them to ask great Wakantanka to forgive their sins.

After prayer and weeping, and offerings have been made to the sacred pole, the dance is started again.  The dancers go rather slowly at first, and as the priests in the center begin to shout and leap about, the dancers partake of the enthusiasm.  Instead of moving with a regular step, each person jumps backward and forward, up and down, as hard as he or she can without relinquishing their hold upon their neighbor's hand.  One by one the dancers fall out of the ranks, some staggering like drunken men, others wildly rushing here and there almost bereft of reason.  Many fall upon the earth to writhe about as if possessed of demons, while blinded women throw their clothes over their heads and run through brush or against trees.  The priests are kept busy waving eagle-feathers in the faces of the most violent worshippers.  The feather is considered sacred, and its use, together with the mesmeric glance and motion of the priest, soon causes the victim to fall into a trance or deep sleep. Whether this sleep is real or feigned the writer does not pretend to say, but sufficiently deep is it that Whites visiting the dance have been unable to rouse the sleepers by jest or blow.

Unquestionably the priests exercise an influence over the more susceptible of the dancers akin to hypnotism. One of the young men, who danced in the ghost circle twenty times, told me that the priest "Looked very hard at us. Some of the young men and women could not withstand his snake-like gaze, and did whatever he told them."

Regarding what is seen by the converts when in the spirit land, I have secured interviews with three prominent Oglalas touching upon this matter.

Little Wound said:

"When I fell in the trance a great and grand eagle came and carried me over a great hill, where there was a village where the tipis were all of buffalo hides, and we made use of the bow and arrow, there being nothing of white man's manufacture in the beautiful land. Nor were any Whites permitted to live there. The broad and fertile lands stretched in every direction, and were most pleasing to my eyes.

"I was taken into the presence of the great Messiah, and he spoke to me these words:

"'My child, I am glad to see you. Do you want to see your children and relations who are dead?'

"I replied: 'Yes, I would like to see my relations who have been dead a long time. The God then called my friends to come up to where I was. They appeared, riding the finest horses I ever saw, dressed in superb and most brilliant garments, and seeming very happy. As they approached, I recognized the playmates of my childhood, and I ran forward to embrace them while the tears of joy ran down my cheeks.

"We all went together to another village, where there were very large lodges of buffalo hide, and there held a long talk with the great Wakantanka. Then he had some squaws prepare us a meal of many herbs, meat, and wild fruits and 'wasna' (pounded beef and choke-cherries). After we had eaten, the Great Spirit prayed for our people upon the earth, and then we all took a smoke out of a fine pipe ornamented with the most beautiful feathers and porcupine quills. Then we left the city and looked into a great valley where there were thousands of buffalo, deer and elk feeding.

"After seeing the valley, we returned to the city, the Great Spirit speaking meanwhile. He told me that the earth was now bad and worn out; that we needed a new dwelling-place where the rascally Whites could not disturb us. He further instructed me to return to my people, the Sioux, and say to them that if they would be constant in the dance and pay no attention to the Whites he would shortly come to their aid. If the high priests would make for the dancers medicine-shirts and pray over them no harm could come to the wearer; that the bullets of any Whites that desired to stop the Messiah dance would fall to the ground without doing anyone harm, and the person firing such shots would drop dead. He said that he had prepared a hole in the ground filled with hot water and fire for the reception of all white men and non-believers. With these parting words I was commanded to return to earth."

GHOST DANCE AT NO WATER'S CAMP, 1890. Sketch by Husté

Just after the dancers have been crying and moaning about their sins the priests strike up the first song, in which all join, singing with deafening loudness. Some man or woman may be at this moment at the tree, with his or her arms thrown about the rushes, sobbing as if their heart would break; or another may be walking and crying, wringing his hands, or going through some motion to indicate the deepest sorrow for his transgressions. So the singer cries aloud to his mother to be present and aid him. The appeal to the father refers, of course, to the Messiah, and its use in this connection is supposed to give emphasis to the demand for the mother's presence and hasten her coming.

## Ghost Dance

I na hé ku wo' Mi sún ka la ché' ya o mán i ye Mi sún ka la ché ya

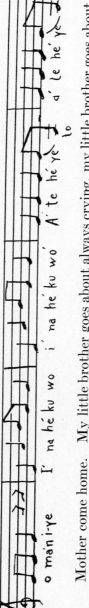

o mán i ye   Ï na hé ku wo   i' na hé ku wo'  A' te hé yè   a' te hé'ye lo

Mother come home.  My little brother goes about always crying, my little brother goes about
always crying.  Mother come home;  Mother come home.  This the father says;  this the father
says.

## Ghost Dance

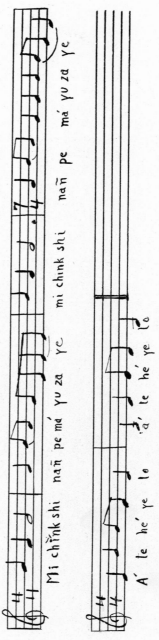

Mi chĭnk shi  nañ pe má' yu za ye  mi chink shi  nañ pe  má' yu za ye

A' te hé' ye lo  'a' te hé ye lo

My son, let me grasp your hand.  My son, let me grasp your hand.  This the father says,
This the father says.

The second song requires a longer explanation. It expresses in brief the goodness of the father. Some one of the dancers has come to life from the trance, and has just related his or her experience in the other world. The Messiah, or Father, has been very near to the subject, and the high priest, enlarging upon the importance of this fact, runs about the interior of the circle handing several pipes around, exclaiming that these pipes were received direct from the Great Spirit, and that all who smoke them will live. The people are worked up to such a pitch of religious frenzy that their minds are now willing to receive any utterance as truth undisputable, so they pass around the pipes, singing the song meanwhile. The repetition of the words, "This the Father says," indicates that the God inspires all that is done.

One of the visions seen by a young woman when under the influence of the trance, varied somewhat from the others. She told the following story:

"I was carried into the beautiful land as others have been, and there I saw a small but well-made lodge constructed entirely of rushes and reeds. These were woven closely together and resembled the fine basket-work that many of our squaws make during the winter. The tipi was provided with a stone wall, which was composed of small, flat stones laid up against the walls to the height of three or four feet. In this lodge the great Wakantanka dwelt and would issue forth at noon. Promptly at the time when the sun was above me the lodge trembled violently and then began its descent toward the earth. It landed near the dance-ground, and there stepped forth a man clothed in a blanket of rabbit-hides. This was the Messiah, and he had come to save us."

The vision of Little Horse is still more remarkable. He said:

"Two holy eagles transported me to the Happy Hunting Grounds. They showed me the Great Messiah there, and as I looked upon his fair countenance I wept, for there were nail-prints in his hands and feet where the cruel Whites had once fastened him to a large cross. There was a small wound in his side also, but as he kept himself covered with a beautiful mantle of feathers this wound could only be seen when he shifted his blanket. He insisted that we continue the dance, and promised me that no Whites should enter his city nor partake of the good things he had prepared for the Indians. The earth, he said, was now worn out and it should be repeopled.

"He had a long beard and long hair, and was the most handsome man I ever looked upon."

Before concluding my description of the dance as it appeared during the first few months of its existence at Pine Ridge, I would like to add that the dances were held throughout the day usually, but that once in a while, when a village was especially devout, they were continued all night. In that event food was prepared in large quantities, so that the worshippers could partake of refreshments when they desired.

The high priest frequently announces in a loud tone the visions related to him by the converts. His discourse is often interrupted by loud grunts of approval on the part of the assembled natives. The personal experience of the Weasel may be of interest:

"While dancing I saw no visions, but the other Indians told me to not think of anything in particular, but keep my eyes fastened upon the priests, and soon I would see all that they saw.

"The first large dance held was on Wounded Knee Creek under the guidance of Big Road. I attended this one, but did not observe Two Strike in the audience. We had been dancing irregularly for several weeks when a runner came into camp greatly excited, one night, and said that the soldiers had arrived at Pine Ridge and were sent by the Great Father at Washington. The priests called upon the young men at this juncture not to become angry but to continue the dance, but have horses ready so that all could flee were the military to charge the village. So we mounted our ponies and rode around the hills all night singing our two songs."

I asked the Weasel: "Did you ever see the medicine-shirt worn?"

"Yes, they wore blessed shirts that night. The priests had said prayers over these garments, and they were bullet-proof. One girl tried to gash herself with a butcher-knife on the arm, but the blade was bent and the edge turned, so powerful was the medicine in the shirt."

# CHAPTER XI.  LOUIS SHANGRAUX AND THE TROOPS

About December 8th Louis Shangraux and some prominent Indians were sent out by the military to persuade the dancers to come in.  December 15th we heard singing, and running out of our quarters, beheld thirty horsemen advancing upon the agency.  Following them were large numbers of the "hostiles".  Every man was superbly mounted and well armed. Six-shooters were hung at their sides, while the gun-cases, neatly beaded and ornamented, were strapped and hung along the saddles.  The warriors drew up in front of the general's (Brooke) headquarters, and as the last notes of the song died away leaped from the animals' backs.  As they crowded into the commanding officer's presence, we who stood near had the honor of shaking hands with these men.  The general himself welcomed them with words of commendation, for he thoroughly appreciated the efforts of the "friendlies" in the desire to prevent bloodshed.

That night, accompanied by my interpreter Bartlett, I visited the lodge of Scout Shangraux, and secured the following narrative regarding the expedition and the intentions of the hostiles.

"One week ago (the 8th) the general called me (Shangraux) into his office, and told me he was very desirous of bringing in the hostiles without bloodshed.  He said that the mission of Father Jutz had resulted in great good, that the Government scouts sent out had failed to reach the camp-site of Short Bull and Kicking Bear, and that all information regarding the strength of the hostiles was entirely unreliable."

Louis was given the power to select his party, and accordingly chose some good, true men whom he knew could be depended upon in case of trouble.  No white man went with him, for it was believed the hostiles would kill anyone not an Indian who should venture near the camp.  From subsequent events this was found to be true.

The camp is located on a plateau, 130 feet above the valley.  But one approach is observed — a narrow path.  Louis claimed the Indians had piled stones, or made breastworks.  They possessed much ammunition and food; two springs afforded plenty of water, and their situation appears to have been secure.  Some little way off, in the valley, was a large village. "When we entered there were about 262 lodges present.  One hundred and seventeen of these remained and 145 returned with us to the agency.  The squaws and men came forward to greet us, and all seemed very friendly.

They supposed at first that we had come to join them, but when they learned our true mission they seemed very suspicious, and refused for some time to have anything to do with us. Just before we began the council, which lasted the greater part of four days, the high-priest and his helpers came forward and announced that there would be a Ghost-dance. They formed a circle about the sacred tree and began their chant.

"Of all the wild dancing I saw on Wounded Knee, this beat the record. People went into trances by the dozen, and the priests were kept busy relating the experiences of the fainters. Several remained in trances as long as twelve hours, and gave evidences of utter exhaustion when the directors aroused them.

"Short Bull said: 'I see the Messiah coming from the West. He is riding in a plain-wagon drawn by two mules and looks very much like a black man. If he is our Messiah we are greatly fooled. Now I see him again, and he is an Indian. Ah! wait; I see him the third time, and he is a white man. He tells me to send my children to school, to make large farms, and not to fight any more. Do not fight, my children, unless the soldiers first fire upon you.'

"People were so excited they trembled all over, their eyes rolled, and the muscles of their faces twitched. They were the most crazy Indians I ever beheld."

The dancing continued for nearly thirty hours; then there was an intermission of several hours, during which a council was held in order to give audience to the friendlies. Short Bull and Two Strike (his real name is Nompagahpa, and a literal translation is, "Knocks down Two"), aided by Crow Dog, championed the cause of the hostiles, while No Neck and Louis Shangraux spoke on behalf of the friendlies. Louis does not remember what he said in the first council, but the substance of his remarks could be put into one sentence:

"The Agent will forgive you if you will return now, give you more rations, but not permit you to dance."

Short Bull's (Tatankaptecelan) reply was so forcible as to remain in Louis's memory in the exact words of the speaker, and ran as follows:

"I have risen today to tell you something of importance. You have heard the words of the brothers from the agency camps, and if you have done as myself, you have weighed them carefully. If the Great Father would permit us to continue the dance, would give more rations, and quit taking away portions of the reservation, I would be in favor of returning. But even if you (turning to Louis) say that he will, how can we know whether you are telling the truth? We have been lied to so many times

that we will not believe any words that your Agent sends to us.  If we
return he will take away our guns and ponies, put some of us in jail for
stealing cattle and plundering houses.  We prefer to stay here and die,
if necessary, to loss of liberty.  We are free now and have plenty of beef,
can dance all the time in obedience to the command of the Great Wakantanka.  We tell you to return to your Agent and say to him that the
Dakotas in the Bad Lands are not going to come in."

No Neck rejoined:

"Think, my people, how foolish is this action!  Do come in, and all
will be well; remain out here and you will be killed."

Short Bull added:

"It is better to die here as brave men, and in obedience to the commands of the Good Spirit, than to live like cowards at the agency on scanty
rations, disarmed, without horses or guns.  No, we will not return.  If we
dance, our Good Spirit will protect us, and if all dancers are sincere, the
bullets of the soldiers will fall harmlessly to the ground without power
to hurt.  There is no army so powerful that it can contend with Wakantanka; therefore we are not afraid to remain here."

The gathering broke up, and nearly every one continued in the Ghost-
dance.  For two days the hostiles would not have further words with
the friendly scouts.  Friday and Saturday, the 12th and 13th, the last
council was held.  The scenes accompanying the closing of this gathering,
Saturday afternoon, were very thrilling, and for a period of two hours it
seemed as if a general battle would ensue between those who desired to
return to the agency and the hostiles.

About noon, Saturday, Two Strike — who had been one of the leaders
in the dance — arose and announced his intention to return to the agency
with the scouts, accompanied by about 145 lodges.  Crow Dog (Kangi-
sunka, the Indian who killed Spotted Tail about ten years ago) also
announced his intention of returning.  At this declaration from two
such prominent men, Short Bull sprang to his feet and cried out,
angrily:

"At such a time as this we should all stick together like brothers.
Do not leave; remain with us.  These men from the agency are not telling
us the truth; they will conduct you back to the agency and they will place
you in jail there.  Louis is at the bottom of this affair."

And, running to the place where the guns were stacked, Short Bull
grasped his gun and, followed by many of his young men, surrounded
Shangraux.  Louis's situation was desperate.  He knew these furious men
might kill him at the slightest resistance, so he laughed as good-naturedly

as possible under the circumstances and told them to put up their guns, as he was their friend instead of their enemy.

"No, do not let the friendlies return," cried the young men; "kill them, or compel them to remain with us. They will tell the Agent all they have seen and the soldiers will know how to enter our camp."

With clubbed guns many of the desperate youths rushed upon the friendlies and scouts, others cocked their Winchesters, and for a few moments it looked as if poor Louis and No Neck, Two Strike and Crow Dog, would lose their lives. Crow Dog sat upon the ground and drew his blanket over his head.

The wiser counsel prevailed, however, and after a great hubbub, in which several young men were knocked down, order was restored. One of the horses and several of the dogs of the friendlies were shot during the mélee. When the 145 lodges started from the camp another difficulty arose. It was during this trouble that Crow Dog made his famous, though brief speech:

"I am going back to White Clay (the location of the agency); you can kill me if you want to, now, and prevent my starting. The Agent's words are true, and it is better to return than to stay here. I am not afraid to die."

So, they started for home.

Imagine the surprise of the friendlies when, upon looking back from the top of a ridge two miles distant, they saw the 117 lodges of hostiles coming after them. They halted to wait for Short Bull to catch up, and then the entire outfit moved toward the agency, all happy in the prospect of peace and forgiveness.

But the hopes of the friendlies were short-lived, for Short Bull became scared after having proceeded four miles farther, and together with his band, left the rear of the column and returned to the Bad Lands. Sunday and Monday morning the Indians moved along the trail, reaching Red Cloud's camp, in sight of the agency headquarters just before noon, Monday. Louis and the scouts had ridden ahead and reached the general's presence as narrated in the forepart of this chapter.

These friendlies, added to the large number already in camp near the agency buildings, led all of us to hope the trouble was over. But during all the Pine Ridge excitement, up on the Missouri river, at Standing Rock, Sitting Bull was in evidence, with some 150 followers.

In the midst of the excitement, when Superintendent McLaughlin went to see Sitting Bull at his camp on Grand River, and argued with him, contending that the Messiah doctrine was false, Sitting Bull suggested that both McLaughlin and himself together with attendants should visit the Messiah in the far West. The truth or falsity of his doctrine would then be apparent. If McLaughlin had agreed to this sensible proposition, much evil might have been avoided, but the Major refused to go, and thereby missed an opportunity of doing the Indians a service and preventing the subsequent massacre.

In November, the President ordered the Secretary of War to prepare for action, and Major John R. Brooke (now General) went to Pine Ridge. These troops (of which we have seen there were a large number) were scattered about through the Indian country.

The troops until the end of December, were either in camp near Pine Ridge, or were scouting about in the country pursuing scattered bands of Indians. In the meantime, Sitting Bull was preparing to leave his reservation (Standing Rock) and flee into the Bad Lands to join the Ghost dancers who had fled there from Pine Ridge. Both Mooney and Major McLaughlin give accounts of what occurred at Sitting Bull's. As McLaughlin's is the lengthier of the two, I shall reproduce that portion of it relating immediately to the death of Sitting Bull.

THE "INDIAN GATE," PINE RIDGE, 1890
Down a ravine, to the right, the interpreter and myself used to creep at night. Thus we reached the "hostiles' camp" and obtained news

## CHAPTER XII: THE DEATH OF SITTING BULL, AND A TRAGEDY AT WOUNDED KNEE

It seems that the Indian police brought Major McLaughlin information as to the intentions of the famous medicine man. The Major became convinced that Sitting Bull must be arrested and confined, and he therefore sent a squad of police under Lieutenant Bull Head. Among the thirty-nine Indian policemen who made the arrest were four relatives. Aside from the officer in charge, Bull Head, Red Tomahawk and Shave Head seem to have been the most prominent.

Sitting Bull's settlement consisted of a number of houses stretched on the banks of the Grand River for a distance of four or five miles. The group surrounding Sitting Bull's cabin was comprised of half a dozen log-cabins and a corral.

The police entered upon their mission in the night and arrived at daylight. "Many of the houses were deserted, the Indians having been engaged in dancing the greater part of the previous night. The entrance of the policemen awakened the camp, but they saw no one, as Bull Head wheeled his men between the Sitting Bull houses and ordered them to dismount. Ten policemen, headed by Bull Head and Shave Head, entered one of the houses, eight policemen the other. In the house entered by Bull Head's party they found the old medicine man, his two wives, and Crow Foot his son, a youth of seventeen years.

"The women were very much frightened and began to cry. Sitting Bull sat up and asked what was the matter.

" 'You are under arrest and must go to the agency,' said Bull Head.

" 'Very well,' said Sitting Bull, 'I will go with you.' And he told one of his wives to go to the other house and bring him his best clothes. He showed no concern at his arrest, but evidently wanted to make a good impression and dressed himself with some care. He had also asked that his best horse, a gray one, be saddled, and an Indian policeman had the animal at the door by the time Sitting Bull was dressed and ready to leave.

"There had been no trouble in the house, and the police, when they walked out, were surprised at the extent of the demonstration. They came out of the building in a little knot, Bull Head on one side of Sitting Bull, Shave Head on the other, and Red Tomahawk directly behind. They had been twenty minutes or more in Sitting Bull's house, and it was in the gray of the morning when they came out. They stepped out into a mass of greatly excited Ghost dancers, nearly all armed and crowding about the main body of the police, who had held the way clear at the door. As Sitting Bull stepped out with his captors he walked directly toward the horse, with the evident intention of mounting and accompanying the police. He was some distance from the door when his son, Crow Foot, seeing that the old man intended to make no resistance, began to revile him: —

"'You call yourself a brave man and you have declared that you would never surrender to a blue-coat, and now you give yourself up to Indians in blue uniforms,' the young man shouted.

"The taunt hit Sitting Bull hard. He looked into the mass of dark, excited faces, and commenced to talk volubly and shrilly, and there was a menacing movement in the crowd.

"The last moment of Sitting Bull's life showed him in a better light, so far as physical courage goes, than all the rest of it. He looked about him and saw his faithful adherents — about 160 crazed Ghost dancers — who would have gone through fire at his bidding; to submit to arrest meant the end of his power and his probable imprisonment; he had sure news from Pine Ridge that he, only, was needed to head the hostiles there in a war of extermination against the white settlers. He made up his mind to take his chance, and screamed out an order to his people to attack the police.

"Instantly Catch-the-Bear and Strikes-the-Kettle, who were in the front rank of the crowd, fired at point-blank range, Catch-the-Bear mortally wounding First Lieutenant Bull Head, and Strikes-the-Kettle shooting First Sergeant Shave Head in the abdomen. Lieutenant Bull Head was a few yards to the left and front of Sitting Bull when hit, and immediately wheeling, he shot Sitting Bull through the body, and at the same instant Second Sergeant Red Tomahawk, who with revolver in hand was rear-guard, shot him in the right cheek, killing him instantly; the lieutenant, the first sergeant, and Sitting Bull falling together.

"Sitting Bull's medicine had not saved him, and the shot that killed him put a stop forever to the domination of the ancient régime among the Sioux of the Standing Rock reservation.

"The tale of the bloody fight that ensued has been told, and the world knows how those thirty-nine Indian policemen, with four of their relatives who volunteered to accompany them, — a total of forty-three in all — fought off 160 Ghost dancers, eight of whom were killed and five wounded; how Second Sergeant Red Tomahawk, after the two higher ranking police officers had been mortally wounded, took command and drove the Indians to the timber; how Hawk Man No. 1 ran through a hail of bullets to get the news to the cavalry detachment, and how six faithful friends of the Whites, policemen of the Standing Rock reservation, laid down their lives in doing their duty that morning. Two days later, on December 17, 1890, we buried Shave Head and four other Indian policemen with military honors in the cemetery at Standing Rock, and, while Captain Miner's entire company of the Twenty-Second U. S. Infantry fired three volleys over the graves of these red heroes, and a great concourse of the Sioux of the reservation stood in the chill bright sunlight of a fair winter's day, mourning aloud for their dead, I quietly left the enclosure and joined a little burial-party in the military cemetery at Fort Yates, situated about five hundred yards south of the agency cemetery. Four military prisoners dug the grave, and in the presence of A. R. Chapin, Assistant Surgeon, U. S. A., H. M. Deeble, Acting Assistant Surgeon, U. S. A., Lieutenant P. G. Wood, U. S. A., Post Quartermaster, now Brigadier General, retired, and myself, the body of Sitting Bull, wrapped in canvas and placed in a coffin, was lowered into the grave."*

Naturally the death of Sitting Bull caused great commotion and many Indians joined the Ghost dancers. In spite of promises to the contrary, they imagined that all those who had incurred the ill will of the authorities were to be killed.

About this time Major Brooke sent out American Horse with Two Strike and others to persuade the rest of the Ghost dancers to come in. There were a number of skirmishes in which a few persons were killed on each side.

On December 28th, Major Whitside in charge of the Seventh Cavalry came up with Big Foot's band. This same Indian, Big Foot, and his people were traveling toward Pine Ridge agency. According to Mooney's account, Whitside demanded unconditional surrender which was at once given. The Indians and the soldiers went into camp twenty miles northeast of Pine Ridge agency. All of this was communicated to Major Brooke, who sent Colonel Forsythe with four companies of the Seventh Cavalry to join Whitside. This gave Whitside a total of 470 men as against 106 warriors and a number of women and children, frequently estimated from 200 to 250. The other Ghost dancers under Kicking Bear and Short Bull had been persuaded by American Horse and Little Wound to come in to the agency and were encamped at the Catholic mission, five miles out. December 29th (the next day) the officers ordered the Indians to be disarmed. In the center of the camp of the Indians a white flag had been erected. Early in the morning a battery of four Hotchkiss guns had been posted,

---

* My Friend the Indian, pages, 219-222.

THE CATHOLIC MISSION NEAR WOUNDED KNEE BATTLEFIELD, PINE RIDGE

and these were trained on the Indian camp. The cavalry was placed in squads at various angles, almost entirely surrounding the Indians, or at least on the flank. Chief Big Foot was ill with pneumonia, and the troops had provided him with a tent warmed by a camp stove. About eight o'clock in the morning the men were ordered to give up their guns. Following Mooney's account further, twenty of them came out with only two guns. The Indians seemed unwilling to give them up, and some of the soldiers were ordered to go into the tents and secure them. Mooney says that this search consumed time and created excitement. My information is to the effect that the soldiers threw things about in the tents and took guns away from those who had them; many children were badly frightened and began to cry, and the Indians were now told by the shaman, Yellow Bird, that they were to be disarmed and then killed. I was told that the medicine man threw dust high in the air and it broke like a little cloud and then the massacre began. Mooney presents the same idea, in a little different form.

While this searching had continued, a large part of the soldiers had been ordered up to within ten yards of the Indians, which further added to their terror and convinced them that Yellow Bird spoke the truth, that they were all to be shot down.

One or two Indians drew revolvers or rifles and fired upon the soldiers, who returned the fire, killing almost half the warriors at the first discharge of their guns. Many sticks were afterwards set up at this place by the Indians. The survivors sprang to their feet, seized knives, clubs or the few remaining guns, and fought desperately.

While this was going on, other troops operated the Hotchkiss guns and sent a storm of shells and bullets among the women and children standing or running about the tipis. Mooney says "the guns poured in two-pound explosive shells at the rate of fifty per minute, mowing down everything alive.

"The terrible effect may be judged from the fact that one woman survivor, Blue Whirlwind, with whom the author conversed, received fourteen wounds, while each of her two little boys were also wounded by her side. In a few minutes 200 Indian men, women and children, with sixty soldiers, were lying dead and wounded on the ground, the tipis had been torn down by the shells and some of them were burning above the helpless wounded, and the surviving handful of Indians were flying in wild panic to the shelter of the ravine, pursued by hundreds of maddened soldiers and followed up by a raking fire from the Hotchkiss guns, which had been moved into position to sweep the ravine.

"There can be no question that the pursuit was simply a massacre, where fleeing women, with infants in their arms, were shot down after resistance had ceased and when almost every warrior was stretched dead or dying on the ground.  On this point such a careful writer as Herbert Welsh says: 'From the fact that so many women and children were killed, and that their bodies were found far from the scene of action, and as though they were shot down while flying, it would look as though blind rage had been at work, in striking contrast to the moderation of the Indian police at the Sitting Bull fight when they were assailed by women.'  The testimony of American Horse and other friendlies is strong in the same direction.  Commissioner Morgan in his official report says that 'Most of the men, including Big Foot, were killed around his tent, where he lay sick. The bodies of the women and children were scattered along a distance of two miles from the scene of the encounter'."

I agree with Mooney, that a man should not criticize the soldiers of his own country.  As for the shooting of armed warriors, we will all give assent.  As to the murder of women and children, whose only thought was to escape with their lives, one may not trust himself to write in moderation. The Indians told me that many of the Seventh Cavalry troops cried out, "Remember Custer," as they pursued little boys and girls and destroyed them.  We might as well draw the veil of charity over the concluding scene — the pursuit and the butchery.

There was one heroic character, Father Kraft, of the Catholic mission, Pine Ridge.  He spoke Sioux fluently and endeavored to stop the fight. He was stabbed through the lungs, yet with bullets flying about him, he administered the last rites of the church to the dying until he fell unconscious.  Mooney pays him a deserved tribute.  The Indians were so excited that they did not recognize him, claiming that he had on a soldier's overcoat because of the cold.  Mooney affirms this is not correct, but that he wore his priestly robes.

The immediate result of the massacre of Wounded Knee was the stampeding of all the Indians into the hills.  They believed that they were to be murdered.

General Miles adopted harsh measures against the Indians and they soon surrendered all their guns and came in to the agency.

Doctor McGillicuddy, the former Agent at Pine Ridge, who was entirely familiar with the events, stated to Mooney on January 15, 1891, "Up to date there has been neither a Sioux outbreak nor war.  No citizen in Nebraska or Dakota has been killed, molested, or can show the scratch of a pin, and no property has been destroyed off the reservation.  Only a single non-combatant was killed by the Indians, and that was close to the agency. The entire time occupied by the campaign, from the killing of Sitting Bull to the surrender at Pine Ridge, was only thirty-two days. The late hostiles were returned to their homes as speedily as possible."

The Indians quit, but the white people did not. On January 11th, some white people led by three brothers named Culbertson,* pursued an aged Oglala, who was a very friendly Indian, for many miles. His name was Few Tails, and he was accompanied by his wife, another Indian named One Feather, his wife and two children. They had been hunting in the Black Hills and had a pass from the agency. They were returning in two wagons loaded with meat. The Culbertson brothers and these other white men fired on Few Tails, killing that Indian and both ponies attached to that wagon. His wife jumped out and received two bullets, bringing her down. Mooney says that the murderers then attacked the other wagon shooting the wife of One Feather, but as she was not badly hurt, she drove away as rapidly as possible and the Indian leaped upon one of the spare ponies and held off the white men for eight or ten miles. They again came up, and he turned and fought them off while his wife drove ahead with the wagon.

The senseless panic had seized upon all settlers in the country because of the Ghost dance and the Wounded Knee fight. This is illustrated by Mooney's concluding description of the first part of the fight.

"As they drove they passed near a house, from which several other shots were fired at the flying mother, when her husband again rode up and kept off the whole party until the wagon could get ahead. Finally, as the ponies were tired out, this heroic man abandoned the wagon and put the two children on one of the spare ponies and his wounded wife and himself upon another and continued to retreat until the Whites gave up the pursuit. He finally reached the agency with the wife and children."

To give readers an adequate conception of what has too frequently occurred in the West, I desire to state that while One Feather and his family escaped, wounded, the wife of the other Indian, Few Tails, was shot twice, and lay helpless on the ground all night. In the morning she found one of the ponies alive, and mounted it and reached a settler's house fifteen miles away.

"Instead of meeting help and sympathy, however, she was driven off by the two men there with loaded rifles, and leaving her horse in her fright, she hurried away as well as she could with a bullet in her leg and another in her breast, passing by the trail of One Feather's wagon with the tracks of his pursuers fresh behind it, until she came near a trader's store about

---

* One had served time in the penitentiary.

twenty miles farther south.  Afraid to go near it on account of her last experience, the poor woman circled around it, and continued, wounded, cold, and starving as she was, to travel by night and hide by day until she reached the Bad Lands.  The rest may be told in her own words:

" 'After that I traveled every night, resting daytime, until I got here at the beef corral.  Then I was very tired, and was near the military camp, and early in the morning a soldier came out and he shouted something back, and in a few minutes fifty men were there, and they got a blanket and took me to a tent.  I had no blanket and my feet were swelled, and I was about ready to die.  After I got to the tent a doctor came in — a soldier doctor, because he had straps on his shoulders — and washed me and treated me well."

"A few of the soldiers camped near the scene of the attack had joined in the pursuit at the beginning, on the representations of some of the murderers, but abandoned it as soon as they found their mistake.  According to all the testimony, the killing was a wanton, unprovoked, and deliberate murder, yet the criminals were acquitted in the local courts.  The apathy displayed by the authorities of Meade county, South Dakota, in which the murder was committed, called forth some vigorous protests.  Colonel Shafter, in his statement of the case, concludes, referring to the recent killing of Lieutenant Casey: 'So long as Indians are being arrested and held for killing armed men under conditions of war, it seems to me that the white murderers of a part of a band of peaceful Indians should not be permitted to escape punishment.'  The Indians took the same view of the case, and when General Miles demanded of Young-man-afraid-of-his-horses the surrender of the slayers of Casey and the herder Miller, the old chief indignantly replied: 'No; I will not surrender them, but if you will bring the white men who killed Few Tails, I will bring the Indians who killed the white soldier and the herder; and right out here in front of your tipi I will have my young men shoot the Indians and you have your soldiers shoot the white men, and we will be done with the whole business."

"In regard to the heroic conduct of One Feather, the officer then in charge of the agency says: 'The determination and genuine courage, as well as the generalship he manifested in keeping at a distance the six men who were pursuing him, and the devotion he showed toward his family, risking his life against great odds, designate him as entitled to a place on the list of heroes'."

I present as an illustration in this book, the little monument erected on the Wounded Knee battlefield by the Sioux themselves some years

"This monument is erected by surviving relatives and other Oglala and Cheyenne River Sioux Indians in memory of the Chief Big Foot Massacre, Dec. 29, 1890.

"Col. Forsythe in command of U. S. Troops.

"Big Foot was a great Chief of the Sioux Indians. He often said 'I will stand in peace till my last day comes.' He did many good and brave deeds for the White man and the Redman.

"Many innocent women and children who knew no wrong, died here.

"The erection of this monument is largely due to the financial assistance of Joseph Horncloud, whose father was killed here."

This was paid for, and put up by Indians — not white people.

after the massacre. It was dedicated in the presence of a great concourse of Indians. The inscription is given in Sioux on one side of the shaft, in English on the other. The War Department rather objected to it, so I was told, but it still stands as a monument typifying our treatment of the Indian in these modern days.

Some of the Sioux are still backward, and there are quite a number who do not attend the Protestant or Catholic missions. If one will talk with these so-called "non-progressives," one may hear them say, "We have not forgotten Wounded Knee."

A few brief concluding statements are in order. A perusal of this long narrative indicates that at the first the dance was a purely religious ceremony. The Sioux were deadly in earnest, they were sincere. They danced day and night until they dropped from exhaustion. There was nothing like it, so far as I can ascertain, in recent times in North America. They were in a frenzy. Yet there was no thought of war. Revivals among Protestant denominations in this country (especially in remote districts) frequently develop religious mania. Many older persons remember the "Camp Meetings" of the West and South in which people "got religion." The interference of police or troops at such a gathering would bring on a riot among the white Christians participating in the services.

Negroes of the South have been known to become insensible for hours — to enter a cataleptic state — and to relate visions on recovering. Hysteria at religious gatherings in the South is common among negroes.

In view of these facts, a religious mania is not surprising among Indians, who sought, as we have seen, salvation out of troubles. In fact the craze was induced by their wretched condition.

There was no danger at any time at Pine Ridge. What we did, not once, but on many nights, is proof of the assertion. There were a number of newspaper men in the little log hotel at Pine Ridge, and they sent many sensational accounts to the Eastern papers. Not one of them ever left the agency, until the battle of Wounded Knee had occurred, when a few went out to look over the field. Mr. Bartlett, who spoke Sioux quite well, and myself, were the only men to my knowledge who left the agency and visited the camps in the valley, one or two miles distant. The fact that we were able to do so, is sufficient refutation of the statement that the Indians desired to fight, or were savages. Both of us would have been killed were this statement true. We never experienced the slightest trouble, but on the contrary were afforded every facility. We often felt guns and revolvers under the blankets on which we reclined in the tipis. Force caused Wounded Knee. Humanity would have prevented it.

# CHAPTER XIII. THE FIVE CIVILIZED TRIBES

This is the largest body of Indians in the United States. They reside in the State of Oklahoma and number, according to the Commissioner's report,* 101,216. The Five Civilized Tribes are composed of southern Indians. A consideration of their tribal customs and ethnology will be presented in the next volume of my history. While the Indians follow some of their ancient customs, the bulk of them have so far departed from the faith of their fathers, that it is advisable to consider their present life and needs, rather than their past.

The report on these Indians for the year ending June 30th, 1913, and signed by J. George Wright, Commissioner to the Five Civilized Tribes, Dana H. Kelsey, Superintendent of Union Agency, and John B. Brown, Supervisor of Education, lies before me. According to this, they are divided among the tribes as follows:—

| | | | |
|---|---|---|---|
| Cherokees | 41,706 | Chickasaws | 10,989 |
| Choctaws | 24,973 | Seminoles | 3,119 |
| Creeks | 18,700 | Mississippi Choctaws | 1,639 |

These Indians are known by ethnologists to belong to the great Muskhogean stock, and lived in the South, east of the Mississippi. They constitute a third of our Indian population. As to why they were removed—that is another story. Suffice it to say that the year 1850 found them in that region known as Indian Territory. Here they located upon large tracts of tribal land amounting to 19,475,614 acres.

Treaties setting forth that they were to remain in undisturbed possession of their new homes were duly signed by the United States Government. Although the treaty of 1866 stipulated that they were entitled to send a delegate to our Congress, when Congress authorized the admission of a representative from Indian Territory, and in spite of the fact that some of the tribes made an effort to bring about this result, nothing effectual was ever accomplished.

May 2, 1890, the laws of Arkansas were extended to cover Indian Territory, and March 3, 1901, every Indian of the Territory was declared to be a citizen of the United States.

March 3, 1893, President Cleveland appointed the famous Dawes Commission. This undertook to allot to all the Indians of the Five Civilized Tribes lands in severalty. There were 200,000 claimants and about 90,000 were allotted.

---

* Report Commissioner Indian Affairs, 1913.

Although I am tempted to present a mass of statistics and facts proving that these most advanced Indians were robbed and despoiled, without let or hindrance, that the treaties made with them were cooly set aside, statehood promises broken, and finally even the very farms and tracts, on which they were to live as citizens and enjoy the blessings of liberty and equality, were taken away, I must confine myself to a consideration of the subject in its broad aspect.

It is stated by apologists that Indian Territory became an impossible country in which to live, that crime was rampant, and that the Five Nations included among their membership thousands of outlaws and robbers. This is a gross exaggeration. There were some hundreds of undesirable citizens who made Indian Territory their habitat from just previous to the Civil War to about the year 1880. Most of these were white men, although there was a sprinkling of mixed-bloods and that worst citizen, the individual whose blood is made up of a mixture of negro, Indian and white. The older Indians, who are more competent to judge, and many of the white persons who long ago settled in Oklahoma, maintain that while this class of citizens caused a good deal of trouble, yet on the whole the Indians were vastly better off between the years 1855 and 1900 than they are at the present time.* There was some violence, murder, train robbing and attendant evils. As against this, however, the great body of Indians were self-supporting, there was no general graft, and very little pauperism.† There is evidence of the correctness of this statement even at the present time. In traveling through Oklahoma, overland, for 600 miles, I noticed in scores of places the type of house erected by the Indians forty or fifty years ago either still standing or in ruins. Their houses were superior, as a rule, to the present flimsy, cheap structures erected either by the natives themselves, or by Government or State employees for the Indians. The old houses were of logs, or heavy boards, the walls being thick. They were thus cool in summer and warm in winter. Near every house was an orchard. The tracts owned by the Indians were extensive, and cattle, horses and hogs had free range. Thus, every Indian family was assured necessary beasts of burden and meat for winter use. Now that the allotments have passed into the hands of white persons, or are restricted in size, or are leased, practically everything is fenced, there are no ranges of consequence; the old-style house is gone, the trees in the orchards have decayed and fallen, or are cut down, most of the remaining orchards are those of white people, although, of course, a few Indian orchards survive. The houses built for

---

* Indians of the Territory legislating wisely. Report Board Indian Comissioners to President Grant, 1871.
† Report of Indian Commissioners, 1872. Indians progressive and raising large crops.

the Indians, or by them, are wretched affairs, small, the walls thin, and not substantial. They are hot in summer and cold in winter.

The Indians having settled down in Oklahoma under their various tribal governments, made great progress.* They published papers in their own language. The Cherokee capital at Talequah contained creditable buildings — a good administration building and two fine Indian schools, which may be seen on pages 138 and 146. This school, by the way, built by the Cherokee Indians with their own money, is now occupied by white pupils. It was the finest building I observed in all Oklahoma, and it is a standing repudiation to the statement that the Indians were not progressing and that they did not afford proper educational facilities to their own people.

At the end of the Civil War, a number of outlaws belonging to guerilla bands, both North and South, came into the State. White persons migrated to the country and occupied it. The Indians complained, and our authorities at Washington made a few abortive attempts to keep them out, but, as inevitably, the whites dominated. The Dawes Commission was formed, and after years of negotiation and coercion, enrollment of the Indians began. The rolls are now completed and include the totals mentioned in my statistics upon a previous page.

There were a few Indians who held out against this arbitrary action on our part, and right here I wish to pay a compliment to a few old men and women, who were treated with contempt, who were called "Snakes" in the Creek and "Nighthawks" in the Cherokee nation by the unthinking. Why? For the reason that they have a simple, a child-like faith in the great United States Nation. They believe that we will keep our pledged word. They are not educated and therefore they cannot grasp the essentials of our civilization as it applies toward Indians; that when we execute a ninety-nine year lease among ourselves, we keep it; but that a solemn covenant entered into with the Indians is a very different matter. So these poor old Snakes and Nighthawks refused to be enrolled and to receive allotments, trusting in the honesty and integrity of the Great Father at Washington. One of the most pathetic sights I ever witnessed in my life, was when old Fixico Harjo and Okoskee Miller, and a few other fine old men, of the best type of American Indian, called my attention to our solemn covenant with these people, stating that they were helpless, that allotments had been forced upon them, that they expected to see even these little tracts taken away from them, that they could not understand

---

* Capt. G. W. Grayson, official interpreter to the Creek Nation — lived with these Indians sixty years — confirms statement of former well-being and progress.

the speeches of the clever, shrewd, oily, forked-tongued lawyers and land-buyers who came among them; they asked not charity but justice. The only thing in this world that was positive, that was true, that was inevitable, was this fact: that every time they touched a pen they lost something; that every promise made to them by a white man was broken; that they had abandoned all hope save one — that when they are gathered to their fathers, in the great beyond, they hope to find some place where they may live in peace and contentment, as in ancient days.

## The Crisis in Oklahoma

Whenever a crisis arises in the affairs of the Nation, there are always men to meet it, and while the forces of evil have conspired against the Indian, there have arisen a few champions, and we should not forget the service such persons have rendered. Some of them have gone down to honorable defeat induced by hatred, treachery, malice and the love of gain. Others continue in office, escaping the wiles of the enemy, not through a miracle, but through the arousing of the public conscience. Today there are some 2,000,000 people in the State of Oklahoma, and as in every other State, the great majority of them are upright citizens. They have not taken a firm stand for the Indian in the past, for the reason that they did not realize what was going on in the eastern part of their State. The grafters controlled a tremendous and effective propaganda. The extent of this is surprising, and I have received scores of circulars, copies of speeches, etc., as evidence of the determined action of those who covet the oil, coal, gas, asphalt, farm lands, and timber tracts of the Five Civilized Tribes. Every person who is endeavoring to bring about fair play in eastern Oklahoma was charged with being "perniciously active in politics", if he lived in the State of Oklahoma. If he happened to reside in the East, he was either a "sentimentalist", unfamiliar with Indian affairs, or guilty of besmirching the fair name of the State of Oklahoma. The better class of citizens in the State of Oklahoma became, at last, aroused to the deplorable conditions obtaining among these Indians and they succeeded in influencing not only the members of Congress but also the Secretary of the Interior and Commissioner of Indian Affairs to call a halt.

The lengths to which a few people went in order to despoil the Indians seems incredible in this day of Christianity and civilization. Some men made contracts with Indians on a basis of fees of high percentage and sought to secure control of Indian moneys in the United States Treasury Others made contracts with thousands of Indians to represent them in the sale of vast tribal estates — tens of millions of dollars — on a liberal commission basis. Others became guardians and administrators of estates; and there were thousands of these professional guardians. The thing became a national scandal. Covetousness overwhelmed eastern Oklahoma. Now and then some man sought to stem the tide. A judge was assaulted in court by a grafter. He called upon his court officers. They, sympathizing with the assailant, did not aid his honor, but merely looked on while the grafter beat the judge into insensibility.

An editor commented upon a certain county judge, before whom guardians and administrators had appeared, and told some plain truths concerning the manner in which minors' estates were being dissipated. The judge drew a knife and stabbed the editor. In neither of these cases were the guilty persons punished. What went on throughout the length and breadth of eastern Oklahoma seems incredible. I refer readers to the various articles cited in my bibliography at the conclusion of Chapter XVI for details.

Matters became so serious that Hon. M. L. Mott, attorney for the Creek Indians, decided to sacrifice his career in that country in order to obtain justice. He sent the facts concerning the despoilation of thousands of Creek minors and incompetents to Honorable Charles H. Burke, Representative from South Dakota. On December 13, 1912, Honorable Mr. Burke made a speech in the House of Representatives which aroused the good people of Oklahoma and Congress itself to immediate action.*

Rev. J. S. Murrow, in charge of a large and successful mission at Atoka, Oklahoma, published a pamphlet, at his own expense, of thirty-nine pages covering the present condition of the Five Civilized Tribes and pleading that the ministers of the gospel residing in the State, without regard to denomination, do what they could to secure humane and just treatment for the Indians.

Miss Kate Barnard, Commissioner of Charities and Corrections for the State, also entered the righteous cause, exposing conditions among orphan children, and pointed out how that thousands of paupers would have to be supported by the National Government, or the State of Oklahoma, if more restrictions to the alienation of Indian lands were removed. As a reward for her faithful and humane efforts, Miss Barnard's office is virtually abolished, since appropriations are cut off.

Grant Foreman is an attorney living in Muskogee. He has made particular study of the Indian situation and is entirely familiar with all the legal aspects, as well as the Indians themselves. Mr. Foreman has

---

* I have extra copies of Burke's speech, and shall be glad to mail copies to those who desire them.

CHEROKEE FEMALE SEMINARY AT TALEQUAH, OKLAHOMA
Built with Indian money twenty years ago. Now used as a White Normal School.

rendered valuable assistance to Mr. Mott, but has never held office in
the State, or been employed in the Indian Service.

The Department of Justice was represented by A. N. Frost, Esq.,
and J. E. Gresham, Esq. Both of these men proceeded against grafters,
and both are out of the Service.

The Federal supervision of the Five Civilized Tribes has rested in
Commissioner J. George Wright and Dana H. Kelsey, Superintendent of
the Union Agency. These men have been years in the Service. They have
shown high integrity, tact and wisdom in handling a most delicate situation.
Under them are employed hundreds of persons—District Agents, teachers,
clerks, farmers, matrons, etc. Because of the rapid expansion of the oil
industry in Oklahoma and the discovery of new fields, many of the Indian
allotments have become very valuable. Naturally, these are coveted by
white men who never seek Indian property unless it is valuable. In this
connection I wish to call attention to what, in Oklahoma, is considered
a great joke on certain white men. Before the discovery of oil, these men
secured, where possible, large tracts of rich agricultural land. The hilly
sections were allotted to the more ignorant Indians, the shrewder selected
the bottom-lands. Through the irony of fate, the richest oilfields have
been discovered in these same hilly or worthless tracts passed up by the
first grafters. So, in spite of all that has been done to seize Indian lands,
many of the incompetent Indians receive large royalties from the oil wells.*
As these incompetents are under Government supervision, bills to remove
restrictions have been agitated. Many of the candidates for Congress
ran upon a platform which may be described as anti-Indian—contrary to
all State promises, sacredly made. I have original handbills, such as are
used in Oklahoma elections. Mr. J. H. Maxey presents his portrait and
says:

"The Government Must Pay the Taxes on All Non-Taxable Indian
Land"; "The Affairs of the Five Tribes Must Be Settled." Mr. Reuben
M. Roddie is even more frank. Over his picture appears in large letters:—
"Pay the Indians Their Money and Remove all Restrictions." Mr.
Roddie was defeated and the Hon. Wm. M. Murray, long a friend of the
Indian, was returned to Congress.

Mr. Foreman prepared for me a comprehensive statement of conditions in Oklahoma. It is the best presentation of the subject that I
have seen and I herewith include it, in the following eight pages.

"The lands of the Indians were allotted to them with restrictions
against alienation or encumbrance. The Creek land was restricted to

* See Reports Commissioner Wright and Superintendent Kelsey as to value of oil properties—1909-1914.

August 8, 1907; the Choctaw and Chickasaw lands could be sold one-fourth in one year, one-fourth in three years and the remainder in five years from date of patent. The Cherokee land could not be sold for five years. Out of each allotment a homestead was reserved, which under the law allotting it, could not be sold or taxed for twenty-one years. This was a condition agreed to by the Government in order to get the Indians to consent to the allotment of their lands. The Creek, Seminole and Cherokee homestead was 40 acres and the Choctaw and Chickasaw 160 acres. Directly after the allotting began, a great clamor went up from the white people to Congress to remove the restrictions on the sale of a part of the lands allotted. In response to this demand, on April 21, 1904, an act was passed removing the restrictions against the sale of the lands except homesteads of the adult members of the Five Civilized Tribes not of Indian blood, which included mainly freedmen citizens of the tribes and affected 1,500,000 acres of land.

"In the next month, May, 1904, President Roosevelt commissioned Mr. M. L. Mott of North Carolina to act as National Attorney for the Creek Tribe of Indians. This appointment was important to the Indians of the Five Civilized Tribes, for Mr. Mott took a deep interest in their condition and became a forceful advocate for them; he was instrumental in impressing enactments upon the Federal statutes and securing from the Supreme Court constructions of the statutes that are essential to the Indians' welfare and that will secure to them their property rights for many years beyond the time allotted by local consent.

"Soon after Mr. Mott assumed his duties he observed that a large part of the land made salable by the Act of April 21, 1904, almost immediately had passed into the hands of white people and the grossly inadequate consideration received by the allottees had been wasted. This was food for serious thought.

"In response to a popular demand Congress had removed the restriction against sale three years before the land was to become alienable according to the agreements under which it was allotted. The land and money had been frittered away. Under the law, all restrictions on the sale of all lands of full-bloods and mixed-bloods, except homesteads, of the Creeks, Cherokees, Choctaws, and Chickasaws were to expire by limitation within three or four years. In the light of the experience under the Act of April 21, 1904, it was not difficult to foretell what would happen when these restrictions expired under the impending statehood regime.

"To avert the calamity threatening the Indians, Mr. Mott bent all of his energies to securing an amendment of the law, extending the re-

strictions against the sale of all Indians' land. In the face of strong opposition he failed to secure an extension as to mixed-bloods, but Congress
was prevailed upon to pass a measure extending until 1931 the restrictions
against the sale of all lands of full-blood Indians except under the supervision of the Secretary of the Interior. This was part of an act of April
26, 1906, entitled 'An Act for the final disposition of the affairs of the Five
Civilized Tribes in the Indian Territory, and for other purposes,' which
was framed to adjust conditions for the inauguration of the new State
of Oklahoma, then practically assured.

"The section of the Act extending restrictions was known as the
McCumber amendment. In urging its passage Senator McCumber read
to the Senate an argument by Mr. Mott in which he made the statement
that within thirty days after the Act of April 21, 1904, became effective,
not ten per cent of the land made salable by that act remained in the
hands of the allottees, and within sixty days not ten per cent of the allottees
who had sold possessed a dollar to show for the heritage so improvidently
disposed of. Senator McCumber and Senator Teller expressed doubt of
the constitutionality of the amendment, but impressed by the necessities
of the situation solved the doubt in favor of the Indians by voting for its
enactment. The wisdom of this measure was vindicated and its constitutionality was established by the United States Supreme Court on
May 15, 1911, in the Marchie Tiger case, reported in 221 U. S. Supreme
Court Reports, page 738.

"This suit grew out of the fact that after August 8, 1907, conveyances
were taken from full-blood Creek Indians on the theory that the McCumber
amendment could not prevent it, in that Congress had not the power
and had not intended to extend the restrictions to land so purchased. On
the advice of Mr. Mott the Council of the Creek Nation made an appropriation for the purpose of testing this contention and authorized the
employment of Mr. W. L. Sturdevant of St. Louis, who was retained by
Mr. Mott, with the concurrence of the Interior Department, to aid in establishing in the courts the binding force of the McCumber amendment.

"The Oklahoma trial court held against the contention of the Indians
and the Supreme Court of Oklahoma said that as the lands involved in
the Tiger case were inherited, Congress did not intend to restrict the sale
of them, and that therefore the constitutionality of the Act was not drawn
in question; but the attorneys were convinced that the local courts did
not see this Indian question in the light with which grave considerations
of public policy and conscience illuminated it before the nation, and they
appealed the case to the United States Supreme Court. This court re-

versed the holding of the Oklahoma courts and established the force and effectiveness of the McCumber amendment, for the much-needed protection of the 40,000 full-blood Indians of the Five Civilized Tribes as to all their lands; the court said that it rests with Congress to say when its guardianship of the Indians shall cease and that it had not surrendered this right by creating the State of Oklahoma. This decision established the power of Congress in the future to impose such additional safeguards for the protection of the Indians in Oklahoma as their necessities may require. On the strength of the principle established in this case, the Government in behalf of the Indians brought suits involving 30,000 causes of action against white people who had taken deeds from Indians who were restricted under the McCumber amendment, the most of which are now settled favorably to the Indians.

"Oklahoma with 1,500,000 population, became a State on November 16, 1907, upon a pledge contained in her constitution that she would never question the jurisdiction of the Federal Government over the Indians and their lands or its power to legislate by law or regulation concerning their rights or property. Immediately she had a delegation in Congress and at once began a determined campaign for further repeal of the laws enacted for the protection of the Indians. The main argument employed was that the Indians were competent to care for their property and needed no legislative protection against improvidence; that the State could be trusted to afford them all the protection they required and that Federal guardianship and supervision should cease, as an interference with the personal privileges and rights of citizens of Oklahoma. And they made much of the fact that among the mixed-bloods there are a few individuals who are quite shrewd enough to look out for themselves.

"This fight was highly successful to the white contenders and resulted in the enactment of a law on May 27, 1908, exective July 27, 1908, repealing the restrictions on the sale of a large class of land including all homesteads of freedmen and of mixed-bloods of less than half blood, freeing from restrictions all told, over 9,720,000 acres. It provided also that all homesteads, as well as all other lands from which restrictions against sale were removed, should become taxable the same as lands of white people, whether sold by the allottee or not. This late act violated the terms of the agreements made with the Indians under which the homesteads of the Creeks and the allotments, or parts thereof, of the Choctaw and other tribes were exempted from taxation for a given period.

"While this measure was being opposed before the House Committee on Indian Affairs, in illustrating the disastrous policy toward the Indians

© by Rodman Wanamaker 1913                    Chief Plenty Coups

that Congress was entering upon, Mr. Mott referred to the 8th day of August, 1907, when restrictions automatically expired on all lands in the Creek Nation, except homesteads, of all allottees of less than full blood. He stated that by one o'clock of the morning of the 8th day of August, deeds conveying one-half of the lands of the Creek Nation so affected were executed and delivered to well-organized land buyers, in many cases for inadequate considerations, and that these considerations were frittered away in a few weeks. This statement was not controverted.

"The part of this Act which undertook to subject to taxation the homesteads and other lands of the Indians was regarded as destructive of their property rights. The Indians had agreed to the allotment of their lands upon the condition contained in their treaties that certain exemptions from taxation should be observed. The Choctaw and Chickasaw lands were to be exempt while owned by the allottees. It was provided that in the Creek, Cherokee and Seminole tribes, a homestead of forty acres should be reserved from each allotment, which should be non-taxable for twenty-one years. This arrangement was favored by the Government as a wise policy of equalizing to the Indians the handicap under which they were about to enter upon a new method of living. It was seen that the destruction of this safeguard would bring disaster to the Indians as it would introduce a most insidious agency for divesting the Indians of their land under the power to sell for delinquent taxes; and it was realized that withdrawing the exemption was the arbitrary taking of property without due process of law, which the courts should be asked to prevent.

"These considerations were presented to the Creek Council by their attorney soon after the passage of the Act and upon his advice they again took an advanced position and decided to test the power of Congress to take away from them the right of tax exemption. A resolution to that effect was passed by the Creek Council in October, 1908, but it needed the approval of the President of the United States to make it effective. And here arose a peculiar situation.

"When Mr. Mott presented the resolution to Mr. Garfield, the Secretary of the Interior, and the President, they stated that they had approved and the President had signed the bill removing restrictions and making the unrestricted homesteads taxable. It was represented to the latter in reply that the Indians believed they were wronged by the Act, and that if the President refused to aid them in getting into court to have their rights measured and determined, the Indians would feel that the Government was not acting in good faith toward them and was afraid to have its actions inquired into by the courts.   President Roosevelt admitted the force of their position and approved the resolution.

"Mr. Sturdevant again was retained to present this question to the courts, together with a similar question arising in the Choctaw Nation, the question being common to all the tribes.   As in the Marchie Tiger restriction case the Oklahoma trial and Supreme courts held against the contention of the Indians.   They decided that the Indians must pay taxes on homesteads as well as on all other land from which restrictions against sale were removed.   Mr. Sturdevant, confident of his position, appealed to the United States Supreme Court and argued the novel question to an interested bench which handed down an opinion on May 13, 1912, reversing the courts below.   It held that the Indians' exemption from taxation was a property right that had become vested in exchange for a valuable consideration, to wit, the consent of each allottee to take his portion of land and yield any claim to all other tribal property, and that Congress had no more power to destroy, impair or withdraw that exemption than it had to take the land itself.

"In the opinion the Supreme Court stated a rule by which the rights of Indians should always be measured, whether in the courts or in Congress.   It was said that '*the construction* (of statutes) *instead of being strict, is liberal; doubtful expressions, instead of being resolved in favor of the United States, are to be resolved in favor of a weak and defenseless people, who are wards of the nation, and dependent wholly upon its protection and good faith.*'

"Thus was settled a question of far-reaching importance to the Indians and particularly to those who have not sold their homesteads.   Congress cannot take away from the Indians this right established by the Supreme Court.   But Congress can repeal all the restrictions on the sale of all Indians' land and expose them to their own ignorance and improvidence; if the present tendency continues, this backward movement will be completely consummated in a few years, and at present there is nothing in sight to indicate a change of policy.

"In a recent primary campaign in Oklahoma there were sixty candidates for Congress of both parties, from whom eight members were to be selected.   Nearly all of these aspirants for seats in Congress solicited support on the promise that if elected they would work for the removal of all restrictions on the sale of all Indian land of the Five Civilized Tribes in Oklahoma, and for the 'emancipation of eastern Oklahoma from Federal supervision.'   And they were all in earnest for they knew that to be elected they must favor that policy, and the sentiment that sent the winners to Congress would exact a strict compliance with that agreement.

"It has been said by members of the Oklahoma delegation in Congress that the Indian question is a local question with which the rest of the country has no concern, and that the people of Oklahoma should be permitted to work out their own policy toward the Indian and solve the question in their own way.

"To a limited extent only is this true. The Indian question is a National problem which we assumed when we as a nation appropriated their land, took them under our protection and arrogated the right to control their destinies. We made definite promises to them and mutual agreements with them, in reliance upon which they consented to changes in their forms of living which the exigencies of our rapidly growing nation demanded. If in the next six or eight years these 40,000 full-bloods and more than 60,000 mixed-bloods and freedmen shall have frittered away their great estate and half of them are paupers, it will not be a State question merely — it will be a National scandal.

"A prophet need not draw deeply for inspiration to see in 1919 the Oklahoma delegation rising in Congress and demanding of the Government: —'What of your stewardship of these Indians, these children of nature, whose vast property they entrusted to your protection? Fifteen years ago they owned in fee simple — by the same title that we own our homes — an estate which today is worth a thousand million dollars, and one-half of them are paupers. Look upon your work for just one generation. Their property was hedged about by every conceivable legislative protection. Treaty after treaty and statute after statute were enacted to secure the Indian against his own improvidence and helplessness by you, the Government, the only power in the world which could protect or despoil him at will. Then you began only a little while ago to tear down this protection and to expose him to perils with which he was inexperienced. You withdrew a little protection here, you tore down something there, time after time, and by your own deliberate acts the Indian was invited to pauperize himself until today he is a wanderer upon the earth. Did your previous one hundred years of experience with the Indians teach you nothing, that you might avoid rewriting some of the miserable chapters of history we have been trying to forget?

" 'He who in 1904 was the independent owner of broad acres of hill and valley, of billowing prairie, timbered mountain side and shady streams, has not land enough on which to erect a shelter against the storm, nor money to build it. His land is making thousands of fortunes annually and supporting millions of thrifty white people who know nothing of the Indian's sacrifice and care less.'

CHEROKEE MALE ACADEMY NEAR TALEQUAH, OKLAHOMA

Burned a few years ago. The contrast between this dignified structure, and the glaring, modern school
buildings has caused much comment

"It seems clear that further removal of restrictions should be discouraged. Under the present law any land of the Five Civilized Tribes other than homesteads may be sold under the watchful eye of the Secretary of the Interior. There should be no objection to this method. True, before the Secretary will authorize a sale he investigates the proposed transaction and he must be satisfied that the Indian wants to sell, that he understands the deal, that the consideration offered is adequate and that it is actually paid to the Indian, or to the Department, for him — in other words, that the Indian is not defrauded.

"To say in the face of the experience of the past eight years that this supervision of the Indian is an unwarranted, unreasonable interference with the rights of citizens of a sovereign State, is the shallowest sophistry. Under the wise policy of the Interior Department the consideration paid for lands of a restricted Indian is received by the Department and expended in the construction of improvements on his homestead and for farm implements, livestock and other necessities of life. Or the money is turned over to the Indian in small instalments, the exact course to be pursued in each case being determined by an investigation of the Indian's capacity and needs. In this way his money is not foolishly spent and he is not cheated by unscrupulous white men who too often take advantage of the Indian's ignorance and improvidence. Certainly this cannot be objected to by the good people of Oklahoma who have no desire to see the Indian plundered.

"The decisions of the Supreme Court have established the right of Congress to pass all needful laws for the protection of these Indians and to impose necessary supervision of their affairs, and have hereby clearly shown that Congress alone is responsible for the fate of these friendless people. The objective point of assault will be the next Congress. Will it be able to resist the pressure that will be brought to tear down the pitiful remnant of protection that remains to these wards of our country? The attitide of the Supreme Court and the Interior Department has placed the whole Nation under obligation to them, for they have saved us as a people from standing pilloried before mankind as entirely faithless to our fair promises made to a weaker people. If their illustrious example shall awaken the legislative conscience, the Indians who are yet restricted need not view with despair the convening of another Congress. But if the present tendency is not arrested, within five years these Indians will be stripped of every measure of protection against their own incompetency. Our wards who less than ten years ago were in the full enjoyment of all their property rights will have experienced a swift impoverishment without parallel in our history."

## CHAPTER XIV.   CAPTAIN GRAYSON'S VIEWS; MISS BARNARD'S WORK; THE MINORS' ESTATES

Captain G. W. Grayson of Eufala, who has served many years as official interpreter to the Creeks, and who is frequently employed by the Smithsonian savants in their studies of Indians, read my Oklahoma manuscript and commented as follows: —

"It is proper to state that in the Creek Nation, excluding negroes, some degree of protection and supervision should be extended over two-thirds of the people.  Some time since, the inquiry was propounded to Mr. Kelsey as to why the Government officials found it necessary to withhold from the allotee the proceeds of the sale of lands in which he in interested, paying it out in small amounts from time to time to him as his need required.  He promptly replied that the experience of the office had very decidedly indicated this to be the humane thing to do.  That there were many instances where a full-blood Indian was paid a considerable sum of royalty money accruing from oil wells on his lands, who was taken in charge by bad white men as soon as he left the office, who immediately conducted him to some convenient brothel where drink is one of the allurements, and rob him of every penny of the money paid to him.  This happens usually during the night following the payment, when on the morning after the robbery, appears the Indian pleading to be again paid at least sufficient to pay his railroad fare so he can get out of town.  To this officer of the Government, it appeared very clear that it was the duty of the Agents of the Department who, in a large sense, had assumed the guardianship of these Indians, to adopt such precautions as would prevent a recurrence of like enormities.

"Another method adopted, and in many cases practiced, is that of allowing the visiting payee only sufficient money to purchase his immediate necessities while in the city, advising him to call at the postoffice in his home town, where the rest of his money due him is sent to him in the form of a check.

"The theory on which such action is based is, that the Indian receiving his money at his home, where he is free from the influence of intoxicants and bad white men, he can wisely advise his wife as to what use to which this money may be appropriated, and in these cool and sober moments, plan and adopt ways of disbursement that will actually benefit the family."

On May 17th, 1912, the Chairman of the Board of Indian Commissioners, Honorable George Vaux, Jr., visited Oklahoma and spent some time traveling through the Cherokee, Creek and Seminole countries. He was accompanied by Dana H. Kelsey, Esq., Superintendent of the Union Indian Agency, having in charge the Five Civilized Tribes. Mr. Vaux's findings were published in the 43rd Annual Report of the Board, 1912.

Desiring to study the Oklahoma situation in its broader aspects, I visited Oklahoma in March, 1913, in company with J. Weston Allen, Esq., who represented the Boston Indian Citizenship Committee and other organizations. We spent considerable time not only in consultation with various Government officials and private citizens, but also in driving over the Creek, Seminole and Cherokee countries.

Mr. Allen remained after I returned East, and drove many miles through the region inhabited by the Choctaw and Chickasaw Indians, and made a report to me on the situation as he found it.

Both of us took numerous photographs showing the actual conditions under which the Indians are living.

I made a report on conditions and submitted recommendations to our Chairman, Mr. Vaux, and to the Honorable Secretary of the Interior. This report was criticised in Congress by Honorable Mr. Stephens, Representative from Texas. Apparently Mr. Stephens did not read the report. He stated in his speech of July 27th, during discussion of the Indian appropriation bill: —

"Mr. Moorehead, the Commissioner mentioned by the gentleman from Illinois (Mr. Graham) a few moments ago, went to Oklahoma last year and by unjust criticism of Indian officials there stirred up more trouble for the Indian Bureau than has ever before occurred in the settlement of the matters of the Five Tribes."

Mr. Stephens desired to see the Board of Indian Commissioners abolished. Speaking for myself personally, and not for the Board, I desire to say that a few years ago it was stated that the Board was not active. Immediately the Board extended its work and projected a number of important investigations, which were carried to a successful end. In the last Congress the Board was criticised for being too active, especially in Oklahoma. Friends of the Board rallied to its support and the former appropriation of $4,000 was raised to the present amount of $10,000.

The past two years studies of Indian conditions by members of the Board have been carried on in Wisconsin, Oklahoma, New Mexico and Arizona. This winter the Board intends to investigate conditions on the Pacific Coast, in the Northwest, Oklahoma, Montana and elsewhere.

In reply to Mr. Stephens' two speeches, I wrote to him and pointed out wherein he was in error. No answer has been received to these letters. Careful reading of my report will convince any unprejudiced person of this fact—that instead of criticising the Indian Office officials in Oklahoma, I commended them. The only criticisms were those aimed at the grafters, and in nearly fifty instances I gave names of guardians or administrators, who had swindled Indians, giving details gleaned from court records. The report urged the Congressional delegation from Oklahoma to take a firm stand in behalf of the Indians.

Much injury is done to the cause for which we are all striving by such speeches as the one cited above. In closing my comments on this unfortunate matter, I desire to state that friendly relations exist between myself and all the Government officials, and that without exception, everyone of them has furnished, or offered, information for this book.

Miss Kate Barnard last winter began a radical campaign on behalf of the Oklahoma Indians. I am sorry space does not permit the recital of Miss Barnard's dramatic story. It seems that for years she was in charge of the Department of Charities and Corrections, for the State. She found in the orphans' homes and poorhouses, large numbers of small children, chiefly Indians. Investigation proved that these children were once possessed of valuable property, out of which guardians had swindled them. After the robbery became complete, the guardians avoided personal responsibility by persuading judges to declare the children homeless paupers; and placed them in State institutions, where they were supported at public expense. The number of children declared paupers mounted into the thousands. The thing became a national scandal, and Miss Barnard soon found herself involved in a fight with the politicians and grafters who profited by these wholesale swindles. Miss Barnard's official reports for the years 1909 to 1913 describe many of these cases in heart-rending detail. The appropriations for her department were wholly inadequate to care for more than a fraction of the State wards, and she was compelled to cooperate with the Federal authorities. This brought her department in line with Mr. Mott, Mr. Kelsey and others who were fighting to bring about similar reforms.

Naturally, she aroused powerful opposition in her own State. The cry of "Eastern sentimentalism" could not be raised against her, she being a State employee. Her campaign seriously affected oil, land and other interests. Hence, the Legislature cut off her appropriation, allowing her salary, but no funds for publication, employment of assistants, travel or other necessary items, whereupon Miss Barnard visited Chicago and raised some thousands of dollars with which to wage a campaign of education. She has organized eleven counties, and although hampered in every way by the grafters, speaks to large gatherings throughout the State. At one meeting 8000 persons assembled to hear her.

She delivered a stirring address at the Lake Mohonk Conference October 21st, this year, and through her efforts the Conference introduced a plank in its platform to the effect that if Oklahoma failed to properly protect her restricted Indians, the Federal Government should resume jurisdiction over them.

Miss Kate Barnard is justly called the "Joan of Arc of Oklahoma".

Of slight figure — even frail — she is possessed of lion's courage and is a most direct, forceful and dramatic speaker. I asked her able assistant and attorney, Mr. Huson, "Where are all these big men of the West, the fellows of the big and courageous hearts, the men we read so much about? Why are they not supporting this woman in her heroic fight?"

He replied: "Oh, they have hearts, all right, when it comes to other matters. But so long as they can make millions out of the Indians, it's no use to talk the humanities to them. They all follow David Harum's golden rule."

In a letter dated July 23, 1912, Mr. H. Huson, Assistant Commissioner of the State Department of Charities and Corrections, which was presented to Congress by President Taft in his veto of the bill attempting to validate inherited land titles, it was also said:

"Armed with this authority Miss Barnard has intervened in behalf of approximately 3,000 orphans, nearly all of these Indian children whose estates were being exploited or disposed of by incompetent or grafting guardians. We have had many guardians removed, and we have saved for these children since this law became operative something like $100,000 in money and prevented the sale or return of something like 115,000 acres of land."

Yet in spite of her good work she is now compelled to fight for existence.

The Indian Office decided to take a hand in the struggle, and Honorable Cato Sells, Commissioner of Indian Affairs, visited Oklahoma early this year, brought together all the probate judges and other officials and made a plea for cooperation in the prevention of further despoiling of the Indian. A set of rules, or method of procedure, was adopted, and the probate judges of Oklahoma have agreed to follow them. Everyone hopes Mr. Sells' plan will work to the advantage of the minors and dependents.

Of the thousands of cases where minors and incompetents were swindled out of property, I present but three or four typical of the larger number. These are from official records.

One man was guardian in thirty-one cases involving more than fifty minors. In all but one case this man as guardian had been dealing with his brothers in the purchase of merchandise for his wards. There is but one exception, that of a minor eighteen years old who was away at school. A Government officer on behalf of these minors protested against such practice and asked to file exceptions and proceed in all of these cases. I am informed that the judge did nothing.

A guardian had a ward, Sam Bighead, a full-blood Indian boy five years of age, who owned 560 acres of valuable land, much of which produced oil. Eighty acres of this land was sold for the sum of $10,000.00 cash. Although this boy owned 480 acres of land and $10,000.00 cash, he was placed in the Creek Orphan Asylum where he died May 18, 1910. This boy, entitled to proper care and treatment, was placed with the children of paupers. Why the guardian wished to have on hand such a large sum of cash, all of which was unnecessary for the maintenance of the ward, since the ward was a public charge, passes comprehension.

When the poor boy died, there was left of this $10,000.00, $2,884.30 in cash, and a $5,000.00 loan on first mortgage.

Death did not stay the actions of the guardian; he became appointed administrator. As administrator he accounted for $11,424.30. He reported that $6,074.96 was the balance on hand of the estate. Of this sum $5,627.00 was divided into four equal parts for four heirs. However, the Government special agent Farrar contends that in three of these cases attorney fees of 25% each were charged. So finally, out of the estate of $11,424.00, $4,405.85 was placed in the hands of the heirs. How can some Oklahoma citizens clamor for withdrawal of Government supervision after reading this story?

A man named Jerry Bunce was guardian of an Indian boy (Choctaw) named Tonihka. Some of the inherited land of the boy had been sold by the guardian through the probate court, and there were in the possession of the guardian funds belonging to his ward amounting to $1100. The guardian bought a cow and calf for the ward; the boy slipped the calf away and sold it and with the proceeds bought him some clothes. The guardian employed an attorney and had the boy arrested charging him with larceny of the calf. Other attorneys were employed to defend the boy. The guardian paid the attorneys on both sides of the case $900 of the boy's money — one side for prosecuting and the other side for an alleged defense;

when the case came up for trial the attorney defending plead guilty for the boy, who was convicted without a word of evidence, and sent to the reform school. Bunce died, and his successor as guardian told my informant the above facts, and said that when he talked with the attorneys involved they treated the matter as a great joke.

In 1910 a full-blood Choctaw Indian named Simon Wakaya was found dead and charred in the ashes of his cabin. An investigation showed that he had been shot before the cabin was burned. This Indian had dealt in cattle and owned a small herd of stock in addition to his allotment. Two or three days after the death, there was filed in the county offices a bill of sale conveying all of his cattle to a man named Bill ————.* At the same time there was filed for probate in the county court, a will purporting to have been executed by Wakaya conveying his allotment to Henry ————.* A Government representative satisfied himself that the will was a forgery and induced a relative to contest the will. After a preliminary hearing occurred in the county court, the matter was appealed to the district court and full disclosure of all the facts was had.

The judge issued a bench warrant, charging them all with murder, perjury, forgery and arson. These men gave bond at the time and for two years they have been at liberty and have never been brought to trial. This last remark merely illustrates the apathy of the white people of this State in matters involving the welfare of the Indians. It is a fact demonstrated a hundred times a day in this State that the white population cares very little about the rights of the Indians and it is difficult to secure a conviction of white people for many felonies committed upon Indians. This is most frequently illustrated in the matter of forgeries in the securing of pretended deeds from unrestricted Indians. Upon failure to secure a deed the white man is not yet at the end of his resources, for he can still either forge a deed or get some Indian or freedman to impersonate the owner of the land and execute a conveyance, acknowledge it before a notary and have it recorded.

A full-blood Cherokee, now about twenty-six, was allotted valuable land in the vicinity of Bartlesville. She had no relatives, and at the age of four years she was taken into the family of a white man, but not formally adopted. When the allotments were made he was appointed her guardian. When she became of age he was discharged. During his guardianship about $4500.00 came into the guardian's hands as guardian. Upon a final accounting he filed receipts for over $2,000 as having been paid to his ward, but which it is claimed he admitted really never was paid to her.

---

* Names omitted.

When this girl became of age a new oil lease was made with her for which a bonus of $8,000 was paid, which money went into the hands of the guardian and which it is alleged he likewise admitted he diverted to his own use. It is also claimed that approximately $2500 royalty has been received by the guardian for this girl. It is claimed that the guardian has admitted that he owed this girl approximately $20,000. The ward lived in the home of her guardian ostensibly as a servant. She is of weak mind and really an incompetent. In September, 1910, the guardian secured a divorce from his wife, and afterwards, it is claimed, continued to live with his ward.

As an illustration of the extremes to which these grafters sometimes resort, my attention was called to a case of an adult who had died and left a valuable property. In order to get large allowances from the estate padded expense accounts were put in for the burial robes, metallic caskets, etc., although the relatives who attended the burial stoutly insisted that only a box, and the cheapest clothes were used. In this instance, the grafters, knowing that an investigation was to be made, exhumed the body and placed same in a metallic casket, and carried off and destroyed the pine box in which the burial had originally been made!

Miss Barnard found a pauper child in an almshouse. Investigation proved that the guardian disposed of a valuable "oil allotment" for $50,000. Instead of using a part of this money for the child's education, he appropriated it to his own use. A portion of the money was recovered and the child placed in an educational institution.

Indians about to become of age possessing valuable allotments, were taken to remote points — Denver, Minneapolis, etc. Henry Purchase was taken to St. Louis, and detained until he signed a deed to his property. Marcus Corey was found by Secret Service men in Southampton, England, and returned after much trouble to his parents. Marcus possessed property worth $40,000.

Cases are on record where Indians were poisoned, or confined in rooms in obscure hotels, until they signed away their property. The ignorant were easy prey to the grafters, as this newspaper clipping of 1913 attests:

Oklahoma City, June 25.—In an opinion handed down today by Associate Justice Jesse Dunn, of the supreme court that body holds that two Mississippi Choctaw Indian girls who were so ignorant that they would have sold their allotments on which were valuable asphalt deposits and which are worth $40,000 for $850 came under the statutory terms of mentally incompetent persons and that the county court of Marshall County should appoint a guardian for them. The girls admitted that they could neither read nor write, did not know when their mother died or how many $5 bills it would take to make a hundred.

In most States guardian and administrator fees range from as low as 2% to as high as 5% or 6%. In Oklahoma, the administrators and guardians charged from 3% to as high as 80% for service and costs in settling up the affairs of these defenseless people. I present a random page from Mr. Mott's long report. This was included by the Honorable Mr. Burke in his speech.

SHACK OF A POOR CREEK INDIAN, OKLAHOMA
Photographed in 1913

In defending such charges, one gentleman claimed that some of these estates consisted of small tracts, widely scattered. Therefore, the charges must of necessity be high. This is true of very few cases, especially since small tracts widely separated were rarely ever sought after by the grafter guardians, who in some localities were opprobiously designated as *professional guardians*. The figures speak for themselves, and should be considered by every thoughtful man and woman in this country, as they tell a story of robbery unparalleled in American history.

No. 626. Amount handled, $2,085, at cost of $1,494.93, or 71.2 per cent.
Nos. 1411–1412. Amount handled, $65,266.92, at cost of $19,315.23, or 29.4 per cent.
No. 1133. Amount handled, $3,286.94, at cost of $1,721.52, or 52.3 per cent.
No. 1556. Amount handled, $41,502.16, at cost of $21,953.60, or 52.8 per cent.

The following cases will be found in McIntosh County, Exhibit C:

No.   32.   Amount handled, $1,328.52, at cost of $937.89, or 70.5 per cent.
No.   310.   Amount handled, $600, at cost of $305.50, or 50.9 per cent.
No.   359.   Amount handled, $1,960, at cost of $695.50, or 35.4 per cent.
No.   428.   Amount handled, $17,944.26, at cost of $3,043.07, or 16.9 per cent.
No.   669.   Amount handled, $1,787.50, at cost of $609.49, or 34 per cent.

In Exhibit D, for Tulsa County, will be found the following cases:

No.   7.   Amount handled, $14,944.37, at cost of $3,267, or 21.8 per cent.
No.   110.   Amount handled, $2,094.28, at cost of $1,274.75, or 60.8 per cent.
No.   273 (a).   Amount handled, $9,520.12, at cost of $2,487.67, or 26.1 per cent.
No.   273 (c).   Amount handled, $29,296.76, at cost of $6,523.15, or 22.2 per cent.
No.   1014 (b).   Amount handled, $19,534.12, at cost of $3,644.30, or 18.6 per cent.

Exhibit E, for Creek County, contains the following cases:

No.   16.   Amount handled, $13,675.37, at cost of $3,099.60, or 22.6 per cent.
No.   36.   Amount handled, $54,968.10, at cost of $10,650.43, or 19.9 per cent.
No.   182.   Amount handled, $64,863.42, at cost of $11,810.59, or 18.2 per cent.
    (The above three cases were under the same guardianship).
No.   42.   Amount handled, $1,740, at cost of $793.75, or 45.7 per cent.
No.   188.   Amount handled, $1,347.78, at cost of $759.37, or 56.3 per cent.

The cases below will be found in Exhibit F, for Okmulgee County:

No.   10.   Amount handled, $8,688.21, at cost of $2,243.85, or 25.8 per cent.
No.   280.   Amount handled, $2,855, at cost of $1,038.82, or 36.3 per cent.
No.   152.   Amount handled, $1,321.50, at cost of $1,196.50, or 90.5 per cent.
No.   136.   Amount handled, $2,026.55, at cost of $778.95, or 38.4 per cent.
No.   540.   Amount handled, $2,570, at cost of $1,684.64, or 65.5 per cent.

In Exhibit G, for Okfuskee County, will be found the following cases:

No.   271.   Amount handled, $3,270, at cost of $911.96, or 27.8 per cent.
No.   237.   Amount handled, $698.60, at cost of $364, or 52.1 per cent.
No.   179.   Amount handled, $3,208.05, at cost of $983.10, or 30.6 per cent.
No.   98.   Amount handled, $1,674.40, at cost of $482.57, or 28.8 per cent.

I also call attention to the following cases found in Exhibit H, for Hughes County:

No.   223.   Amoung handled, $2,372.50, at cost of $909.58, or 38.3 per cent.
No.   305.   Amount handled, $4,939, at cost of $1,147, or 23.2 per cent.
No.   480.   Amount handled, $1,950, at cost of $717.95, or 36.8 per cent.
No.   984.   Amount handled, $2,847.79, at cost of $744.44, or 26.2 per cent.
No.   1039.   Amount handled, $806.40, at cost of $407.64, or 50.5 per cent.

It will thus be seen that these methods and practices apply generally throughout the Creek Nation, and while they may exist in a greater degree in one county than another, the general situation is substantially the same. It is reasonable to presume also that in that large number of cases, as above pointed out, to wit, 4,339, where no reports of guardians have been made, and where files are out, equally bad or even worse conditions prevail.

## CHAPTER XV. WHAT IS LEFT OF INDIAN PROPERTY IN OKLAHOMA

We have looked upon the dark side of Oklahoma Affairs, let us look on the bright side for a moment. From last year's report of J. George Wright, Commissioner to the Five Civilized Tribes, it is learned that there are 32,939 restricted Indians. These are still protected by the Government, and all own homesteads. Notwithstanding the thousands of Indians who have been swindled out of their property, or sold same at ridiculously low prices, a great deal remains — sufficient to provide every Indian of the tribes with a homestead and enough agricultural land to maintain himself and family, provided he is protected in his rights; all hinges upon that word *provided*.

As to the true value of this land, I shall not present the statistics, but the entire 19,000,000 acres, held by Indians and Whites, because of the great oilfields, coal and asphalt lands timber and farm lands, must be worth at least $1,000,000,000. About half of this, or $500,000,000, it is claimed that the Indians still own, largely because of the restrictions placed upon their property

Much of this land is what is known as tribal land, and when sold the amount is placed to the credit of the tribe. The tribal attorneys, the Government officials, and practically everyone believes that the lands should be sold, and the money divided up among the Indians. The reasons for this, I have briefly presented on page 28, when speaking of Indians in general. By this method, we will rid the Indians of an ever-increasing swarm of attorneys and remove all incentive to unwise legislation.

Of the number of Indians at work, the value of their crops and labor, no man may know. Estimates vary, but I suppose that it is no exaggeration to state that about a third of the males belonging to the Five Civilized Tribes work — thousands of them regularly. The Government has encouraged this through the District Agents, or field helpers, whose duty it is to instruct the Indians in farming, to protect them in their rights and to exercise a general supervision over them. These field agents stood between the Indian and the grafter, and there was a determined effort on the part of a few men to have the entire number dismissed from the Service. However, Congress continued the appropriation and these worthy men are assured of another year's effort on behalf of the Indians.

Some of the illustrations presented in these chapters are from photographs taken by Mr. Allen and myself in Oklahoma and will give an idea

**OLD-STYLE CABIN, 1850-1890**
Cherokee, Oklahoma. Photographed, 1913

of the homes of the Indians, and some of the farms they have brought under cultivation.

The unallotted lands have usually been sold at auction and since November 1, 1910, 1,838,921 acres have been sold for $10,458,945, or an average of $5.68 per acre. This seems rather low price, but as most of the lands were not developed and many tracts had grown up to bushes, it is the best that could be obtained under the circumstances.

Of immense value are the segregated coal and asphalt lands in Choctaw and Chickasaw nations. These total 455,303 acres. The value has been variously estimated, and it is impossible to accurately or even approximately state the amount. Coal tracts, in the eastern part of the United States, have been known to sell as high as $1,000 an acre. The price may vary from $50 for tracts wherein the veins are thin, to $500 for heavy vein of the best grades of bituminous coal. It will thus be seen that at the lowest estimate coal contained in this enormous area is of exceeding value, and this statement does not take into account the great asphalt deposit of undoubted value. Up to the present, the Government has successfully resisted attempts of those who would secure control of this property. Commissioner Wright, on page 28 of his report, states that there is in cash deposited to the credit of the Indians, in banks in the State of Oklahoma, $4,474,189.45. The interest paid on this sum varies from 4% to 6%.

Some of the coal and asphalt lands have been leased to mining companies and during the year ending June 30, 1913, 3,103,071 tons of coal and 4,752 tons of asphalt were mined; the royalty on the coal being eight cents per ton and on crude asphalt ten cents, refined asphalt sixty cents per ton.

The tribal attorneys, acting for these Five Civilized Tribes, and occupying high positions of trust and responsibility, have, without exception, done what they could to further the interests of their clients.

The existence of the Cherokee terminated June 30, 1914, and all tribal offices were abolished. Whether the Cherokees will prosper remains to be seen.

In addition to the totals presented, it must be recorded that $2,480,739.35 were distributed to individual Indians. This sum was received from oil royalties, lease privileges, mining royalties, rents, bonuses, etc.

Dana H. Kelsey, Superintendent of the Union Agency, and acting in conjunction with Commissioner Wright last year handled a grand total of $8,215,989.71. Some idea of the enormous amount of business transacted by his office may be gleaned from the statement that pieces of mail matter (over half of which were letters) during the year totaled 364,218. His office investigated about 18,000 leases, land cases, complaints and probate cases all relating to Indian property. The net saving to the Indians by this governmental supervision was $667,352.25.

Mr. Kelsey states: "At the advent of statehood there were no ample facilities to afford proper protection to the minor and incompetent Indians, the former of which number approximately 60,000."

Some of the difficulties with which his office has had to contend may be imagined from the following quotation: —

"Many parties who sought to secure these lands either controlled the appointment of the guardian or connived with the guardian to purchase the land at grossly inadequate prices, the difference between the purchase price and the actual price of the land being the profit realized by the guardian and the purchaser. In other instances parents who were appointed guardians of their children sold their children's allotments and dissipated the proceeds. This work discloses many instances where parties desiring to lease minor allotments secured the appointment of themselves or employees as guardian, and by so controlling the land sought they were able to profit to a considerable extent in subleasing lands for, in some instances, many times the amount paid. Many of these leases provided for the improvement of the land in lieu of cash rental, while none of the improvements were made. Many complaints lodged with the field clerks are from the unrestricted Indians, who, upon attaining their majority, find that their allotments have been sold and the funds dissipated by the guardian, leaving them penniless."

I visited Mr. Kelsey's office and spent a number of days there watching the conduct of business. The tremendous activity in the oilfields, and the thousands of applications for oil leases or purchase of Indian lands pass, for the most part, through his hands and those of his able assistants. If it were not for his efforts and those of Commissioner Wright, and the tribal attorneys (and not to omit Mr. Mott, Mr. Foreman and Miss Barnard), in other words, if there had not appeared before those who sought to despoil the Indians this "stone wall defense", there would be little to record today beyond the fact that the Five Civilized Tribes at one time possessed a great deal of property.

Mr. Kelsey served over ten years as Superintendent of the Union Agency and is thoroughly familiar with conditions in Oklahoma. His recommendations, therefore, should carry weight. They are found on page 93 of his report.

"1.   Continued and more practical care of the health and property of the older, uneducated, full-blood Indian, and the disposition, under proper supervision, of his excess land holdings.

"2.   The immediate placing of all mature, able-bodied Indians entirely upon their own resources when shown that they have had sufficient experience or education to enable them to earn a livelihood.

"3.   Systematic and compulsory education of every Indian child, and conservation of his property in the meantime."

He emphasizes the education of Indian children for the reason that back in the hills in Oklahoma there are several thousand children not officially recognized as members of the tribes, for the reason that they have been born since the rolls were closed.  As no provision is made for the education of these, he properly claims that these children constitute one of the great problems in Oklahoma.  He also states that most of the adult Indians have remaining more or less property or money.  I would add to his recommendations that this property and money must be wisely safeguarded else the Indians will become paupers.  Already a few of them are living on the section lines, along the county roads.  And this number will increase rapidly, unless we make the citizenship real and effective.

The office held by Mr. Wright now being consolidated with that of Mr. Kelsey, he acts as Supervisor.  I wrote him a long letter concerning the Oklahoma situation, and a portion of his reply should be included in this book: —

     \*     \*     \*     \*     \*     \*

"So far as the consolidation of the two offices is concerned, I rather feel that you were unduly anxious over its effect.  I have had the responsibility of the entire work now for nearly two months, and am more than ever convinced that the time was ripe for it and it was good administration to have it all under one head, provided that head is the right sort of a man, and that there will be no ill effects therefrom.  It was bound to come, and had better come while there was somebody here who knew how to do it than later.  I am having such fun getting it working smoothly that it will soon be only an incident.  I am happy to say that the good work to protect the Indians goes on I think better now than ever.  We are getting excellent results from the new probate attorney organization, in cooperation with our former field force (which is still intact), and not only preventing new abuses, but, as time permits, delving into and correcting many old and rotten ones affecting minors, and I think the cooperation of the probate courts — especially since the earnest entrance into the thing by the Commissioner personally — is a hundred per cent better than it was before, all of which I helped plan, and with which I feel I have had much to do. "Muskogee, Oct. 23rd, 1914."

All of the above is very encouraging, and I hope the consolidation and the probate attorneys will work together for the result we all desire.

It would not be proper to close the Oklahoma affair without saying a few words concerning Mr. Mott and Captain Grayson.

Captain George W. Grayson has served as official Creek interpreter for many years. He understands the history of his tribe, is entirely in sympathy with their aims, and has done much to aid the various tribal attorneys in Oklahoma. With a fine Indian, Moty Tiger, Chief of the Creek Nation, he has frequently visited Washington. I asked Captain Grayson to read the manuscript of my Oklahoma section prior to publication, and am indebted to him for valuable suggestions and information. Captain Grayson as interpreter has been made use of by the Smithsonian Institution men in their investigations of Creek language, mythology and family life. There is no more able interpreter in all the State of Oklahoma.

Mr. M. L. Mott has been referred to in previous pages of this chapter. In closing, I would call attention to a remarkable scene which occurred in the office of the Secretary of the Interior in February, 1914. The Oklahoma delegation in Congress from the state of Oklahoma, had opposed the reappointment of Mott as attorney for the Creek Indians. As we have seen in previous pages, Mott put up a heroic fight on behalf of his clients, thereby incurring the ill will of many persons. Each afternoon for five days, were arrayed against him all the Congressmen from Oklahoma. At the conclusion of these lengthy sessions, in which the opponents were unable to prove anything of consequence against Mr. Mott, the Secretary of the Interior issued him the following letter:

THE SECRETARY OF THE INTERIOR
WASHINGTON

February 14, 1914.

My dear Mr. Mott:

Chief Moty Tiger and myself have agreed upon Judge Allen as your successor as Attorney for the Creek Nation.

\*        \*        \*        \*        \*        \*

I shall always take pleasure in contemplating the manner in which you conducted yourself during the inquiry here. That you have been honest under difficulties and fearless at all times in doing your duty, seems to be admitted even by those to whom you have been most antipathetic.

I am glad to know that you are going to return to Oklahoma and I trust that by mingling freely with those people they will come to see you as a man of ideals.

Cordially yours,<br>(Signed) FRANKLIN K. LANE

M. L. Mott, Esq.,
Washington, D. C.

We may search governmental records in vain for a parallel case. Here was a faithful servant of the public, a loyal friend to the Indians. The Congressmen appeared against him in force and brought up every conceivable charge, in order to encompass his fall; striving to preserve official peace in Oklahoma, the Honorable Secretary was forced to replace him, yet at the same time wrote a commendatory letter in Mott's behalf.

The night following his honorable defeat, I saw Mott in his room at the National Hotel. With him were two staunch friends of the Creeks, Chief Moty Tiger and Captain G. W. Grayson. Mott uttered a remarkable prophecy: "Moorehead, they are rid of me. The next step will be to force out the Department of Justice men, Gresham and Frost; then Kelsey and Wright will have to go; Kate Barnard must stop protecting minor heirs, or her board will be abolished; also your Indian Commissioners. Having cut off the real fighters, then they will remove restrictions. A few years hence — and do not forget this — the Oklahoma Congressmen will ask the American people to support Indian paupers, claiming that Federal negligence has brought distress to thousands, and that the State of Oklahoma must not be called upon to care for these indigents. Most people who took Indian lands will not be compelled to return them, and the Federal slate will be wiped clean of the 30,000 land suits now pending."

In eight months, nearly half of Mott's prophecy has been verified.

## CHAPTER XVI.  THE LEASING SYSTEM; CHOCTAW AND CHICKASAW; FINAL RECOMMENDATIONS

Few Indian matters in our honorable Congress have had more publicity than the so-called McMurray contracts.  Several chapters of this book could be devoted to describing the propositions made by Mr. McMurray and his associates and the far-reaching effects on the Indians of Oklahoma were these carried into effect.  But I must content myself with calling attention to the bibliography at the end of this chapter.  The testimony and investigations cover hundreds of pages.

Mr. McMurray made contracts with thousands of Indians on a percentage basis.  P. J. Hurley, Esq., attorney for the Choctaw Indians, opposed the McMurray contracts before Congressional Committees and in court.  Hurley contended that McMurray would receive at the least possible estimate $3,500,000 in fees, the undistributed portion of the Choctaw and Chickasaw estate being $35,000,000 minimum valuation.  The struggle for so large a stake has extended through a number of years.  So far Mr. Hurley, and other friends of the Indians, have succeeded in preventing McMurray carrying his contracts into effect.

The Choctaw and Chickasaw affairs are both interesting and complicated, and tell a different story from that of the Creeks.  Further reference to Cherokees and Seminoles may be omitted, as their story is practically that of the Creeks.

A little more than two-thirds of the entire acreage — a vast domain over 200 miles east and west, and an average of approximately 100 miles north and south — was allotted and sold for the benefit of these three classes of Indians, the Choctaws, Chickasaws and Mississippi Choctaws, about 37,600 in number — a little more than one-third of the total Oklahoma enrollment.

The eastern third of this territory is especially rich in coal and hardwood timber.  What is shown upon the map as the Choctaw Nation contains the largest coal deposits in what is generally known as the Mississippi valley, and when allotment of lands began in 1903, this country was practically covered with a rich growth of pine timber of the finest quality.

The Chickasaw Nation comprised the greatest agricultural and stock-raising lands, some of which had been under cultivation for half a century.  By the use of these vast estates, they became well-to-do and self-supporting.  The richness of the country becoming known, Whites and negroes flocked to Indian Territory with the idea prominent that they were going to be permitted to homestead the surplus land, as had been the custom in breaking up Indian reservations. With the opening of the Cherokee strip, the Cheyenne and Arapaho and the Iowa and Comanche reservations on the west, comprising all of the western half of Oklahoma, immigrants flocked to these openings. Some of the best of them remained as farmers in that great western country. The riff-raff, after exploiting those western and northern reservations, came back to Indian Territory to ply their vocations at the various allotting agencies among the Five Civilized Tribes.

By 1903 all kinds of land, livestock and timber companies were at work; skillful lawyers schemed to change the laws. More than one Indian, disgusted with the "Christian" white man, stayed in the Choctaw hills among the pine forests and refused to come out and perform the duties necessary under the laws made for him in order that he might receive his allotment. Each man, woman and child was to receive $1040 worth of land, appraised at from twenty-five cents to $6.50 per acre; also 320 acres of average land. He was supposed to look it over, and being satisfied with it, come to the land office and file his "descriptions" with an affidavit that he owned such improvements, if any there were, and the possessary right to the land selected. He could not be induced to come. It cost money to go 200 miles over into the Chickasaw Nation, or even to find suitable land in the Choctaw Nation.

Under the allotment act the members of the tribes were given the right to alienate one-half their lands within five years from date of patents. The more ignorant classes were more easily influenced, and runners were employed to go over in the Choctaw Nation and "shell the woods" for Indians. Sufficient quantities of whiskey, an interpreter, and expense money were all that was necessary. Indians were brought into the allotting agencies by the score. He was taken out in a conveyance and driven a few miles from the agency and shown the best improved farm in the country, a deal made with him to lease the land for five years in consideration of the purchase of the possessary right to the land. His plans were prepared for him. His allotment known as surplus which would be alienable within five years, was plotted upon improved lands which he had never seen and the balance of his land known as homestead selected for him in some out of the way place, generally upon the hills. To this day most of these full-blood Indians have never seen nor set foot upon their several allotments.

A case or two illustrating Choctaw and Chickasaw affairs is illuminating of general conditions. Addie B. Fasler was a minor full-blood Indian about twelve years of age in 1907, and a certain man was made guardian for her. Under a new act of Congress an additional judge had been appointed in the southern district, Judge J. T. Dickenson, and he had been assigned the northern half of the district by agreement between himself and the other judge. This application was presented to him for approval. Judge Dickenson refused to appoint the one requested, but upon his own motion selected a man by the name of Wright living at Sulphur. Up to this time such independence on the part of the judiciary was unusual and war from this time on existed between the old and the new judge. Wright found his ward in squalor. He found that she owned, by reason of the death of her family, four allotments besides her own — that they consisted of something like a thousand acres of improved land, the larger part in cultivation; that all of this land had been in the possession of a Mr. Mullen since allotment, and was at that time being rented out by Mr. Mullen for an average rental of $2.50 per acre per year. Mr. Wright employed attorneys and began proceedings to recover these lands for his ward. He was met at the hearing by a subsequently appointed guardian from the central district who had been appointed at the instance of Mullen. The hearing was had before the old judge who promptly held that the domicile of the minor was in the central district and that the United States Court for the southern district had no jurisdiction to appoint Mr. Wright guardian. What has become of Addie B. Fasler or her vast estates? She is one of the many now "unknown" since her property is gone.

After statehood, the Chocktaw and Chickasaw Nations were cut up into many counties and probate matters transferred to the County Courts of the counties which included the court towns. Provisions were made to transfer probate cases to the county which would have had jurisdiction had such case been inaugurated after statehood.

Little effort has been made to transfer these cases, because the Indians themselves are ignorant of the fact that administrators and guardians have been appointed elsewhere and only in those instances where the grafter wants to sell or lease the land is any pretense made to have everything regular. This condition has resulted in the appointment of guardians in the counties of the residence of the minors to recover lands and rentals. Much litigation has grown out of these conflicts, and it is safe to say that in very few instances have the grafters surrendered to the Indian lands allotted to him.

Charles McKinney is an ignorant, easy-going quarter-blood Chickasaw with four or five minor children. Their lands were scattered in Poulatre, Johnson, Marshall and Carter Counties. He was their guardian. He sold these various allotments through the County Court of ——— County and received something like $7000. The mayor of the city was on his bond. A certain judge, the mayor and several other politicians decided to buy a local newspaper which was too independent for the good of the party. This money was loaned to the mayor, who gave as security a mortgage upon several tracts of land which he did not own, and used the money in the purchase of the newspaper plant; the latter became insolvent and was sold by its creditors, and the guardian squandered the balance of the money.

The Mississippi Choctaws are Indians of a low order of intelligence. They were imported into this country in 1902 and 1903 by land companies, among which was the Choctaw Investment Company, now defunct, and J. E. Arnold. They were herded in barracks around Ardmore and other places during 1902, 1903 and 1904; the smallpox broke out among them and they died like sheep. Before they left Mississippi, contracts were made with them in which they agreed to prove up on their lands and sell them to the promoters.

The stockholders of the Chocktaw Investment Company and other non-residents furnished the money and have stood the loss, but J. E. Arnold and Senator Owen are now pressing before the Court of Claims large accounts for allowance. To secure these claims if allowed, J. E. Arnold has filed a lien upon almost every allotment of a Mississippi Choctaw in these two nations. Congress has recognized these claims by permitting them to be litigated.

### RECOMMENDATIONS

Except a few persons, everybody agrees that affairs in Oklahoma are in a bad shape. The Indian Office is doing all that it can through Mr. Sells' attorneys to bring about desired reforms and protection, but it is exceedingly slow work. We must adopt Miss Barnard's plan if we desire to save the remaining Indian peoples in Oklahoma. That is, briefly, to arouse the conscience in hundreds of thousands of good citizens in Oklahoma and persuade them to take a firm stand against further despoilation of Indians. The grafters, through their newspapers, have exerted an influence out of all proportion to their strength. They have dominated in Oklahoma. They have even subsidized. One of the newspapers which attacked Hon. George Vaux, Jr., and afterwards was very bitter toward Mr. Mott and myself, received thousands of dollars from an Indian minor child's estate. This money was used to boom a political journal.

All who would save the Indian must stimulate the better class of citizens into action. Attacking grafters, is not bringing into discredit

the good name of a great State.  I mention this because the grafters raise
the cry of State persecution.  They do not, however, deny the pauperizing
of Indians, or the 30,000 specific cases of fraud.  Miss Barnard well answers
critics with the statement that we are merely attacking forces of evil.
The people of Oklahoma themselves can solve the problem promptly and
satisfactorily, if they will assert their rights.  All the protection and publicity, and legal procedures in the world will not save the Oklahoma Indians, if the better class of citizens (the great majority) do not take a firm
stand for right and justice.  The ministers, Miss Barnard claims, are
already beginning to preach sermons against graft — all of which indicates
a trend of healthy public opinion.

Mr. Foreman, who has worked along the same lines as Department of
Justice officials, Miss Barnard and Mr. Kelsey, and has been associated with
Mr. Mott, takes a rather gloomy view.  I present his paragraphs herewith:

"In a few short years, Congress has removed the restrictions on the
sale of nearly 70 per cent of the 100,000 Indians of the tribes — on all
but the full-bloods.  The inevitable has overtaken these mixed-bloods
from whom Congress released its protecting supervision, and probably
not one in ten of them retains even a considerable part of his original
allotment of land.

"The experiment of turning these mixed-blood Indians loose has been
a lamentable mistake.  But at least some good should be extracted from
it.  The lesson should be employed to emphasize the need for protection
of the full-blood.  The mixed-blood as a land owner is no more.  He is
gone and there is practically nothing to be done for his class except in the
protection of his minor children.

"But the full-blood still has his land, for his restrictions have never
been released.  There is no obligation to these Indians so commanding as
the duty of seeing to it that they are protected in their property; this means
that the restrictions against the sale of their lands must not be relaxed
except under the supervision of the Interior Department.  To permit them
to sell their lands without this protection would expose them to their own
inexperience and improvidence, to the cunning of the shameless horde of
white land grafters.

"It was claimed that at least the mixed-bloods are competent to handle
their property, and developments have shown the fallacy of that claim.
Many of the full-bloods are but little more fortunate.  Totally unprepared
they have had thrust upon them individual ownership of their lands.  In
1906 Congress provided that full-blood Indians might sell lands inherited
from deceased relatives.  As the rate of mortality is high among these

© By Rodman Wanamaker—1913

Chief Koon-Kah-Za-Tha-Chy addressing the Council

people, there are many such inheritances and many such sales have been made. In a great number of instances they have been swindled out of their inheritances for a pittance.

"Congress unwisely permitted these full-bloods to lease most of their land for five years without supervision. Thousands of them were induced by white speculators to lease their land, including their homes and little cultivated farms which were capable of making them comfortable. Inexperienced in such transactions, they gave the white man their home for five years for little or nothing, the consideration depending on the extent of fraud practiced on them. The speculator in turn sublets the land to a renter and makes a handsome profit on the transaction. The Indian was then forced to move on the land of a relative, or into the hills on unimproved land, with practically nothing to sustain his family. In many cases only the first year's rent is paid the Indian and the lessee refuses to pay more. The Indian in his helplessness knows no remedy and suffers almost a total loss of the consideration agreed upon. This situation is particularly distressing in the Choctaw and Chickasaw Nations.

"These leases are extended by methods which the mind of the Indian cannot comprehend, and once out of possession it is practically impossible for the Indian to get his land back. When the restrictions are removed from the sale of this class of land, which is looked forward to by the people holding them, they will make the most of their advantage over the Indian, by making it practically impossible for the Indian to get any other buyers than the lessees, who will buy on their own terms. This mean advantage is evidenced now in another way. The Indian Department can sell part of the Indian's allotment for the Indian's benefit, but in many cases a sale for an adequate consideration is defeated by the presence of leases often taken by white speculators for no other purpose than to prevent anyone else buying the land, or to demand a heavy tribute for a surrender of the lease.

"The newspapers and the court files of the eastern half of Oklahoma for several years have been filled with the stories of the Indians' undoing which explains the swift impoverishment of the mixed-blood Indian. If the mixed-bloods could not stand up against this condition, what chance, would the full-bloods have?

"When the hardy pioneer ventured within the domain of the aboriginal proprietors of this country he found himself among what are often described as "hostile" people. It is a strange caprice of fortune that with the coming of the white man's civilizing influence, the description "hostile" should be shifted from the Indian to the white man, and the submissive red man, remaining upon his own land, should discover himself surrounded by the perils of hostile white people.  Perils less bloody but more insidious and relentless; the thirst for blood supplanted by the thirst for the Indian's property; the Indian's ambush exchanged for the white man's ambush of intrigue and deception; conquest of the stout of heart and arm routed by the conquest of the pen and deceit and of the brain befuddled by the devastating alcohol.

"The Indian is groping his way through the dusk of his day upon earth and soon he will pass from our sight and the sound of his footsteps will cease.  As he proceeds falteringly, this shred of a great race is comforted by no expressions of good will.  The road is rough and the guide-posts are far between and hard to read.  The only light that would reveal his path to him shines distantly but faithfully.  From this light, from the voices and counsels of a few distant friends unselfishly striving for him, comes the only promise of amelioration."

Miss Barnard's assistant, Mr. Huston, at Lake Mohonk, dictated to me the following two paragraphs as indicative of the essential things for which the Department of Charities and Corrections is fighting.  It must be understood that the second paragraph from the end is not aimed at the Indian Office personnel.  It is merely a statement of fact, that the new attorneys labor under disadvantage.

1st.  To elect a Legislature pledged to appropriate sufficient funds to make effective the Department of Charities and Corrections,— the only arm of Government, Federal or State, which is clothed with legal authority to intervene in the probate courts of Oklahoma on behalf of Indian minor heirs.

2nd.  To enact a law embodying adequate probate procedure.  The probate procedure recently agreed to between the probate judges of Oklahoma and the Commissioner of Indian Affairs is substantially the same procedure which was prepared by M. L. Mott and put into effect in five out of the eight counties of the Creek Nation several years previous to the present administration.  Mr. Mott had this procedure embodied in a bill which passed the lower house of the Oklahoma Legislature two years ago, but which was defeated through the influence of grafters in the Senate. Mott knew that the probate procedure, depending for its force and effect merely upon the personal agreement of county judges elected by a constituency hostile to the Indians, would be ineffective to protect Indian minors, unless the same had the force of law, and provided adequate penalties for violation of same.

Finally, all good citizens in the United States must rally to the support of those who are making a fight for simple justice and decency in Oklahoma. If the better element in that State is defeated by a combination of oil, coal, gas, timber, land, and asphalt interests, the taxpayers of this country will be called upon to support 100,000 homeless paupers. Nowhere else in the United States are 100,000 citizens to be dispossessed, and if this calamity is permitted to occur, the blackest page in all American history shall have been written. A helpless, a trusting, and a dependent people look to us to keep the final one of all our promises.

---

## PARTIAL BIBLIOGRAPHY ON OKLAHOMA

Lengthy discussion of Indian Affairs. Both branches of Congress. *Congressional Record* for 1914. Jan. 22; Feb., 10, 11, 12, 13, 17, 16, 17, 19, 20, 26, 28; March, 10, 11, 12, 21, 26, 27, 28, 31; Apr., 24, 28, 29; May 4; also Dec. 20, 1913.

Detailed reviews of satisfactory conditions of Five Civilized Tribes; statistics of some; need of protection; legislation recommended. Board of Indian Commissioners reports to President and Secretary of Interior. 1869-1890.

Letters expressing the favorable cooperation indorsing the work of, or urging the retention of District Agents in the Five Civilized Tribes. Washington 1912. Printed for the use of the Committee on Indian Affairs.

Choctaw-Chickasaw Tribal Affairs. *Patrick J. Hurley.* Thirty-first Annual Report Lake Mohonk Conference, P. 29. 1913.

Toward "Restricted" and "Unrestricted" Indians of Five Civilized Tribes, Should the Law and its Administration be the same?—*William H. Murray.* Thirty-first Annual Report Lake Mohonk Conference. P. 35. 1913.

Memorial of the Choctaw and Chickasaw Nations, Relative to the Rights of the Mississippi Choctaws. Submitted for consideration in connection with H. R. 19213. 1913.

Five Civilized Tribes, Conditions — *George Vaux, Jr.* The Red Man. Dec., 1912. P. 135.

Report of the Commission to the Five Civilized Tribes to the Secretary of the Interior. June 30, 1912.

The Reorganized Schools in the Five Tribes.—*J. P. Brown.* Twenty-eighth Annual Report Lake Mohonk Conference, 1910. P. 79.

Report on School Taxation in Indian Territory. House of Representatives Doc. No. 34. Fifty-eighth Congress, 3rd Session, Dec. 6, 1907.

Education Among the Five Civilized Tribes.—*J. P. Brown.* Quarterly Journal of the Soc. Amer. Indians, Oct.-Dec., 1913. P. 416.

Veto Message of the President of the United States, without approval Senate Bill 7978, entitled "An Act Relating to inherited estates in the Five Civilized Tribes in Oklahoma." Senate Doc. 899, 62nd Congress, 2nd Session, August 6, 1912.

Laws and Regulations, Relating to Indians and their Lands.—*Oscar H. Lipps.* 1913.

Suppressing the Liquor Traffic in Indian Territory and Oklahoma.—*William E. Johnson.* Twenty-fifth Report Lake Mohonk Conference, 1907. P. 27.

Indian Appropriation Bill, Hearings before the Committee on Indian Affairs, U. S. Senate. Parts 1, 2, 7, and 5. Ending June 30, 1915.

Hearing before Committee on Indian Affairs of the U. S. Senate. Appropriation Bill. Jan. 28 to Feb. 10, 1905.

Suits in Court of Claims by the Choctaw and Chickasaw Indians. "To authorize the Choctaw and Chickasaw Nations to bring suit in the Court of Claims and for other Purposes." Doc. No. 1010, 62nd Congress, 3rd Session. 1913.

The Grace Cox Inheritance Case. Decision of Comm. of Indian Affairs which relates to the Determination of Heirs of Deceased Indians. Jan. 22, 1914.

Letter from Dept. of Interior to Chairman of the Committee on Indian Affairs, transmitting detailed statement of all expenditures and disbursements from various funds on account of the Five Civilized Tribes from 1908 to 1911 inclusive. Senate, 62d Congress, 2d Session, June 30, 1911.

The U. S. Government and the Indian Problem.—*Hon James S. Sherman.* Twenty-seventh Annual Conference Lake Mohonk, 1909. P. 74.

Status and Needs of the Five Civilized Tribes. Thirty-first Annual Report Lake Mohonk Conference, 1913. P. 16.

The Need of Publicity in Indian Affairs.—*John M. Oskisen.* Twenty-fourth Annual Report Lake Mohonk Conference, 1906. P. 38.

Indian Territory Tribes. The Cherokees, Chapter VIII, Pp. 257-297. Indian Territory pp. 425-431. Century of Dishonor.—*Helen Hunt Jackson.* 1886.

The Five Civilized Tribes — Why They Employ Attorneys.—*Speech of Hon. William H. Murray, Congressional Record,* No. 78, Vol. 51. Feb. 11, 1914.

Oklahoma Red Book, 1909-14. Oklahoma City.

Fort Sill Indians, Report of Condition of.— *William H. Ketcham,* Member Board of Indian Commissioners, Jan. 5, 1914.

The Shawnee Indians: Their Customs, Traditions, and Folk-lore.— *Rev. Jacob Spencer.* Kansas City Historical Society, 1907-1908. P. 382.

Reports of the Dawes Commission to the Five Civilized Tribes. 1894-1895.

Five Civilized Tribes. Handbook of American Indians. Vol. I. P. 463.

Seminole. Handbook of American Indians. Vol. II. P. 500.

Creek. Handbook of American Indians. Vol. I. P. 362.

Choctaw. Handbook of American Indians. Vol. I. P. 288.

Chickasaw. Handbook of American Indians. Vol. I. P. 260.

Cherokee. Handbook of American Indians. Vol. I. P. 245.

Sank and Fox Agency, Oklahoma. Report of the Department of the Interior. 1900. P. 348.

Indian Territory. Fourth Annual Report of the Board of Indian Commissioners. 1872. P. 14.

Osages. Third Annual Report of the Board of Indian Commissioners. 1871. P. 5.

Cherokees, General Condition of the Eastern. Twenty-eighth Annual Report of the Board of Indian Commissioners. 1896. P. 13.

Choctaws and Chickasaws. Fifth Annual Report of the Board of Indian Commissioners. 1873. P. 52.

First to Fifth Annual Reports of the Commissioner of Charities and Corrections of the State of Oklahoma. Dec. 10, 1908 to 1913.—*Kate Barnard.*

McMurray Contracts. Hearings Before the Committee on Indian Affairs. U. S. Senate, 63rd Congress. First Session on H. R. 1917. pp. 338-353, 354-456.

Our National Problem. The Sad Condition of the Oklahoma Indians.— *Warren K. Moorehead.* 1913.

Kiowa Agency, Anadarko, Oklahoma. General Condition of Agency Indians.— Report of Department of the Interior, 1904. P. 293.

Habits of the Indians. Kiowa Agency, Oklahoma.— Department Interior Report, 1900. P. 332.

Kiowa Agency, General Condition of the Indians of.— Report of the Department of the Interior, 1902. P. 287.

Pawnee Agency, Oklahoma.— Report of the Department of the Interior, 1904. P. 302.

Cantonment Training School, Oklahoma.— Report of the Department of the Interior, 1904. P. 283.

Cantonment Training School, Oklahoma.— Report of the Department of the Interior, 1903. P. 252.

Mott Report Relative to Indian Guardianships in the Probate Courts of Oklahoma.— *Honorable Charles H. Burke.* House of Representatives, Dec. 13, 1912.

# CHAPTER XVII. RED CLOUD. THE GREATEST INDIAN OF MODERN TIMES

He belonged to the Oglala division of Teton Sioux. He was born at the forks of the Platte River and died at Pine Ridge, South Dakota, 1909.

It is said that he counted coups — that is, he touched the bodies of enemies—eighty times with his coup-stick.

The band of the Sioux to which he belonged is known as Iteshicha. As no comprehensive account of his life has ever been published, I intend to devote this entire chapter to him and his activities. He first comes into prominence in 1865, when the Government undertook to build a road from Fort Laramie, Wyoming, to the gold regions of Montana. Red Cloud captured a detachment of troops and held same prisoners for two weeks and then released them without injury. Commissioners were sent out from Washington that fall to treat with him, and he refused to meet with them.*

Of the individuals who exerted an influence upon the various bands of Sioux something can be learned by a search of the records. Perhaps Sitting Bull and Red Cloud are more popularly known than others. Every plainsman worthy of the name has had an encounter at some time during the past with Red Cloud's warriors. Army officers stationed on the frontier in the '60's or '70's testify to the courage and dash of these sons of the Plains. The War Department records contain more frequent mention of Red Cloud than of any other American Indian; and the pictographic accounts made by the Sioux themselves upon tanned buffalo hides, many years ago, are filled with evidences of the prowess of this chief.

Makh-piya-lúta, or Red Cloud, has said in his pictographic history of his life, that he was born in the year 1822.† His parents were not prominent among the tribe. He calls this year "Star-passed-by-with-a-loud-noise-winter." The Sioux, in their winter-counts, designate each year by some particular or striking occurrence. For instance, in Red Cloud's winter-counts, or census, one winter is called "Winter-in-which-many-died-of-smallpox"; another, "Winter-we-killed-one-hundred-white-men." There are several of these winter-counts made by different chiefs in possession of the Government, which agree as to the naming of each year, and only

---

*Handbook of American Indians, page 358.

†Garrick Mallery, in the Fourth Report of the Bureau of Ethnology, in an illustrated article entitled "Pictographs of the North-American Indians," includes the Dakota winter-counts of Lone Dog, an aged Indian of the Yanktonai tribe of Dakotas, which covers the winters from 1800-'01 to 1876-'77.

vary in minor details.  Two of them cover a surprisingly long period of time, from 1800 to 1877.  Both have been carefully studied by ethnologists and interpreters, and accurate translations prove them of special value to history students.

Of the extreme youth of Red Cloud we know nothing.  An old Indian, when asked at Pine Ridge, shrugged his shoulders and said, "All great men were once boys."  He was trained as became a young Lakota.  All Indian children learn to ride when extremely young.  General Dodge says that, whether men or boys, the Plains tribes, or, as most officers call them, "Horse Indians," produced the finest horsemen in the world.  Red Cloud was not a hereditary chief, but arose to distinction through merit.

Red Cloud was about sixteen when he became a leader among the other boys, signalizing himself in skirmishes and battles with the Crows, Pawnees, and other hereditary enemies of the Sioux.  The various winter-counts tell us that many severe engagements occurred between the Crows and the Sioux, and it is doubtless true that he charged and yelled, scalped and tortured just as energetically as his companions.

Mr. C. W. Allen, who is well acquainted with Red Cloud, prepared a manuscript some years ago, before the chief's memory failed.  Because the chief presents his version of Plains history, the work is unique and merits publication.  Heretofore we have had only the white man's narratives.

Between 1840 and 1849 there were but few attacks against Whites on the Plains, and most of these occurred to the south, in Texas, or along the old Santa Fe trail.  It was not until and during 1849 that extensive emigration set in towards California.  As the wagon-trains increased, the hunting of the Indians was seriously interfered with.  Expeditions, not only of United States troops but of adventurers, buffalo hunters, and miners, penetrated to various parts of the great West.  Among these travelers were men who regarded an Indian no higher than a dog, and fired upon peaceful parties of hunting Indians without the slightest provocation.  Wagon-trains were often in charge of men from the East who knew nothing whatever of Indians or their habits, and becoming insanely frightened at the approach of either friendly or hostile red men, opened fire without the slightest thought of consequences.  It is therefore not surprising that all the Plains Indians soon assumed a hostile attitude toward any being with a white skin.

I have talked with many old Indians of Pine Ridge, Red Cloud's home, and they have agreed that the destruction of the buffalo was the greatest calamity ever brought upon their race.  They could forgive the

Whites for attacking their villages, and for the disregard of treaty promises, and overlook the seizure of their lands, but they could not forget that the Americans made useless and unnecessary slaughter of that grand, majestic native animal, typical of the "spirit of the Plains." But few men appreciate what the buffalo was to the Indian. Thousands of men flocked west to hunt buffalo solely for their hides. Most of them were inexperienced and destroyed many animals before they learned how to properly prepare a robe for sale. The great Platte valley, the Arkansas, the Niobrara and other Plains rivers, were in a few years lined with millions of skeletons — a pitiful spectacle — wretched relics of a once noble creature. Complaints were made by the Indians, who depended solely upon the buffalo for existence, to the Government at Washington, but without avail. More butchers, attracted by the alluring and exciting life of the hunter, flocked to the West. They strained every nerve to make a "record" in destroying these animals. To be a buffalo-hunter became popular, and a number of persons have since carried through life names distinguishing them from their fellows because of the exceeding slaughter which they made. Col. Dodge, who spent from 1849 to 1884 on the frontier, blames the hunters, miners, and cowboys for the Indian wars. This class of people regarded the rights of no persons, save themselves. While our Government was supposed to protect, it did little save send out Peace Commissions and armies in rotation. The lawless white men were never controlled. But the day of retribution was at hand. The Sioux held a great council, which was attended by the dissatisfied element of other bands, and decided to drive out all the whites found in their hunting territory. They split up into small bands, attacked emigrant trains, killed hunters, and at the time of the Civil War were carrying on a general warfare from the Black Hills to the frontiers of Texas.

After the terrible massacre of 1862 in Minnesota* the Indians became bolder, and having received recruits from the bands who had

*From the Minnesota Historical Collections, page 434, volume 9, we learn than on Sunday, August 17, 1862, a small party of Sioux, belonging to Little Crow's band, while out ostensibly hunting and fishing at Acton, Meeker county, Minnesota, obtained from a white man some spirituous liquor, became intoxicated, and murdered a white man and part of his family, and this act precipitated the Sioux war. Little Crow said that since blood had been spilled the war would have to go on, and he summoned warriors from Montana and what is now North and South Dakota. The war began August 18 and lasted about twelve days. The number of white people killed was about 500. The whole or a large part of some fifteen or twenty counties was fearfully desolated, and for a time almost entirely depopulated. In one of the engagements between the Indians and a company of regular troops, twenty-three soldiers were killed and about sixty wounded, and also ninety-two horses were killed. Chief Big Eagle makes a statement of the causes which led up to the trouble. The Whites were constantly urging the Indians to live like the white man. Some were willing, but others were not and could not — the Indians were annoyed, and wanted to do as they pleased. "Then," he says, "some of the white men abused the Indian women in a certain way and disgraced them, and surely there was no excuse for that."

RED CLOUD AND PROFESSOR MARSH

The illustration is reproduced from a photograph in the possession of Miss Fannie
Brown, of Andover. The date is uncertain, but supposed to be 1874 or '75

fled from Minnesota they held up several large wagon-trains, killed or captured the escorts and appropriated the goods.  When the news of this affair reached Washington, Colonels Carrington and Fetterman were ordered to subdue the Plains Indians, and were sent to Wyoming, where they established Fort Phil. Kearny on the Piney fork of the Powder River. Not only was this movement necessary on the part of the Government because of the hostility of the Sioux, but it was desired to open a road through the Powder River country to Virginia City and other mining towns in the mountains, and also to the coast.  Part of the territory was owned by the Crows, but the Dakotas had usurped most of it as hunting-grounds for themselves.  Several conferences between the authorities and the Indians were held, but as dissatisfaction among the Indians was manifest, no settlement could be effected.  "We will lose," said they, "all our best hunting territory if this route is established."  Red Cloud and other chiefs (Crazy Horse, American Horse, etc.) saw opportunity for war and openly urged hostilities.  Clouds of warriors flocked to his standard. During the long and tedious struggle he won great reputation as a leader. General Dodge said:*  "Several forts were established, but they only protected what was inside the palisades.  A load of wood for fuel could not be cut outside without a conflict."

During these troublous times Fort Laramie was the center of importance, peace conferences, Indians coming and going, troops and supplies arriving from the East.  When Colonel Carrington and his troops left Laramie, June, 1866, they were constantly watched by Red Cloud, and a reliable report states that upon the visit of some Indians at headquarters the commander was informed of his movements, in detail, during the entire journey.  With the troops was Capt. Frederick H. Brown, noted for his bravery and contempt of Indians, and after the establishment of the post he infused in Col. William J. Fetterman some of his own spirit. Both officers declared that a nervy White could put to flight a hundred Sioux.  When calling one evening, Brown told Colonel Carrington's wife that he must have Red Cloud's scalp before he returned East, but, instead, Red Cloud took *his* scalp on the day of the Fetterman fight, December 21, 1866.

The warriors harassed the garrison of Fort Phil. Kearny constantly, killing small parties of wood-cutters.  It became necessary to send out a guard of fifty to eighty men with every wood-train.  Red Cloud drilled his warriors daily, seeming to possess a system of signals equally as good

* Our Wild Indians, pp. 83, 84, by Col. H. I. Dodge.

as those in use at the fort.  Colonel Carrington, in his description of the events at the post, says on one occasion Red Cloud's signals covered a line of seven miles, and were rapidly and accurately displayed.  Again, on December 6, a number of soldiers were killed.  On the 21st the picket signaled that the wagon-train was surrounded, and ninety-seven men were sent to its relief.  Afterward it was ascertained that the train was threatened but not attacked; in fact, the teams and escort came in safely that night. Red Cloud had made a feint to draw troops some distance from the post that he might engage them successfully.  The world knows the result, and it is not necessary for me to enter into details here.  The entire command under Fetterman and Brown was killed, including several citizens accompanying it.  Col. H. B. Carrington, in his official report, says: "The officers who fell believed that no Indian force could overwhelm that number of troops well held in hand."

Red Cloud's name was heard throughout the land, and among his own people he arose to be supreme chief; hundreds of recruits joined his camp, and he was given an immense medicine dance and heralded as invincible.

August 2, 1867, Major James Powell was attacked by a large force under the command of Red Cloud and Spotted Tail.  In this fight Red Cloud and his warriors exhibited, with scarcely an exception, the greatest bravery ever shown by Indians in the history of the West.  Unknown to the Indians, special wagon-beds, constructed of iron, were mounted on wheels by the Government blacksmiths.  As soon as the attack began, the troops removed these from the trucks and placed them in a small circle, the men concealing themselves beneath.  The iron was sufficiently heavy to stop or deflect bullets, and the men were armed with the first repeating rifles brought on the Plains.  They were thus better equipped than their adversaries.  Red Cloud charged no less than eight or ten times, frequently coming within thirty or forty feet, many of his dead falling less than twenty or thirty yards from the improvised fortification.  The Indians could not understand how so small a body of men could fire with such rapidity.  Red Cloud said to Spotted Tail, as the two sat their horses on a little knoll a few hundred yards distant, that he believed the Americans had "medicine guns," which never ceased firing.  The entire force of the Sioux and Cheyennes was hurled against the enemy, Red Cloud's nephew distinguishing himself by riding among the foremost and the two chiefs accompanying the charge.  One Indian fell near enough to touch the beds with his coup-stick before he died.  But for the protection, the Whites would have been wiped out of existence, for nearly every spot on the outer surface of the iron as large as one's hand showed a bullet mark. An Indian chief told Colonel Dodge afterwards that they lost 1137 in the fight. A famous scout said to Major Powell that at least a thousand were struck, and the most conservative estimate places the number at three or four hundred. Not only was great bravery manifested in these charges, but after the battle many of the dead and wounded were recovered in spite of a heavy fire kept up by the troops. In the Fetterman fight Red Cloud had been victorious. In the Powell engagement he was badly defeated.

These two fights, and the series of peace treaties held by the Indian Peace Commissioners August 13 to September 13, 1867, brought about what the Sioux desired — the evacuation and destruction of several forts in favorite hunting territory, the promise of extra annuities and rations, and paved the way for the great Dakota treaty of 1868.

In 1868-'69 Hon. William Blackmore of London, visited the Plains tribes and made a lasting friendship with Red Cloud. At that time Red Cloud scorned the "white man's road" and refused to have his photograph taken; but it is noteworthy that he made an exception in favor of Mr. Blackmore, and in the first portrait of this distinguished red man we see him standing side by side with the patron of the great South Kensington (Blackmore) museum. Why did he do this? Because he knew that the British treated the Indians well, and that for a century Indians in Canada lived unmolested, whereas just over the American border bloodshed and robbery were rampant.

After the treaty Red Cloud himself went to war no more, but instead became distinguished as a councilman and treaty maker. He was, with Spotted Trail, uncompromising, and insisted upon the fulfillment of every condition of the later treaties.

Sitting Bull, a shaman, had made "medicine" for most of the battles, and about the year 1870 came into prominence. To the Indian "medicine" means much. Upon going into action he places implicit confidence in the efficacy of his medicine first, in his own courage second. Sitting Bull, being very crafty, a schemer and a politician, became known as the "battle-medicine maker" of the Dakotas. Before the Custer fight he made several dozen medicine sacks, filled them with the "mystery," and hastily distributed them among the chief warriors and sub-chiefs. After the fight he and his friends claimed the honor of the victory, saying that it was through his miraculous medicine alone that the Sioux prevailed over the soldiers. Sitting Bull seldom was a warrior, claimed little distinction as a fighter, and owes his reputation among the Whites as the leader of the forces on the Little Big Horn to the misdirected energy of the newspapers. Red Cloud was friendly with Sitting Bull, but was seldom associated with him either in councils or upon the field. The two present marked contrasts. The latter was very outspoken in his hatred of the Whites, lacked the tact and judgment displayed by Red Cloud in his later years, and appears decidedly the inferior man of the two. Sitting Bull's temper was easily ruffled, and even as late as 1890 (he was killed December 15, 1890) he persisted in open censure of Government authorities. To give an idea of his language, he told General Miles, upon the occasion of their first meeting, that "God Almighty made me; God Almighty did not make me an agency Indian, and I'll fight and die fighting before any white man can make me an agency Indian." His prophecy was fulfilled.

So when Red Cloud settled down upon his reservation near Fort Robinson, Sitting Bull continued to range about the Plains and in the valleys of the Tongue, Powder, Yellowstone and Big Horn Rivers. Some of the turbulent element in Red Cloud's camp joined him, but by far the greater portion of those who followed Sitting Bull until after the Custer fight were not Oglalas. In 1874-'75, when Professor Marsh of Yale, passed through the agency, he noted that there were some 13,000 Indians under the care of the authorities. He reported that the provisions issued them were of poor quality and insufficient, and tardily delivered. Lieutenant Carpenter also complained that the Indians were compelled to eat ponies, dogs and wolves to avoid starvation. Professor Marsh stated that the goods purchased by the Government, carefully and honestly delivered and distributed, would prevent all suffering. Eastern newspapers published Marsh's charges, and the "Indian ring" of politicians was defeated. Marsh was well received by Red Cloud, who accompanied him East. The two were photographed together, holding the peace-pipe in common. The Sioux called Professor Marsh the "Big Bone Chief," because he hunted fossils in the Bad Lands. And while Bills and Dicks of frontier fame howled about the "hostile Injuns" and engaged in frequent fights with the Sioux, Marsh came and went in that wild country *safe*. The "murderers" knew he was to be trusted! (*See page 176*)

**JACK RED CLOUD**

Son of the War Chief of all the Sioux.   Pine Ridge, 1909.   Photographed by
W. K. Moorehead.   The older Indians say Jack looks exactly
as did his father in the early seventies

# CHAPTER XVIII. RED CLOUD'S LATER YEARS

It is no secret that Red Cloud's ponies were looked upon as legitimate prey by the Whites living near the reservation. One man told me he had seen a bunch of cattle driven around the beef corral twice in order to figure in a double count, and corn and provisions had been passed twice through a certain building in order that some one might make just 100 per cent off the Indians. During the early '70's horse-stealing was carried on to a surprising extent, and Indian ponies were openly sold in frontier towns. A deputy United States marshal, who had twenty years' experience on the reservation of the Sioux, told me that some detectives and trailers employed by the Government were in league with the thieves and received two compensations — one from the Government and the other from their confederates. Stolen stock was seldom recovered. The warriors, becoming desperate, would steal stock from some ranchman in retaliation. Another method of getting even was to complain to the officers at Fort Robinson, who would give the Sioux an escort of troops. Along the trail of the robbers the combined forces traveled as rapidly as possible, and, upon reaching any ranch or town where ponies were assembled in large numbers, the warriors would claim, and apparently identify as their property, a number of horses. Protests on the part of the Whites were of no avail, and the triumphant party would return with some of the stolen stock, and, perhaps, some which had never been on their pastures. I asked an old Indian about this and he said it seldom happened, but as they lost thousands of horses which were never recovered, and as nearly all white men living near the reservation were there to rob the Indians, and as every white man (whether he had or had not Sioux ponies on hand) would deny knowledge of the location of stolen stock, he thought it was fair and just to seize everything in sight!

In spite of suffering, privation and thefts of every description, the Red Cloud tribe kept their faith. Would that white men had been as faithful to their treaty promises. They complained to the Great Father that they had been moved eight times since 1863. Exclaimed Red Cloud: "How can you expect us to take the white man's road when you move us before we have time to plant and grow corn, to clear the ground and raise cattle?" In 1874 the Red Cloud and Spotted Tail reservations were in Western Nebraska, the nearest railroad point being Sidney, on the Union Pacific. Except in spots the land was barren — absolutely worthless. Red Cloud said that the Whites gave it to his people because they could

THE HIDE HUNTER'S WORK. 40,000 BUFFALO HIDES AT DODGE CITY, KANSAS, 1876

Drawn from a print owned by R. M. Wright

not use it themselves.  A delegation of Indians went to Washington, were talked to in the usual patronizing manner, flattered, promised, and returned to their agency.  Some one suggested to the Commissioner of Indian Affairs to remove the Indians to the Missouri River, where some good soil assured corn and wheat.  Red Cloud and Spotted Tail begged that they be not sent there, for whisky was brought up the river and sold to their young men, to the injury of the entire tribe.  Being assured that their supplies had all been sent to the old Ponca reservation, they consented to go there provided they would be sent to a new reservation in the spring.

I can best describe what ensued by use of Mrs. Helen Hunt Jackson's words:* "In the spring no orders came for the removal.  March passed, April passed — no orders.  The chiefs sent word to their friend, General Crook, who replied to them with messages sent by swift runner, begging them not to break away, but to wait a little longer.  Finally, in May, the Commissioner of Indian Affairs went himself to hold a council with them. When he rose to speak, Chief Spotted Tail sprang up, walked toward him, waving in his hand the paper containing the promise of the Government to return them to White Clay creek, and exclaimed: 'All the men who come from Washington are liars, and the bald-headed ones are the worst of all!  I don't want to hear one word from you — you are a bald-headed old liar!  You have but one thing to do here, and that is to give an order for us to return to White Clay Creek.  Here are your written words, and if you don't give this order, and everything here is not on wheels inside of ten days, I'll order my young men to tear down and burn everything in this part of the country!  I don't want to hear anything more from you, and I've got nothing more to say to you,' and he turned his back on the Commissioner and walked away.  Such language would not have been borne from unarmed and helpless Indians; but when it came from a chief with 4000 armed warriors at his back, it was another affair altogether. The order was written.  In less than ten days everything was 'on wheels' and the whole body of these Sioux on the move to the country they had indicated, and the Secretary of the Interior says, naively, in his report: 'The Indians were found to be quite determined to move westward, and the promise of the Government in that respect was faithfully kept'." It had been decided in council that Spotted Tail would do the talking, while Red Cloud and his followers held themselves in readiness for any emergency which might arise.

* Mrs. Jackson's "Century of Dishonor," page 183.

Crazy Horse as war chief, and Sitting Bull as the most prominent of the shamans, engage our attention during 1875-'76. A continual warfare was kept up against the Whites. Gold was discovered in the Black Hills, and settlers and miners flocked into the new territory, committing en route depredations against the Sioux. They promptly retaliated, and our Government sent General Custer to remove the miners from the new gold-fields, and history records that he successfully scattered the obnoxious invaders. During his famous march not one shot was fired at Indians. Red Cloud had kept his treaty promise, but peace was not long to be maintained. The frontier towns began to fill up with outcasts of civilization. Breeders of mischief, they instilled into the minds of the Oglalas love of gain. "You should have more money, more rations," said they. "These lands to the north (Black Hills) are full of valuable mines which are yours. Drive out the miners and we will show you how to develop the country." Custer had returned from his expedition and the miners flocked back to the gulches about Deadwood. Buffalo-hunters were fast destroying the great north and south herds, and Red Cloud beheld the encroachments with a heavy heart. The death-knell of his people's freedom and prosperity on the Plains was sounded in the noise of the train, the blast in the mine, and the hum in the town. Civilization was advancing, savagery must die! He could not go to war himself, he must look after his people on the reservations; but he sent many of his best warriors to join Crazy Horse and American Horse. Murders and robberies followed in rapid succession. Custer was ordered to the Little Big Horn to destroy the villages of the hostiles.

As to the battle which followed, the Bureau of Ethnology Report, 1888-'89, gives a series of pictographic paintings made by Chief Red Horse, which are considered the most accurate we possess of the Sioux side of that unfortunate affair. I can only refer to it briefly. People digging wild turnips saw a cloud of dust in the distance. Supposing it to be made by a herd of buffalo, they informed the end of the village (scattered for three miles along the river) nearest them. Before any persons were armed a runner came up in great excitement and said, "Soldiers are coming." There was no time to hold a council. The chiefs shouted their orders. At first it seemed as if the whites would take the whole village, but as warriors hastened up from the main body of the camp, the flanks as well as the front were attacked, and the troops forced across the river. Red Horse says there were two men with long yellow hair. One wore a buckskin coat.

Captain French was the bravest man the Sioux ever fought. Red Horse says he repeatedly covered the retreat of his men. Finally the soldiers gained the top of the hill and began to throw up little earthworks, but were all killed. Red Horse said some of the soldiers became demoralized and begged the Sioux to take them prisoners but not to kill them.

At Pine Ridge agency I was told that Flat Hip, an Uncapapa Sioux, claimed to have killed Custer. Flat Hip died of consumption a few years after the battle. No one knew positively as to Custer's manner of death, but two men, dressed alike, were noticed for their bravery. Oglalas at Pine Ridge said Sitting Bull was not in the fight, but made medicine while it was in progress. Eastman's account is probably more correct.

Many Sioux surrendered after the summer of 1876, and were returned to their respective agencies. Sitting Bull and his most faithful followers fled to Canada, where he remained some time. General MacKenzie took nearly all of Red Cloud's horses shortly after the Custer battle, thus effectively preventing further hostilities.

September 3, 1877, a soldier ran a bayonet into Crazy Horse while the latter was confined as a prisoner of war in the guard-house of Fort Robinson. The murder occasioned much talk among the Sioux, and, but for the interference of Red Cloud, who counseled peace, would have resulted in a war of revenge. Crazy Horse was a desperate but withal, a brave Indian.

During the latter part of 1876 and 1877, Red Cloud gave General Crook a party of young men to help him fight the Cheyennes, which was greatly to his credit, considering his treatment at the hands of the Whites.

After the removal of his people to Pine Ridge agency he was somewhat dissatisfied because of the poor land given him as a reservation. He also appealed to Washington for reimbursement for the ponies stolen by lawless men. There are voluminous reports, Congressional and Interior Department, filled with speeches of Red Cloud and his people, and all more or less pathetic. They ask for fulfillment of treaty stipulations, for money due, and for cattle and goods. At the time of the visit of the Congressional Committee in 1883 he had 8000 people under him. The flag from Fort Robinson agency was there, and, by the way, there is an incident regarding that flag. Their Agent had cut and hauled a long pole, upon which he proposed to raise a flag. Red Cloud said he wanted no flag over his reservation, and so his men cut to pieces the flagstaff, but the Agent saved the colors and sent them to Pine Ridge.

Red Cloud last achieved prominence in the Messiah craze of 1890.* Whether he believed in the coming of an Indian Savior is uncertain, but I know that he used his influence to preserve peace.

*Commissioner of Indian Affairs, Report 1890, page 49; 1891, pages 125, 410.

When the news of the Wounded Knee massacre reached Pine Ridge, a few miles distant, most of the friendlies "stampeded," tore down their lodges and fled north.  Red Cloud and his daughter and son, in spite of protests, were compelled to accompany them.  Jack Red Cloud, his son, smuggled him out of camp, and his daughter led him eighteen miles through a severe blizzard, back to Pine Ridge.  I mention this incident to show the faithfulness of the man.

Red Cloud was nearly blind and aged rapidly after 1890.  Eighty-seven years is a long time for an Indian to live.  Continual exposure, uncertain food supply, and frail habitation, break down the constitution, and one rarely sees an Indian more than sixty years of age.  During the last years of his life Red Cloud enjoyed the comforts of a two-story frame-house.  It was given him by the Government as a special mark of honor.  During the presence of the troops he kept a little American flag and a white peace flag constantly floating above it.  He bemoaned the fate of his race, and from his conversation one could easily discern that he had done his duty, had defended the claims of the Dakotas in adversity as in prosperity.  Over twenty years ago I had several conversations with him through the interpreter.  He dwelt upon the happy "buffalo days", and the free life of the Plains sixty years ago.  We stepped outside the house and he told me to look about over the valley, for his eyes were dim; but he knew its character.  I cannot give the exact words of his speech, but it was somewhat as follows: "You see this barren waste.  We have a little land along the creek which affords good grazing, but we must use some of it for corn and wheat.  There are other creeks which have bottoms like this, but most of the land is poor and worthless.  Think of it! I, who used to own rich soil in a well-watered country so extensive that I could not ride through it in a week on my fastest pony, am put down here!  Why, I have to go five miles for wood for my fire.  Washington took our lands and promised to feed and support us.  Now I, who used to control 5000 warriors, must tell Washington when I am hungry.  I must beg for that which I own.  If I beg hard, they put me in the guard-house.  We have trouble.  Our girls are getting bad.  Coughing sickness every winter (consumption) carries away our best people.  My heart is heavy, I am old, I cannot do much more.  Young man, I wish there was some one to help my poor people when I am gone."

It is a singular anomaly that the character of an Indian should not be gauged by the same standards employed in measuring the virtues and worth of a white man.  To my mind Red Cloud's high character places him on an equality with prominent men of America, irrespective of color.

In considering the Indian, while most persons recognize the disadvantages under which he has labored, yet I am persuaded that very few realize the great, almost overwhelming difficulty, which must be overcome before a truly strong and high character can be developed.  With but few exceptions, nearly every white man who went on the frontier as a scout, miner, trader, hunter or explorer, exhibited the worst side of his character when among Indians.  It is natural that when a man is in a new and wild country, far from restraint, untrammeled by laws, unchecked by society or the refining influence of women, all that is bad in him comes to the surface. Many men died in defense of a woman or child, underwent great hardship to succor a comrade in danger, exhibited personal bravery in the defense of claims, wagon-trains, ranches, etc., but, admitting all this in their favor, most of them were destitute of a regard for the rights of Indians. Such men inspired hatred in their dealings with the Sioux.

The Indian became acquainted with all that was bad, and saw but little of the real good of civilization.  He heard more oaths than prayers, saw more saloons than churches or schools.  The men whom he met were not calculated, by their acts, to inspire him with any confidence or respect for the white race.  If the Plains tribes had associated with a better class of citizens before they had learned the vices of civilization, I am satisfied that the historian would not be compelled to write so dark and tragic a narrative; nor would he feel constrained to hold them up as fit subjects for pity and compassion.

Considering that Red Cloud came in contact with a class of white men whose presence would not be tolerated in a respectable community; his high character, his forbearance, his submission to the unjust acts of his conquerors, places him, in my opinion, among the great men of America, regardless of color, birth or ancestry.  His career exhibits a degree of mental capacity, a knowledge of human nature and an acquaintance with the affairs of men which we would not expect in the mind of a savage. Red Cloud's bearing towards the Government in the Leavenworth and Fort Robinson treaties, in having secured his end in both instances, indicates a knowledge of diplomacy of no mean order.

His people were suddenly confronted with a high civilization which they could neither understand nor follow.  For centuries they had been schooled in the simple life of the Plains (and it ranked below the culture of the bronze age of man in Europe), unmolested by any extensive or exterminating war, content with their lot.  To be suddenly brought face to face with a question, the issue of which was not a matter of temporary supremacy, but involved the very existence of themselves as a nation —

to have bravely met it, mustered every available young man and fought their superior forces for a period of nearly thirty years, and then to have ceased only when resistance was no longer possible — presents an heroic spectacle. All through this stormy period, Red Cloud figures as a brave warrior, dignified counselor, and staunch advocate of the welfare of his people.

After the treaty, he and his immediate followers, or those directly under his control, observed their part of the agreement, although the white people gave them every pretext for violation. A weaker man, one of less character, would have taken his warriors, as Sitting Bull did, and have fought until there was not a man left.

Red Cloud possessed more human kindness than any of his red contemporaries. It has been affirmed that after the Fetterman fight, he assisted the young men in scalping and mutilating the bodies of the dead. There is no direct evidence as to this. Red Cloud himself says he never tortured a living person nor mutilated a dead body, and that those under his control were no more cruel than the Colorado citizens at the Sand Creek massacre, the soldiers in the battle of Washita, or the Seventh Cavalry at Wounded Knee. He cites the murder of Crazy Horse and several subchiefs after they had surrendered and were held as hostages in one of the forts. He also says that some Whites, many years ago, visited the camps of the Sioux under the guise of friendship, and presented the Indians with whiskey which contained strychnine. Nineteen who partook of it died in terrible agony. He claims that in all his fights and raids he never perpetrated cruelties like these; that he was either a staunch friend or a bitter enemy.

In his later years he rather inclined towards the faith of the Catholics, but when younger he was reported to have said that he believed in no white man's God, but held to the Great Spirit, Waukantanka, and propitiated the evil spirit also; that, if he tried to do his duty, help his people and was a good man, he should not fear to meet the Great Spirit in the hereafter. That so far he agreed with the missionaries of different denominations, but because they were in discord among themselves as to just how the Great Spirit should be worshipped, he considered that not one of them was better than another; that his religion was as good as theirs, and that he would do as his heart prompted him.

He has always been a little vainglorious, but not more so than other prominent men. His twenty years' residence at Pine Ridge exhibited a quiet and gentle demeanor. He ever lamented the fate of his people, but there was no bitterness, and his bearing was such as one might expect in a man who has faced death upon the field of battle.

© by Rodman Wanamaker 1913

*The Last Arrow*

After his removal to Pine Ridge, a petty Agent arrested this great man, on a trivial charge, and confined him in the guardhouse. Immediately his warriors armed, and a great number of Indians prepared to attack the agency.

When some of the subchiefs after his release said, "Let us kill our women and children and fight until we are gone, that is preferable to starvation here on the reservation," he is reported to have made a dignified and manly speech, in which he maintained that the Almighty had decreed that they should continue on the reservation, virtually as prisoners of their conquerors, and resistance would only result in suffering and bloodshed, and could accomplish no good.

An intelligent savage, reared upon the Plains amidst surroundings not calculated to develop other than the lowest desires, and possessing a primitive idea of the true type of manhood, he has presented us with a career which shall endure in American history long after the frontiersmen shall have been forgotten.

### War Dance

Sung by a party of Warm Spring Indians (Oregon) about 1889. A few of these Indians traveled in the East and gave entertainments. This song is repeated many times, rapidly.

I have no Sioux war-dance music, but the above is the most weird Indian song ever brought to my attention.

# CHAPTER XIX.   SITTING BULL—THE IRRECONCILABLE

Among other prominent Indians, this man presents a stern and dramatic figure.  He has been praised and censured, flattered and abhorred; called brave by some, cowardly by others.  He is an anomaly if we judge him by Departmental standards.  More properly, he typifies the Plains spirit of 1840, and he was out of place in the reservation life of 1880–1890.

He bluntly told white people they lied;  he refused to accept substitutes for solemn treaties;  he met falsehoods with trickery of his own.  He lived and died a strong, resentful man — his hand against white domination, even as white men's hands were against him.

Sitting Bull (*Tataⁿka Yotaⁿka*, "sitting buffalo bull") was a noted medicine man, or shaman, of the Sioux Indians.  He belonged to the Tetons and was of the Hunkpapa division.  According to the Handbook of American Indians,* he was born in 1834.  He presents one of the most picturesque characters among all our Indians in any period of American history.  He was called Jumping Badger as a boy and manifested a great deal of ability in buffalo hunting in his extreme youth.

At the age of fourteen he accompanied his father on the warpath against the Crows, and counted his first coup on the enemy.  His name (after boyhood) was Four Horn, but when he became a medicine man in 1857, his name was changed to Sitting Bull.

The Handbook presents a brief sketch, part of which I quote.

"He rapidly acquired influence in his own band, being especially skillful in the character of peacemaker.  He took an active part in the Plains wars of the '60's, and first became widely known to the whites in 1866, when he led a memorable raid against Ft. Buford.  Sitting Bull was on the warpath with his band of followers from various tribes almost continuously from 1869 to 1876, either raiding the frontier posts or making war on the Crows or the Shoshoni, especially the former.  His autographic pictorial record in the Army Medical Museum at Washington refers chiefly to contests with the Crows and to horse-stealing.  His refusal to go upon a reservation in 1876 led General Sheridan to begin against him and his followers the campaign which resulted in the surprise and annihilation of Custer's troops on Little Big Horn River, Montana, in June.  During this battle, in which 2,500 to 3,000 Indian warriors were engaged, Sitting Bull was in the hills 'making medicine,' and his accurate foretelling of the

---

* Handbook, Vol. II. p. 583.

battle enabled him 'to come out of the affair with higher honor than he possessed when he went into it' (McLaughlin). After this fight the hostiles separated into two parties. Sitting Bull, in command of the western party, was attacked by General Miles and routed; a large number of his followers surrendered, but the remainder of the band, including Sitting Bull himself, escaped to Canada, where they remained until 1881, when he surrendered at Ft. Buford under promise of amnesty and was confined at Ft. Randall until 1883. Although he had surrendered and gone upon a reservation, Sitting Bull continued unreconciled. It was through his influence that the Sioux refused to sell their lands in 1888; and it was at his camp at Standing Rock agency and at his invitation that Kicking Bear organized the Ghost dance on the reservation. The demand for his arrest was followed by an attempt on the part of some of his people to rescue him, during which he was shot and killed. (*See page 124*). Although a chief by inheritance, it was rather Sitting Bull's success as an organizer and his later reputation as a sacred dreamer that brought him into prominence. According to McLaughlin, "his accuracy of judgment, knowledge of men, a student-like disposition to observe natural phenomena, and a deep insight into affairs among Indians and such white people as he came into contact with, made his stock in trade, and he made 'good medicine'. He stood well among his own people and was respected for his generosity, quiet disposition, and steadfast adherence to Indian ideals. He had two wives at the time of his death (one of whom was known as Pretty Plume), and was the father of nine children. His eldest son was called Louis."

This in brief is an account of his life, but it fails to give a thorough conception of the man.

He is referred to in many of the War Department reports, between 1860 and 1890. A Mr. W. F. Johnson wrote a book upon his career entitled, "The Life of Sitting Bull," in 1891; Major McLaughlin has devoted a great deal of space to him, as has Mr. Mooney and others.

Sitting Bull's favorite declaration which he was wont to inflict on peace commissions from Washington, is an index to the character of the man: "God Almighty made me. He never made me an agency Indian."

Attuned to this strong chord, was his whole life. He was not a pleasant man, and he incurred the dislike of his Agent, Major McLaughlin, and many others. I do not agree with Major McLaughlin, that Sitting Bull was altogether a coward. If he had been such, we would not have found him associated with the hostile element in the later sixties and all through the seventies. Neither would he have opposed the authorities at the time of the Ghost dance.  He knew that opposition must bring imprisonment, and probably execution, and it did.

His boyhood, as was that of Red Cloud and other prominent Indians, was spent among his own people in the chase, about the village, and occasionally he accompanied war parties.

I suppose that he was present during the Fetterman massacre in 1869, and the fact that he is not mentioned by Colonel Carrington and other officers does not necessarily imply that he was absent.  Carrington would naturally record the names of such Indians as he met, and Sitting Bull was not a man to seek interviews until he became, against his will, a reservation Indian.

At the Custer fight he made the medicine.  I have not presented an account of the battle of the Little Big Horn, for the reason that practically every other writer of modern days has mentioned it at length, and several have devoted chapters to the subject.*

He made the medicine for the fight, and I have understood from the Sioux at Pine Ridge that Sitting Bull sat on a hill, some distance from the action, and went through with his incantations in plain view of many of the warriors.  McLaughlin states that Sitting Bull and his family fled when the shooting began.  Be that as it may, the success of the fight was attributed, in no small part, to the efficacy of Sitting Bull's medicine, and he became a great man thereafter.

After the Custer fight the Indians separated into two parties, one soon surrendering to the military, and the other, under Sitting Bull, continuing fighting.  Various army officers pursued them, and Sitting Bull continued his flight towards the north, to escape capture.  The pursuit by General Miles occupied some time and the Indians were continually harassed, and driven here and there, until finally they found an asylum in Canada.  Toward the close of the seventies a Commission was appointed to visit him, and persuade Sitting Bull and his followers to return to this country.  In view of the dislike on the part of our authorities toward him, it is incomprehensible that they should seek his return.  He was very abrupt in his treatment of the Commission, and publicly shook hands with Her Majesty's representatives and declined to return to this country.

His later life was much embittered by his confinement at Fort Randall, contrary to the promise made him.

Sitting Bull possessed a grim humor.  He knew more of our ways than he admitted, and always availed himself of the opportunity to get the better of white people.  McLaughlin tells this story: —

* Consult Writings of Doctor Eastman, Doctor Joseph K Dixon, Major James McLaughlin, Mrs. George A. Custer, Colonel Richard I. Dodge, etc.

"He was not a nice character, Sitting Bull; he took what looked good to him, whether it was a woman or property of other sort, and he was not in any sense typical of his people. I never heard that he had a love-affair, and the measure of the man was shown when Bishop Marty tried to induce him to put away one of his wives. He went to see the Bishop, who was visiting the missions. The Bishop pointed out to him the evil of his ways, and the bad influence he exerted among the people, finally asking him if he would not put away one of his wives. Sitting Bull was crafty.

" 'You think that I should put away one wife and that would be good?' he asked.

" 'It would, and the woman would be taken care of. You should keep only your first wife.'

" 'But I cannot put one away; I like them both and would not like to treat them differently.'

"The Bishop admitted that it might be hard, but one should be put away; the second wife.

" 'But I could put them both away without injuring either one,' said Sitting Bull.

" 'You could do that,' was the reply of the good man, thinking he was making some headway.

" 'The black gown is my friend,' rejoined Sitting Bull, 'and I will do this for him; I will put away both my wives, and the black gown will get me a white wife.'

"The Bishop gave him up as incorrigible, and the old chief retained both his wives to the end."*

In 1883 a Congressional Commission composed of Honorable H. L. Dawes, John A. Logan, Angus Cameron, John T. Morgan and George G. Vest, visited Standing Rock agency to investigate conditions. There had been great discontent because of the failure of the Government to fulfill the stipulations set forth in the treaty of 1868 (*See pages 103-104.*) Most of the Indians, while mindful of their rights, exhibited no ill will toward the Government, although they were insistent that the cattle and goods promised them be forthcoming and were rather against the further division of the reservation. After the conference had been in session a day or two, the Chairman said to the interpreter, "Ask Sitting Bull if he has anything to say to the Committee."

The Committee, having the services of excellent interpreters, we may assume that what followed is a literal translation of Sitting Bull's words.

---

* My Friend The Indian, p. 65.

As they are very interesting, and the mind responsible for the utterance of these words was the mind of an Indian who lived in the past, I reproduce the conversation in full.

SITTING BULL: "Of course I will speak to you if you desire me to do so. I suppose it is only such men as you desire to speak who must say anything."

THE CHAIRMAN: "We supposed the Indians would select men to speak for them, but any man who desires to speak, or any man the Indians here desire shall talk for them we will be glad to hear if he has anything to say."

SITTING BULL: "Do you not know who I am, that you speak as you do?"

THE CHAIRMAN: "I know that you are Sitting Bull, and if you have anything to say we will be glad to hear you."

SITTING BULL: "Do you recognize me; do you know who I am?"

THE CHAIRMAN: "I know you are Sitting Bull."

SITTING BULL: "You say you know I am Sitting Bull, but do you know what position I hold?"

THE CHAIRMAN: "I do not know any difference between you and the other Indians at this agency."

SITTING BULL: "I am here by the will of the Great Spirit, and by his will I am a chief. My heart is red and sweet, and I know it is sweet, because whatever passes near me puts out its tongue to me;[*] and yet you men have come here to talk with us, and you say you do not know who I am. I want to tell you that if the Great Spirit has chosen anyone to be the chief of this country it is myself."

THE CHAIRMAN: "In whatever capacity you may be here today, if you desire to say anything to us we will listen to you; otherwise we will dismiss this council."

SITTING BULL: "Yes; that is all right. You have conducted yourselves like men who have been drinking whiskey, and I came here to give you some advice." (Here Sitting Bull waved his hand, and at once the Indians left the room in a body).[†]

A little later, some of the Indians having told Sitting Bull that he had treated the Committee very harshly and should apologize, he appeared and made a much longer speech. In this he asked for many things; he pointed out that the Whites were responsible for the destruction of the

---

[*] That his heart was "good." He was a firm believer in signs.

[†] The power of the man is here exhibited.

buffalo — the Indians' means of sustenance.  He seemed to be aware that his speech had caused ill feeling for his opening sentences are: —

"I came in with a glad heart to shake hands with you, my friends, for I feel that I have displeased you; and I am here to apologize to you for my bad conduct and to take back what I said.  I will take it back because I consider I have made your hearts bad.  I heard that you were coming here from the Great Father's house some time before you came, and I have been sitting here like a prisoner waiting for some one to release me.  I was looking for you everywhere, and I considered that when we talked with you it was the same as if we were talking with the Great Father; and I believe that what I pour out from my heart the Great Father will hear.  What I take back is what I said to cause the people to leave the council, and want to apologize for leaving myself.  The people acted like children, and I am sorry for it.  I was very sorry when I found out that your intentions were good and entirely different from what I supposed they were.  Now I will tell you my mind and I will tell everything straight. I know the Great Spirit is looking down upon me from above and will hear what I say, therefore I will do my best to talk straight; and I am in hopes that some one will listen to my wishes and help me to carry them out. I have always been a chief, and have been made chief of all the land. Thirty-two years ago I was present at councils with the white man, and at the time of the Fort Rice council I was on the prairie listening to it, and since then a great many questions have been asked me about it, and I always said wait; and when the Black Hills council was held, and they asked me to give up that land, I said they must wait.  I remember well all the promises that were made about that land because I have thought a great deal about them since that time.  Of course I know that the Great Spirit provided me with animals for my food, but I did not stay out on the prairie because I did not wish to accept the offers of the Great Father, for I sent in a great many of my people and I told them that the Great Father was providing for them and keeping his agreements with them, and I was sending the Indians word all the time I was out that they must remember their agreements and fulfill them, and carry them out straight. When the English authorities were looking for me I heard that the Great Father's people were looking for me too.  I was not lost.  I knew where I was going all the time.  Previous to that time, when a Catholic priest called 'White Hair' (meaning Bishop Marty) came to see me, I told him all these things plainly.  I meant to fulfill, and did fulfill; and when I went over into the British possessions he followed me, and I told him everything that was in my heart, and sent him back to tell the Great Father what

I told him; and General Terry sent me word afterwards to come in, because he had big promises to make me, and I sent him word that I would not throw my country away; that I considered it all mine still, and I wanted him to wait just four years for me; that I had gone over there to attend to some business of my own, and my people were doing just as other people would do. If a man loses anything and goes back and looks carefully for it he will find it, and that is what the Indians are doing now when they ask you to give them the things that were promised them in the past; and I do not consider that they should be treated like beasts, and that is the reason I have grown up with the feelings I have. Whatever you wanted of me I have obeyed, and I have come when you called me. The Great Father sent me word that whatever he had against me in the past had been forgiven and thrown aside, and he would have nothing against me in the future, and I accepted his promises and came in; and he told me not to step aside from the white man's path, and I told him I would not, and I am doing my best to travel in that path. I feel that my country has gotten a bad name, and I want it to have a good name; it used to have a good name; and I sit sometimes and wonder who it is that has given it a bad name. You are the only people now who can give it a good name, and I want you to take good care of my country and respect it. When we sold the Black Hills we got a very small price for it, and not what we ought to have received. I used to think that the size of the payments would remain the same all the time, but they are growing smaller all the time. I want you to tell the Great Father everything I have said, and that we want some benefit from the promises he has made us; and I don't think I should be tormented with anything about giving up any part of my land until those promises are fulfilled — I would rather wait until that time, when I will be ready to transact any business he may desire. I consider that my country takes in the Black Hills, and runs from the Powder River to the Missouri; and that all of this land belongs to me. Our reservation is not as large as we want it to be, and I suppose the Great Father owes us money now for land he has taken from us in the past. You white men advise us to follow your ways, and therefore I talk as I do. When you have a piece of land, and anything trespasses on it, you catch it and keep it until you get damages, and I am doing the same thing now; and I want you to tell all this to the Great Father for me. I am looking into the future for the benefit of my children, and that is what I mean, when I say I want my country taken care of for me. My children will grow up here, and I am looking ahead for their benefit, and for the benefit of my children's children, too; and even beyond that again. I sit here and look around me

SITTING BULL 197

now, and I see my people starving, and I want the Great Father to make an increase in the amount of food that is allowed us now, so that they may be able to live."*

In Sitting Bull's speech, we have the thoughts and the desires of the native Indian. It is the speech of a strong man. Omitting much that followed, I desire to state that General Logan replied in a severe manner to Sitting Bull.

There is a great deal of good advice in Logan's speech. It indicates the domination the authorities wished to exercise over the Indians. On page 82 of the report the following words occur: — "Here the interpreter said that Two Bears desired to say a few words to the Committee, and permission was given." This would indicate that the Committee dominated and had the right to designate such Indians as should speak, or withhold permission from those who desired to talk. Most white men's councils are foreign to Indian methods of council. Where the white man sought to make of the council a one-sided affair, friction was quite certain to develop.

However, the Commission did what it could for the Indians and made a very voluminous report to Congress.

There were numberless peace conferences in the early days, and we do not lack Congressional committees at the present time, and with such an Indian as Sitting Bull, most any of them might have had trouble. McLaughlin himself found Sitting Bull a pretty handful, and much of his dislike of the Indian is probably entirely justified.

Sitting Bull was never an agency Indian. He lived in the past. He was tolerant of the white man and his ways because he was compelled to subsist on the bounty of the white man. His own son, Crow Foot, believed in his father's medicine and died with him. Truly, greater proof of faith could not be produced.

If Sitting Bull had been as cowardly as McLaughlin states, he would rather have surrendered. Instead, he fought his way to Canada. He would have spent his days on the reservation, meekly accepting whatever the authorities wished to dole out to him. But he was the incarnation of the fighting spirit of the Sioux. I think that a man possessed of the ability of Sitting Bull, under different environment, would have become an Indian Bismarck. He was a man of blood and iron, and accustomed to scenes of bloodshed. He was unscrupulous — so was Bismarck — he tried to lead his followers into action; although the cause for which he fought was

---

* Senate Report, No. 283, 48th Congress, 1st Session, pp. 79, 80. 82.

well-nigh hopeless. He realized that one person cannot single-handed fight a regiment, yet he often fought when his support was meagre. He brooded over the past greatness of his people. He saw little good in the white race. If we are to judge Sitting Bull by our standards, we must consider him a "bad Indian." If we are to analyze Sitting Bull as a Sioux of the old type, a man who desires to have our Government fulfill its obligations, and having established certain Indians upon a tract of land the boundaries of which are definitely defined, expects them to live there and enjoy peace, liberty and happiness, Sitting Bull was right. Sitting Bull could not fathom the intricacies and the duplicity of the average white man's mind. During his stormy career, he had met more bad than decent white men. He had faith in the medicine of his fathers, and he lived and died in that faith. He was consistent in his belief and consistent in his hatred to the end.

He had been dissatisfied with life at Standing Rock, where those who sought to cultivate the good will of the Superintendent carried stories of his doings. Doubtless these lost none of their force in the transmission. He could not dance, visit his relatives or friends at a distance, because of continual espionage. To a man of strong feelings this was intolerable and hastened the end. He believed all were against him. "They have taken our game, our lands, our health, and now they take our religion." Well might he have said these words — as did another prominent Indian.

So he broke his peace-pipe — deliberately. All his followers saw him. He had kept it since his return from Canada in 1881. But now it was destroyed. This was equivalent to saying to Washington, "I break with you." The word was carried to McLaughlin, and the police redoubled their watch. The end came speedily and the curtain fell upon the last act of Sitting Bull's life.

A parallel between Sitting Bull and Geronimo is easily drawn. They were not pleasant persons. They rendered an eye for an eye and a tooth for a tooth, and by so doing they won more than did the leaders of the California, or the Chippewa bands, whose last days have been pathetic in the extreme.

The times in which Sitting Bull lived, and the incidents surrounding him were such as will produce an unscrupulous, crafty, and cruel man. Yet, with all of that, we must admit that he was a great man and that the words of his prediction were verified — he never became a reservation Indian.

After writing this chapter, the proofs were sent to my friend Dr. Eastman. His reply is interesting.

Dear Mr. Moorehead:

I have read with interest your chapter on Sitting Bull. You are right in believing that he was present at the Fetterman fight. In regard to the Custer fight, I have carefully compared many stories of Indians who were there, including several of my own relatives. Sitting Bull did not run away, neither was he "making medicine" at the time. He was on the Reno side of the fight at the first, and later, when Custer appeared, was heard in a loud voice urging the young men to be steady, etc. Most certainly I agree with you that he was no coward, and do not agree with Major McLaughlin in his estimate of Sitting Bull's character. According to all my researches, he was no medicine man, but a statesman, one of the most far-sighted we have had, and as such I have represented him in my study of his career, which has not yet been published. In his early days, he won distinction as a warrior. After he came in from Canada, his character was ruined by the humiliation to which he was subjected, followed by his exhibition all over this country and Europe by "Buffalo Bill," and being lionized and his photographs and autographs sold, etc. Then he was brought back to the agency and again humiliated, and crushed by the Agent until he was both spoiled and embittered. The weakest thing he ever did was to take up the Ghost dance craze, which led to his death.

As to Red Cloud's warriors, it must be remembered that the number of Indians engaged in a fight with U. S. troops is nearly always exaggerated in the military reports. They have no means of counting the warriors, and their estimates are more than liberal, for obvious reasons. At the Custer fight, for example, not more than 1,400 warriors were probably present.

You are welcome to use any or all of this letter in your book. I wish to say that I like the tone of your work very much and agree with most of what you say. I do not desire to idealize Sitting Bull, but what he did, and the conditions of the period, and the Indians' own estimate of him at the time, will tell their own story. It is not the story of an Indian Agent, or an Indian on the reservation who is very apt to say things to soothe the savage white man's ear for the favor he may receive.

Yours sincerely,

CHARLES A. EASTMAN
(OHIYESA)

# CHAPTER XX.  EDUCATION

Shortly after 1850, it became apparent to our authorities that education of Indians was the most important service that our Government could render them. Pursuing this policy, schools and appropriations, both governmental and sectarian (as well as non-sectarian) have increased until most of the Indians have been, or are, in school. I have referred on page 25 to the Honorable Commissioner's report in which there are but 17,500 Indian children listed as out of school.

Naturally, this tremendous activity on the part of all these good people, has had an effect on the entire Indian body. If there have been retrogressions, it is not the fault of the educational system. This should be understood in the beginning.

The subject is so comprehensive that this entire volume could be devoted to its consideration. But we must needs confine our observations to two chapters.

Between 1850 and 1875 the education of Indian children was confined to various missionary and philanthropic organizations. Indians could avail themselves of collegiate education in the East, notably at Dartmouth College, which was founded for the education of Indian youth. But there seems to have been no systematic, or persistent attempt to educate Indians until 1879, when Captain R. H. Pratt, U. S. A., began the education of Indian boys and girls. In September that year, the Carlisle barracks were transferred by the War Department to the Interior Department for Indian school purposes. By the end of October, General Pratt gathered together 136 Indians. The number steadily increased; in 1905 there were about a thousand; and at the present time the school cares for, during the course of a year, something like 1200 pupils. This remarkable school had up to 1905 admitted 5,170 Indians. Early in General Pratt's administration, an outing system was inaugurated. Most of the boys and girls were placed in families of prosperous citizens of Pennsylvania, New York or Massachusetts during the summer months. This brought them in direct contact with the best elements of the white race and served a double purpose. It not only taught them industry and proper methods of living, but brought home to the youth of both sexes the vast difference between the life of white citizens in Massachusetts, Pennsylvania, New York, New Jersey or elsewhere, and the frontier element with which so many of the Indians had come in contact. This does not necessarily imply that all persons living near Indian reservations were undesirable citizens. It means that entirely too many white persons by their example did not impress the Indian with any respect for the white race, and that such individuals set a very low standard. This feature of Indian (or white) life has had a tremendous effect on the Indians. Other writers have not emphasized its importance, and its pernicious effect. Beyond question the fact that the Indians came in contact with those who were not "substantial citizens," as we understand the term, is responsible for many evils, and a general lack of progress, and a widespread inclination to accept merely the veneer of our civilization.

General Pratt's plans, therefore, were not only sound, but of great benefit in the uplifting of the race. Other schools have followed the excellent example set by Carlisle, and it is now pretty generally recognized that the Indian youth must be made to realize that the majority of American citizens are not of the type of the Indian trader, the grafter, the squaw-man, etc.

The illustrations presented throughout this and the succeeding chapter will give an idea of the various activities followed at Carlisle, Chilocco, Haskell and other schools.

General Pratt remained in charge of Carlisle for about twenty-five years, when he was succeeded by Major William A. Mercer, who was replaced a few years ago by Mr. Moses Friedman. The present superintendent in charge, Oscar H. Lipps, Esq., has had years of experience in the Indian Service, and is maintaining the high standard established by General Pratt and followed through the administrations of his successors.

For some years there was a leaning in this school toward the higher education of Indians, but that policy was not carried to any extent and need not be referred to in detail here. It is now recognized that the schools and colleges of the United States afford abundant opportunity for any Indian who is sufficiently bright, and has the energy and determination to win scholastic honors. It is neither necessary nor advisable that the Government should attempt the higher education of Indians. Most of the successful Indians today were originally trained in Government schools, and such as exhibited marked ability, left what might be termed secondary schools and entered colleges. There occurs to me at this moment Henry Roe Cloud, a Sioux, who graduated from Yale a few years ago; Doctor Charles A. Eastman, a distinguished author and lecturer, Dartmouth; Charles E. Dagenett, Supervisor of Employment, United States Indian Service, who graduated from Eastman Business College; Arthur C. Parker, State Archaeologist of New York, Albany, who studied under Professor Putnam of Harvard; Rev. Sherman Coolidge, Arapaho, graduate of

DR. CHARLES A. EASTMAN, SIOUX (OHIYESA)
Educated at Dartmouth. Writer and Lecturer

Hobart College and Seabury Divinity School Dr. Carlos Montezuma, Apache, University of Illinois; Howard E. Gainsworth, Tuscarora, business expert, Princeton; Rev. Frank W. Wright, Revivalist, Choctaw, graduate of Union College; Doctor Olephant Wright, Choctaw, Union College; Miss Bee Mayes (Pe-ahm-ees-queet), Ojibwa, educated in Boston, musician; Louis Shotrige, Chilkoot, Chief of his tribe, graduated from the University of Pennsylvania; Nicholas Longfeather, Pueblo, inventor and tree doctor, graduated from Syracuse; Marvin Jack, Tuscarora, horticulturalist, Cornell; Rev. Philip B. Gordon, Chippewa, priest, graduate of St. Paul's; Mrs. Marie L. Baldwin, Chippewa, lawyer, graduate of Washington College of Law; Dennison Wheelock, Oneida, lawyer, Dickinson College; Thomas St. Germain, Chippewa, business, Yale; John M. Oskison, Cherokee, newspaper business, Harvard; William F. Bourland, Chickasaw, lawyer, graduate of Berkley; Asa F. Hill, Mohawk, minister, Denison; Francis La Flesche, Omaha, author; Angel Deceva-Deetz, Winnebago, artist; Zitkal-a-sa, Sioux, writer; Elmer La Fouso, California, singer; Tscawina Redfeather, Creek, singer; Jeff. D. Goulett, Sioux, politician; Gabe E. Parker, Choctaw, Registrar of the Treasury, Washington; Charles D. Carter, Cherokee, Congressman; F. E. Parker, Seneca, business expert in New York City.

These all availed themselves of advantages other than those afforded by the Government schools. There is no reason why many Indians should not occupy high positions and become distinguished citzens. I include Honorable Senator Robert L. Owen and one or two people serving in Congress, although in them the white blood predominates. My list is confined to those in whom Indian blood is in excess of white, with two or three exceptions.

The plant at Carlisle has been extended year after year until there are at present fifty buildings. There are upwards of one hundred instructors, clerks, and other employees.

Carlisle produced the first newspaper printed by Indian boys. This, *The Indian Helper*, became in later years *The Red Man*. The Indians are trained in every conceivable industry necessary to the welfare of Indian men and women. The following trades are taught in well-equipped buildings: tailoring, carpentry, blacksmithing, wagon-making, printing, dairying, stock-raising, general agriculture, gardening, engineering, irrigation, brick-laying, plumbing, etc. There is also a shoe shop, tin shop, paint shop, etc.

There is instruction in music, and the Carlisle military band is a feature of the parades and entertainments. There is a gymnasium, and outdoor recreation, exercises and athletics have had a beneficial effect on the student body. The football and baseball teams, as well as the track squad, have made Carlisle a formidable rival of Harvard, the University of Pennsylvania, Mercersburg and numerous colleges and schools. The famous athlete, James Thorpe (*See page 39*), was trained at Carlisle and at the time of the Olympic games in Stockholm, was awarded first prize as the ranking athlete in the world. The sturdy football eleven has on more than one occasion been pitted against the best football material produced by Harvard, and the West Point eleven, during the annual fall contests. Apropos of these games an interesting story was told me by an interpreter in Minnesota. He had played on the Carlisle eleven many years ago. At that time most of the team was composed of Ojibwa (Chippewa) with a few Sioux and other Indians, practically all of whom understood more or less of the Ojibwa language. The signals were, of course, called out by numbers, but during one of the plays, the quarterback became confused. The play was misunderstood and the opponents gained. He became angry, dropped his numerical system and called out to the other players in Ojibwa what they should do. The succeeding play was a success and from that until the end of the game, the quarterback called out his signals in Indian, and the game was won.

In all schools girls are trained in the domestic arts, and this covers every conceivable duty connected with home-life. Both boys and girls are thoroughly grounded in primary education which includes the common branches, and a sufficient training in the handling of moneys and accounts, the buying and selling of produce, and general mercantile affairs to enable them to cope with the white people in managing their farms.

What is said of Carlisle is also applicable to the great Chilocco school in Oklahoma. Chilocco Indian School was established May 17, 1882, and opened January 15, 1884, with 123 pupils from Kiowa, Comanche and Wichita, and Cheyenne and Arapaho Agencies.

The school is located at Chilocco, Oklahoma, and was established primarily for the Poncas and Pawnees and other Indians of Oklahoma, exclusive of the Five Civilized Tribes. However, the student body has for years included youth from all parts of the country, and since 1910 restricted numbers of the Five Civilized Tribes have been admitted. W. J. Hadley was the first superintendent. A dozen other men held this office, and April, 1911, Edgar A. Allen, Esq., was appointed, and still remains. The school, under his management, has done excellent work.

The maximum attendance at any one time at this school during the past year was 561 and the total attendance 692. Since the school was established in 1884 it is impossible to tell how many students have gone through it, but it is likely that the number would not be fewer than 5000.

In addition to the non-reservation schools conducted by the Government, there is the school at Hampton, Virginia, where both colored and Indian youths are trained. The Hampton Normal and Agricultural Institute was established in 1868 by General C. S. Armstrong. After ten years of success in training negroes, Indians were included. Since that time about 1500 boys and girls have been trained at this place. It is stated that five-sixths of them are industrious and are a credit to the institution. The academic course covers four years. There are normal courses, and business, agriculture, and the trades. In connection with the school there is a stock farm of 600 acres, together with a model farm, dairy, orchards, poultry yards, gardens, etc. The equipment is about sixty buildings. The Government pays $167 a year for each of its 120 Indian pupils. There never has been any discrimination against the Indian on account of his color. This is seen in many of our Eastern institutions where Indian boys are received on the same footing as Whites. But there is a feeling against the negro — not a feeling of hostility, but a general disinclination to associate with him on terms of equality. That is seen in some of the schools. The negro is received as a student, but not as a social equal. I have always thought that the mixing of negroes and Indians at Hampton was unnecessary. Hampton is not a Government school, but is maintained by private subscription and the Government pays a certain sum per pupil for Indians who are there educated. The system has worked satisfactorily, and Hampton has turned out many excellent and worthy graduates. But it would be better, it seems to me, if the Indians and the negroes were educated in separate schools, just as today we do not consider it advisable to educate Whites and negroes in the same school. At Harvard University, colored students are admitted, and in the classes and through the general University life, there is no discrimination made against them, and they are on an absolute equality with the white students. But in the real life of the world there is a line drawn between them, and no man or woman can blind himself or herself to this fact.

The association of Indians and negroes in Oklahoma has not helped the Indian, and a careful study of the situation there would lead one to suggest that the policy be discontinued in the best interests of both the races. The union of the negro and the white is not to the advantage of either, and it is even more true of negro-Indian marriages, according to my way of thinking.

It was found that the boarding-school and the non-reservation school did not entirely supply the needs of the Indians, and so was organized the day school.  Mr. Leupp, who made a great improvement in the administration of day schools, hit the nail on the head when he stated: —

"To me the most pathetic sight in the world is a score of little red children of nature coralled in a close room, and required to recite lessons in concert and go through the conventional daily programme of one of our graded common schools.  The white child, born into a home that has a permanent building for its axis, passing most of its time within four solid walls, and breathing from its cradle days the atmosphere of wholesale discipline, is in a way prepared for the confinement and the mechanical processes of our system of juvenile instruction.  The little Indian, on the other hand, is descended from a long line of ancestors who have always lived in the open and have never done anything in mass routine; and what sort of antecedents are these to fit him for the bodily restraints and the cut-and-dried mental exercises of his period of pupilage?  Our ways are hard enough for him when he is pretty well grown; but in his comparative babyhood — usually his condition when first captured for school purposes — I can conceive of nothing more trying.

"My heart warmed toward an eminent educator who once told me that if he could have the training of our Indian children he would make his teachers spend the first two years lying on the ground in the midst of the little ones, and, making a play of study, convey to them from the natural objects right at hand certain fundamental principles of all knowledge.  I dare say that this plan, just as stated, would be impracticable under the auspices of a Government whose purse-strings are slow to respond to the pull of any innovation.  But I should like to see the younger classes in all the schools hold their exercises in the open air whenever the weather permits.  Indeed, during the last year of my administration I established a few experimental schoolhouses, in regions where the climate did not present too serious obstacles, which had no side-walls except fly-screen nailed to studding, with flaps to let down on the windward sides in stormy weather."*

The day schools, for the most part, are of simple construction.  The teachers' quarters are built adjoining, or the teacher occupies the ell or detached cottage.  There is usually attractive land large enough for a garden.  Except in the northern reservations, the day schools are more or less open-air affairs.  In many of them the children are provided with a luncheon at noon.  Among the poorer Indians, the school luncheon fur-

---

* The Indian and his Problem, page 126.

nished by the Government constitutes the only substantial meal the Indian children receive. Most observers agree that boys and girls six to thirteen years of age should not be separated from their homes during the entire year. The day school surrounds the children during school hours with a wholesome environment and encourages them to work at home in the field and garden and promotes real education, culture and advancement.

The boarding-schools on reservations were considered by Mr. Leupp to be an anomaly in the American educational system. He aptly states:—

"They furnish gratuitously not only tuition, but food, clothing, lodging, and medical supervision during the whole period for which a pupil is enrolled. In other words, they are simply educational almshouses. Nay, though ostensibly designed to stimulate a manly spirit of independence in their beneficiaries, their charitable phase is obtrusively pushed forward as an attraction, instead of wearing the brand which makes the almshouse so repugnant to Caucasian sentiment. Thus is fostered in the Indian an ignoble willingness to accept unearned privileges; from learning to accept them he gradually comes to demand them as a right; with the result that in certain parts of the West the only conception his white neighbors entertain of him is that of a beggar as aggressive as he is shameless. Was ever a worse wrong perpetrated upon a weaker by a stronger race?"*

The boarding-schools have somewhat changed their character, and they are certainly reduced in numbers since Mr. Leupp's administration. His successor, Honorable Robert G. Valentine, recommended their restriction, and the present administration has still further curtailed them. The day schools are far preferable, also are the non-reservation schools. Indians who are exceptionally bright need not attend reservation boarding-schools, but will find opportunity to study under better conditions elsewhere; like Eastman at Dartmouth; Roe Cloud at Yale.

Of Indian education at the present time there is little criticism to be offered. The tendency seems to be toward agricultural training with a sufficient grounding in primary and secondary education to enable the pupils to write intelligent letters, keep accounts and become familiar with American history, etc. This is all that need be expected of the Government schools, and advanced learning may be obtained in the colleges.

While all this is true, we must record, that in the early years of Indian education grievous mistakes were made. These have had their effect on the Indian body at large. Chief among these were the contract schools established years ago by act of Congress. These were schools located either on the reservations and known as boarding schools, or at a distance.

* Leupp, page 137.

Years ago, when the Government was pushing allotting and educating of Indians to the exclusion of pretty much everything else, there sprang up a pernicious system, which I am happy to say has been abolished. Schools were erected in a number of localities, and agents were sent hither and thither to gather Indian pupils. The Government allowed quite a sum of money per head for the support and education of these Indian

CLASS IN AGRICULTURE JUDGING CORN, CHILACCO INDIAN SCHOOL

children. I have forgotten whether it was $200 or $400 per capita, but it was quite a sum. One of the reasons tuberculosis and trachoma became so prevalent was on account of these schools and the crowding of the children into small quarters. The more children, the larger financial returns to those conducting the school. Extensive enrollments were regarded with great favor at Washington and so, the system continued to expand until the Government officials awakened to its distressing effect.

Honorable O. H. Lipps, supervisor in charge of the United States Indian School, Carlisle, writes me regarding these contract schools as follows: —

"Referring further to the inquiry in your former letter, I might add that when I took charge of the contract boarding-schools in the Five Civilized Tribes four years ago, I found in some of those schools conditions that were almost shocking. For instance, in the school near Okmulgee, Oklahoma, not only were two and three sleeping in one bed, but the beds were double-deckers and pupils were packed in almost like sardines in a can. The same was true in some of the other schools. It is needless to state, however, that this condition was immediately remedied so that those schools are now among the best boarding-schools we have in the service. The contract system was abolished and the superintendents are now bonded officers and under the direct supervision of the Indian Office."

It is unnecessary to go into details, and we should not blame the authorities at Washington. The whole matter of education was largely an experiment; and mistakes must needs be made.

A great deal of the tuberculosis and trachoma is, beyond question, due to the crowding in these schools. There is absolutely no excuse for such system and it is surprising that it continued as long as it did. The fact that children came home from these schools to die, or to become permanently disabled, had a deterring effect on the Government's educational policy. It was quite natural that Indian parents did decline to send their children to school under such conditions. No white parent would send his son or daughter to a school if by so doing that child contracted disease. Yet we were expecting the Indian to cheerfully accept a scheme of education which we would not countenance among ourselves for a moment.

I have tried to ascertain the number of children sent away to school who came home and died. It has been impossible to secure any reliable statistics. Miss Caroline W. Andrus of the Indian Record Office, Hampton Normal and Agricultural Institute, under date of September 2d, 1914, writes me that: —

"The death rate was high among our Indians for the first few years, but no physical examination was then required before they left their homes, and a good many died within a few weeks or months after they arrived. Homesickness probably had a good deal to do with it, but some were certainly far gone with tuberculosis when they reached here. Any statistics we might get together would be for so small a number that I think they would be useless, particularly as we have never used large dormitories, but have an average of two students in a room, and therefore no over-crowding."

In a table of statistics presented in a later chapter will be observed that under Question IV, "In your opinion has there been a high percentage of deaths among children suffering from tuberculosis sent from schools to their homes the past ten years?" we addressed a great many persons, including teachers, and asked their opinion. Many of these can give no accurate information, having been recently appointed. Others think that the death rate has not been very high, whereas others claim that many Indians returned from school merely to die from consumption or to become blind from trachoma. It would have surprised all of us, I think, could statistics be compiled with any degree of accuracy. For instance, during the long period that Carlisle has been maintained, it would be illuminating to place before the public in tabulated form how many of the Indians are living and how many have died. Charles F. Lummis, Esq., of California, who has devoted a great many years to the study of Indian problems, is of the opinion that in the early years of our educational system we made almost as many consumptives as educated Indians. He has uttered this opinion in several of his articles in past years. Be that as it may, at present the physicians in charge of the schools and physicians on the reservations are doing all humanly possible to end this evil.

But the opposite still obtains in some quarters. We have been properly ambitious to keep the schools free from disease and we have promptly sent to their homes children who are not strong or healthy, with the result that disease was disseminated on the reservations. While this was good for the school, it was very bad for those who lived at home.

# CHAPTER XXI.  WHY SOME INDIANS OBJECT TO SENDING CHILDREN TO SCHOOL, AND FURTHER COMMENTS ON EDUCATION

There is not a white parent of intelligence in America who would send children to school if in that school there was danger from disease.  When Cornell had a small epidemic of typhoid fever, the institution was closed; the same is true of Milton Academy when a few pupils were taken with scarlet fever.  Phillips Academy, at Andover, closed its doors some years ago when less than four per cent of the student body became affected with measles.  Yet in past years these Indian schools have continued in the even tenor of their way, including among their membership children suffering from some form of tuberculosis or trachoma.  I observed that with my own eyes in Minnesota in 1909.

You cannot expect the Indian — who is just as human as we are ourselves — to wax enthusiastic over education when such intolerable conditions obtain.  All the Indian knows is that the child comes home sick, and he having no facilities for proper treatment, unless the child's constitution is unusually strong, the child dies or is disabled.

Right here I wish to pay a tribute to one of the leading Sioux, Chief White Horse.  He said: "I sent my own boy to school first, as an example to the others.  I sent my children to a nearby school until they were old enough, and then I was one of the first to send them to Hampton, Virginia, to school.  They all came home and died of consumption."*

While we all believe in education, yet I affirm that there is neither a man nor a woman in all America who would willingly, and gladly, send one child after another to a school so managed that the children contracted tuberculosis and died.  The average white man and woman would refuse to send other children to such a school, after the first one had died; and a system of education productive of consumptives, would be indignantly denounced in unmeasured terms.  President Lincoln wrote a beautiful letter to Mrs. Bixby, when she gave to her country five sons who were killed in battle during the Civil War.  Mrs. Bixby was a white woman, and of some education.  Lincoln's letter to her is celebrated in the United States.  Poor old White Horse was an untutored Indian, and yet his faith in the white man and his ways rose to sublime heights.  He deserves a

---

* The Vanishing Race, page 93.

place among the heroes of peace. In return for his simple trust, we murdered his sons and daughters.

There has been a wide diversity of opinion among persons as to the wisdom of our general educational policy for Indians. This is not confined to those employed by the Interior Department, who serve as Superintendents and teachers. It is more largely shared by missionaries and other observers.

Many of the persons who furnished me with data for my table of statistics also wrote out their views at considerable length. These are valuable in that they are sincere; they come from men and women who are in direct contact with the people. We will omit all those who agree with our present policy. It may be summed up thus: to give the Indians vocational training; to ground them in the rudiments and to make of them farmers, mechanics, carpenters, stockmen, lumbermen, weavers, etc., rather than to attempt to fit so many of them for higher callings. It is well to consider the opinions of several persons residing in separate communities in the great West, and I herewith append their statements, but omit the names of the writers.

"Allow me to make one more remark. As far as I can see, the fact that the condition of the Indians is not satisfactory is due largely to the nature of the education provided for them. I think that the education given them is too high and far above their condition in life. It seems to me to be an attempt to make them leap from the bottom to the top rung of the ladder of civilization without having them touch those that lie between. They are not yet far enough advanced in civilization and culture to enable them to follow successfully the higher pursuits of civilized social life, against which the present educational methods try to put them. Thus when leaving school, they are unable to compete with Whites of equal education, while they are unwilling and often unqualified to take up farming or mechanics.

Naturally they all will have to work for a living, and the proper and only occupation that would make them self-supporting will be farming or other manual labor. But having passed ten or more years at Carlisle, Hampton, etc., and coming home to the reservation, serious work is no longer to their liking. Playing and spending money for amusement is about the only thing they know and care for. If they get a position in the Indian Service, they get along as long as they are able to hold it. But the day they are discharged for any reason, they join the army of grumblers and idlers, and help to raise the howl — the Indians are cheated, robbed and trodden under foot.

The fact is, as long as they go to school they are coddled and furnished with everything, as only children of well-to-do parents are in a position to enjoy. Then when they are finished, so that they have to stand on their own feet and make their own living, they are not able to do it. Whatever has been used for their education is worn, then thrown away. It has been used to spoil and enervate them, has made honest work hateful to them, has certainly not fitted them for the task of earning an honest livelihood suited to their condition of life.

"It is my opinion that a thorough eighth-grade common school education along with a good training in industrial and economic habits would bring far more satisfactory results. It would be more suited to their present stage in their advancement towards civilization, they would then more easily take to farming and other general work, and train them to be self-supporting. This would fill out the gap, which men have been trying to bridge over by forcing an intellectual education upon semi-barbaric Indian children. This is, however, not saying that a higher education should be denied to those that show inclination, talent and character for advancement."

Correspondent, Keshena, Wisconsin

"The white people will not allow the Indian children to go to the country schools. The Indians in some places have no schools for their own children, and are left without any opportunity to give their children the ordinary, elementary education of a grammar school. In two places under our care here the circumstances are as stated above.

"What the Indians want is a public Government school. If you have any influence and can rouse the Government to action in this matter, I wish you would use your influence. You would be doing a good work.

"The Indian children do better when educated near home. The children want to remain near home; and the parents also like to have them at home."

Correspondent, Ukiah, California

The next letter is from a full-blood Indian. Some of the sentences are a trifle ambiguous. I know the man to be one who labors under disadvantages. He is doing a good work among his more ignorant fellows.

"Any Superintendent will say that, let a discovery of oil be made upon any child's land and that boy or girl rises in distinction, develops relatives, friends, and a fond guardian at an alarming rate. Then one of the first moves, after this discovery, is to take the child from school. They can't bear that the searchlight of learning be turned into the black corners of their schemes. The situation in Oklahoma is indeed alarming! I believe there are more lawyers and land men in Eufaula than in any other little town outside the State, in the United States, and we know they have acquired and are acquiring, fortunes at the expense of the benighted Indian and his allotments.

"In time the 'benighted Indian' will be spoken of in the past tense. The rich Indian in this locality is truly an object of pity. The weight of his fortune, the world of uncertainty, indecision and fear in which he lives, is pitiable indeed. If the Indian is sagacious at all, it has to be brought out by the slow process of education and this 'drawing out' process is worse than the 'pouring in'. Eternal vigilance and a world of patience, all tempered with common sense and good judgment, are the tools with which to work against this grafting, and schools, SCHOOLS. These institutions should be continued indefinitely. As an illustration to the fact that the Creek tribe is waking to the possibilities these schools afford — our capacity is 125 and I venture to say we could have enrolled 300. It was pitiful to turn them away, yet our files were closed early in August!"

Correspondent, Eufaula, Oklahoma

"Those educated away from the reservation have too much done for them to make life a pleasure — they learn and see the easy side of life and the methods by which it can be obtained easily — but when they return home the picture is not so alluring, and when they find that they must depend upon themselves they also realize that they did not learn how to depend upon themselves, and they as a rule give up and go back to the old Indian life more or less, and in the majority of cases altogether.

"In my opinion Indian Agents should have full control of their Agencies and Indians in order to push their people to the front. Indians like men who can do things, but in so many cases the Agent must go to higher authority and this delay has a bad effect in most cases. The Agent should be strictly responsible to the Commissioner for his action — there should be frequent and searching inspections of his work and if it is found wanting, he should be removed."

Correspondent, Anadarko, Oklahoma

One correspondent living in Sapulpa, Oklahoma, writes at length concerning the immorality in Indian schools ten years ago. Happily, such things are not possible at the present time. A number of correspondents have referred to most distressing moral conditions (in past years) in certain schools. It is incomprehensible that such conditions should have been permitted to obtain. The effect on the children was exceedingly bad, as it is impossible to keep such things a secret, especially in communities where two or three hundred persons are assembled together.

IMPROVED INDIAN HOME IN THE SOUTHWEST

There are statistics available on this unpleasant subject, although I shall not refer to them. Suffice it to say that because immorality was not prevented in past years, we cannot expect a high moral tone among all Indians. Too many of them have profited to their own detriment, by the bad example set them.

While these are varied and present a diversity of opinion as to detail, they strike at the greater evil. Far too many of our Indians on returning from such schools as Carlisle are inclined to look for clerkships or occupations in towns, and are not willing to perform tasks requiring hard labor. They moved along the paths of least resistance. This does not apply to all, but quite a number of them, which gives rise to the popular conception that educated Indians will not work. There is also another problem to be considered. The Indian comes home and he finds that he does not regard the community and people as he did previous to his education. His case may be compared with the son of a small farmer in one of the eastern states, who, given advantages of a higher education, comes home without determining in his own mind what he shall do and is dissatisfied with his surroundings. Formerly, the farm, the home life and the neighborhood did not appear to him to bespeak a small and narrow world. He feels himself out of his environment. He becomes dissatisfied. Such young white men become failures in life. It is similar with the Indians. He has seen all that is best in the East, and his eyes are opened to the poverty and the dull monotony of reservation, or Indian community life. Unless he is willing to put his hand to the plow and work for his living, he is pretty apt to fall into ways of idleness, to draw inheritance money, or annuity, or sell a piece of land. One of the problems in Indian education is to overcome this. It is, to a great extent, due to the Indian himself, as one of the most competent workers in the United States Indian Service has pointed out. Mrs. Elsie E. Newton in answering my circular at length says: —

"For success in their home environment, the Indian educated at or near home is better qualified, if the training has been good in itself. If highly trained away from home, it is more difficult, just as in the case of Whites, to adapt themselves to home environment, the conservatism of the old and a difficult economic state, or to struggle against such conditions where he should."

In addition to all that has been said on the preceding pages, it must be remembered that there is yet another reason why some of the educated Indians do not progress as satisfactorily as we would desire. And this latter is, perhaps, the most significant of all. With such, it is, it seems to me, after due deliberation, due to the impression that after all, our civilization holds little for the Indian. He has lost faith in us and in our institutions. This statement, let me repeat, applies only to the educated Indians who have been trained, or have been told year upon year what to do and how to do it, but still persist in the old ways. This also has a direct bearing on the greater question, the lack of progress in the entire Indian body; for education, property, health, citizenship and all the rest are but a part of this great problem. I shall further discuss it in a subsequent chapter.

In addition to the long bibliography on Indian education presented in the Handbook of American Indians, there are quite a number of articles, speeches and reports mentioned in the following brief bibliography which students of educational problems among Indians will do well to consult. These cover, in a general way, all phases of education, although in the general references, in the chapters on agriculture, irrigation and industries, there are many references which might apply to general education.

———————

The Carlisle Graduate and the Returned Students.— *Siceni J. Nori.* Twenty-ninth Annual Report of the Lake Mohonk Conference, 1911. P. 17.

History and Purposes of the Carlisle Indian Industrial School.— *Brig.-Gen. P. H. Pratt.* The Hamilton Library Association, 1908.

Carlisle Indian School. Hearings before the joint Commission of the 63rd Congress of the United States to Investigate Indian Affairs. 1914.

Education Among the Five Civilized Tribes.— *J. P. Brown.* Quarterly Journal of the Society of American Indians. Oct.-Dec., 1913. P. 416.

Educating Indians for Citizenship.— *John Francis, Jr.,* Chief of the Education Division of the Indian Bureau. The Red Man. June, 1914. P. 430.

Education of Indians. Handbook of American Indians, p. 414. A lengthy account of educational activities, and full bibliography of publications dealing with Indian training.

Indian School, Chilocca, Oklahoma, Some History and Work of the.— *Indian School Journal,* June, 1914. pp. 791 and 553.

Indian Day School. Purpose and Results. Table giving location, capacity, enrolment, and average attendance of Government day schools during fiscal year ended June 30, 1904.— Report of the Department of the Interior, 1904 P. 41.

Indian Education, Interesting facts concerning.— *Indian School Journal,* June, 1914. P. 518.

Indian Education, Present and Future.— *H. B. Peairs.* The Red Man. Feb., 1914. P. 211.

Indian Education, Some Facts and Figures on.— *Laura C. Kellogg.* Quarterly Journal Society of American Indians. Jan.–April, 1913. P. 36.

A Reorganized School in the Five Tribes.— *Gabe E. Parker.* Twenty-eighth Annual Report of the Lake Mohonk Conference, 1910. P. 51.

The Reorganized Schools in the Five Tribes.— *J. B. Brown.* Twenty-eighth Annual Report of the Lake Mohonk Conference, 1910. P. 79.

Educational Conditions in the Five Civilized Tribes.— *John B. Brown,* Supervisor, United States Indian Service. Thirty-first Annual Report of the Lake Mohonk Conference, 1913. P. 24.

Flandreau Indian School, A Little History of the.— *Indian School Journal,* April, 1914. P. 356.

The Fort McDermitt Indian Day School — Illustrated.— *The Indian School Journal,* March, 1914. P. 298.

Haskell Institute, Lawrence, Kanses. Table showing location, date of opening, capacity, attendance, etc., of non-reservation schools during fiscal year ended June 30, 1904. — Report of the Department of the Interior, 1904. P. 39.

Higher Education for the Indian.— *Joseph M. Burnett.* Quarterly Journal of the Society of American Indians. July-September, 1913.   P. 285.

Industrial Education for the Indian.— *Charles Doxon.* Twenty-fourth Annual Report of the Lake Mohonk Conference, 1906.   P. 37.

Educational Activities in the Indian Service.— *H. B. Peairs.* Twenty-ninth Annual Report of the Lake Mohonk Conference, 1911.   P. 36.

Mt. Pleasant Indian School, A Short History of the.— *Indian School Journal*, May, 1914.   P. 445.

Moral Education, Vital Interest in.— *Milton Fairchild.  The Indian School Journal*, September, 1913.   P. 7.

Moral Education in Indian Schools.— *Milton Fairchild.* The Red Man.   December, 1912.   P. 157.

Educating the Morals, Colonel Roosevelt on.— *Indian School Journal*, March, 1914.   P. 310.

Indians in Public Schools.— *Peton Carter,* Indian Office.   The Red Man.   June, 1914.   P. 427.

Report of School Taxation in Indian Territory.   House of Representatives, Doc. No. 34.   Fifty-eighth Congress 3d Session, Dec. 6, 1904.

A Segregated Indian University Unnecessary.— *M. Friedman, Litt. D.*   The Red Man.   January, 1914.   P. 182

# CHAPTER XXII. THE APACHES, PAPAGO AND PUEBLO. THE DESERT INDIANS

Arizona, New Mexico and southern California, together with portions of Nevada and Texas, were inhabited by the Yuman, Piman and Athapascan stocks. I have devoted an entire chapter to the Navaho, and shall confine this to the Pima, Papago, Pueblo and Apache.

The past fifty years the population of these Indians has not varied to any appreciable extent. The enumeration of 1906 indicates that there are about as many Pimas and Apaches as at the present time, although the Papago have increased.

These tribes are desert Indians, pure and simple. The Pima and the Papago present many characteristics in common, and remain long in the same locality; the chief difference being that they belong to totally distinct linguistic stocks. The Apaches, however, are far more nomadic in character, not given to agriculture, and were never known to construct irrigation ditches to any extent, and beyond raising a few vegetables and a little corn on restricted tracts, were not given to labor.

The chapter of our dealings with the Apaches is one of the bloodiest, considering the small number of persons engaged on each side, in American history. Notwithstanding much said against them, they were not beyond the pale of civilizing influences. Many of the outbreaks could have been prevented, but our policy toward these Indians was vacillating and shortsighted.

Doctor F. W. Hodge of the Smithsonian Institution, long a student of Indians in the Southwest, presented a sketch of the Apaches in the Handbook of American Indians.* This covers their complete history. I here insert portions relating to Apache history the past sixty years. It will be observed that the Apaches were frequently located on reservations, but because of change in management, or friction, or incompetency on our part, they were compelled to flee, and such flights were merely to better their condition.

"No group of tribes has caused greater confusion to writers, from the fact that the popular names of the tribes are derived from some local or temporary habitat, owing to their shifting propensities, or were given by the Spaniards on account of some tribal characteristic; hence, some of the common names of apparently different Apache tribes or bands are

* Vol. I. pages 63-66.

synonymous, or practically so; again, as employed by some writers, a name may include much more or much less than when employed by others. Although most of the Apache have been hostile since they have been known to history, the most serious modern outbreaks have been attributed to mismanagement on the part of civil authorities. The most important recent hostilities were those of the Chiricahua under Cochise, and later Victorio, who, together with 500 Mimbrenos, Mogollones, and Mescaleros, were assigned, about 1870, to the Ojo Caliente reserve in W. N. Mex. Cochise, who had repeatedly refused to be confined within reservation limits, fled with his band, but returned in 1871, at which time 1,200 to 1,900 Apache were on the reservation. Complaints from neighboring settlers caused their removal to Tularosa, 60 m. to the N.W., but 1,000 fled to the Mescalero reserve on Pecos r., while Cochise went on another raid. Efforts of the military agent in 1873 to compel the restoration of some stolen cattle caused the rest, numbering 700, again to decamp, but they were soon captured. In compliance with the wishes of the Indians, they were returned to Ojo Caliente in 1874. Soon afterward Cochise died, and the Indians began to show such interest in agriculture that by 1875 there were 1,700 Apache at Ojo Caliente, and no depredations were reported. In the following year the Chiricahua reserve in Arizona was abolished, and 325 of the Indians were removed to the San Carlos agency; others joined their kindred at Ojo Caliente, while some either remained on the mountains of their old reservation or fled across the Mexican border. This removal of Indians from their ancestral homes was in pursuance of a policy of concentration,which was tested in the Chiricahua removal in Arizona. In April, 1877, Geronimo and other chiefs, with the remnant of the band left on the old reservation, and evidently the Mexican refugees, began depredations in S. Arizona and N. Chihuahua, but in May 433 were captured and returned to San Carlos. At the same time the policy was applied to the Ojo Caliente Apache of New Mexico, who were making good progress in civilized pursuits; but when the plan was put in action only 450 of 2,000 Indians were found, the remainder forming into predatory bands under Victorio. In September 300 Chiricahua mainly of the Ojo Caliente band, escaped from San Carlos, but surrendered after many engagements. These were returned to Ojo Caliente, but they soon ran off again. In February, 1878, Victorio surrendered in the hope that he and his people might remain on their former reservation, but another attempt was made to force the Indians to go to San Carlos, with the same result. In June the fugitives again appeared at the Mescalero agency, and arrangements were at last made for them to settle there; but, as the local authorities found indictments against Victorio and others, charging them with murder and robbery, this chief, with his few immediate followers and some Mescaleros, fled from the reservation and resumed marauding. A call was made for an increased force of military, but in the skirmishes in which they were engaged the Chiricahua met with remarkable success, while 70 settlers were murdered during a single raid. Victorio was joined before April, 1880, by 350 Mescaleros and Chiricahua refugees from Mexico, and the repeated raids which followed struck terror to the inhabitants of New Mexico, Arizona, and Chihuahua. On April 13, 1,000 troops arrived, and their number was later greatly augmented. Victorio's band was frequently encountered by superior forces, and although supported during most of the time by only 250 or 300 fighting men, this warrior usually inflicted severer punishment than he suffered. In these raids 200 citizens of New Mexico, and as many more in Mexico, were killed. At one time the band was virtually surrounded by a force of more than 2,000 cavalry and several hundred Indian scouts, but Victorio eluded capture and fled across the Mexican border, where he continued his bloody campaign. Pressed on both sides of the international boundary, and at times harassed by United States and Mexican troops combined, Victorio finally suffered severe losses and his band became divided. In October, 1880, Mexican troops encountered Victorio's party, comprising 100 warriors, with 400 women and children, at Tres Castillos; the Indians were surrounded and attacked in the evening, the fight continuing throughout the night; in the morning the ammunition of the Indians became exhausted, but although rapidly losing strength, the remnant refused to surrender until Victorio, who had been wounded several times, finally fell dead. This disaster to the Indians did not quell their hostility. Victorio was succeeded by Nana, who collected the divided force, received reinforcements from the Mescaleros and the San Carlos Chiricahua, and between July, 1881, and April, 1882, continued the raids across the border until he was again driven back in Chihuahua. While these hostilities were in progress in New Mexico and Chihuahua, the Chiricahua of San Carlos were striking terror to the settlements of Arizona. In 1880 Juh and Geronimo with 108 followers were captured and returned to San Carlos. In 1881 trouble arose among the White Mountain Coyoteros on Cibicu cr., owing to a medicine-man named Nakaidoklini, who pretended power to revive the dead. After paying him liberally for his services, his adherents awaited the resurrection until August, when Nakaidoklini avowed that his incantations failed because of the presence of Whites. Since affairs were assuming a serious aspect, the arrest of the prophet was ordered; he surrendered quietly, but as the troops were making camp the scouts and other Indians opened fire on them. After a sharp fight Nakaidoklini was killed and his adherents were repulsed. Skirmishes continued the next day, but the troops were reinforced, and the Indians soon surrendered in small bands.  *  *  *  *

"In March, 1883, Chato with twenty-six followers made a dash into New Mexico, murdering a dozen persons. Meanwhile the white settlers on the upper Gila consumed so much of the water of that stream as to threaten the Indian crops; then coal was discovered on the reservation, which brought an influx of miners, and an investigation by the Federal grand jury of Arizona on Oct. 24, 1882, charged the mismanagement of Indian affairs on San Carlos res. to local civil authorities.

PIMA HOME, ARIZONA
Aboriginal house type

"Gen. G. H. Crook having been reassigned to the command, in 1882 induced about 1,500 of the hostiles to return to the reservation and subsist by their own exertions. The others, about three-fourths of the tribe, refused to settle down to reservation life and repeatedly went on the warpath; when promptly followed by Crook they would surrender and agree to peace, but would soon break their promises. To this officer had been assigned the task of bringing the raiding Apache to terms in cooperating with the Mexican troops of Sonora and Chihuahua. In May, 1883, Crook crossed the boundary to the headwaters of the Rio Vaqui with 50 troops and 163 Apache scouts; on the 13th the camp of Chato and Bonito was discovered and attacked with some loss to the Indians. Through two captives employed as emissaries, communication was soon had with the others, and by May 29, 354 Chiricahua had surrendered. On July 7 the War Department assumed police control of the San Carlos res., and on Sept. 1 the Apache were placed under the sole charge of Crook, who began to train them in the ways of civilization, with such success that in 1884 over 4,000 tons of grain, vegetables, and fruits were harvested. In Feb., 1885, Crook's powers were curtailed, an act that led to conflict of authority between the civil and military officers, and before matters could be adjusted half the Chiricahua left the reservation in May and fled to their favorite haunts. Troops and Apache scouts were again sent forward, and many skirmishes took place, but the Indians were wary and again Arizona and New Mexico were thrown into a state of excitement and dread by raids across the American border, resulting in the murder of 73 white people and many friendly Apache. In Jan., 1886, the American camp under Capt. Crawford was attacked through misunderstanding by Mexican irregular Indian troops, resulting in Crawford's death. By the following March the Apache became tired of the war and asked for a parley, which Crook granted as formerly, but before the time for the actual surrender of the entire force arrived the wily Geronimo changed his mind and with his immediate band again fled beyond reach. * * * *

"Being a nomadic people, the Apache practised agriculture only to a limited extent before their permanent establishment on reservations. They subsisted chiefly on the products of the chase and on roots (especially that of the maguey) and berries. Although fish and bear were found in abundance in their country they were not eaten, being tabooed as food. They had few arts, but the women attained high skill in making baskets. Their dwellings were shelters of brush, which were easily erected by the women and were well adapted to their arid environment and constant shifting. In physical appearance the Apache vary greatly, but are rather above the medium height. They are good talkers, are not readily deceived, and are honest in protecting property placed in their care, although they formerly obtained their chief support from plunder seized in their forays."

Of the other Indians in the southwest there are some 3800 Yuma, 4,000 Pima and nearly 6,000 Papago.

These three bands occupy the lower Colorado basin. At one time they constructed extensive irrigation ditches and raised large crops. The history of the Pimas has been set forth at length by Mrs. Jackson and Mr. Humphrey.

As the country settled up, white settlers appropriated the water from the Gila, Salt and other streams and these Indians were much reduced. Many of them became paupers. The larger portion of the Papago left their ancient homes and located on the public domain, seeking only to be removed from white persons.

As in the case of all other Indians, the Government has established schools, and Agents, Superintendents, physicians, and employees may be found wherever there are a considerable number of Indians congregated together.

It became known that the very existence of the Pima and the Papago, as well as the Yuma, was threatened because of the changed conditions, the influx of Whites, and the haste on our part to make of these Indians citizens in the full sense of the word. Water is the very life of all desert Indians. With white people appropriating the bulk of it, very little was left for the Indians. Hence various irrigation schemes were set on foot. It would be very interesting to discuss how that we have improved their condition and made available a large acreage in some places, yet in others we carelessly sank wells deep into alkali-bearing ground and thus ruined unnumbered acres; but space forbids discussion of this subject.

The Board of Indian Commissioners late last year, through its Chairman, Honorable George Vaux, Jr., commissioned Rev. William H. Ketcham, Director of Catholic Missions, and Rev. Samuel A. Eliot, President of the Unitarian Association, and both members of our Board, to visit these various Indians and recommend what should be done for them. Their findings were published in pamphlet form, but merit wider circulation. I herewith append their remarks on the Papago.

"*Land.* Approximately 5,000 Papago Indians are living, as they have lived since they were first known to history, on the public domain in Pima and Pinal Counties. They are an industrious and self-supporting people and maintain the habits of life that have been theirs for many generations. They know no other home than the desert and are able to sustain life under conditions which would be difficult, if not impossible, for white people. These Indians on the public domain are more or less nomadic, moving from two to four times each year from their farms in the valleys to the ranges on the foothills. They are scattered in some fifty or sixty small villages over a vast tract of desert and mountain country. On their farms, which they break out of the desert wherever water can be obtained, they raise two crops a year, in summer raising beans, peas, squashes, melons and corn, and in winter wheat and a little barley. Each family or village owns some cattle, horses and mules. Their tribal customs are good and the habits of family life, while exceedingly primitive, are excellent. The Franciscan Fathers have for some time maintained missions and a few schools among these nomadic Papagoes and the Presbyterian Board of Missions has also several chapels and schools in the chief villages.

"These Papagoes on the public domain have no title whatsoever to the lands where they have made their homes from time immemorial The desert nature of their country is such that thus far they have had little contact with white settlers. The time is, however, fast approaching when the better parts of the land which they occupy will be desired by white settlers or prospectors. A railroad project, the Tucson-Ajo Railroad, has already put a survey through the Santa Rosa Valley for the purpose of transporting the output of the Ajo Mines in Southern Arizona to market and opening the country to settlement. If this project is completed it will mean the coming of Whites into this territory and inevitably imperil the continued occupation by the Indians of the irrigable lands. In order to preserve the rights of these people it is our judgment that a number of Executive Order Reservations drawn upon lines to be recommended by the Department of the Interior should at once be made. The reservations should contain the lands adjacent to the villages which are needed for farming and grazing purposes and sufficient sources of water supply for irrigation, stock and domestic use. The village sites and the water sources should be held in common. The allotments heretofore made to Indians upon the public domain should then be cancelled where actual residence has not been established. Any delay will greatly imperil the character and prospects of these self-sustaining Indians, who have never had any trouble with white men, and who deserve the sympathy and protection of the Government.

"An almost equally urgent situation exists on the Papago Reservation itself. The Indian population on the reservation is mostly centered about the Agency at San Xavier. This is the only part of the reservation where there is water. The remainder is arid and uninhabitable. These Indians are also self-supporting and well governed by their own tribal laws and chiefs. Their farms are productive, wherever water can be secured, and they have good habits, so long as they remain beyond the evil influences of the neighboring city. Their continued welfare is obviously dependent upon the supply of water. The Tucson Farms Company has acquired practically all the land between the Agency and the City of Tucson, and is opening this land for cultivation. The Farms Company also owns the land bordering the reservation on the east and a considerable tract to the south of the reservation.  There is naturally some conflict as to the water rights between the Farms Company and the Indians.  The welfare of the City of Tucson can evidently be promoted by increasing the agricultural productiveness of the land held by the Farms Company and the plans by which the Farms Company hopes to encourage settlement are well-devised, but it must be borne in mind that the Indians, who have lived at San Xavier for many generations, have the prior claim upon the water supply. It is hoped and expected that there is in the Santa Cruz Valley enough water for both the Indians and the incoming white settlers, but the utmost vigilance will be necessary to protect the rights of the Indians to the water which is absolutely essential to their well-being.

"The trust patents under which most of the Indians near the Agency hold their allotments will expire in the course of the next two or three years.  The officers of the Farms Company evidently expect at that time to acquire title to the Indian lands together with any improvements which the Indians or the Indian Service may have made.  It is much to be feared that the Indians will too readily yield to this temptation to sell their lands. We earnestly recommend that these trust patents be extended and the Indians thus protected.  It appears that the lines of the original allotments were badly surveyed, and the present fences or boundaries of the Indian allotments do not conform to the survey.  If, therefore, an Indian should sell his allotment, he will very probably be selling the land occupied by the homestead of another Indian.  We recommend, therefore, that new allotments be made to the Papago Indians living at San Xavier, and that trust patents be dated from the time of the new allotment.  By the adoption of this plan not only the lines of the allotments will be correctly adjusted, but also the Indians will be protected in the possession of their lands.

"We understand there is litigation pending between the Government and the Tucson Farms Company in regard to the title to the Berger Ranch at San Xavier.  The Agency offices and residence have always been located in the buildings of this ranch and it is obvious that the Government must own and control the property.  The suit should be pressed to settlement and title established.

"*Irrigation.*  The plans for the irrigating of the Indian land at San Xavier have been well studied and the report of the Superintendent of Irrigation is on file at the Indian Bureau (Senate Document No. 973, 62d Congress, 3rd Session).  We recommend the adoption of the plan there suggested, but only if the trust patents can first be extended.  In other words, it is obviously undesirable for the Government to expend a con-

*The Voice of the Water Spirits*

siderable sum of money for irrigating Indian lands which in the course of
two years may become the property of the Tucson Farms Company. It
is true that better irrigation will increase the value of the Indian lands
and the Indians will secure more for their property than they otherwise
would, but it is to be feared that this increase in price will simply accrue
to the benefit of the saloon keepers at Tucson and other persons eager to
prey upon the Indians. In order to save these self-respecting, industrious
and peaceful Indians from demoralization and vagabondage, we earnestly
recommend: (1) The extension of the trust patents under which they now
hold their lands, and (2) the prompt adoption and carrying out of the
plans by which they will obtain an adequate and reliable supply of water.

"*Schools*. The Government maintains only two small day schools
for the Papagoes, whether living on the reservation or upon the public
domain. A few elementary schools are also maintained by the Catholic
and Presbyterian Missions. It is not necessary for the Government to
duplicate these schools. They cannot, however, reach more than a small
proportion of the school population. Without further and more careful
survey of the best centers of population, we do not wish to recommend
the establishment of any considerable number of Government day schools.
They will naturally be established where permanent water supplies can
be developed. We believe, however, that provisions should at once be
made for the opening of day schools at the villages known as Indian Oasis
and Coyote, which are natural centers of population within the proposed
new Executive Order Reservations. We understand that plans have already
been formed for the establishment of the first of these schools.

"*Health*. The health conditions among the Papagoes are not different
from those on other Indian reservations. There is a great deal of tuberculosis and trachoma, and there are no hospital provisions whatever. We
earnestly recommend the establishment of field hospitals at San Xavier
and at Indian Oasis. These hospitals should be of slight construction,
but they are greatly needed for the welfare of the Indians.

"*Liquor*. The Indians living on the Papago Reservation and on the
public domain seem to be well protected because of their remoteness from
white settlements, their own good habits, the vigilance of the Agency
officers, and the influence of the missionaries. The Indians living near
Tucson, Casa Grande or Maricopa are much more exposed to temptation
and are too often demoralized and vicious.

"*Native Industries*. It is highly desirable that the Papagoes should
be encouraged both in the industries by which they have always sustained
themselves and also in the arts which they practice. They are remarkably

successful desert cultivators. They have more to teach Whites about desert farming than the Whites can teach them. Nevertheless, there are certain methods of farming which can be brought to their attention by skilful and tactful Government farmers, and we commend the present activity of these officers. In particular the Indians can be helped in the use and conservation of water, and in the securing of water for domestic purposes apart from its use for stock. The Superintendent of Irrigation has now at his disposal a small appropriation which he is using to discover and develop new sources of water supply and in teaching the Indians to separate their own drinking-water from the water used for the stock.

INDIAN BUILDINGS OF RECENT CONSTRUCTION
On an allotment near Wewoka, Okla.

"The Papago Indians are at present a primitive, but self-supporting people. The Government does very little for them. Their livelihood is now seriously threatened. A failure on the part of the Government to protect them in their land and water rights, will be most disastrous. The Indians will become homeless outcasts and a menace to all southern Arizona. There is abundant evidence to justify the conviction that neglect of the Papagoes at this time will result in the corruption and degredation of these worthy Indians, and write another chapter of disgrace in the history of our dealings with our Indian wards. Now, before irreparable harm is done, is the time to act. An ounce of prevention now, will be worth pounds of cure later. To prevent the threatening abuse, to protect these deserving Indians and to promote their permanent welfare, it is necessary; 1st, To establish Executive Order Reservations on that part of the public domain where some 5000 Papagoes have always made their homes, and provide for their efficient administration. 2nd, To extend the trust patents of the Indians holding allotments at San Xavier and provide for the adequate irrigation of their lands. 3rd, To establish schools at Indian Oasis and Coyote, and hospitals at San Xavier and Indian Oasis."

The Pueblos present a very interesting spectacle. Living as they do in a number of stone and adobe villages, carrying on a highly developed communistic life, practicing ceremonies the like of which does not exist elsewhere in America, if anywhere in the world — they have been the subject of numerous ethnological investigations. Mrs. Matilda Stevenson published a volume through the Bureau of American Ethnology relating to the ethnology of these strange folk. The late Frank Hamilton Cushing lived for years in Zuni Pueblo, was adopted, mastered the language, joined the secret society, and presented us with a great deal of valuable and technical information. After Cushing's death, Doctor J. Walter Fewkes spent years in studying the various Pueblos. Mr. Charles L. Owen of the Field Museum, Chicago, and other investigators have approached the subject from various angles. We have, all told, a score of books relating to the life and beliefs of the Pueblos; their famous snake dance has been repeatedly described until it would seem that not a single detail has escaped publication. Others have concerned themselves with Pueblo arts, the origin of the Pueblo and the relation between the Pueblo and the Cliff Dweller. Few tribes in America have been more thoroughly studied, and it is safe to say that the various departments of the Smithsonian Institution, the past thirty years, have published 5,000 or more pages relating to these people. As the peculiar customs are handed down from antiquity, we shall study them in detail at some future time and adhere to our rule of confining this book to the modern Pueblo. The following report submitted by Messrs. Eliot and Ketcham is self-explanatory and covers their activities, their needs, and warns us against the dangers with which they are threatened.

"*Land.* The primary need of all the Pueblos is for a determination of the boundaries of their grants. The encroachment of squatters on the

Indian lands is constantly increasing and producing friction and litigation. These trespassers are not always blameworthy because the limits of the Indian lands are so indistinct. There is urgent need of surveys and of definite marks or bounds with indestructible monuments. When these have been established, vigorous action should be taken for the eviction of trespassers who have not established a legal right to occupancy. We earnestly recommend an appropriation for the immediate survey of all the Pueblo grants.

"We recommend an Act of Congress prohibiting any Pueblo Indian from selling land. Such an Act will prevent endless misunderstandings and litigation. All the land problems of the Pueblos would be settled by accepting the proposal of the Indians to place all their lands in trust with the Department of the Interior. We believe this proposed course of action to be wise and just.

"The liquor question is at the front in nearly every pueblo. Illegal selling and bootlegging are very prevalent and as a rule public opinion among the Indians does not condemn the use of liquor. In spite of the vigilance of the officers of the Government bad whiskey is demoralizing many of these Indians. The efforts of the Superintendents and their policemen for the suppression of this traffic should be heartily supported by the Indian Office and the superintendents should be authorized to employ additional policemen.

"The prosecution and punishment of land thieves and liquor sellers put a very heavy burden upon the attorney for the Indians. We particularly commend the able, alert and disinterested service of Mr. Francis C. Wilson, who with very small resources has been remarkably successful in protecting the Indians and punishing those who would rob or degrade them. We earnestly recommend that his salary be put at $3,000 and that at least $1,000 be allowed him for the prosecution of the suits now pending.

"We commend the good sense, vigor and assiduity of Superintendents Perry, Lonergan, Coggeshall and Mr. Snyder. They understand these Indians and without pampering or pauperizing them have their real interests at heart.

"*Irrigation.* Owing to the sandy nature of the soil of the Rio Grande Valley the seepage from the irrigation canals is excessive. We recommend that the canals at Isleta and Laguna, where conditions are particularly bad, be concreted. A reservoir is urgently needed at Taos.

"*Health.* In spite of pernicious inbreeding and unsanitary conditions the health of the Pueblos is comparatively good. Instruction is needed in elementary sanitation.

"*Education.*  While heartily commending the work and efficiency of the boarding schools at Albuquerque and Santa Fe, we are clearly of the opinion that the best education for these Indians can be obtained in the day schools.  Boarding schools are well adapted to nomadic Indians, but the Pueblos have always lived in permanent villages and the best schools for them are the day schools in or immediately adjoining the villages.  The

SOUTHERN UTE, COLORADO
Modern Indian pictographs in the rear.  1902.  Photograph by E. R. Forrest

new day schools are well planned, but there is urgent need of more of them. The school accommodations at Isleta are a disgrace to the Government. They are unsafe and unsanitary and there is not room for half the children of school age.  New school buildings should also be provided at Acoma, Acomita and Encinal.  A farmer is greatly needed to give agricultural instruction at Isleta and Laguna.  The needs of the boarding schools have been sufficiently set forth in the recommendations of the superintendents. We especially commend the application for appropriations to buy additional land at Albuquerque and to build a dairy barn at Santa Fe.

"We recommend the applications of Superintendents Lonergan and Coggeshall for additional policemen, and for authority to hire laborers when needed. It is absurd to have to request a physician to milk the cow or for a superintendent to personally have to carry the chain for his surveyors.

"The training of the Pueblo Indians for life in a civilized environment must be slow. Their inherited habits and customs are exceedingly rigid and their prejudices are stubborn. The educated or progressive Indians among them have now a very hard road to travel. They need not only moral support, but sometimes actual physical protection. The superintendents should be encouraged tactfully but firmly to break up the personal despotism which often rules the villages, to protect the right of the individual to personal liberty, to insist upon the gradual adaptation of the pueblo life to its new environment. The Pueblos are now in a transition stage. They cannot pass through it without some bitter feelings and some hard experiences. They need the consistent, sympathetic, courageous leadership of their guardians, in whose good intentions they are beginning to trust."

In closing the chapter on the desert Indians I desire to suggest that the older Pueblos be permitted to continue their weaving and pottery-making in their own way. It is perfectly proper to train the young in our arts, but the superb native arts of the old Indians should be encouraged. With the death of these old people, the art will deteriorate and disappear. I mention this particularly for the reason that several well-meaning, but misguided persons sent one or two representatives to Zuni and attempted to instruct the women in the manufacture of pottery. They even persuaded them to glaze the pottery and to make tiles. The movement, if continued on a large scale, would result in ruining an art which is fast disappearing.

The population is about stationary. The ceremonies of the antelope and snake societies are becoming more and more public. Recent photographs of them show hundreds of white persons, teams and automobiles, and admission is now charged, for the dances and attendant ceremonies are fast becoming commercialized. They have persisted because of the curious life of these people — a people who live, as it were, in a different world. With the extension of education, the allotment system, and the continual effort of Government employees to break down the old and insert the new, the real life of the Pueblos will soon pass away forever.

## CHAPTER XXIII. THE CAREER OF GERONIMO

This fighting man was for many years feared and hated. He was not a docile person, and his tribe did not tamely submit to kicks and curses — the treatment meted out to his more gentle red brothers in California and Arizona. They were despised, trodden under foot, cast aside; not so with the Apaches and Geronimo. It required more than two years' labor on the part of hundreds of our cavalry to catch him, and when he surrendered there were but seventy-four in his band.

Now that everything regarding the Indian is being made public, I deem it important that the true history of Geronimo be set forth.

In 1905 this chief published the story of his life. His book is a remarkable production, and gives the Indian point of view, which is rare indeed.*

Mr. Barrett, who wrote the story at Geronimo's dictation, had much trouble with the War Department. Officers objected to the narrative, and he was compelled to secure permission from President Roosevelt. Even then the War Department advised against publication.

The history of the Apaches dates from the time of Coronado, who is supposed to have penetrated their country in 1541-'43 when he marched north in search of the fabled "seven cities of Cibola." There is no record of the Apaches, or any other Indians for that matter, beginning hostilities against the Spaniards. After Coronado, the Spaniards and the Apaches were at war for three centuries. The Spaniards pursued their usual policy in dealing with these people, and the latter returned an eye for an eye, and a tooth for a tooth. Geronimo and his people had abundant cause for their hatred of the Spaniards. It was a different story in Arizona and northern Mexico from that of California and central Mexico. Today the California Indians are paupers, and the gentle Aztecs have long since perished, but the sturdy Apaches remain and live in more or less prosperity on their several reservations.

Geronimo says he was born in Arizona in 1829.† On the death of his father, Mangus-Colorado became chief of the Bedonkoke Apaches, to which band the subject of this sketch belonged. When a half-grown boy, Geronimo assumed the care of his mother, and in 1846 he joined the council of the warriors. Soon after this he married Alope and three children were born

---

* Geronimo, the story of his life, Recorded by S. W. Barrett. New York ,1906.

† 1834, according to Mooney, in Handbook of American Indians, page 491.

GERONIMO
Photographed at Fort Sill, Oklahoma, about 1905

during the next few years.  In 1858, when he was twenty-nine, his band went into Mexico to trade.  One afternoon while Geronimo and the other men were returning from a visit, they were met by crying women and children who told them that the Mexicans had attacked the camp — a peaceful camp — and had massacred the men and most of the women and children.  Geronimo lost his aged mother, his wife and his three small children.

They decided to retreat to Arizona and as the Mexicans were searching for survivors in order to kill them, the remaining Apaches traveled all night.  The mourning period, according to Indian etiquette, prevented Geronimo, who had lost more relatives than anyone else, from eating or speaking.  He traveled two days and three nights without food and did not open his mouth until the third day.  I quote from his book: —

"Within a few days we arrived at our own settlement.  There were the decorations that Alope had made — and there were the playthings of our little ones.  I burned them all, even our tipi.  I also burned my mother's lodge and destroyed all her property.

"I was never again contented in our quiet home.  True, I could visit my father's grave, but I had vowed vengeance upon the Mexican troopers who had wronged me, and whenever I came near his grave or saw anything to remind me of former happy days, my heart would ache for revenge upon Mexico."

The Apaches collected arms and supplies.  Geronimo visited other bands of his tribe, and in the summer of 1859, a year later, a large force (on foot) entered Old Mexico.  They went light, and without horses, for strategic reasons.  Knowing the country thoroughly — every water-hole, mountain and valley — they could trail unobserved.  On horseback they must follow certain known trails, whereas on foot the band could scatter, travel singly and meet at a common rendezvous.  It was well-nigh impossible to follow unmounted Apaches, as all the military reports admit.  They invariably scattered and sought the most inaccessible, waterless mountain ranges.

Geronimo acted as guide, and near Arispe eight men came out from the village and were killed by the Apaches.  The next day the Mexican troops attacked.  Geronimo says that in one part of the field four Indians, including himself, were charged by four soldiers and in the final fight, two of the Indians were killed and the four troopers were slain, two of them by Geronimo himself.

The art of trailing was developed among the Apaches and Comanches more than among other Indians on this continent.  Possibly a few Delawares might be excepted. The success of Geronimo's operations, as well as those of his able lieutenants, Cochise, Naiche, Mangus-Colorado, was chiefly due to the fact that the trail was to them an open book. As an illustration of the skill of the desert Indians in this respect, I would cite the case of Pedro Espinosa, who, when nine years old was captured by the Comanche and for years lived with the Comanches and Apaches. Colonel Dodge says of him that he was a marvel even to the Indians themselves, and relates this incident:

"I was once sent in pursuit of a party of murdering Comanches, who had been pursued, scattered, and the trail abandoned by a company of so-called Texas rangers. On the eighth day after the scattering, Espinosa took the trail of a single shod horse. When we were fairly into the rough, rocky Guadalope Mountains, he stopped, dismounted, and picked up from the foot of a tree the four shoes of the horse ridden by the Indian. With a grim smile he handed them to me, and informed me that the Indian intended to hide his trail. For six days we journeyed over the roughest mountains, turning and twisting in apparently the most objectless way, not a man in the whole command being able to discover, sometimes for hours, a single mark by which Espinosa might direct himself. Sometimes I lost patience, and demanded that he show us what he was following. 'Poco tiempo,' he would blandly answer, and in a longer or shorter time, show me the clear-cut footprints of the horse in the soft bank of some mountain stream, or point with his long wiping-stick to most unmistakable 'sign' in the droppings of the horse. Following the devious windings of this trail for nearly a hundred and fifty miles, scarcely ever at a loss, and only once or twice dismounting, more closely to examine the ground, he finally brought me to where the Indians had reunited."

On another occasion, the Indians had fired the prairie to hide their trail. The officer in despair went to camp. Espinosa, after working over the ground carefully on his hands and knees, blew away the light ashes until sufficient prints were found to show the direction of the trail. He was compelled to make several circuits, covering a total of six or seven miles, and after weary hours spent in this work, the troops were able to pursue and capture the Indians. Espinosa and the Apaches once found a trail after dark by feeling of the ground with their fingers. This remarkable man, at the outbreak of the Civil War, was selected to carry dispatches from Union men in San Antonio to Colonel Reeve. He was captured and shot to death. The account presented by Dodge of Espinosa is very interesting and indicates that this unknown man in Plains knowledge was far in advance of the white scouts of which we have heard so much. The

Apaches recognized that their only weakness lay in their trail, and they tried by every means to conceal it.

The next few years Geronimo led several expeditions into Mexico, sometimes being defeated, on other occasions returning with much plunder and many scalps. During his career as a fighting man he was wounded seven times. Once, he was left for dead, on the field.

In 1861 the Mexicans attacked an Apache winter village, killing men, women and children.

In 1864, while raiding in Mexico, Geronimo's people captured a mule pack train. Some of the mules were loaded with mescal — an intoxicating drink of the Mexicans. The Apaches began drinking this and Geronimo, fearing the consequences, poured out all of the liquor. On this occasion he captured a herd of cattle, drove the cattle to Arizona, killed them, and dried the meat for winter use.

Geronimo emphasizes in his book something unknown to the general public. Many outlaws, both Americans and Mexicans, stole cattle and committed robberies during these troublous years and the blame was always placed on the Apaches. In spite of all that has been said, the latter were not without their virtues, as the following anecdote attests.

In 1883 two young men from the East, while prospecting in the mountains, saw an old Apache and a young man, apparently his son. In attempting to retreat to camp, one of the white men fell and broke his leg. The old warrior examined the broken limb, removed the shirt of the uninjured youth, tore it up and carefully bound the broken member. Then the old warrior, indicating the direction with his finger said: "Doctor — Lordsburg — three days," and silently rode away.

Up to 1870 the Apaches had had little trouble with the white people, although in 1841, according to testimony presented by Mrs. Jackson, they had abundant grounds for hostility.*

It was not until the 30th of April, 1871, that the real trouble began. The massacre at Camp Grant, in Arizona, of several hundred friendly Apaches, men, women and children, brought on hostilities.

Beyond question, this and several subsequent raids on the part of white people, were responsible for the attitude of Geronimo, Victorio and Cochise. In 1873 and again in 1880 there was hard fighting in Mexico. In 1884 Geronimo was head war chief, and fought his heaviest engagements. How many men were killed in these actions is not stated.

In the early sixties United States troops invited the Apache chiefs into a tent under promise, Geronimo states, that they were to be given a

---

* Century of Dishonor, page 325.

feast.  Geronimo says: "When in the tent they were attacked by soldiers. Our chief, Mangus-Colorado, and several other warriors, by cutting through the tent, escaped; but most of the warriors were killed or captured."  Heavy fighting followed.  Such Apaches as spoke English visited the officers and advised them where were located camps they sought, and while the soldiers hunted for these camps, Geronimo and his warriors, "watched them from our hiding-places and laughed at their failures."

In 1863 the favorite chief, Mangus-Colorado, was put in the guard-house.  He had been told by General West that he would be protected if he made peace.  As the old chief entered he said: "This is my end." During the night some one threw a stone through the window and struck him in the breast.  He sprang up, and as he did so the guard shot and killed him.

In the seventies the United States troops sent for Victorio and Ger-onimo.  As soon as they entered the camp they were taken to headquarters and tried by court-martial.  Victorio was released and Geronimo was put in chains, remaining in shackles four months.

For the next ensuing years there was considerable fighting, the Apaches being afraid to trust the United States authorities and the frontier element anxious that the Apaches be exterminated.  Our troops occasionally defeated the Indians but were more often repulsed.  General Crook took away the Apaches' cattle and horses, and as few of the Apaches were horse Indians, preferring to fight or hunt on foot, and as the cattle were an incen-tive to thrift and industry, this action of General Crook's was not a severe blow to the Indians.

The General followed the Apaches into Mexico and held an interview. I quote Geronimo's description of what occurred.*

"Said the General: 'Why did you leave the reservation?'

"I said: 'You told me that I might live in the reservation the same as white people lived.  One year I raised a crop of corn, and gathered and stored it, and the next year I put in a crop of oats, and when the crop was almost ready to harvest, you told your soldiers to put me in prison, and if I resisted to kill me.  If I had been let alone I would now have been in good circumstances, but instead of that you and the Mexicans were hunting me with soldiers.'

"He said: 'I never gave any such orders; the troops at Fort Apache, who spread this report, knew that it was untrue.'

"Then I agreed to go back with him to San Carlos.

* Geronimo, the Story of his life, Recorded by S. M. Barrett, New York, 1906, page 138.

"It was hard for me to believe him at that time. Now I know that what he said was untrue, and I firmly believe that he did issue the orders for me to be put in prison, or to be killed in case I offered resistance."

On the return march, the Indians left General Crook's command and fled. Geronimo became "a bad Indian" in every sense of the word. He says: "We were reckless of our lives, because we felt that every man's

POMO WOMAN WEAVING A TWINED BASKET, CALIFORNIA

hand was against us. If we returned to the reservation we would be put in prison and killed; if we stayed in Mexico they would continue to send soldiers to fight us; so we gave no quarter to anyone and asked no favors."

The American troops in one action killed seven children, five women and four men. Again, three Apache children were slain. Later, all Geronimo's family was captured.

Naiche, son of the famous fighting chief, Cochise, fought for years with Geronimo and surrendered when further resistance was useless.

The end came suddenly. Geronimo, driven from one side of the American-Mexican border to the other, found no rest for his band, and told Captain Lawton's scouts that he would surrender to General Miles under certain conditions. When Geronimo met General Miles, the interpreter said, "General Miles is your friend." Even in so critical a situation his grim humor asserted itself. Geronimo retorted, "I never saw him, but I have been in need of friends. Why has he not been with me?"

According to the narrative of the Indian chief and other witnesses, Geronimo was to live with his family and be supported by the Government, under certain restrictions. "I said to General Miles: 'All the officers that have been in charge of Indians have talked that way and it sounds like a story to me; I hardly believe you.'

"He said: 'This time it is the truth.'"

Geronimo gave up his arms saying:

" 'I will quit the warpath and live at peace hereafter.'"

"Then General Miles swept a spot of ground clear with his hand and said:

" 'Your past deeds shall be wiped out like this, and you will start a new life.'"

It is unfortunate that when the Apaches were taken East, not only the hostiles but also a few friendlies and some who had helped the troops, were also deported. They were imprisoned in Florida, and Geromino made to labor sawing large logs. One or two of the warriors committed suicide. After some years the prisoners were removed to Fort Sill. Geronimo often complained that the Government did not keep the terms of the Miles surrender. I have never heard that General Miles tried to right this wrong. If he did, I stand corrected.

Geronimo did not see his family for two years — contrary to the terms of the surrender.

The foregoing sums up in a brief way the career of Geronimo. Under similar circumstances any white man of spirit and independence, and who was not a coward, would become "a bad Indian." After many appeals by the Board of Indian Commissioners, the Indian Rights Association and others, these Apache prisoners were removed to their ancient homes. About seventy elected to remain near Fort Sill, Okla., and have been given farms.

Practically all of them are doing well — industrious and capable.

# CHAPTER XXIV.  THE NAVAHO

The great Shoshonean and Athapascan stocks extended from the Northwest down into the Southwest. The States of Nevada, Utah, Arizona, New Mexico, southwestern Colorado, western Texas and southern California prior to 1860 were known as the "Great American Desert." The Yuman, Piman and Athapascan, together with a few lesser stocks, inhabited this great region. Chief of the desert tribes is the Navaho. Doctor Washington Matthews has presented considerable literature in the American Anthropologist and elsewhere on this interesting folk; Oscar H. Lipps published a history of the Navaho in 1909; George Wharton James, Esq., refers to them at considerable length in his publications. The Franciscan Fathers, having a mission at St. Michaels, Arizona, published in 1910 a complete ethnologic dictionary of the Navaho customs, legends, and gave large numbers of sentences. This also contained a bibliography of some length. Doctor George W. Pepper of the University of Pennsylvania Museum published a very interesting article on "The Making of a Navaho Blanket" in *Everybody's Magazine*, January, 1902. A volume giving details of blanket and wool industry among the Navaho has just been written by George Wharton James, Esq., entitled "Indian Blankets and Their Makers". This volume of 213 large pages contains many colored plates and is the most comprehensive treatment of the Navaho blanket-weaving industry ever published.

The Navaho are the only really unspoiled Indians left in America, and I trust that readers will pardon repetition, when I again urge that they be let alone to work out their own salvation. That is, while certain safeguards are necessary, we should realize our incompetency and ignorance — not to use a stronger term — in handling the natives of Oklahoma, Minnesota and California, and not repeat our blunders in the "benevolent assimilation" of these intelligent, industrious, and moral people. Here is one splendid racial stock that has thus far escaped the blight of our bureaucracy. The Navaho still stands, frightened, gazing in at the threshold of our civilization. He sees the greed of the white settler for his possessions.

There have been a number of reports on the Navaho, in addition to the ethnological and popular works cited. Any one of these will give readers a fair conception of conditions among these Indians.

Rev. Anselm Weber of the Franciscan Mission published a pamphlet on July 25, 1914. The Indian Rights Association has also taken up officially these Indians in its annual reports, the past two or three years.

Honorable F. H. Abbott, Secretary of the Board of Indian Commissioners, visited the Navaho and made specific recommendations as to allotment and irrigation plans. In December-January, 1913-'14, Rev. Samuel A. Eliot and Rev. William H. Ketcham, members of the Board of Indian Commissioners, officially visited the Navaho and made a report to the Secretary of the Interior. Rev. W. R. Johnson, missionary located at Indian Wells, Arizona, has repeatedly urged in public addresses at Lake Mohonk and elsewhere the need of proper protection of this, the finest body of aboriginal men and women remaining in North America.

It is not necessary to go back to 1850, to state that these Indians were in a satisfactory condition. They *are* in a satisfactory condition today, and are the only band of Indians so situated in this country. The number of them is said by Father Weber to be about 25,000. Rev. Johnson, who traveled extensively over the reservation, claims there are 28,000. Taking into consideration several thousand that live off the reservation on the public domain, there are at least 30,000 Navaho today. The number of sheep they possess has been variously estimated from one million to two million head. The number of blankets the women wove last year, no man may know, but the value of the blanket industry is upwards of a million dollars per annum. A few years ago, Commissioner Valentine stated that the Navaho sold $800,000 worth of blankets. It must be remembered that many of their blankets are sold north of the San Juan river and elsewhere off the reservation, and that traveling traders and buyers continually penetrate beyond the borders of the reserve. The totals obtained by superintendents, teachers and white employees, is doubtless far below the actual volume of business.

As everyone knows, the reservation is a part of our famous "painted desert". It is exceedingly diversified in character, the landscape varying from high mesas to deep canons; from towering mountains to stretches of desert. Fortunately, no mineral deposits aside from coal have been discovered. On three separate occasions, in the '60's, '70's and '80's, prospectors, in defiance of law, entered the Navaho reservation in search of gold, silver or copper. When I was conducting the cliff-dweller expeditions along the San Juan in 1892 and again in 1897, several of the "oldtimers" informed me that these prospectors were never heard of afterward. Accompanying the last expedition, there were several men from north of Durango, Colorado, and their friends threatened reprisals on the Navaho, alleging that the Indians had killed these prospectors. However, aside from talk, nothing was done, the men never returned, and the Indians remained in peaceful possession of their estate. It was considered, in the

'70's and '80's "bad medicine" for white men to depart from certain Navaho trails!

The Navaho reservation embraces 11,887,793 acres, of which approximately 719,360 acres belong to the Santa Fe Pacific Railroad Company, and approximately 55,400 acres to the State of Arizona, leaving 11,113,033 acres. Consequently, if you take the very conservative figure of 25,000 Navahos and 11,113,033 acres belonging to them, you would have 444 acres to the person. But as four-fifths is high, dry mesa or absolute desert, the statement often made that each Indian might have 444 acres is misleading. Each Indian could not have (average) more than twelve or fifteen acres of pasture land.

The Navaho are the only large body of Indians in the United States who keep up ancient customs, arts and ceremonies. They not only enjoy a great variety of games and sports, but they are probably the best and strongest long-distance runners in America. Mr. Lipps has given a very entertaining account of their games, etc., in his book, to which I have referred on a previous page.

They are exceedingly adverse to burying their dead and are quite willing that white people should perform this service for them. Of all the remaining Indian tribes, they furnish the best field for investigation at the present time. Much has been written concerning them, but it will require additional researches in order to complete a satisfactory study of their ethnology.

On the death of the head of the family, his property "descends to his brothers, sisters, uncles and aunts to the exclusion of his wife and children, a custom which is often very harmful in its effects, since if the wife should happen not to be possessed of some property in her own right she and her children are made to suffer penury and want."*

In past years a number of the older men possessed two or three wives. Polygamy was to be expected, for the Mormons settled north of the San Juan, (Utah), long before white settlers came from the East. Although the Navaho probably believed in polygamy long ago, only those who were well-to-do had more than one wife, and the increase in polygamous marriages was undoubtedly due to the example set by the Mormons.

The Government has taken steps to wipe out this practice and no more plural marriages are permitted. Men having more than one wife have been encouraged to give up their plural wives, and this has been done in some cases, mainly where there are no children by the marriage.

* "A Little History of the Navahos." Oscar H. Lipps, page 49.

NAVAHO SILVERSMITH AND HIS OUTFIT

The Navaho are invariably kind and considerate to each other, and their family life is of higher plane than among most Indians. The children are seldom punished, for the good reason that they do not merit punishment. In the case of very old persons, it is sometimes observed that the children do not love and protect them as completely as might be expected.

The chief taboo of the Navaho is the fish. Under no circumstances will a Navaho eat fish. He believes that upon the death of a very evil person, the spirit enters the body of a fish, hence his utter horror and hatred of the finny tribe. An Indian student entered Phillips Academy, Andover, some years ago. He was employed in the dining hall and thus earned his tuition. He informed me that his most disagreeable duty, and that which he loathed, was the preparation of fish for the weekly Friday dinner.

When we were in camp at Chaco canon in 1897, the Navaho came to us in large numbers at meal time. Our larder rapidly diminished. Something must be done. The cook found that one of the packing boxes had a large blue codfish stamped on the side. He placed this box out in plain view and the Indians who had assembled to eat supper with us withdrew to their own camps.

The Navaho had carried on raids against the Mexicans and the frontier of Texas for many years. In 1863 a party of men led by the famous scout, Kit Karson, invaded their territory and killed a large number of Indians. All of the Navaho that could be captured were taken East to the Rio Pecos. Here they were kept until 1867 under military guard, when they were restored to their country and given a large flock of sheep. In 1869 the Government assembled all these Indians and having difficulty to enumerate them because of their nomadic habits, resorted to a novel stratagem. The people were crowded in an enormous corral, and counted as they entered. The Handbook of American Indians states that there were some fewer than 9,000. I cannot believe that this estimate was accurate, for it would be impossible for troops to round up all the Navaho. Doubtless, many fled north of the San Juan, or west to the Colorado, on the appearance of the troops.

They are very highly religious people and possess thousands of significant songs and prayers. The Handbook states that some of the ceremonies continue for nine nights, and that it is necessary for the shamans to spend years of study in order to become perfectly familiar with the complicated ritual.

The Indians were much crowded before permitted to settle upon public lands. To meet this need, Commissioner Leupp in 1908 extended the reservation.  Father Weber covers all the details in his excellent pamphlet.  The white cattlemen and their friends set up a great uproar, indignation meetings were held, and Congress was importuned to prevent the Indians from living on the public domain.  In fact, all sorts of pressure was brought to bear to reduce the size of the reservation — although it was manifestly too small.  None of the Mexicans and Americans, for whom the business men and politicians of the southwest were so concerned, were living on the tracts they sought to control.  On the contrary they

RED GOAT AND HIS MOTHER, NAVAHO, 1902
Photograph by E. R. Forrest

lived in towns or settlements removed from the Indian country, and simply ranged their sheep and cattle over these tracts in charge of herders and cowboys.  The Indians, the Navaho, against whom this hue and cry was raised, actually had their homes upon the tracts, and were dependent upon them for their living.  Many of them lived in the same place for two or three generations.  During all the disputes, no one was shot, and no violence occurred.  Yet all that was possible was done to mislead Congress, as the following speech attests.

"I want to say to the Senator (Bristow) that possibly he does not understand the conditions as they exist in our country.  Possibly he is not aware of the fact that every year, two or three times a year, these Indians are allowed to go from their immensely rich reserves to interfere with white men, American citizens, on the public domain, causing the killing of anywhere from one to a dozen people. This is an unfortunate condition of affairs. I can say to the Senator that we people down in our section of the country can deal with these conditions if we are compelled to; but this sometimes becomes a question of all a man has — of his property rights, of protection to his family and his children. Any white man, any American citizen, will then use such force as is necessary in protecting his family. All that we seek to do is to restrict the further location of these Indians upon the public domain until Congress can act again. The committee is being appointed, and I presume this matter will be investigated. It has been investigated before, and reports made, and no action taken. But this must cease; it must stop; and I tell the Senator from Kansas that it will stop."—(*Congressional Record*, June 17, 1913, page 2320).

Father Weber's comment on it is very apropos: —

"I regret that a Senator made this statement. I have been among the Navaho for sixteen years, and I know of not one single instance where a white man was killed on account of Navahos leaving the reservation, or on account of any grazing or land disputes. If every year the killing of from one to a dozen is occasioned by Navaho leaving their reserve, how is it that no one knows anything about it?"*

In past years I have traveled a good deal over the Navaho reservation. Recently one of my friends, J. Weston Allen, Esq., of Boston, on behalf of the Boston Indian Citizenship Committee, of which he is vice-chairman, made a tour of investigation through the Navaho country, and the conditions as he found them were incorporated in an able report to the Secretary of the Interior. Major John T. Shelton, the Superintendent at Shiprock, who has long lived with these Indians, while differing in some details from the views of Mr. Sniffen, Rev. Johnson and Honorable F. H. Abbott, yet agrees with them in the main issue that the Navaho should not be too much superintended. All he needs is protection — not charity, suggestion, nor interference with his industry. Doctor W. W. Wallace, who has been a trader among the Navaho since 1890, writes me that the Indians have steadily progressed, that they ask no favors, and all they desire is to be permitted to continue on their successful way. My own observation leads me to believe that the reservation should not be reduced; allotments must not be made in any event until irrigation has disclosed the land values; more schools should be established, and above all dams should be

---

* "The Navaho Indians. A Statement of Facts." Rev. Anselm Weber, O. F. M., page 5.

erected to store water during the spring floods so that more acres may be brought under cultivation. There are vast possibilities for irrigation in the Navaho country, as Mr. Abbott has pointed out. The last investigation by two members of our Board (Ketcham and Eliot) was important, and I present two of the seven recommendations they strongly urged.

"*Allotment*. We are thoroughly convinced that the time has not yet come for the allotment of the Indians on the reservation. The Navaho is proceeding along the way of civilization as fast as he can safely travel. He is independent and self-supporting. He is steadily improving his dwelling, his stock and his method of farming. He is learning English, sending his children to school, and increasingly following the advice of the white physicians. He is developing his own water resources, forming good industrial habits and gradually adopting white standards of domestic life. Following their own customs, the Indians divide their common resources with remarkable fairness and live peaceably with one another and with the Whites. They must be permitted slowly to come into an understanding of our customs of private land ownership and inheritance. There is nothing to be gained by hurrying that process. Allotment on the reservation should not be thought of for a good many years to come.

"We are impressed with the exceptional opportunity of the Navaho reservation for the work of field matrons and recommend that an additional force be provided for. The field matrons should work in close cooperation with superintendents, teachers and physicians.

"In general we believe that the condition of the Navaho is promising. The people are virile, industrious and independent. With the exercise of ordinary good judgment, patience and tact, there need never be any serious problem in connection with their development."

Doctor Joseph K. Dixon, representing the Wanamaker Expedition, visited the "painted desert". He took some remarkable motion pictures of Navaho herders driving thousands of sheep down to the waterholes. As I observed these pictures, portraying the peaceful, industrious life of these red nomads of the desert, I wished fondly that all men and women unable to observe Indian life as it is in the Southwest, might see them. They recalled many interesting days spent among these sturdy folk. The natives living as do the Navaho, present an object lesson to all "reformers", and it is to be devoutly hoped that we will heed the lesson and "let well enough alone." To do otherwise will destroy the initiative of a self-supporting and upright people, and deprive the world of a primitive stock of exceptional physical stamina and mental ability.

Mr. Allen's report to the Secretary of the Interior and the Boston Indian Citizenship Committee cannot be reproduced at length, much to my regret, but I herewith append certain sections, as it is a splendid presentation of the Navaho situation and includes valuable recommendations to meet the needs of these Indians.

"Three obvious difficulties immediately present themselves when any plan of Navaho settlement is considered —(1) the great inequality of the land for grazing purposes; (2) the scarcity of water, and the fact that much of the land is far distant from the nearest water supply; (3) the existence of summer and winter ranges and the removal of the sheep from place to place under the changing conditions of different seasons of the year.

"Of the inequality of the land for grazing purposes, it is sufficient to say that there are vast areas of rock and sand where an allotment of 160 acres would not support a single sheep. Of the inaccessibility of water, it may be similarly stated that there are sections of land within the reservation which are so far from water during the dry season that sheep would die from exhaustion before they could reach it. Of the necessity of moving the sheep from one part of the reservation to another, it is perhaps sufficient to point out that in the winter the sheep must have the protection of the sheltered valleys and in the summer they are driven by the heat and the scarcity of water into the mountains.

"A matter of far greater importance in the consideration of any equitable allotment is the determination of the location and extent of the land within the limitations of the reservation which can be claimed by irrigation."

Mr. Allen points out the difficulties in allotting a nomadic people permanent homes. He is opposed to any allotment under existing conditions. It may have to come in time, doubtless prematurely as in the case of other reservations, but on the Navaho reservation there are difficulties which have not been encountered in our experience with other tribes.

Mr. Allen's report may be summed up as follows: —There should be a commission appointed composed of engineers and stockmen to thoroughly investigate the possibilities of the reservation, both through means of storage dams to conserve the mountain freshets in the springtime, and also to divert the water from the rivers as is being done along the San Juan river to the north. This stream carries a large volume of water, and although there are many white persons living north of the river in Utah and New Mexico and much water is used, the river is very high from May 1st to July 1st. It therefore affords great possibilities in the way of water storage.

He recommends a detailed study of the coalbeds and timber tracts on the reservation, and the improvement of the Navaho sheep, by the introduction of better stock.

While tuberculosis is found in about 10% of the Navaho, trachoma is much more prevalent, and he records the usual story of afflicted Indian children, men and women. The hospital facilities are totally inadequate.

NAVAHO WINTER HOGAN
Photographed by E. R. Forrest; 1902

There is a hospital at Indian Wells, Arizona, maintained by the National Indian Association, an Episcopal hospital near Fort Defiance, while another is maintained by the Presbyterians at Ganado. The only large hospital with adequate equipment is at the Government school at Fort Defiance. Doctor Wigglesworth, physician in charge, who has won the confidence of these Indians by long years of constant labor among them, does all in his power to alleviate distress, but the field is entirely too extensive to be covered by one man. Mrs. Mary L. Eldridge, for many years in charge of a mission near Farmington, N. M., does medical work among the Indians. There is a small Government hospital at Shiprock.

The medicine men cause the Government officials and missionaries a great deal of trouble. Mr. Allen presents a number of incidents in his reports explaining their activities. Many Indians will not take treatment in the hospitals through fear of the shamans, and in more than one instance a sick Indian has been removed by his friends from the mission hospital during the night, and carried off to the village where he might be treated by the shaman.

MODERN INDIAN HOUSE, SYLVIAN, OKLAHOMA
This type is inferior in construction to the houses built in pre-statehood days

Educational facilities are inadequate to care for half the children of school age. In many of the schools, trachoma has afflicted numbers of the children. When tuberculosis develops among the school children they are sent home from the school to die without medical attendance. Mr. Allen suggests that more physicians, qualified to treat trachoma and tuberculosis, be appointed to service among the Navaho, and that each one be assigned a territory fifty miles square, with a field sanitarium located near the center of the territory. He also suggests that young Navaho women, selected from the larger boarding schools, be trained as nurses, since many of these Indians do not take kindly to treatment by white persons, and it is difficult to secure competent nurses who are willing to remain long in the small frontier hospitals of the Navaho desert.

At Shiprock, Superintendent Shelton has developed a large school with extensive farms and industrial buildings. The settlement at Shiprock is justly considered one of the show places in the Indian Service. Here the desert is made to blossom as the rose. Mr. Shelton admits few small children in his school and keeps his scholars until they reach adult age. He is thus able to make a better showing in his farms and gardens than do those who receive the children at an earlier age, and return them to their homes after four or five years of training. Mr. Shelton's work at Shiprock could now be carried on by some one else, and his recognized ability used in a new field to develop another section of the reservation further west. By creating another Shiprock, he could do more to raise the standard of of living among his people.

Superintendent Parquette at Fort Defiance is extending education work throughout his reservation, and reaches a larger percentage of children of school age than are being reached elsewhere in the Navaho country.

In concluding his report, Mr. Allen points out the failure of the returned student to make good and the reasons for it.

"The problem of the returned student is a serious one among the Navaho. The boys and girls who have been for years in school come back to their people without a training for taking care of the flocks, and are outdone by those who remain at home. They are for this reason more or less looked down upon, with the result that they have no inclination to continue the habits of study and cleanliness which they have acquired at school and which are not appreciated in the home. The effort of the old men of the tribe is to keep the children who return from school from seeking any higher place than is enjoyed by other members of the family. If the young men and the young women of the tribe, who have received an education and who have acquired an appreciation of what they learned in school, intermarried, the benefits of their education would be more permanent, but many of the girls upon their return from school are given in marriage by their parents to old men of the tribe, and many of the boys return only to find that they are required to marry old women, or at best, 'camp girls' as they are called — the uneducated girls of the hogan. The inevitable result is that they go back to the old life."

# CHAPTER XXV.  INDIANS OF THE NORTHWEST

The Indians of the great Northwest, are today of many diversified and small bands, chief among which are the Crows, Utes, Nez Perces, Paiutes, Northern Cheyennes, Blackfeet, and Yakimas, and various Columbia River bands.  Linguistically they are Athapascan, Salishan and Shoshonean stocks with remnants of other stocks along the Pacific coast. Practically all of them live on reservations.  As in the case of the other tribes described in this volume, the children have been educated, allotments have been granted to most of the individuals, irrigation schemes either projected or carried into effect, timber sold, or Government sawmills established, and the entire life of the Indians changed.  The narrative, therefore, must be along historical and philanthropic lines rather than ethnologic.  True, up to about 1880 many of these Indians lived in their original condition, and particularly is this true of the Paiute and Modoc bands located far from the established routes of travel.  The Indians of the Northwest came in contact with the trappers and gold-hunters flocking to the new country made familiar by the Lewis and Clark expedition.  As an inevitable result, a number of wars occurred in which all of the Indians were more or less engaged.  The most noted of these was the Nez Perce war of 1877, in which Chief Joseph led his Indians on a magnificent retreat through the mountains for upwards of 1100 miles to nearly the Canadian border.  The story of our broken faith with the Nez Perces is set forth in many documents and by General Howard himself in his book, "Chief Joseph.  His Pursuit and Capture."

Following the Nez Perce war, in 1878, the Bannock Indians, a numerous division of the Shoshonean stock, were so harassed by white people that they went upon the warpath.  A number of settlers and soldiers were killed, and in September, 1878, the outbreak came to an end after the military had killed all the women and children in a village of twenty lodges.

In 1870 the Modocs in southeastern Oregon had obtained a very unsavory reputation.  This was due to their resenting the encroachments of the Whites.  Many settlers, and also friendly Indians, were killed during various encounters.  The trouble culminated in the famous siege of the lava beds, on the California frontier between Oregon and California.  Here the Indians located in an almost impregnable stronghold and withstood the attacks of troops from January to April, 1873.  Some Peace Commissioners, headed by General Camby, were sent to treat with the Indians and these were treacherously murdered.  After hard fighting the stronghold was taken and five of the leaders captured and hanged. Like other Northwest tribes (except larger bands) the Modocs have so dwindled in numbers that they now cease to be a factor in Indian life. The northern Cheyennes now located on a reservation at Lame Deer, Montana, have long been known as a fighting people. Two generations ago the Cheyennes were much in evidence with the Sioux and other tribes in an attempt to prevent the usurpation of their hunting grounds and grazing lands on the part of the Whites. One of the Department Inspectors recently visited their reservation and under date of September 17th, writes me as follows:

"I am very busy and am finding conditions here about as bad as they were at White Earth except that these Indians have not been allotted and are not losing their land, but they are just as poor and are eating dogs, horseflesh, prairie dogs, porcupines and skunks. Conditions are disgraceful but will be properly presented, you may be sure."

The Crow Indians, an offshoot of the Siouan stock, in Montana, are numerically the strongest of any of the mountain tribes. They possess a very large reservation, abundant grazing lands, timber and agricultural possibilities. However, as in the case of the Cheyennes, they have been backward in spite of all efforts on the part of the Government to educate them. The problem on their reservation relates chiefly to the grazing privilege. The Indians were leasing a vast tract of land to white men for the pasturing of cattle and horses at so much per head. The Whites took advantage of the Indians' ignorance and it was necessary for the Indian Rights Association to conduct a thorough investigation. I quote from the Association's report as to former conditions among the Crows, and the present improvement.

"The Crow Reservation, in Montana, had for years been controlled by a small ring of men, who boasted of strong political backing, and they used it for their private gain at the expense of those Indians, through the connivance of the Agent, who had formerly been employed in a bank of which the leader of this ring was the principal stockholder. For three years the Indian Rights Association sought to have a real investigation made at that point by the Department, but instead of receiving any encouragement, its efforts were blocked at every turn. Secretary Garfield had said to us, 'bring me facts, and I will investigate them,' but he refused to give us a formal permit to enable us to go on to the reservation and get those facts. When our Secretary was sent there for that purpose, a little later, he was promptly arrested and ordered off the reservation at his earliest convenience.

"When Commissioner Valentine assumed office, however, he promptly afforded our Secretary every courtesy and facility that were required to go unmolested over the reservation; and when the result of a month's sifting was brought to his attention, he not only ordered an immediate investigation, but Mr. Sniffen was requested to be present to represent the Indians — an invitation that was, of course, accepted.

"On the basis of the information gathered by our Secretary, the chief Supervisor of the Indian Office conducted an investigation during October and November, 1909, and his treatment of the Crow Indians was in decided contrast to their experience with a former Inspector two years previous, when, without provocation, their main witness was brutally cursed and ordered from the tent. When the Supervisor's report was submitted, however, it proved to be one of 'confession and avoidance.' He made it plain, certainly in a number of respects, what some of the conditions were, but he avoided placing the responsibility where it belonged — upon the then Superintendent. It was clearly proved that this Superintendent knowingly and wilfully permitted the violation of a United States statute by the man he regarded as his real superior, who was NOT an official of the Government, and that provisions of the grazing permits had not been respected. In spite of this and more, however, the Supervisor recommended that the Superintendent be 'assured of the confidence of the Indian Office in his integrity, business ability and moral character.' A few months later (in 1910), the Superintendent was forced by pressure to resign, notwithstanding the 'confidence of the Indian Office in his integrity,' etc. He was succeeded by an honest and efficient high-grade man, and conditions on the reservation have greatly improved. It is significant that the revenue derived from the grazing privileges under the new management will amount during the fiscal year ending June 30, 1913, to $160,000, whereas under the former Superintendent it was $33,001.27."

All of these tribes mentioned in this chapter still possess sufficient property for their maintenance, and some of them a great deal. The conditions are not intolerable as elsewhere, and most of the educated Indians have become self-supporting and are successful farmers, teachers, lumbermen, etc. Along the Columbia river the salmon industry affords employment to hundreds of men and women, and the vast extent of orchards and vineyards presents an opportunity for other hundreds of Indians to earn money picking fruit and hops, harvesting grains and hay, picking apples, etc.

One of the richest reservations in point of natural resources is that inhabited by the Yakima of the same linguistic family as the Nez Perces (Shahaptian). A gentleman whom I have known for many years, L. V. McWhorter, Esq., has a ranch adjoining the reservation, and has lived

GRAIN, VEGETABLES AND FRUITS, BEAD-WORK AND BASKETS
This Exhibit took several prizes at the State Fair, Spokane, Wash., 1913

among these Indians until he has become entirely familiar with the situation and their needs. The problem in the Northwest, being totally different from that elsewhere in the United States, I herewith reprint a number of paragraphs from Mr. McWhorter's recent pamphlet "The Crime Against the Yakimas."

It indicates how that the white people have dispossessed these Indians and taken advantage of the wonderful agricultural, timber and water-power resources. There are a number of other places in the United States where at present similar conditions to that on the Yakima reservation face the Indians, and this may serve to illustrate other sections of the country where irrigation schemes on Indian lands are under consideration.

"The Yakima Indian Reservation, Washington, was created at the Walla Walla Treaty in 1855, for the Fourteen Confederated Tribes, and covers approximately 1,000,000 acres of diversified country, including a vast body of fine desert lands susceptible to irrigation, which last has been allotted in severalty to the Indians, numbering 3,046 souls. About 42,000 acres of this is under a good system of irrigation, some private ditches, the canals being paid for by the Indians and by special appropriations by the Government. Crops are produced on 10,000 acres additional by sub-irrigation, while perhaps 20,000 acres of the allotted lands have been purchased by the Whites. This irrigable region, fertile beyond conception when watered, has long been coveted by the white man. The first attempt at irrigation on this reservation was in 1859.

"In 1895 the Commercial Club of North Yakima, Wash., petitioned Congress to sell the surplus lands of the Yakimas, and to open the reservation for settlement. Two years later Commissioners were sent to negotiate with the tribe. It was estimated that 200,000 acres of land would suffice for all allotments, and for the residue the Government offered $1,400,000, deferred payments to bear four per cent interest. The Yakimas refused this offer.

\*    \*    \*    \*    \*    \*

"Aside from the Jones Bill, December 21, 1904, which provides for the opening of the reservation and the sale and settlement of unallotted tribal lands, the next serious attempt to amputate the Yakimas from their lands culminated in the notorious Jones Bill, March 6, 1906, which provides that the irrigable lands of the Reservation be cared for by the United States Reclamation Service. This bill, with the consent of the Indian, authorizes the Secretary of the Interior to sell sixty acres of each eighty-acre allotment; the twenty acres retained by the Indian to be furnished with a water right, to be paid for from the sale of the sixty acres. After the payment of such water right, 'the balance, if any, shall be deposited in the treasury of the United States, to the credit of the individual Indian, and may be paid to any of them, if, in the opinion of the Secretary of the Interior, such payments will tend to improve the condition and advance the progress of said Indian, but not otherwise.' Under this act the Wapato Project to water about 120,000 acres, was launched. The estimated cost for a water right for the Indian's twenty acres, including storage, is $30.00 per acre."

We have no space for a full discussion of the attempt to rob the Yakimas. Friends rallied to their support — notably the Indian Rights Association. McWhorter saw the fruits of his toil ripening, and it now appears that these Indians will be protected in part, if not entirely.

June 8th, 1912, the Indians themselves sent a long petition to Hon. J. H. Stephens, Chairman of the House Committee on Indian Affairs. The closing paragraphs are characteristically Indian: —

"On Ahtanum River divide of our reservation where white man have most land, the Secretary of the Interior gives three-fourths of water to white man. Now, when red man have most land to water, he gives nearly all water to white man. This was done and we could not help ourselves. We want only what is right. God wants the white man and the red man to live in peace. We try hard to do right and obey the white man's laws. We want you to help us.

"Our friend in Congress introduced 'House joint resolution 250' for Attorney General to settle our water rights. This is good, but Secretary Interior hold up this resolution and try to make Jones bill 6693 law, so Reclamation will own all water and have us flat. We want you to stop Jones bill and make law the resolution 250. Then Attorney General will settle all justly. If this is not done we are bringing suit in United States court to settle our water rights. We want the white man to be honest and treat us right. Our words are done.

"Our friend, help us. We want to hear from you.

"Your friends,

"(Signed)        WE-YAL-LUP WA-YA-CI-KA (his x mark),
            "*Chief Judge of the Yakima Tribal Courts,*
                    "*Clan Chief of the Ahtanum.*

"(Signed)        LOUIS MANN,
            "*Corresponding Secretary of the [Indian] Councils.*

The Utes of Utah and Colorado never have been progressive, though some of them do work. They require special treatment. A Government employee remedied conditions among them in August, 1912, and wrote me, giving sensible advice, as follows: —

"What good does it do to send out circulars on sanitary conditions and dairying, when some of these Indians are in destitute circumstances? The poor Utes down at Navaho Springs need something to eat and wear, and some blankets to keep them warm. They sleep on sheepskins on the floors of their tipis. They get but little rations. They have been compelled to sell their ponies and buckskin suits, and beadwork, and Navaho blankets, to get something to eat for themselves and their children. They have no allotments, do not farm and have no way to make a dollar.

INDIAN PACK-TRAIN IN THE MOUNTAINS
Photographed by E. R. Forrest, Washington, Pa.

"Here at this reservation I have found that the Indians have been defrauded in their lands and moneys. They sold their lands under direction of the Agent, and then the scheme was to get their money away as soon as possible. It was done through the dishonest Indian trader in every possible manner. Indians' checks were drawn, of which the Indian knew nothing, in favor of some Indian trader for horses, wagons and other things of which the Indian had no knowledge and which he did not get. Although the checks are drawn in his name and charged to the Indian, no credit is given the Indian on the books of the trader. This is just a sample. One poor Indian who lives at Navaho Springs, had his allotment of 160 acres sold for $245. This was put on the books to his credit. Then a check was drawn for a horse and saddle in favor of Mr. Trader for $165 to pay for same. He never bought same and never had this horse and saddle. No credit for this check on the Trader's books. Then another check was drawn in the sum of $67 against this Indian account, of which he knows nothing, for a saddle, bridle, and tent. He never bought or got the bridle, saddle, or tent and knows nothing of the transaction. He never put his thumb mark to either check. So out of the little pittance he got for his land, a little more than a dollar an acre, he has had stolen from him out of that $245, the sum of $232."

Several correspondents in the Northwest give their opinions on what should be done, and I submit extracts from their letters.

"The Government, in my judgment, should further strengthen its work in suppressing the liquor traffic among the Indians. A large appropriation should be asked for each year, and good, competent men should be employed to break up the traffic. In my opinion, it is useless to educate the Indian to grow up and drink himself to death, and if the United States laws are too little enforced with relation to the liquor traffic among Indians, it is not because they are not violated, but because the Government has not yet secured sufficient assistance to see that the law-violators are punished.

Correspondent, Pendleton, Oregon

"I have always believed that unallotted Indians who have large grazing areas on their reservation should be the direct beneficiaries of their own grazing-lands and have continually urged that a reimbursable appropriation be made to stock this reservation. It has also occurred to me that the Indians should be encouraged by the use of large reimbursable appropriations to stock their allotments with tools and livestock and I am glad that the above propositions are being actively pushed as desirable propositions by the present Commissioner of Indian Affairs."

Correspondent, Lame Deer, Montana

"In my opinion, the reservation was opened seventy-five years too soon. With the exception of a few half-breeds, they were absolutely unprepared for the opening of the reservation. Humanly speaking, they are doomed to utter annihilation. In dealing with them, we forgot that they

were savages, and that, as it took centuries to polish our own ancestors
who were vastly more intelligent than these redmen, at least one century,
or one century and a half, would be required to make these people civilized."

Correspondent, St. Ignatius, Montana

"When I took charge, nothing had been done for them by the Government. I at once issued agricultural implements, wire, seeds, etc., and
organized each band and devoted the first efforts to agriculture on individual tracts, but worked all together as a community. By this means
we raised a good crop the first year, in one instance going from almost
starvation to plenty in the short space of four months. Since that time
not a single ration has been issued, and aside from supervisory work and
teaching, which is given by myself and employees, all my Indians are
entirely self-supporting. I am unqualifiedly and absolutely opposed to
all ration and annuity distribution as it has been carried on in our department. I am insisting upon all my Indians caring for and supporting their
old people, and see that it is done. My method of helping Indians is to
work both day and night to inaugurate methods and give opportunities
to enable them to work out their own salvation.

"I have had an unusual opportunity to work out my own ideas, by
reason of beginning in a virgin field. So far I have been remarkably successful. However, there is a strange characteristic apparent among all
Indians, that they have apparently no sense of gratitude, and take everything that is done as a matter of course, and do not seem to have the faculty
of contrasting their situation from year to year and striking a balance, as
it were, to note their material progress.

"I have no suggestions as to reforms, except those directed toward
the Indian himself. In this State he is not discriminated against as in
others. Here he has nothing except his labor to tempt the cupidity of the
Whites. In the past he has been given many opportunities for improvement through the Mormon Church, and he had the chance to become just
as well off as the majority of the Mormon immigrants who came here into
the desert almost with their bare hands. So the fault, if fault it is, lies
entirely with himself. He had the opportunity to observe and profit by
the example of the poor Whites who started on desert ground under the
same environment and made themselves homes; in addition to this just
as soon as the Mormon Church was able, the authorities 'called' some of
its members, sent them to each band, not as preaching missionaries, but
as farmers, and gave them tools and oxen and instructed them how to use
them. This was done with every band under my jurisdiction. As these

THE CHALLENGE. NEZ PERCE WARRIOR
Copyright by L. V. McWhorter, who photographed the Indian, and
permits publication

missionaries were sent without any pay, and were poor, they had their own families to support, and gradually returned to the settlements, leaving the Indians to carry on their work themselves. The Indians simply killed the oxen and kept up their nomadic life to a great extent, simply holding campgrounds on the water courses where their water rights have been protected by the church until I took all the responsibilities over."

Correspondent, Salt Lake City, Utah

"The immorality of our Indians, in my opinion is largely (probably seventy-five per cent) due to the presence of low Whites. Had the Indians been left alone seventy-five years longer; and had they been allowed to continue the time-honored custom of punishing crimes with the whip — they would be today easily and surely seventy-five per cent better men than they are. Here again we forgot that they were savages, absolutely impervious to really noble feelings, such as honor, and that it takes time and careful training to raise them to a higher level. Today, they are incapable of feeling the shame of a prison or penitentiary. When they come back from either, they are treated as heroes. Twenty-five years ago, a whipping solemnly, modestly, and moderately administered to those who had been guilty of thievery, adultery, fornication, gambling or drunkenness, was producing marvelous results. Two years ago, a deputation of Kootenay Indians came to beg me to write in their name to the Great Father (the President) and ask him to allow again the use of the whip. They said, 'Tell the Great Father that our young men and women only laugh at the white punishments; it is the whip and the whip alone that kept us straight, and the same punishment alone will correct the generation.'

"Under the present circumstances I believe that the Government has at heart the welfare of its wards and is protecting them. There is only one flaw which I desire to bring to your notice. The real wards of the Government are the full-blood Indians, and they, more than the mixed-bloods, are entitled to the care of the Government, for many reasons, easy to understand; now, in point of fact, mostly all of them, on this reservation, are helpless. They are, if in good health, unable to understand their real interest, and to work as they should. In matters of business they are at the mercy of everyone who chooses to deceive them. But the number of those who are in health is very limited. The vast majority are old, crippled, blind or otherwise helpless. And those, I am sorry to say, are practically left unaided. They need food, raiment, shelter, they should be supported. As it is, they are practically thrown on the charity of the white people. Though possessed of lands, they are unable to draw any profit from them.

Some appropriation is made yearly for those; but it is insufficient to furnish them with food, raiment and shelter. Means should be provided for that purpose. They are doomed to disappear, and in justice their last years should be made comfortable. The Government has been collecting large sums of money from the white settlers; why not dispose of some of this money liberally for the impotent full-blood Indians who are left in destitution, instead of spending it in improving the irrigation of the reservation, which improvement will never benefit the full-blood Indians who are disappearing, but will turn to the advantage of the mixed-bloods who have very little right to the land (some of them none at all) and who, on account of their superior intelligence got the very best part of the allotments at the time of the opening of the reservation. The condition of mostly all the full-bloods is pitiful. If they have leased their lands, it takes them an age to receive their money, the local Agent having no authority to disburse it, and the Indian Bureau being very slow in granting it. It seems to me that provision should be made in favor of destitute Indians to have them receive monthly some food, and a small sum of money to provide themselves with clothes, also to have them provided with decent houses and with fuel when they cannot get it themselves. No one but those who live on the spot have any idea of the privations which this class of full-bloods have to submit to, through no fault of theirs. It seems to me that this evil could easily be remedied. Some people seem to think that a monthly sum of money, $20, should be paid to each destitute Indian, with which he could easily provide for his needs; but knowing them as I do, I would prefer to see them receive only $10 or even $5 with rations, for if they get more money, they will spend it all in the first days of the month."

Correspondent, St. Augustins, Montana

NOTE—A very interesting book, "Life Among the Pai-utes," was written by Sarah Winnemucca in the early '80's. This presents an account of the Nez Perce, Bannock and other wars from the Indian point of view.

# CHAPTER XXVI.  HEALTH OF THE INDIANS
## 1880 TO 1912

That the Indians of the present time are in a deplorable condition as to health, no person familiar with Indian affairs will deny. It is incomprehensible to me that the appropriations for combatting disease are so meagre, and the appropriations for allotting and education so lavish. As a western friend of mine, who had observed Indians for more than thirty years says, "Of what use is education to an Indian with consumption? An Indian child learns to read and write, contracts trachoma, is sent home and goes blind. How does education benefit the blind Indian?"

Doctor Ales Hrdlicka of the Smithsonian Institution recently made an investigation of health conditions among the Indians. His report is statistical in character, and will be found in Bulletin 42, Smithsonian Institution, 1909.

Following this, the Public Health and Marine Hospital Service made a thorough investigation in 1912-13 of health conditions among the Indians and published another statistical report, "Contagious and Infectious Diseases Among the Indians", Document No. 1038, 62nd Congress, 3d Session. Investigations were conducted in twenty-five states by competent corps of medical observers. No trachoma was found in Florida. Among the New York Indians there was but .2 of one per cent; Wisconsin 6.86 per cent. In the other states the percentages rise rapidly, reaching 15.5 per cent in Minnesota; 22.38 per cent in New Mexico; 24.9 per cent in Arizona; 68.72 per cent in Oklahoma.

As to tuberculosis, but 1.27 per cent was observed among the New York Indians. But the investigation set forth in the Public Health report related mainly to trachoma and there were limitations placed on tuberculosis research.

Although the Commissioner of Indian Affairs states that there are 25,000 Indians suffering from tuberculosis, the number is probably greatly in excess of that figure. In Minnesota alone, in 1909, I found the greater majority of the Indians suffering from tuberculosis, trachoma, or some form of scrofulous disease. It is not necessary to go into this subject in any detail. That disease among these poor people is rampant, is inexcusable. It is heart-rending. It is a blot on our escutcheon, and should have been removed long ago. Whether the delay in establishing preventive measures, until trachoma and tuberculosis became widespread, is due to ignorance, incompetency or carelessness, it is not my purpose

SANATORIUM SCHOOL, FORT LAPWAI, IDAHO

No. 1. Superintendent's house, employees, mess, and official guest room.  No. 2. Commissary.  No. 3. Laundry and Carpenter shop.  No. 4. Employees' dormitory (not completed when picture was taken).  No. 5. Residence of physician, Nez Perce Agency.  No. 6. Engineer's residence.  No. 7. Nez Perce Agency.  No. 8. School building and chapel.  No. 9. Girls' building and dining-room.  No. 10. Boys' building.  No. 11 and 12. Buildings belonging to school district No. 57, Nez Perce County.  No. 13. Top of chimney, barely seen, office of the Sanatorium.  No. 14 Employees' quarters, Nez Perce Agency.

to state. I have high respect for the personnel of the medical branch of the Service. The fault is not theirs, but solely due to meagre appropriations, and lack of proper reports from the inspection corps. I simply desire to cover this unpleasant subject with a blanket statement of facts that the condition is intolerable, and all of us have been criminally negligent. We introduced tuberculosis, trachoma, smallpox, measles, diphtheria and most of the other diseases. If any man or woman doubts the statement, let him or her read the narratives of travelers among Indians two centuries ago and compare the condition then, with that today. There is no earthly excuse why instead of three or four, there should not be fifteen or twenty doctors on every reservation. There is no reason why our rich, powerful Government does not appropriate two or three million dollars a year to put an end to the miseries we ourselves have introduced.

Persons of prominence have called attention to the spread of disease in past years. Commissioner Leupp first noted that health conditions were bad, and increased his medical corps. But his successor, Honorable R. G. Valentine, made a health campaign the chief thing of his administration. He went before Congress and plead for increased appropriations. Great credit is due him for his humane efforts, which are continued by the present Service head, Mr. Sells.

Before the Government awoke to the need of health protection, a gentleman in California was a pioneer in the fight against disease. He has lived to see the fruits of his planting, but for many years his voice was that of one crying in the wilderness, and few there were who thought of repentance. I refer to Charles F. Lummis, Esq., an authority upon the Pueblo and California Indians. Mr. Lummis has written me a long letter in which he sets forth the difficulties under which he labored, and how that he was roundly denounced because he opposed the scheme of taking children accustomed to open-air life, shipping them East, crowding them into contract schools — thus making of strong, healthy boys and girls, consumptives. Lummis fought — not education, but this pernicious and wicked policy. Some of his experiences were interesting. He speaks of the former school conditions, and I take it that his strictures do not apply to the past two or three years.

"It is obvious that to take children from the high, dry climate of New Mexico and the general Southwest, back to the Eastern winters and to steam-heated halls, can have but one effect. That is no theory. I have seen the practical workings for more than a quarter of a century; and it is my sincere conviction that Carlisle and similar schools away from home have graduated more consumptives and more sons and daughters forever alienated from their parents and kin, than they have produced of scholars or other people seriously useful in any walk of life.

"I do know that thirty years ago consumption was almost unknown in most of the Pueblos in New Mexico. I do know that the first consumptive Pueblo I ever saw was from Carlisle; and that most of the consumptive Indians that I have known in my thirty years acquaintance with New Mexico have come back thus infected from these Eastern Government Schools".

"At a meeting of the National Educational Association in this city in July, 1899, I had a serious clash with a distinguished Indian educator. An Indian convention was held in conjunction with the N. E. A. I was busy; but seeing the daily reports finally became so incensed at the inhuman and stupid proceedings, that on the last day I went to the Convention and took the floor almost by force, after listening to most of the afternoon's proceedings.

"This man had with him two very charming and well-schooled Indians — a young man and a young woman, who were called up by him to answer some of my strictures as to the Carlisle methods. And they made eloquent and loyal defences. The audience (being as unobservant as American audiences generally are) were very much surprised when in my reply I called attention to the fact that the two model students that Mr. Educator brought with him were both consumptives, and I asked him point blank if they were consumptive when they entered Carlisle.

"Of course I got no answer — and I was lucky in getting out of the hall alive."

Los Angeles, Sept. 14th, 1914.

Doctor Ales Hrdlicka, in the year 1908, acting for the Indian Office and the Smithsonian Institution, investigated health conditions with reference to tuberculosis among five selected tribes of the United States.

On page 7 of the report Doctor Hrdlicka states: —

"The investigations on which this report is based were pursued in five of the tribes, shown in the above-mentioned data to be most afflicted with tuberculosis, and in one of the large non-reservation schools. The tribes in question are the Menominee in northeastern Wisconsin; the Oglala Sioux in South Dakota; the Quinaielt on the seacoast and along the river of the same name in northwestern Washington; the Hupa in northwestern California; and the Mohave, on the Colorado river between Needles, Cal., and Yuma, Ariz. These tribes were selected not only because of the prevalence among them of tuberculosis, but also because they live under widely differing conditions of climate, environment, civilization, and contact with the Whites. The school visited is the one at Phoenix, Arizona. The investigation was carried on during the two months of midsummer when people everywhere are most free from the various bronchial and pulmonary affections that might complicate a diagnosis.

"On account of the short time available, and the extensive ground to be covered, the study had to be limited to what was most essential toward obtaining reliable statistics. In the smaller tribes, as the Hupa and the Mohave, nearly all the dwellings were visited, and all the members of the tribe who were not far distant were studied. In the larger tribes,

AGED WOMAN NEARLY BLIND FROM TRACHOMA

as the Menominee and the Oglala, the examinations were limited to one hundred families. Among the Oglala, these one hundred families included only full-bloods, who in this tribe suffer more from tuberculosis than do the half-breeds.

"The actual work consisted in visiting the dwellings consecutively and making a personal examination of each member of every family, healthy or not healthy. In many families absent members were brought from many miles away by the Indians themselves for examination. This examination embraced the lungs, heart, glands of the neck, and skeleton, and was supplemented by inquiries. * * *

"The investigation was everywhere promoted by the Indians them-selves, who welcomed an inquiry into the disease which is deciminating them, the gravity of which they well appreciate, but against which they feel utterly helpless."    *    *    *

He found the Oglala Sioux, of Pine Ridge reservation, numbering 6,663, very susceptible to tuberculosis; the number of individuals in a thousand affected with pulmonary tuberculosis being 30.8, bones and joints 6.8, and glandular 57.7.   The highest number of persons suffering from this disease was found among the Hupa Indians of California, where the number of individuals per thousand arose to 60.4, pulmonary tuberculosis.

"In regard to civilization, the Oglala are in the transition period, which generally means partial degeneration.   They live in small or fair-sized log houses of one room, each provided with one or two small windows that are never opened.   The houses have earthen floors and sod roofs. In summer almost every family constructs from poles and boughs, or from young pine trees, a more or less open shelter in which, while it is warm, they spend most of their time.   Usually, each family has also a light, easily portable tent, which represents the ancient tipi.   These tents are erected near the house and are occupied by the aged, by some relative or visitor of the family, or serve to sleep in.   When the family leaves home, such a tent is packed, together with bedding, kitchen utensils, etc., into the wagon, and is pitched whenever a stop is made for the night.   Indeed, there will be at times one or more villages of these tents near the agency, or about a house where some particular feast is being given.   In summer these tents are oppressively hot during the day, though they become cool if the sides are raised.   As they are made of very light fabric, they are cold at night, and afford but poor protection during a severe rain or hail storm, as the writer personally experienced.    *    *    *

"As to clothing, the Oglala now dress like the Whites in most respects, though the majority still persist in wearing moccasins.   The women wear leggings and always a blanket or shawl when going about.   A tendency to wear too much clothing, even on the hottest day, was again noticed and is very prevalent.   This is due partly to ignorance and partly to vanity. The garments are usually far from clean.   The writer learned of several instances in which the clothing of tuberculous persons was given or sold to others.

"In diet the Sioux are chiefly meat eaters, the principal kind of meat consumed being beef.   They cook this fresh, or cut it into strips and dry it on cords stretched outside their dwellings.   Other common articles of diet are badly made wheat bread and large quantities of coffee.   When they have money they purchase crackers and canned foods. They eat very irregularly, both as to time and quantity. During feasts and when visitors are present, they not infrequently use the same wooden spoon or other utensil, one after another, and eat from the same dish, the bones and other remnants being freely strewn over the floor.

"In many of the dwellings it was seen that the denizens lack in both quantity and quality of food on account of their poverty. * * * Numerous cases were seen where the whole meal consisted of a few crackers and black coffee. In several instances cattle which had died of disease had been consumed, both flesh and viscera. According to the resident physician, Doctor Walker, the Oglala eat not only cattle but even horses and dogs that die of disease. The people are not emaciated; in fact, many look well nourished. Yet there is no doubt that many do not receive, except on rare occasions, all the nourishment they require. This doubtless induces indolence and disease. It would also strongly promote the spread of alcoholism, but fortunately there are very few chances for obtaining liquor on or near the reservation.

"Few of the Oglala men have any steady occupation. They do very little farming. During the summer they cut some hay in the valleys, which brings fair prices. Cattle and horses are being distributed by the Government to the different families, and stock-raising is being encouraged with some success. * * *

"The people of this tribe are quite shrewd, tractable, and glad to be instructed, though the instruction given does not always have practical results. Their most striking peculiarities are the above-mentioned tendency to a seminomadic life and the disinclination to steady manual work. They are very ignorant of all matters regarding hygiene. One of the most reprehensible customs among them is the so-called 'passing of the pipe.' Whenever a number of men have gathered in a house, there is passed from mouth to mouth a lighted pipe, the mouthpiece of which is never cleaned. As there is often in such a group an individual in the earlier stages of consumption, the habit must be regarded as providing a direct mode of infection with the disease."*

This description of the Oglala Sioux by Doctor Hrdlicka, who is one of our most expert and competent scientists, might well be applied to other bands and tribes of Indians in the transition period. As has been suggested elsewhere, it emphasizes the immediate need of larger appropriations, the employment of numerous physicians and sanitary officials, if we would save the full-blood Indians.

* Bureau of American Ethnology, Bulletin 42, Washington, 1909. Pages 11-14.

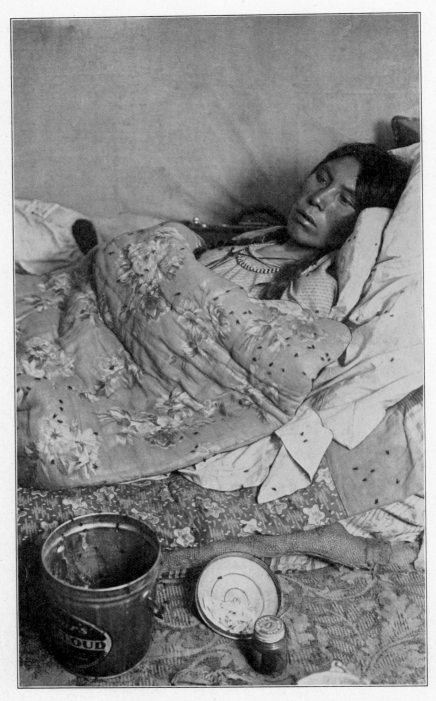

A TUBERCULOSIS PATIENT. BEDDING COVERED WITH FLIES

Dr. Joseph A. Murphy is medical supervisor of the Indian Service, and a more competent man cannot be found. I have received a number of reports covering his activities the past two years. That the Indians are suffering, is no fault of Dr. Murphy's, or his assistants. He has recently established hospitals and increased the medical corps. If the present ratio of increase in physicians and buildings continues, much alleviation will result.

Dark as is our picture, recently it has become brighter. The past two years conditions have greatly improved. There are more adequate appropriations. But this realization of our responsibilities at a late day, does not absolve us from past responsibility. We had been repeatedly told — nay, warned of the consequences, yet we continued our "same old story, in the same old way," until the white people living in Indian communities complained. Now, when Indians complain we pay little heed, but when the representatives of the white people cry, "menace to public health", we heed and we speedily send help to allay the fears of the good and substantial citizens. The appeal from Macedonia is not uttered in vain.

We now have hospitals building, and they may take care of a third of the sick. We also enforce stricter sanitary laws. So we may look forward to saving some of those who suffer from the "coughing sickness", and as to the other scourge, it is so contagious that heroic measures have been adopted, and the light will not go out forever from Indian childrens' eyes.

I present two field reports, sent by competent observers who traveled extensively in Wisconsin and Oklahoma, and both of whom have long resided among Indians there.

"When I came to the Lake Superior country in 1878, I found the Indians of Lac Courte Oreille Reservation and of Lac du Flambeau, living almost entirely in birch-bark wigwams, also in Bad River Reserve, near Ashland, Wis. In Courte Oreille, I counted about six log houses, mostly inhabited by French half-breeds. In Bad River Reserve (now Odanah) perhaps about the same number; in Lac du Flambeau also about six log houses. But as soon as the Indians got their pine-money and their allotments, they immediately began to build houses, many of which were large and commodious. Others were of hewn logs, rather small and low and very unhealthy on that account, as there was very little ventilation, and in the winter they would be huddled together, most of them sleeping on the floor in a blanket, or poor bedclothes. The stove was very hot until after the fire went out, when, of course, towards morning they would be shivering with the cold. Cooking, smoking, living, in such a small room would naturally cause colds, and consumption. This may be justly called *the Indian's Disease*, as it is the most common sickness of which they die; they generally die of consumption, brought on by their total disregard of the laws of health. Sugar-making early in spring, when they used to gather the maple-sap in the woods, walking in the wet snow and cold water, shod with soft moccasins, made of deerskin, and not much better than common stockings; then went the whole day with wet feet — this no doubt laid for many, the seeds of future consumption. Then, gathering cranberries in swamps, wading in the water for hours and hours, was also highly unhealthy. Their cooking was also very poor. Bread, tea, and pork their principal food, the bread badly made, hard and heavy. The Indian's natural home is the woods, like that of the deer; the white man's natural home is the clearing, in open country. Civilization is coming on the Indian too fast — it effeminates and weakens him. The Indian woman is naturally industrious, the Indian man is lazy; that's about the way to put it.

"The Franciscans in California solved the Indian problem in the best and most practical way: they first made Christians — and then civilized the people."

Correspondent, Bayfield, Wis.

"Surrounded by wretched conditions, it is not surprising that the incidence of tuberculosis, trachoma, and other diseases is large among these Indians. Although tuberculosis can hardly be considered as prevalent here as among some of the other reservation tribes, it nevertheless occurs to an alarming extent. It appears to be more prevalent in some localities than in others, and, in some sections, seems to be on the increase. The home conditions of many of these Indians are such that, if a case of tuberculosis or other infectious disease occurs in a household, the probability is that the disease will, in time, go through the entire family.

"During my drive among the Cherokee full-bloods, probably forty families were visited, many of which either have, or have not, one or more cases of tuberculosis. In the vicinity of Barber, twenty miles from Talequah, there occurred three deaths from tuberculosis within three weeks of the time of my visit. Two of the cases, one a baby in the arms and the other a woman, the head of the family, were seen by me. The latter case was particularly pathetic and deserves special mention. The sick woman, dying of tuberculosis, was found in the one room of the house, which, though small, illy ventilated, and poorly lighted, was occupied by nine other people, including six small children. Being wholly ignorant of the dangerous and infectious nature of the disease, this condition continued until the death of the patient, which occurred two weeks later. Another family visited, had lost three members from tuberculosis within the past few years.

"When the housing conditions encountered here are taken into consideration, it seems remarkable that tuberculosis does not spread among the people even more rapidly than it does. This can be partially explained, however, by the fact that they are sometimes widely scattered, the houses, in many instances, being several miles apart.

NATIONAL INDIAN ASSOCIATION HOSPITAL AT
INDIAN WELLS, ARIZONA

"In another family near the little village of Eucha, a girl fourteen or fifteen years of age was seen to wipe her trachomatous eyes with the end of a shawl, worn about her mother's head. The mother held a young baby in her arms, and it would seem that a failure to infect the baby's eyes with the contaminated shawl would be nothing short of marvelous.

"The civilizing influences that surround these people are far from good. The class of people that are frequently found as neighbors are a shiftless, undesirable class. These Whites live amidst unsanitary, meagre surroundings. It is due to this class of citizens that the use of cocaine has of recent years assumed alarming proportions. This habit has become quite common among the full-bloods in some sections, and I heard of several deaths that were attributed directly to this cause.

"The use of alcoholic liquor is, no doubt, a positive detriment to the Choctaw Indians, particularly in those districts close to the Arkansas border. Many crimes have been committed among the Indians that can be attributed directly to the use of liquor, given to them by unscrupulous bootleggers from across the border.

"Trachoma appears to be even more universal among the Creeks and Seminoles than it is among the Indians farther south, and many cases are observed. Trachoma is, no doubt, a positive menace to the usefulness

INDIAN CABIN, NORTH DAKOTA
Six of the seven inmates had trachoma

and well-being of many of these people, and should be met by a vigorous campaign for its control.

"The native medicine man appears to play a more important part among the Creeks and Seminoles than among the other Indians of the Five Civilized Tribes. The full-blood Indians seldom call on the local white physician for treatment, but depend almost entirely upon their own medicine men, and the use of patent remedies, purchased at the local country stores. Several bottles of a patent consumption "cure" were seen in a number of homes visited.

"After a careful survey of the conditions existing among the full-blood Indians of the Five Civilized Tribes, it seems highly important that there should be a well-organized system of medical treatment provided. Tuberculosis and trachoma, the two most important diseases to be combatted among Indians generally prevail among these people to an alarming extent, and both appear to be steadily on the increase. It is unquestionably true that many of these Indians sicken and die without any medical aid whatever. Many of them are too poor to employ white physicians, with the result that the physician is either not called at all, or only when it is too late to be of any avail.

"Too much emphasis cannot be placed upon the need for hospital facilities for these Indians. There is, at present, no place available in which to place the needy sick except in local city hospitals. This necessarily entails considerable expense on the individual and, in many instances, there is a prejudice against going away from their homes to enter a strange hospital. The several sanitariums throughout the Service are usually already filled beyond their capacity, and it is seldom possible to secure their admission to the institutions.

"In view of the extremely unsanitary conditions existing in many of the full-blood homes throughout the Five Civilized Tribes, it would appear that field matrons would here find a large field for usefulness. The people with whom she comes in contact are easy of approach and tractable. They are also readily susceptible to teaching, and would, no doubt, welcome the assistance that the field matron would be able to give."

Correspondent, Muskogee, Okla.

---

Five Civilized Tribes. Reports of the Commissioners of Indian Affairs, 1893-1905.

Health Conditions Among Indians.— *Edgar B. Meritt.* The Red Man. May, 1914. P. 347.

Tuberculosis, Saving Indians from.— *Frank H. Wright.* Twenty-fifth Annual Report Lake Mohonk Conference 1907. P. 38.

Sanitary Homes for Indians.— *Edgar B. Meritt.* The Red Man. June, 1912. P. 439.

Sanitorium Schools: Fort Lapwai, East Farm, Laquna (Tuberculosis Sanitorium), Toledo. From Articles pp. 356, 362, 368, 385, The Red Man. May, 1914.

Indian Medical Service, Organizing the.— *J. A. Murphy.* Twenty-seventh Annual Report Lake Mohonk Conference, 1909. P. 23.

"White Plague" of Red Man.— *George P. Donehoo, D.D.* The Red Man. September, 1912. P. 3.

The Trachoma Problem.— *W. H. Harrison, M.D.* The Red Man. May, 1914. P. 377.

Tuberculosis Problem, Important Phases of.— *Dr. F. Shoemaker.* The Red Man. May, 1914. P. 351.

Indian Tuberculosis Sanitarium and Yakima Indian Reservation.— *Congressional Record,* 63rd Congress. Dec. 20, 1913.

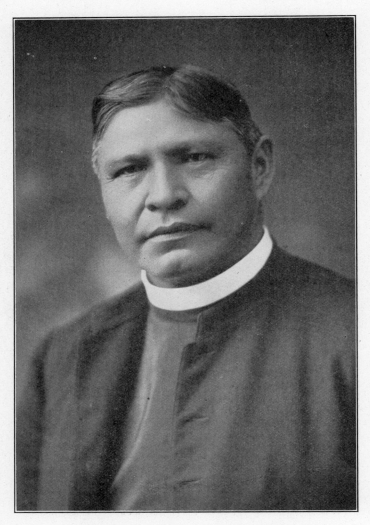

**REV. SHERMAN COOLIDGE; ARAPAHO**
Missionary at Fort Washakie, Wyoming

# CHAPTER XXVII. THE INDIAN'S RELIGION; HIS CHARACTER; PHILANTHROPIC ORGANIZATIONS

Since 1850, the Indian's belief in the hereafter has undergone a very marked change. It is extremely difficult to find individuals, among most of our tribes, who can give us any clear conception of the Indian's religious belief. The Navaho preserve much of their original religion, for the reason that these Indians have been remote from contact with the Whites. As has been stated in this book, the greater part of the 28,000 Navaho do not speak English and continue in the faith of their fathers. There are also scattered tribes or bands of other Indians who keep up, to a greater or less degree, their religious belief, have confidence in their shamans, and resort to the white men's ministers and doctors only under compulsion. But while this is true, the vast bulk of our Indians today have adopted the God of our Bible, and recognize his opposite, the evil spirit. If one takes the pains to read a number of the reports of competent ethnologists who have studied the religious activities of various tribes recently, one is impressed with the complications presented. In fact, it is no reflection on these able and competent workers and observers to state that it is extremely difficult (if not impossible) to cover the Indian's religious belief in one blanket paragraph or statement. Beliefs vary among different tribes, and we must go far back of the year 1850 would we find primitive American religion, practiced in its purity. We cannot now affirm that the religious life of all tribes is the same; that the deities and spirits are alike.

Generally throughout the United States the tradition of the Thunder Bird obtains, and it typifies the supernatural. In the desert areas, water is more precious than soil, or any other necessity. It is therefore quite natural that the Earth Mother and Water Spirit enter very largely into the religion of that region. Some of the older Sioux, even in recent times, believed in spirits, or ghosts, and any Sioux man or woman having heard the calling of the ghosts at night, prepared himself (or herself) to join his ancestors in the spirit world. Major McLaughlin presents one or two instances in his book* where Indians have actually given up, taken to their beds and died, firm in the belief that the ghosts were calling.

Doctor Eastman in his remarkable book, "The Soul of the Indian," defines that indefinite thing, the belief in the supernatural, in a beautiful and striking manner.

---

* My Friend the Indian, Pages 80, 242, 245.

The whole subject of religion among Indian tribes comprehends mythology, shamanism, totemism, and the taboo. There is so great variance among the different linguistic stocks as to belief in the super-natural, religious rites and incantations, that one must study extensively did one desire to obtain any clear conception of ancient Indian religion. In fact, the subject is so beset by uncertainties that we may well omit a consideration of it from this volume. Pure Indian religion — generally speaking — does not exist in the transition period of today.

We may defer to scientific workers the conflicting beliefs among Indians of the present. The labors of the missionaries, both Catholic and Protestant, have instilled into the minds of the Indians the teaching of our Scriptures. Missionary labors, having continued for more than two cen-turies, (and three centuries in some parts of the country) have had their effect, and as I stated above, the Indian today believes as do ourselves. As I pointed out in referring to Miss Densmore's excellent study of Ojibwa music (*page 20*) all the investigators invariably seek out the older Indians and glean from them such fragments as remain of the Indians' former faith. We never hear of ethnologists talking to educated Indians, and recording their opinions.

Among the Navaho, the taboo is more strongly pronounced than, possibly, among other tribes. The totem and the phratry doubtless had their origin in certain religious beliefs. But these are not observed today, to any appreciable extent outside of the Navaho and the scattered bands referred to. We must consider, in studying the Indian of the transition period, not the exceptions, but that which predominates. This has been my aim. Many of the lesser important customs and taboo (bordering upon the religious side of the Indians' nature) obtain. As an illustration, the taboo against the mother-in-law is still in effect in many places. Also, certain rites are performed when a death occurs. Such are clearly survivals of more primitive beliefs.

In a general review of the Indians' religion it must be admitted that while our missionaries and teachers have converted thousands of Indians and these are today faithful members of churches and missions, it is doubt-ful if the bulk of our 330,000 red brothers has been improved spiritually by contact with the white people. I have presented sufficient number of specific instances in this book to prove that where they meet one missionary, priest or teacher, they come in contact with a dozen white persons ranking spiritually and morally far below American standards.

Along with the Indian's religion, he possessed a high sense of honor, or responsibility, and integrity. Judge Thomas, long a resident of

Oklahoma, informed me of cases wherein Indians under sentence of death, were permitted by the authorities to visit distant villages for a few days. There are a number of such instances on record. The Indians invariably returned and were executed according to law. This occurred many years ago. If any modern Indian, or white man under sentence of death, was released by the authorities, it is doubtful if he would consider himself bound to keep his word.

Because the Indian was cruel to his enemies, it does not necessarily follow that he was bad. Among every band there were bad and wild young men who could not be restrained. This has been admitted in the testimony of Red Cloud, Spotted Tail, and many other prominent Indians. Red Cloud, from the Indian point of view, considered it no more cruel to kill his enemies than for us to compel people to work as slaves. He heard we made women and children labor from daylight to dark. This, as well as our long hours for mill-hands and laborers, he considered cruelty. He indicated this in a conversation with me many years ago. One of the prominent Southwestern Indians, when asked by Colonel Dodge, "Why are you Indians so cruel?" cited many things of common occurrence among white people which were considered perfectly proper by them, but which the Indians would not tolerate. It all depends on one's point of view. In condemning Indians for cruelties, we must remember that the patriarchs of the Old Testament, in the name of religion, destroyed more innocent persons in a few of their wars than have the Indians in all of their wars.

I do not agree with the widespread belief that through our general education of Indians, we have raised their moral and religious tone. We have improved some thousands, but the greater number of Indians, observing from the treatment accorded them that we do not practice what we preach, have less realization of their responsibilities and exhibit less integrity than formerly. A letter addressed to the average Indian trader who has done business with Indians more than twenty years, will bring a reply to the effect that their business obligations were more faithfully kept in the past than at present.

As to missionary endeavor among the Indians during the past sixty years, I find that there are upwards of fifty Protestant denominations who maintain mission stations in various parts of the Indian country. These include every denomination, but those most prominent are the Presbyterians, Baptists, Friends, Congregationalists, Methodists, Episcopalians, Moravians, Lutherans. In addition there are the Home Missionary Associations (interdenominational) and the National Indian Association. It is impracticable to present details of their work. The National Indian

Association is one of the strongest of these bodies, and was organized thirty-five years ago. It has fifty-two stations scattered throughout the West, and some idea of its good work may be had by the illustration presented of the Good Samaritan hospital maintained at Indian Wells, Arizona. (*page 275*)

The educational and humanitarian work of the Association has been the helping to right political wrongs; gathering of Indian children into schools; stimulating and preparing capable Indians for wise leadership among their people; loans of money to Indians to enable them to build homes or to carry on business. The Association has done a large and influential educational work, and through its Home Building and Loan Department has enabled Indians to build homes which have become civilizing centers of family life. It has also made loans to Indians for the purchase of implements of labor or for stock needed to begin some useful and paying industry. By such methods the Association seeks to put the Indian in a position to earn his own living and to become self-supporting and self-reliant. It has maintained library, temperance, hospital, and other departments; trained Indian young women as nurses, and assisted Indian young men and women to obtain training as physicians and teachers, some of whom have long been working to help their own people. The Cambridge (Mass.) branch of this organization is especially active and has contributed generously. The work of the missions maintained by the Congregationalists, Episcopalians, Baptists, Methodists, etc., comprehends general religious education and charitable work among the Indians.

Rev. Thomas C. Moffett, Chairman of the committee on Indian work of the "home missions council", has just published an interesting book entitled, "The American Indian on the New Trail." This presents an excellent review of missionary labors among Indians, including much of a statistical character. The review is broad, and covers the entire United States.

The Bureau of Catholic Missions, Washington, has in charge the many missions maintained by the Catholics. I have visited a number of these in various parts of the West, along with the Protestant missions, and find most of them well equipped and doing splendid work.

The California Indian Association has concerned itself more with the securing of homes for dispossessed Indians. In Chapter XXXI, dealing with California conditions, the secretary, Mr. C. E. Kelsey, has commented on the work of the association.

The Indian Rights Association is the most famous of all the benevolent organizations. Organized in 1882, its work has grown and expanded until at the present time its activities cover most of the reservations of the United States. It has frequently been in sharp conflict with the Indian Office, but at the present time the relations between Commissioner Sells and his able assistants and this and other organizations, are most friendly and helpful. The pamphlet, covering the activities of the organization, the number of steals of land it has prevented, the reforms instituted, dishonest employees forced out of the Service and all other recommendations, covers some hundred or more instances and places.

Its corresponding secretary, Mr. Mathew K. Sniffen, returned from Alaska in September of this year, after having spent three months investigating the most deplorable condition of the Alaska Indians.

The Indian Industries League of Boston was organized in 1901 and has done much to encourage arts and industries among certain Indian tribes. It does not attempt to do missionary work, although it has educated a number of Indians. In recent years the League has held fairs and disposed of large quantities of blankets, baskets, beadwork, etc., thus aiding many old Indian women in New Mexico, California, Washington and elsewhere.

I have always been a believer in the work of these organizations, and I have no criticism, but rather a suggestion to offer. The missionary and other organizations had a great opportunity for good during the Messiah craze, and with one accord they let it pass. At the Lake Mohonk Conference this year, a minister from South Dakota spoke of the evil effects of the Messiah craze. In Chapters IX–XI I have described it. There were no evil effects until the troops and Sitting Bull dominated. Had the missionaries seized upon the religious mania when it began, they might have turned it to good account. It was, at first, a purely religious ceremony of high and noble type.

Among the Indians of Oklahoma there is great religious activity. Last year I met many native preachers, and heard of numerous meetings at various campgrounds. I was surprised at the extent of these, and the number of Indians attending such gatherings. The meetings may be a trifle sentimental, but the intentions of the worshippers are excellent. Here is presented a great field for missionary labors, and if the good people would take full advantage of it, a lasting impression and the furtherance of religious activity would ensue.

The modern missionary spirit among most of the workers in the field has changed in recent years. There is more medical activity, more endeavor to stimulate interest in fairs, school exhibitions, etc. Thus the Indians are brought nearer the real life and spirit of the missions, than in the older days where on stated intervals they were assembled for worship. Aside from mere biblical instruction little was done for them. This was all right and proper, but the Indian needed more.

The most potent influence in shaping public opinion, with reference to Indian affairs the past thirty years, has been the annual Conference of Friends of the Indian and Other Dependent Peoples held each year at Lake Mohonk. This was begun in 1882 by Honorable Albert K. Smiley. Since Mr. Smiley's death, the conferences are continued by Honorable Daniel Smiley.

At these conferences are assembled men and women from the United States, Europe and Canada interested in Indian affairs, the Philippines, etc. The conference consists of addresses by persons familiar with Indian topics, which are followed by general discussion. For two or three years the conference seemed to its friends to be somewhat dominated by the Indian Office, but a few years ago it became again a real open parliament. Conflicting views are often expressed, and both the dark and the bright sides of our Indian picture are presented. The conference last year was devoted almost exclusively to a discussion of Oklahoma affairs.

An annual report is published and circulated throughout the world. The meetings have been productive of a great deal of good. Those who attend are invited as the personal guests of Mr. and Mrs. Smiley and enjoy the privileges of their magnificent estate in the heart of the Catskills, while attending the conference.

The Society of American Indians was organized at Ohio State University in 1911. It came into being in response to a feeling on the part of the educated Indians of the country that the "Indian problem" could best be solved through an awakening of the race itself, through its leaders, in cooperation with white friends.

The organization of the society is due to the efforts of Prof. F. A. McKenzie of Ohio State University. The founders of the Society were such men and women as Dr. Charles A. Eastman (Sioux), Dr. Carlos Montezuma (Apache), Rev. Sherman Coolidge (Arapaho), Laura Cornelius (Oneida), Henry Standing Bear (Sioux), Charles E. Dagenett (Peoria), Rosa B. LaFlesche (Chippewa), Arthur C. Parker (Seneca), Thomas L. Sloan (Omaha), Emma D. Goulette (Pottawatomie), Marie L. Baldwin (Chippewa), Henry Roe-Cloud (Winnebago), and Hiram Chase (Omaha).

The high stand taken by the Society and its elimination of all selfish motives led to an unqualified endorsement of its objects by the most earnest friends of the Indian in this country and in Europe.

The Society though only four years old has a membership of about 1500. Hundreds of the most progressive Indians in the country are members and almost all trades and professions are represented. More than 500 citizens of the white race, including both men and women, are associate members of the Society. Most of them have for years demonstrated their earnest and unselfish interest in the welfare of the Indian and have now united their interests with the Indian.

The Society is not connected with any other organization. It is governed entirely by its own membership and has no connection with the Indian Bureau or the Government. Indians and their friends of every shade of opinion are members.

The Society of American Indians seeks to bring about better conditions so that the Indian may develop normally as an American people in America. The Society has asserted that it believes that the full response to the duties of life is more important than constant demands for rights; for with the performance of duties, rights will come as a matter of course. The Society thus seeks to urge the Indian to avail himself of every opportunity to learn the ways of "civilized" life, in order that he may become able to compete and cooperate successfully with other men. The members believe *Indian progress depends upon awakening the abilities of every individual Indian to the realization of personal responsibility, for self, for race and for country, and the duty of responding to the call to activity.* When the nation remedies the laws now hindering Indian progress, work, thrift, education and clean morals will then secure for the Indian all the rights that may be given a man and a citizen.

The Society is not an organization devoted to complaining. Its aim is to suggest and bring about better conditions wherein the old evils cannot exist. The Society does not seek to continually fight over local matters; it does seek to abolish the cause of the misery and the disability of the race. It strikes at the root of evil, yet it does not ignore the individual case of injustice. Nearly one hundred applications each month come from Indians asking legal information.

The annual platform adopted by the Denver Conference and reaffirmed at the Wisconsin University Conference in 1914 demands: First, the passage of the Carter Code Bill, by which a commission will draft a codified law, recommend new legislation and the abolition of laws no longer operative; and the establishment of the definite status of every tribe, band or group of Indians in the United States. The Indian cannot progress until he knows his legal status and how he may advance from a lower to a higher civic status; Second, the Society demands the passage of the amended

Stephens Bill, through which the Indians may place their claims directly in the Court of Claims without specific permission of Congress in each instance.  Indian progress will be retarded as long as real or fancied claims against the Government are unsettled;  Third, the Society asks that the tribal funds be apportioned to each individual's personal account, so that each Indian may know exactly what the nation holds in trust for him. Individual effort and progress will come with an awakened interest in personal resources and personal property, as opposed to bulk holdings; Fourth, better educational advantages and better sanitary protection are demanded.  An ignorant and a sick race cannot be an efficient, useful race. Wisdom, health and thrift will bring to the red man the greater rights he craves.

The Society publishes a *Quarterly Journal* of unique interest.  It contains contributions from the pens of Indians who have the true welfare of the race at heart, and from friends of the red man who have a constructive message.  All shades of thought are given.  The discussion is open, free and earnest.  The editorial board consists of five Indians who are university graduates.  The editor-general is connected officially with the University of the State of New York.  The *Quarterly Journal* is a high-grade publication, and is an epoch-making departure in the history of the race.

There are three general classes of membership, Active, Associate, and Junior.  Active members are persons of Indian blood; Associates are persons not Indians; Juniors are persons less than twenty-one years of age.

Each year a national conference is held at some convenient point, and in connection with some great university.  Four successful conferences have been held.  Each has been of great importance to the Indian race and has assisted materially in bringing the Indian problem to a point where it is nearer solution.

The old-time, non-English-speaking Indian was reverent towards the "unknown" or mystery.  He did not blaspheme.  "Why do the white men ask the Great Spirit to curse them so often?"  This was uttered by a pagan, White Head, a Cheyenne chief, in the presence of Col. Carrington at Fort Phil Kearney in 1866.

There were a vast number of good traits in the old Indian and we must not overlook them.  Mr. Wright (*page 314*) has referred to theft. They stole from other tribes — that was proper — but not from each other.  Frankness was a trait everywhere apparent, and Indians spoke their minds freely.  Deceit was for the enemy — deceit as to trail, purpose, trade and so forth.  Among themselves (in the tribe) there was no such thing as trickery.  Exaggerations were indulged in by story-tellers, of course. But such deceit as white people practice upon each other was unknown in the olden days.

All the writers, past and present, agree that the bulk of our Indians were governed by certain moral codes. There never was a real degenerate among Indians, until white people came among them. In all our efforts to uplift the Indian during the present crucial transition period, we should encourage those good qualities (even though they be tinged with superstition). We should build upon the natural foundation of Indian character. If we utterly destroy the past, we cannot save the Indian.

I am no idealist. I am quite aware that there are good Indians and bad Indians, as there are good white people and bad white people; but I contend that if there is a general breaking down of the Indian character — which may or may not be true — it is due to us and not to the Indian.

As to his sense of honor, and his morality, Leupp presents the following: —

"Has the Indian a basic sense of moral responsibility sufficiently robust to be capable of high religious development? Let me tell you a true story. A number of years ago a group of twenty Indians who had been in controversy with the authorities in Washington entered into a solemn pact not to accept certain money which the Government was preparing to distribute among their tribe in three or four successive payments, because they believed that that would be a surrender of the principle for which they had been contending. Later the questions at issue were cleared up by a judicial decision which left the Indians' protest not a leg to stand on. Nineteen of the twenty, including a candidate for the chiefship who had led the party into their attempt at resistance, bowed to the inevitable, took the money offered them at the next payment, and applied for the instalments then in arrears. The twentieth man, whose English name was Bill, stood out alone in his refusal to touch anything, but refused to tell why. Soon afterward I visited the reservation on business, and he sought me privately and opened his heart. He was poor, and his family were actually in need of some things the money would buy; so I tried to make him feel more comfortable by assuring him that the withdrawal of the others from their mutual agreement left him free to do as he wished.

" 'No,' he declared; adding, in a phraseology which I shall not try to imitate, 'we are all bound by a vow. I swore that I would not take my share of that money, and I must not. The others may change if they choose, but they cannot release me from my oath.'

" 'That is honorable, certainly,' I answered; 'but if you feel so strongly about it, why did you come to me for advice?'

" 'There is something you can tell me, and I am afraid to trust the others. I vowed for myself and not for my family, though they have not drawn their shares either. Now, can they get their money even if I don't touch mine?'

"I said that I could get it for them.

" 'What becomes of my money if I don't take it?'

" 'It will accumulate in the Treasury, and be paid to your heirs after your death.'

" 'You have made my heart glad,' exclaimed Bill, laying his hand affectionately on my shoulder while his face beamed with satisfaction. 'That is the way I would have it. I felt right in standing out, but I did not want my wife and children to suffer if I were wrong.'

"A cynic might find the moral of this story to be that only one Indian in twenty is high-minded enough to hold his ground against such temptation. But it would be fairer to temper that judgment with the inquiry, how the proportions would have arranged themselves in a like number of any other race?"*

Two years ago, when the Board of United States Indian Commissioners met in Washington, the representatives of practically all the missionary organizations appeared and a full and frank discussion ensued. It is no exaggeration to state that all of these persons representing varied interests (and twenty years ago these very people might have been considered rivals) left with a resolve to carry on their work with due regard for the rights of others. It is quite clear that if the Catholics have a successful mission on Reservation A, and the Presbyterians on Reservation B, that the good work should continue, and those in charge of mission A should not seek to establish a post on Reservation B, unless it is perfectly clear that Mission B is unable to care for more than a portion of the Indians. That where different denominations are located on the larger reservations, they should all work in harmony, looking toward the great purpose for which such worthy organizations exist.

It is true that the Indians in former years did not understand our religion, and that confusion existed in the minds of the untutored aborigines in the past for the very reason that representatives of different sects worked at cross-purposes. This is said in no disrespect whatsoever, it is merely a statement of facts. Mr. Leupp presents an illuminating illustration on this subject.

"Indians are always greatly puzzled by the differences between the sects, and the appearance of hostility so often assumed by one toward

---

* The Indian and His Problem, page 303.

another. It has little effect to assure them that all the sects are but parts of one religious body, worshipping the same deity. Doctrinal subtleties are of course beyond the reach of the ordinary Indian's mind, but in matters of discipline he discovers what seem to him serious incongruities. An old chief once expressed to me his deep concern because a missionary had warned his children that they would be punished after death if they broke the Sabbath with their accustomed games, yet he had seen with his own eyes a missionary playing tennis on Sunday. Another raised in my presence, with a sly suggestion of satire in his tone, the question of marriage. One missionary, he told us — referring to a visit from a Mormon apostle several years before — had four wives, and said it was good in the sight of the white man's God; the missionary who preached at the agency school had only one wife, and said that that was all right, but it would be wicked for him to marry any more; but the priest who came once in a while to bless the children had no wife at all, and said that the white man's God would be displeased with him if he took even one."*

The powerful missionary organizations, comprising as they do, hundreds of earnest workers, will accomplish much more for "Indian uplift" if they devote their energies to "pagan Whites ' as well as to the pagan Indians. The worst people I have met had white, and not red skins. These men swarm about all Indian communities. Enough evidence against their character has been brought before the benevolent organizations and Washington, to convince the most skeptical. Suppose the Indians of a certain region were found to be swindling each other, importing whiskey, gambling, stealing and committing all sorts of crimes. Immediately half a dozen organizations would raise funds and send their best workers to "lead the pagans from darkness into light." It has been clearly shown that the worst elements of our white race are responsible for the deplorable condition of thousands of Indians. Yet, I fail to observe any concerted effort to check this evil at its source. No one seems to realize that the "pagan White" is vastly more in need of reformation than his red brother. We have tried to save the Indian — meanwhile permitting whiskey and graft, immorality and greed, to continue virtually unchecked. We tell him to be upright, yet we surround him by examples of civilization, the antithesis of that which we preach. No wonder the Indian loses faith in us and our culture. Some wealthy man or woman will do the Indian a great and good service by liberally endowing a score of missions to labor among the "pagan Whites", living near (or in) Indian communities.

* Page 296.

NAVAHO WOMAN WEAVING A BLANKET

From "Indian Blankets and their Makers," by G. W. James

# CHAPTER XXVIII. IRRIGATION PROJECTS

The Indians of the Southwest in both ancient and modern times built dams, dug irrigation canals and watered certain tracts more or less extensive in area. The subject of agriculture as conducted in arid regions by the Indians is an exceedingly interesting one and has been treated briefly by Doctor Hodge in the Handbook of American Indians. Many of the modern canals in Arizona, New Mexico and California follow the old ditches dug by the Cliff Dwellers, Pueblos and other tribes. Excepting the Apaches and Comanches, probably all southwestern Indians understood and made use of irrigation in the raising of crops.

Some of the military and scientific expeditions to the Southwest in early times found the Pima, Maricopa, Papago, Pueblo and other Indians in possession of large, cultivated fields. With the influx of white settlers in the later '70's and early '80's, not only was much of this land appropriated by the Whites, but the water was diverted, thus causing the Indians great privations. I have referred elsewhere in this book to the case of the Pimas, and that of the Maricopas, Yumas and Pueblos, and it has been commented upon in a score of reports. Briefly summed up, we have well-nigh destroyed (or rather appropriated) the entire irrigation zone formerly controlled by the Indians. Their fields and ditches have passed to us.

A movement has been inaugurated to save what little remains. In this humane work the Indian Rights Association and the Board of Indian Commissioners, as well as the Indian Office, have all played prominent parts. When Hon. F. H. Abbott became acting Commissioner he made a study of this subject, and later, as Secretary of the Board of Indian Commissioners, he prepared an exhaustive paper entitled, "Briefs on Indian Irrigation and Indian Forests." This was presented to the Senate Committee on Indian Affairs, February 9th, 1914. It covers the entire irrigation problem, and I insert most of it herewith.

"The proposed amendment relating to Indian irrigation, you will observe, is sweeping in character. Its main and central purpose is to stop the gratuitous use of tribal and Government funds in the construction and maintenance of irrigation projects, to charge the costs thereof against the lands benefited or against the pro rata shares in the tribal funds, when distributed, of the individual Indians whose lands are benefited, and to give the Indians a voice in the expenditure of their own funds for irrigation purposes and make them share the responsibility of maintaining and operating the completed projects.  If this amendment is enacted into law nearly $400,000 carried each year in the Indian appropriation acts as gratuity items will become reimbursable.  The facts relating to existing irrigation law and practice and arguments in support of the proposed amendment are fully elaborated in the brief submitted herewith, to which I invite your careful attention.

"The proposed amendment relating to the care, protection, and sale of Indian timber is also supported by a carefully prepared statement, herewith submitted.  This amendment, if enacted into law, will save the Government in the neighborhood of $75,000 a year.  *  *  *  *

"The difficulties of the complex problems relating to the education and civilization of the Indians of this country and to the handling of their vast property resources are increasing in direct ratio with the increase in the value of that property and the individualization thereof.

"The eyes cannot be closed to the constantly increasing administrative burdens of the Indian Bureau.  This increase can not be explained away on the ground of alleged bad administration; it is due, in large part, to the carrying out of laws enacted by Congress for the breaking up of the vast tribal estates of the Indians and to the establishment of the policy of individualization in connection therewith.  Before the volume of the business of the Indian Bureau will begin to grow less, it will become very much greater; and the value of Indian property over which the Indian Bureau is required by law to exercise supervision, now estimated at nearly one billion dollars, will undoubtedly be very much greater before it begins to grow less.

"How is the Government going to meet this growing problem?  Will Congress increase appropriations to meet the increased demands imposed by law and changing economic conditions upon the Indian Bureau?  Is there any other way out?

"Those who answer by saying, 'Give the Indians immediate citizenship and full control of their property and thus keep down the appropriations for Indian administration,' offer a correct solution only for that class of Indians who are sufficiently educated and advanced in civilization to accept the full responsibility for handling their property.  Accepting this solution for that class of Indians — and it is undoubtedly the correct solution for this class — it still remains true that the increasing value of the lands and minerals and forests on Indian reservations which are still closed to settlement, and of the property of individual Indians who are still unprepared to protect it, and the future individual allotment of lands to nearly 50 per cent of the Indians of the country, will make the administration of Indian Affairs for some years to come one of increasing difficulty and expense. * * * *

"The reclamation of arid lands on Indian reservations by irrigation, to provide better homes for Indian families, and to bring to them the benefits of civilized society through the agricultural development of their lands, is one of the most beneficent policies the Government has ever inaugurated in dealing with their affairs. Too much credit can not be given to Senators and Congressmen and administrative officers of the Government who have had to do with the enactment of laws and the securing of appropriations to carry out this policy. The motives of legislators have been benevolent and patriotic, and the work of the Government engineers and other officials who have constructed the projects has been honest and comparatively efficient and economical. However, a careful examination of Indian irrigation laws and conditions prevailing in connection with their administration reveals defects which need remedy. It is no reflection upon the high motives of those responsible for present law and present conditions that these defects exist. It was a new legislative and administrative field. Irrigation laws were not uniform in the several States. Conditions varied on different Indian reservations. The legislation was necessarily experimental. Nevertheless, the defects are serious, they should be faced frankly, and the remedies needed should be applied promptly to preserve the good in the existing order of things and eliminate the bad before greater harm results.

"Lack of uniformity in Indian irrigation laws, lack of utilization by Indians of their irrigated lands, lack of a voice on the part of the Indians in the expenditure of their funds for the construction and maintenance of their irrigation projects, and failure to individualize the reclamation costs by charging them against the lands benefited are the most serious fundamental defects of the present situation.

"Approximately nine million dollars have been expended for the irrigation of Indian lands. About seven millions of this amount have been charged to tribal funds and the balance expended from gratuity appropriations made by Congress. About 600,000 acres of irrigable Indian lands have been brought under ditch. Of this area less than 100,000 acres are being irrigated by Indians, while a large part of the area thus irrigated is not farmed, but is used to produce hay crops. And, notwithstanding the fact that either tribal or Government funds have been used to irrigate these lands, on all except three reservations, when patents in fee are issued to Indian allottees, and in every case where their lands are sold under the supervision of the Government, either the individual Indian who sells the land or the purchaser thereof puts in his pocket the value of the water right for which the tribe or the Government has paid; and not only are the members of the tribe not consulted with respect to the expenditure of their money, which ultimately passes in this manner either to the individual allottee or to the white purchaser of his land, but the individual whose land is benefited is given no opportunity to assume any responsibility in connection therewith or to appreciate the value of the benefit conferred, while the free-water right thus secured by the individual Indian offers a constant inducement to him to part with his land.

NAVAHO HOME, NEW MEXICO

"Some striking illustrations of the lack of utilization of irrigable Indian lands may be found on the following reservations: On the Crow Reservation, where irrigation ditches have been completed for more than ten years and where the total area under constructed ditches is estimated at 68,756 acres, only 11,376 acres are irrigated by Indians, and most of this is irrigated for hay crops; on the Flathead Reservation the present irrigable area is estimated at 38,000 acres, but only 1,088 acres are irrigated by Indians; on the Fort Belknap Reservation, out of 22,000 acres under ditch, 7,670 acres are irrigated by Indians; on Fort Hall Reservation Indians irrigate only 3,300 acres out of present irrigable area of 35,000 acres; on the Wind River Reservation the Indians are irrigating approximately 5,000 acres out of a total irrigable area of 35,000 acres, and most of this area is irrigated for hay crops; on the Uintah Reservation, out of a total irrigable area of 87,880 acres the Indians are irrigating approximately 6,000 acres; on the Yakima Reservation, where the present irrigable area is 54,000 acres, the Indians are irrigating 5,350 acres; and at Yuma the Indians are irrigating approximately 200 acres out of an irrigable area of 4,000 acres. In the reservations of the Southwest the showing of utilization of irrigable lands is very much better.

"The lack of utilization noted in the foregoing paragraph is serious enough from an industrial standpoint, but it is fraught with peculiar dangers in the case of the reservations where the water rights are subject to the operation of State law. On the Fort Hall Reservation (Idaho) beneficial use must be made of the water for the irrigable lands prior to the year 1916, in order to prevent the appropriation of the water by other water users; on the Wind River Reservation in Wyoming beneficial use must likewise be made before 1916; and on the Uintah Reservation (Utah) beneficial use must be made before 1919. The total investment in the construction of irrigation ditches and the purchase of water rights on these three reservations amounts to approximately $2,000,000, and in the case of the Wind River and Uintah Reservations the expenditure has been made from Indian funds.

"Lack of proper utilization can not be charged to the indolence of the Indian. The present system is doubtless responsible for an undue lack of interest and indifference on his part. He has not been consulted in advance of the expenditure; the cost of the construction and the expense of maintenance on the basis of each acre irrigated have not been explained and brought home to him; the money being taken out of a tribal fund which has never become a part of his individual possession, he has not understood his intimate individual interest in its expenditure, nor has he realized the value, in dollars and cents, of the benefit.

"In many cases irrigation on Indian reservations has been provided for in response to a perfectly natural and normal demand of white settlers, either for the opening to settlement of irrigable lands on Indian reservations or for obtaining water from streams flowing through Indian reservations for the irrigation of their lands on the outside. As a result, the construction of irrigation projects on Indian reservations has often preceded the proper preparation of the Indians for such construction and often has preceded the development of transportation facilities necessary to market the products of the land irrigated, and in the case of the large reservations in the Northwest irrigation has been brought to Indians unskilled in the art of irrigation, strangers to the art of agriculture, trained for generations to the exciting life of the chase, having no knowledge of any of the pursuits of modern civilized life except a somewhat general knowledge of the raising of cattle and horses. Generally, however, this premature development of irrigation has had sufficient justification in the necessity of such development to preserve the rights of the Indians to the water.

"One of the chief reasons for the failure of the Indians on the reservations mentioned to utilize their irrigable lands has been the failure to provide appropriations necessary to enable them to buy teams and tools and other equipment, without which the utilization of their lands is impossible. The main thought apparently has been to build the ditches, and with rare exceptions no provision has been made to use tribal funds for any other purpose than that of reimbursing the Government for the cost of construction of the project. At the same time the Indian has lacked the credit which is available to the white settler living under similar conditions necessary to help himself. Through the policy of reimbursable appropriations established during the last few years Congress has begun to prepare a remedy for these conditions. But on a majority of the reservations mentioned above, Indians are still in a position where they have to sit idly by and witness the expenditure of their own funds in the construction and maintenance of irrigation ditches which, under present conditions, they cannot use and in which expenditures they have no voice — helpless, though they have more than ample resources in their undeveloped lands to secure money advances necessary to make productive use thereof.

"Another reason for the lack of adequate utilization of Indian lands may be found in the failure to adjust the size of the allotment of irrigable land to the conditions of soil and climate and the industrial habits and needs of the Indians. While in the Southwest, on the Colorado River and Yuma Reservations and several others, allotments have been made in 10-acre tracts, and in some cases smaller, suitable to the methods of intensive agriculture practiced in that section of country, this policy has been lacking almost universally in the reservations of the Northwest, where in most cases allotment has been made under the general allotment act, which did not take into consideration the question of possible irrigation. The allotment of 80 acres to each man, woman, and child is found under the irrigation projects on the Yakima, Uintah, Crow, Wind River, Flathead, and Southern Ute (diminished) Reservations while on Blackfeet and Fort Peck the size of the allotment is 40 acres, and on Fort Hall 40 acres to each head of a family and 20 acres to each other member of the tribe. Take the Uintah and Wind River Reservations, for example, where beneficial use is required by State law in order to protect the water rights  The average family of five members would have 400 acres of irrigable land. The average white family in the same section of the country can not utilize satisfactorily over 80, or at the most 160, acres of the same land. How can an Indian family unassisted, and especially without money or credit to buy tools and equipment, be expected to reclaim 400 acres of land?

RINCON RESERVATION, MISSION INDIANS, CALIFORNIA
Grandfather blind (trachoma).   Both children infected

"In striking contrast with the lack of agricultural development on irrigated Indian reservations, under the present system, is the marked development of agriculture during the last few years on a number of reservations in the regions of normal rainfall where Indians have had control of their own funds and the responsibility of expending them in the improvement and development of their lands, under the guidance of practical Indian Service farmers.

"The remedies needed will be suggested briefly, as follows:

"1.   General legislation that will charge the individual land benefited with the cost of construction and maintenance, payment to be made out of the share in the tribal funds of the individual whose land in benefited or from the proceeds of the sale of the land when it passes from Indian ownership where the share of the individual in the tribal fund is insufficient.

"2.   The general legislation suggested in the above paragraph should provide that the tribe whose funds it is proposed to use for the construction of irrigation projects shall be first consulted.

"3.   The proposed general legislation should also provide for charging of costs of maintenance and operation against the lands under the project and should give the Indians whose lands are benefited a voice in said maintenance and operation.

"4.   In order not to overburden irrigated Indian lands by the legislation suggested, especially since the Indians have not heretofore been consulted, the costs of supervisory engineering and of experimental construction and cost of investigations and preliminary surveys should be excluded from the charges made against the lands and paid from gratuity appropriations.

"5.   Reimbursable appropriations from tribal funds should be made immediately for all Indian reservations where the utilization of irrigable lands has not kept pace with the construction of irrigation projects through lack of funds in the hands of individual Indians to make such utilization possible.

"6.   Skilled irrigation farmers should be provided out of gratuity appropriations to give advice and assistance to Indians having irrigable lands."

# CHAPTER XXIX. THE BUFFALO

The American bison, commonly called the buffalo, occupied an extended area of the United States in ancient times. About 1850, the range of the buffalo extended from the Red River valley, Manitoba, to central Texas; through western and central Minnesota and as far west as the arid plains of Colorado, and to near the headwaters of the Missouri River in the Northwest. As settlers pushed west of the Mississippi, the buffalo disappeared from eastern Nebraska, Missouri and western Arkansas. The animal does not appear to have ranged in eastern Arkansas or Louisiana, preferring the portion of the country known as the Great Plains, and the entire Missouri River valley. In the later sixties, when the Union Pacific Railroad was built westward, hundreds of hunters were enabled to ship East unnumbered thousands of robes and great quantities of meat. The herds were further restricted, and by 1885, the buffalo almost entirely disappeared.

Of the numbers of these animals, none of the authorities seem to agree. Robert M. Wright of Dodge City, Kansas, one of the earliest pioneers, recently published a book entitled "Dodge City, the Cowboy Capital." He gives the estimates prepared by men living at the time, as to the number of buffalo. I present his remarks at some length as indicative of the difference of opinion even among those familiar with the Great Plains, of their numerical extent. It is safe to assume, however, that there were between 25,000,000 and 50,000,000 buffalo in the West in the year 1850.

"I wish here to assert a few facts concerning game, and animal life in general, in early days, in the vicinity of Fort Dodge and Dodge City.* There were wonderful herds of buffalo, antelope, deer, elk, and wild horses, big gray wolves and coyotes by the thousand, hundreds of the latter frequently being seen in bands and often from ten to fifty gray wolves in a bunch. There were also black and cinnamon bears, wildcats and mountain lions, though these latter were scarce and seldom seen so far from the mountains. General Sheridan and Major Inman were occupying my office at Fort Dodge one night, having just made a trip from Fort Supply, and called me in to consult as to how many buffaloes there were between Dodge and Supply. Taking a strip fifty miles east and fifty miles west, they had first estimated it ten billion. General Sheridan said, 'That won't do.' They figured it again, and made it one billion. Finally they reached the

---
* Pages 71-6.

conclusion that there must be one hundred million; but said, they were afraid to give out these figures; nevertheless they believed them. This vast herd moved slowly toward the north when spring opened, and moved steadily back again from the north when the grass began to grow short, and winter was setting in.

"Horace Greeley estimated the number of buffaloes at five million. I agree with him, only I think there were nearly five times that number. Mr. Greeley passed through herds of them twice. I lived in the heart of the buffalo range for nearly fifteen years. I am told that some recent writer, who has studied the buffalo closely, has placed their number at ninety million, and I think that he is nearer right than I. Brick Bond, a resident of Dodge, an old, experienced hunter, a great shot, a man of considerable intelligence and judgment, and a most reliable man as to truthfulness, says that he killed 1500 buffaloes in seven days, and his highest killing was 250 in one day; and he had to be on the lookout for hostile Indians all the time. He had fifteen "skinners," and he was only one of many hunters.

"Charles Rath and I shipped over 200,000 buffalo hides the first winter the Atchison, Topeka and Santa Fe Railroad reached Dodge City, and I think there were at least as many more shipped from there, besides 200 cars of hind-quarters and two cars of buffalo tongues."

A Kansas newspaper (*Dodge City Times*, August 18th, 1877) remarks: "Dickinson County has a buffalo hunter by the name of Mr. Warnock, who has killed as high as 658 in one winter.— *Edwards County Leader*.

"Oh, dear, what a mighty hunter! Ford County has twenty men who each have killed five times that many in one winter. The best on record, however, is that of Tom Nickson, who killed 120 at one stand in forty minutes, and who, from the 15th of September to the 20th of October, killed 2,173 buffaloes."

Colonel Richard I. Dodge, who spent thirty years on the Plains, commenting in 1880 on the value of the buffalo to the Indian, says:

"It is almost impossible for a civilized being to realize the value to the Plains Indians of the buffalo. It furnished him with home, food, clothing, bedding, house equipment, almost everything. Without it he is poor as poverty itself, and on the verge of starvation.

"Some years, as in 1871, the buffalo appeared to move northward in one immense column, oftentimes from twenty to fifty miles in width, and of unknown depth from front to rear. Other years the northward journey was made in several parallel columns, moving at the same rate and with their numerous flankers covering a width of a hundred or more miles.

"During the three years 1872-73-74, at least five millions of buffaloes were slaughtered for their hides.

"This slaughter was all in violation of law, and in contravention of solemn treaties made with the Indians, but it was the duty of no special person to put a stop to it. The Indian Bureau made a feeble effort to keep the white hunters out of Indian Territory, but soon gave it up, and these parties spread all over the country, slaughtering the buffalo under the very noses of the Indians.

"Ten years ago the Plains Indians had an ample supply of food, and could support life comfortably without the assistance of the Government. Now everything is gone, and they are reduced to the condition of paupers, without food, shelter, clothing, or any of those necessaries of life which came from the buffalo; and without friends, except the harpies, who, under the guise of friendship, feed upon them."

The first trains on the Union Pacific Railway were frequently compelled to stop for one or two days until these immense herds had crossed the tracks. The Missouri River has been known to be filled with buffalo swimming across; a boat descending or ascending the river was compelled to wait a day or two for the herds to pass. Unnumbered thousands were drowned at the time of these crossings. Prairie fires must have destroyed multitudes of these animals.

The American bison was very easily approached and killed, and a careful reading of the accounts of buffalo-hunts indicates that there was about as much real sport in the slaughter of these animals as in killing domesticated cattle. In fact, the long-horned Texas steer such as used to range the Southwest forty years ago, would probably afford more sport to men engaged in a "running hunt," than the buffalo. The latter were heavy, ponderous animals and save when stampeded, could be shot down from ambush. An "oldtimer", long on the Plains, told me that he frequently killed from fifty to seventy-five buffalo from one stand. He would secret himself on a little bluff, overlooking a ravine where the grass was exceptionally good, and from this vantage-point, using a heavy Sharpes rifle, he shot down one after another. He stated that the bulls would walk up to a fallen animal, smell of the blood, paw the dirt, and perhaps bellow a little, but until the animals got scent of him, they would not move away. Professor William T. Hornaday in the United States National Museum Reports for 1887 and 1889 has given an extended account of the buffalo and its destruction. Catlin has presented us, in earlier years, of a stirring account of a buffalo-hunt. Coming down to later times, General Custer, Colonel William F. Cody and others have pictured the excitement of the

UNITED STATES CAVALRY ATTACKING BLACK KETTLE'S VILLAGE ON THE WASHITA, NOVEMBER 27, 1868

Black Kettle was killed in the fight.   Reproduced from Col. Dodge's "Our Wild Indians"

buffalo-chase. Colonel Cody, in fifteen months, according to his own admission, slaughtered 4280.* He thus obtained the name "Buffalo Bill."

The senseless slaughter of this magnificent creature by thousands of hunters, frontiersmen, Bills and Dicks, and others between 1850 and 1880, soon brought about the near extinction of the species. A few were saved by Messrs. Allard and Conrad of Montana, the Canadian Government, our own Government, Colonel W. A. Jones (Buffalo Jones) and others. The late Senator Corbin secured a number of animals and shipped them to New Hampshire where a tract of several thousand acres was set aside as a park. All of these herds increased, and at the present time in the United States and Canada there must be nearly, if not quite, 1500 head. Thus the species is preserved. The Government had great difficulty in preventing poachers in Yellowstone Park from slaughtering the animals, and in the early nineties there were very few animals left alive. Public opinion has been aroused to the necessity of preserving this typically American animal, and it is now certain that the species will not become extinct.

Buffalo Bill, not content with his records of "big killings", took numbers of bison East during the '80's. Of these, twenty fine specimens died of pleuro-pneumonia while his show was at Madison Square Garden, New York City, during the winter of 1886-'87. The last survivors of this magnificent creature were hauled about the country and exhibited before gaping crowds. At Newark, Ohio, in the early '80's, when a boy I attended Buffalo Bill's "Wild West Show". I shall ever remember my sensations when witnessing the "grand buffalo hunt". Three or four poor, old, scarred bison were driven into the fair-ground enclosure by some whooping cow-punchers. Buffalo Bill himself dashed up alongside the lumbering animals and from a Winchester repeater discharged numerous "blanks" into the already powder-burned sides of the helpless creatures. The crowd roared with appreciation, and as the cow-punchers pursued, and rounded up the hapless bison before the grandstand, Buffalo Bill reined in his steed, and spurring the horse (so he would prance), bowed right and left.

Professor Hornady's report, together with other information, indicates that enough buffalo were carted about the East to have formed a very respectable herd — had they been permitted to remain in some favored spot in the buffalo country.

The killing of the buffalo furnished employment for the type of men who usually flock to any frontier. There was more or less excitement in the chase, the animals were absolutely defenseless, the hides and meat could be sold. But for the hostility of the Plains tribes, the buffalo would

---

* U. S. National Museum Report, 1887, page 478.

long ago have disappeared. But when the Sioux, Pawnee, Cheyenne, Arapaho, Kiowa, Omaha and others saw that the Whites would destroy their means of sustenance, they inaugurated a campaign of hostility throughout the Great Plains and the Upper Missouri country, against the Whites.

Certain communities where a large number of fearless men were assembled (such as Dodge City, Kansas,) became headquarters for the hunters, but the ranging of hunting parties throughout the entire West was restricted. This delayed the destruction of the buffalo. As I have stated, the coming of the railroad, and the subsequent building of other railroads, and steamboat navigation upon the Missouri, brought about curtailment of Indian activities and the ultimate destruction of the buffalo. I present a drawing from Wright's book in which are exhibited upwards of 40,000 buffalo hides stacked up in the corral at Dodge City.* This was in 1876. So many hides were shipped to the eastern market that the price fell to a dollar. Unnumbered thousands were sold at $1.25. I entered a furrier's store in Boston last winter and saw three buffalo robes offered for sale. The ordinary one was $75, another one was $100, and an extra fine robe was priced at $150. A few live buffalo were recently sold and the price was, I have been told, $1,000 each.

The hide-hunters killed the animal for the robe, as the name implies, and left the carcass to rot. Sometimes men took neither the hides nor the tongues, but killed for the mere pleasure of slaughtering.

It is not at all difficult for us to reconstruct the "good old buffalo days" among any of the tribes, from the Comanches of Texas to the Sioux of Minnesota. Many of the Indian bands followed the buffalo in its annual migration north or south, killing such of the animals as were needed for use and permitting the greater number to escape. There is no authentic account of early Indians slaughtering to satisfy a craving for blood. Indians sometimes killed enemies for the sheer love of slaughter, but the buffalo was not an enemy. Having obtained sufficient meat or hides, they simply quit, for they had not become "civilized".

Let us imagine some village of the period between 1850 and 1865. There are numerous accounts of such, and we need read few of them to form an accurate, though composite picture. The camp is located in some favorite spot. Young men, out upon a scout, observe the approach of a great herd, and, lashing their ponies, speed back home with the welcome news. All is excitement in the village some twenty miles to the east. Immediately the village crier gallops from one end of the encampment to the other announcing that a buffalo dance is to be held that night. Every-

* Page 182.

body prepares for the festive occasion; the shamans make their medicine; the buffalo dance paraphernalia is brought out, and until early morning hours the dance continues.

Great merriment is caused when the better dancers try to outdo each other. Much feasting follows — for are they not soon to possess an abundance of meat? An old shaman appears; the dancers pause; he informs them that his medicine is "good." No enemies are near; the dreadful white hunters are not at hand; every lodge will secure at least three buffalo. Therefore, all must prepare and be ready to begin the hunt at daybreak.

Shortly after sunrise a large portion of the Indians mounted on their most reliable "buffalo horses" (which have been trained to skillfully avoid the rushes of the bulls) pursue the herd. Each man selects a well-proportioned beast, and with rifle, arrow or lance, he brings him down.

Now, hunting buffalo with the lance, or bow and arrow, was sport. The use of a rifle required no skill. With the lance, the hunter must ride up close, thrust the lance in and swing his pony suddenly to avoid the charge of any belligerent bull. The steel-pointed arrows must be shot at close range, and when the beast was "on the jump", in order that the arrow penetrate between the ribs to a vital part. Much of the arrow's force was lost, if it struck a rib. Hence, great skill on the hunter's part was required. He must shoot or thrust at the proper moment. This was true sport — just the opposite of still hunting, the favorite pastime of the pot-and-hide hunters; far more exciting than the work of such men as Buffalo Bill, who killed in order to make "big records". When Indians hunted, the women and children and older men followed along in the wake of the advance party, removed the hides and cut up the meat.

Or, if the herd is a small one, it is surrounded by a large number of horsemen and forced to a common center. "Milling", the old frontiersmen used to call it. Indians ride furiously around the herd, making much noise, and the animals seeking to escape, crowd toward the center of the circle. Buffalo were often maimed or crushed as a result of this style of hunt. It afforded the Indians opportunity to shoot down a large number of animals before the buffalo ceased "milling" and fled in various directions.

Again, small herds were run over precipices, or into ravines having steep sides. Sometimes they were pursued to the banks of the Missouri River and shot while swimming.

Often from a village small parties of young men would go out on informal hunts, preceding which there was no special ceremony such as the buffalo dance. But as a rule, the hunts were more or less ceremonial affairs, or at least preceded by certain rites. The introduction of the

THE HIDE HUNTER

Sharpes rifle, and later the Winchester, among the Indians, changed this style of hunt and many of the Indians followed the example of the white men and hunted individually, or in small groups, rather than tribally.

Miss Alice C. Fletcher is considered an authority upon the Omaha and related tribes. Of the buffalo she says: —

"Tribal regulations controlled the cutting up of the animal and the distribution of the parts. The skin and certain parts of the carcass belonged to the man who had slain the buffalo; the remainder was divided according to certain fixed rules among the helpers, which afforded an opportunity for the poor and disabled to procure food. Butchering was generally done by men on the field, each man's portion being taken to his tent and given to the women as their property.

"The buffalo was hunted in the winter by small, independent but organized parties, not subject to the ceremonial exactions of the tribal hunt. The pelts secured at this time were for bedding and for garments of extra weight and warmth. The texture of the buffalo hide did not admit of fine dressing, hence was used for coarse clothing, moccasins, tent covers, parfleche cases, and other articles. The hide of the heifer killed in the fall or early winter made the finest robe.

"The buffalo was supposed to be the instructor of doctors who dealt with the treatment of wounds, teaching them in dreams where to find healing plants and the manner of their use. The multifarious benefits derived from the animal brought the buffalo into close touch with the people. It figured as a gentile totem, its appearance and movements were referred to in gentile names, its habits gave designations to the months, and it became the symbol of the leader and the type of long life and plenty; ceremonies were held in its honor, myths recounted its creation, and its folk-tales delighted old and young."[*]

There were many separate uses to which the entire buffalo carcass was put. I have grouped them thus: —

| FLESH | HIDE | BONES | HORNS | SINEWS | OTHER PARTS |
|---|---|---|---|---|---|
| Ordinary food | House | Shovels of shoulder-blades | Ornaments | Thread | Tallow |
| Dried for winter use | Bedding. | Grooved adzes | Cups | Bow-strings | Pemmican |
| Mixed (pounded) with other foods | Lariat | Scrapers | Club-heads | Ropes | Fuel |
| | Trunk | Flint-chippers | | | Bladder (storage) |
| | Boat | Spoons | | | Hair (Stuffings) |
| | Garments | Needles | | | |
| | Leggins | Awls, etc. | | | |
| | Footwear | Skull for ceremonies | | | |
| | | Hoof-points for rattles | | | |

[*] Handbook of American Indians. Vol. I, page 169.

It will thus be seen that he meant to many of the Plains tribes their very existence. The destruction of the buffalo meant the destruction of all. Indian chiefs were quick to foresee that if indiscriminate slaughter on the part of white people continued, the power of the Indian as a race was doomed. That is, of the Plains or "Horse" tribes. Our own army officers also were aware of this fact, and Custer, Miles, Sherman, Crook and others have stated in their reports that in order to bring the Plains Indians into subjection and control them on reservations, it was necessary to destroy the American bison. All the prominent Sioux, Cheyenne and other chiefs inspired their followers to continue the war against the white people, using as an incentive the phrase —"They are destroying the Indians' means of livelihood." Speeches of this character were always made in councils, or preceding war dances, and never failed to rouse a militant spirit.

As the Indians became settled on reservations and attempted to provide themselves with meat, robes, dwellings, etc., as formerly, they experienced great difficulty on account of the scarcity of the buffalo. It was very natural, therefore, for them to turn to the authorities at Washington for support, since the authorities had permitted the hide-hunters, frontiersmen and numerous persons who flocked to the frontier at the close of the Civil War, to engage in lawless acts. These Indians were not agriculturalists, and yet they had always supported themselves. Their inter-tribal wars, while at some times serious, never resulted in the total destruction of a large band. In fact, too much has been made of the wars between the Crows and the Sioux, or the Ojibwa and the Sioux, or those between other bands. The existence that they led, in the good old buffalo days, was to them ideal. And from their point of view we must admit that they speak truly when they so declare. Many an old Indian has told me he would rather "take chances on a piece of lead" in olden times, than live as he does today. The effect of this lawless element on Indian life has been overlooked by other writers. They have minimized its pernicious effect. We know they were free from disease, until white men came among them; they desired nothing further than to be properly fed, clothed and housed. The destruction of the buffalo put an end to all of this, and the presence of the military further curtailed their activities. Hence the reservation and ration system sprang up.

But it seems to me, we have all minimized one great truth. Having destroyed that which was the very life of these Indians, we should have given them something in its place. The Indian frequently asked for stock, but it was not until years afterwards that stock in any numbers was issued to them. The issue of cattle to the Plains Indians was much curtailed because of reports from Agents and Superintendents, during the eighties, that the Indians killed much of this stock for food. All the Plains tribes were meat-eaters and not vegetarians. We could not expect them to live where there was no meat available, save their own cattle. Agriculture was (and among the Sioux, still is) in its infancy.

A gentleman living in northern Nebraska, who has been familiar with the Sioux for forty years, writes me on this point as follows: —

CREEK CHURCH AND CAMP-MEETING GROUND NEAR SYLVIAN, OKLAHOMA, 1913

"On the spring round-up of the year that Major Clapp left Pine Ridge, (thirty years ago) these Indians branded over 16,000 calves; and horses dotted the hills in herds of from fifty to several hundred head each. At this time there are a few herds of small proportion, and the calves produced by the entire four counties that originally comprised the reservation, is numbered by a paltry few hundred."

What the Government did was to permit the destruction of the buffalo, corral the Indians, expect them to change from the chase to agriculture, or, it utterly destroyed their sustenance and commanded: —"Become as white men," all within one or two decades. This was, manifestly, impossible. The ration system was a necessity, not a mere gratuity, as so many of the writers have maintained. Without a ration system, these Indians would have starved to death. If large numbers of cattle had been issued them, and they had been compelled to save a certain portion of these for breeding purposes, and thus increased their herds, we should certainly have avoided a great deal of misery.

Be this as it may, it is quite clear that the extinction of the bison worked a hardship not only to the Indians, but was a great monetary loss to our own nation. The frontier element responsible should have been controlled. Canada has not been cursed with the class of Bills and Dicks who roamed at will the Great Plains in our own country between 1850 and 1880. Canada had, and has, a great many Indians in her northwestern possessions. Her white population was, numerically, far weaker than our own between these periods of time. Such a united band as Red Cloud led against Fort Fetterman in 1866 could have utterly destroyed all the white settlers in western Canada were the chiefs so inclined. The very fact that they never attacked the Canadians, and that immediately south of the boundary between the two countries, bloodshed was rampant from 1850 to 1880, indicates that the Canadian authorities adopted a much wiser policy than that followed by our easy-going officials at Washington. If we possessed a mounted police service such as that long ago established in the Canadian northwest, roving hunters, and undesirable citizens responsible for most of the Indian wars, could have been held in check.

As time passes, and men view dispassionately the events of the Plains, our historians will record that most of the wars had their origin with ourselves. The Indians never began them.

# CHAPTER XXX.   THE PLAINS INDIANS FIFTY YEARS AGO
## AND TODAY

Robert M. Wright, Esq., of Dodge City, Kansas, located in that State when a boy, in the early '50's.   There are few men living at the present time who have had a more varied and interesting career.

In Mr. Wright's recent book, "Dodge City The Cowboy Capital", I was struck with its frankness.   The book presents a true picture of life among buffalo-hunters, scouts, gamblers, stock-men and others.   I wrote to this aged frontiersman and asked him to give me an absolute, frank opinion as to the cause of the Indian wars, and his views upon our Indian policy.   In return he sent me a lengthy communication which illuminates events on the Plains between the years 1855 and 1890.

Mr. Wright is one of the few living men who observed Indians from the pioneer point of view.   Mr. Wright's observations, which he kindly furnished me, are the more important in that they are offered by one who has not held Indians in very high esteem.   Mr. Wright saw some of his warmest friends shot down during Indian raids.   His narrative, if anything, should be rather prejudiced against the Indians.   Yet it is not so, as will be observed by perusal of the following pages.

Before presenting quotations from his manuscript I shall sum up briefly his general observations.   Looking back upon a career of upwards of sixty years throughout the West (chiefly in Kansas and Nebraska,) Mr. Wright concludes that the Plains Indian was vastly better off when able to roam, unhampered by anyone, throughout the country, than at the present time.   He speaks of the great and interesting Kiowa village located some distance from Dodge City about 1868.   Living in central and southern Kansas, he came in contact, not so much with the Sioux, but with the Pawnees, who occupied the flat country, and the Horse Indians, which included the Kiowa, Comanche, Cheyenne, Arapaho and Prairie Apache.   As to the wars among themselves, he thinks that the number of killed, or damage inflicted upon villages has been exaggerated. Usually, there were few casualties in these actions.   Some writers might not agree with him, but this is his opinion.   Occasionally, one band would surprise a village and take many captives and scalps.   He was impressed in the early days with the good health of these Indians, their hardiness, and that they were seldom visited by epidemics.   Smallpox broke out along the Missouri River, and to the east and north, but seldom in southern Kansas and northern Texas.   He declares that there was no tuberculosis or trachoma when he first went among these people.  The general standard of character and virtue was much higher.

"As has been said, the Indian was by nature a warrior and hunter, and was trained as such from earliest childhood.  It is taken for granted, by the great mass of civilized peoples, that the uncivilized redskin had no idea of education.  This is an error.  For years, I was among the wild Indians of half a century ago, and I know from personal observation that they had as thorough a system of education for their children, in their line, as that boasted by the civilized white race.  From the time the Indian child was able to walk, his or her education began.  The first lesson usually consisted in being strapped upon the back of a docile pony and taking a little practice in riding.  In the second step in education he was made to become familiar with the bow and arrow, which were the Indians' favorite weapons, half a century ago.  At the age of five, perhaps, the father took the boy out upon the hills adjoining the camp and admonished him to be observant of what he saw.  Every ravine and hill, a buffalo skeleton, a rock or tree, a footprint in the sand or grass, the displacement of a stick or stone — all these things and many more a child must study and learn to notice.  He must learn to readily detect the different marks on bows, arrows, and moccasins, distinguishing as to which tribe they belonged, as every tribe had a peculiar mark of its own for its manufactured articles. When the father and child came back to the tipi, after a day of observation, the child was required to give a description of what he had seen during the long tramp, the father or teacher questioning him.  The child must give an intelligent and comprehensive account of his observations, or be taken over the same ground again and again until he could do so and had acquired a thorough knowledge of the territory covered.  As soon as the child had familiarized himself minutely with one section of the country, he was taken to another and yet another, until, finally  he was intimately acquainted with all the territory adjacent to the camp.  These same methods were employed in familiarizing the young Indian with more extended ranges of country until, at last, he thoroughly understood his surroundings for hundreds of miles.

"But there were many other subjects in that course.  For instance, the young Indian was expected to learn signalling, similar to that of our signal corps.  Indians well versed in signalling could communicate accurately with each other though many miles apart.  This knowledge was augmented by detailed instruction and drill in matters of war, the trail, and the chase.  Some of the old-time scouts, who were with us, had been captured in childhood and raised and educated by the Indians.  These were as proficient in Indian tactics as the Indians themselves, and were very valuable to have along with a command in Indian campaigns as scouts and guides. They could follow up a trail, tell the number of ponies, give the number of Indians in the party being trailed, and, in fact, by their Indian lore, could know the movements of such a party about as well as those comprising it knew them. The Indian was as fond of his boys as any white father could be, and took pride in their training."

Of the buffalo, he claims, as have all writers, that the very existence of the Plains Indians was threatened when that noble animal was exterminated. A great enmity sprang up between the Indians and the white hunters.

"With this hatred and enmity, the Indian blended a certain fear of the white hunters, and to the credit of the redskin's courage it can be said that the hunters were the only class on earth that he did fear, while with his fear was mixed also a sort of desperation. The Indian hunted altogether on horseback, with bow and arrow or lance, which they planted in the side of the animal by riding up alongside of him. The Indians claimed they killed only for meat or robes, and, as soon as they had sufficient, they stopped and went home; whereas, the white hunters never knew when they had enough, and were continually harassing the buffaloes from every side, never giving the herds a chance to recover, but keeping up a continual pop-pop from their big guns. Only under the most favorable circumstances would the Indians attack the hunters. They were afraid of the latters' big guns, cool bravery, and, last but not least, of their unerring, deadly aim. The passing of the buffalo herds, because of the white men, was one of the prime causes of Indian hostility.

"But the feeling over the buffalo was only one of the causes of the Plains wars. To understand other causes, one should consider the Indian as he was found by the first white men, and compare him with what he was after his association with the Whites for a term of years. It can clearly be seen, by such a comparison, that a great change took place, in that time, in the Indian's attitude and sentiments toward the Whites, and this change could not have been due to anything but the influence of association. The redskin acquired knowledge, also confidence in himself. Then followed hostile feelings awakened by the mismanagement and needless cruelty of the Whites. The Indian seemed to learn and adopt every vice of the Whites but not one of their virtues.

"When I first crossed the Plains in 1859, we met several bands of Indians. In fact we struck about the first and much the biggest number at the great bend of the Arkansas River, a little east of where the town of Great Bend now stands and from there on we met them up to seventy-five miles west of old Fort Lyon in eastern Colorado. There was no military fort there then, nor any west of Fort Riley to Fort Garland in the mountains, and there was no need of any, for the Indians were supposed to be friendly, which indeed they were. This part of the country was the chief resort of the Kiowas, Comanches, Cheyennes, Arapahoes, and Prairie Apaches. Here, on the Arkansas River, near the present site of Great Bend, is where they all congregated. Up to 1864, all the Indians mentioned were considered peaceable and were so to a great extent. When they caught parties of Whites south of the Arkansas River (which was sacred ground to them, where no trespassers were allowed) there was trouble. Only traders were allowed in that region, and they had to be well known and familiar with the Indians to be safe. If an unknown trader ventured down there, he was stripped of his goods, whipped severely, often killed, and his wagons burned. But along the great Santa Fe Trail small parties of Whites, and even single individuals, went through without being molested, though I have seen these peaceable Indians, at such times, treated with the utmost contempt and actual abuse by the white travelers.

"The propensity to beg or steal seemed born in the original Plains Indian. They made away with any portable article at hand from seemingly sheer love of theft. And beg! they would beg one blind! They wanted everything in sight, yet in early days, they made no disturbance if they were given nothing. It actually seemed as if an Indian could not help begging or stealing, but, instead of accepting this as a fact and treating it accordingly with wise leniency, the Whites made use of needless cruelty. When an Indian picked up something and hid it under his blanket to carry away, he was blacksnaked, or kicked out of camp. I once saw an Indian climb up on the hind wheel of a big freight wagon and lift up the wagon sheet. As he was peeping in, with his back bent and body exposed much as if he were bent over a barrel, a bull-whacker, with a big ox-whip, stood off ten feet and let him have it on the naked skin. That Indian dropped as if he were shot, with a gash where the lash struck as if a sharp knife had cut him. There were many other Indians in camp, and they all jumped up and halloed and laughed uproariously at the discomfited one, who crept humbly out of camp. Many indignities like this were given the Indians without their retaliating, even though there were often many more Indians than Whites in the party, which conclusively proves the superior peacefulness of the redskin. This was as late as 1863. But soon there came a change.

**OGLALA  WOMAN**

Pine Ridge, 1909.   Photographed by W. K. Moorehead

"The Indian wars of the Plains were more the result of a combination of causes, added to those already mentioned. First, our Government commenced a wishy-washy, desultory course with the Indians, instead of taking a bold, firm stand with them, and bringing out enough soldiers to overawe and make them respect the Government by showing them how strong it was, thus making them understand what to expect if they did not behave themselves. The Government policy was so weak at the beginning, that the Indians actually laughed at it and said: 'The Government is afraid of us; it dare not punish us'; and this was their real belief. I heard some Kiowas braggingly say, 'Why, we can whip the United States, for it has been fighting Texas for years and cannot whip her. We go and sweep down upon her settlements, kill, burn, and destroy, drive off stock, take women and children prisoners, and make the settlers glad to hide.' This was at the time of the Civil War, and the Kiowas thought the Government was fighting only Texas.

"Now then, as I have said, the Government began with the Indians in a very feeble way and sent a few troops after them, which, of course, the Indians bested and forced to retreat. Then a large force was sent which also was beaten, and, after repeated little fights and skirmishes, large armies were sent out. Usually, however, the Indians got the best of the troops and were thus emboldened and given new confidence in themselves and their strength.

"I have been a stockman all my life, and whenever my cattle became 'breachy', if the break they made in my fence was poorly mended, it was broken through again and again. Each time we repaired the fence a little better than before, but each time, also, the cattle acquired fresh skill and force in breaking down the fence. At last, it was impossible to fix the fence in a way that my herds could not break through. If I had made the fence good and strong when first repairing it, the trouble would have been settled at once, and the cattle would never have broken it down the second time. A comparison between my haphazard fence and breachy cattle, and the Government's Indian policy of years ago is the most fitting I can make."

Wright believes that the military authorities at Washington were rather responsible for continuation of an unwise policy toward the Indians, and is somewhat critical as to the plans of campaign. It was a great mistake to send infantry against Indians, but this was repeatedly done. In the Fetterman massacre, the troops were infantry. The cavalry horses of the '60's and '70's were grain-fed, and extra large. Cavalry commands were accompanied by a wagon-train in which grain and hay were hauled.

Hence, prior to Custer's later campaigns, the American cavalry made little progress as against Indians. The latter went very light, carrying a little dried buffalo meat, guns and ammunition. Each Indian warrior always possessed an extra horse — his war pony — which was never ridden except in battle. He rode his ordinary pony, and led the other. In this way the Indian soldiers had an advantage over the white cavalry. Mr. Wright says that the Indians feared winter attacks on their camps. They seldom made war during cold weather. The warriors endeavored to lead the troops away from their permanent villages.

"General Sully found this out, in 1868, when he supposed he was marching upon an Indian village from which the families had been removed and hidden in another direction, while the warriors led Sully on a wild-goose chase into the Wichita Mountains. It is a wonder his whole command was not annihilated, and if he had followed the Indians a little further, not a soldier would have escaped, the trap was so well set. But Sully realized the danger just in time, turned around, got out of the mountains almost by a miracle, returning to Fort Dodge for reinforcements, with the Indians harassing him all the way back. This ambush and defeat was a source of great mortification to General Sully. General Custer then took the field with big reinforcements, and surprised the Indian camp on the Wichita River; but, after the attack, Custer, too, was forced to beat a hasty retreat to Camp Supply, as he found himself greatly out-numbered — nearly ten to one. He inflicted on the Indians a severe punishment, taking nearly two hundred women and children prisoners, which greatly disheartened the Indians for a while. But this success was in the dead of winter, and might have resulted differently had it happened in the summer season, with the Indian fighting according to his views of proper war tactics. (*See picture, page 302.*)

"It was a big mistake of the National Government to appoint civilians and representatives of different religious denominations as Government Agents. We should have appointed army officers instead, at a post where there was also an agency. This was merely a necessity of the times and conditions, clearly visible to anybody in the least acquainted with the needs of the situation. Soldiers were always stationed at an agency, the commander of that post was always subject to the orders of the Agent, a civilian often wholly unqualified to direct military movements or frontier exploits, and the ideas of commander and Agent were nearly always in conflict. The officer bitterly resented being subject to the Agent's orders and certainly the former, familiar as he was with the border and Indian, knew better than the Agent could know, coming as he did, as a rule, direct from civilized centers. While treating them kindly and fairly, an army officer would have governed the Indian with a firm hand, and with none of the little less than criminal weakness displayed by many of the Agents. Moreover, most of the Agents were not good men, and not only robbed the Indian but starved him. I personally knew of graft practised by several Agents by which the Indian suffered greatly. Let me cite one of many instances of weakness that fell under my own observation. Mr. Darlington, Agent of the Cheyenne and Arapaho, was a good old Quaker, but weak and unsophisticated to a marked degree. I was sutler for the soldiers at this agency, and these Indians had stolen a lot of horses and mules from me. One issue day, the Indians rode in, and I saw several of my horses and mules, bearing my brand, among their stock. Now, the Indians who had possession of my horses belonged to Stone Calf's band. Stone Calf was one of the head chiefs of the Cheyennes, a man of more than ordinary intelligence, and a pretty truthful Indian. I went to Mr. Darlington, told my story, and asked him to recover my stock for me. He promised to do so, sent for Stone Calf, and said to him: 'This young man is truthful and honest, and he says you have a lot of his stock (describing the brand). Now, Stone Calf, you are a good, honest, truthful Indian, and I have always found you square; give this young man back his stock.' Stone Calf drew himself up with superb dignity and fairly breathed disdain at the Agent's suggestion. 'I have no doubt that this stock *did* belong to the young man,' he replied, 'but it belongs to *me* now. I took it when I was at war, and I never give back anything I take when I am at war.' That settled the matter and I never recovered my stock. An army officer in the Agent's place would have said: 'This stock belongs to Wright; give it up to him at once!' and he would have been obeyed and nothing more would have come of it.

"Again, had military instead of civilian Agents been appointed, the wholesale robbery of the Indians already mentioned, and system of graft in general that went on would have been largely avoided, the Indian benefited, and trouble averted. Remote as he always was from surveillance, with large quantities of Government supplies entrusted to his care for the use of the Indians, the temptation to dishonest practices for private gain was great to every Agent. Mr. Darlington, already mentioned as Agent of the Cheyennes, was as honest an old man as ever lived and, being so, seemed to think everyone else honest too, but his employees stole from the Indians right and left, and robbed them right along, under his very eye, and he was not aware of what was going on. The graft of the agencies was notoriously well-known on the frontier, and many an Agent became actually rich from the spoils of his office.  The Indians realized the state of affairs and resented it, and added it as another brand to the fire of their hostility against the Whites.  The big old chief Red Cloud once said: 'I don't see why the Government changes our Agents.  When one Agent gets rich at his trade of looking after us and has about all he wants, he may stop his stealing and leave us the property which belongs to us, if he keeps his place.  But when one man grows fat at our expense, he is removed and a lean man sent to take his place, and we must fill his belly till he is fat also, and give way to another lean one!' "

Mr. Wright calls attention to the fact that the army officer was a better judge of human nature than the civilian and he further had the advantage of discipline.  Surrounded as he was by numerous associates aspiring to promotion, he dared not steal Government supplies lest he be found out, and drummed out of the army.  With a civilian it was very different.

"History gives no more striking example in proof of feeble Governmental policy with the Plains Indians in combination with the pitiful incapacity of some of the civilian Agents, than the story of the last Indian raid through western Kansas and Nebraska in 1878.  It seems that for no better reason than that they wished to have all the Cheyenne Indians in one band, the Indian officials of the Government gave orders for the removal of the Northern Cheyennes from their agency in Dakota, to that of the Southern Cheyennes at Fort Reno, in what is now Oklahoma.  The Northern Cheyennes did not wish to move and protested vigorously, but in vain.  Being unused to the southern climate, it was not long after their arrival at Fort Reno, before malaria appeared among them, numbers became sick and many died.  Terror-stricken at this almost unknown experience, they became possessed with the idea that the water they had to drink in the new country was poisoned, and that all would die if they remained.  Going to the Agent, they begged to be allowed to return to their northern home, but were refused.  Then provisions began to grow scarce.  The Cheyennes applied to the Agent for permission to go on a buffalo hunt to gain food.  Permission was granted, but the buffalo had been practically exterminated in that locality, and, though they hunted for days, not a buffalo could be found, and the poor savages were in worse condition than before.  They were forced to kill their few scrawny ponies for meat to sustain life until they could return to the agency, and there they killed their dogs and lived upon them for a while.  Again they begged to be permitted to return to the North, and again they were refused.  In pity for their distress, however, the Commander of the fort gave orders that a small ration should be distributed among them, but it is almost certain that a large portion of this was confiscated by unscrupulous assistants, and that very little of it ever reached the needy Indians. Their condition rendered them fairly desperate. They resolved to return to Dakota at any cost. 'We may as well die fighting,' said Dull Knife, the Cheyenne chief and leader, 'as to stay here and die of starvation.' They began stealing and concealing guns, ammunition, and what provisions they could spare from their scanty stock. When ready to start, they stole horses, and, with a few mounted warriors, their foraging operations were rapidly extended until an abundance of mounts, arms, and provisions were obtained. Women and children took part in the exodus, and the march was very leisurely, but notwithstanding this fact, the troops sent in pursuit were defeated in battle about sixty miles from Reno, and afterwards proceeded in so careless a fashion, that the Indians were not again overtaken till they reached Sand Creek, about forty miles south of Dodge City. Here, however, the troops completely surrounded the Indian camp and might have recaptured the fugitives with ease, but the superior cunning and energy of the Indians were here again strikingly apparent, for they managed to slip away in safety during the night, the soldiers not discovering the escape until two days after it occurred. The flight and leisurely pursuit was resumed, but the Indians had killed very few Whites until they reached White Woman creek in Western Kansas. Here they were again overtaken by the soldiers and an engagement fought. If Colonel Lewis, who had joined the pursuing detachment with reinforcements, had not been killed, it is probable the Indians would have been defeated and recaptured, but the troops, deprived of a leader in Lewis's death, showed the white feather, and once more allowed the Cheyennes to slip away in safety. From thence onward, emboldened by success and filled with contempt for the Whites by the indolence of the troops, the progress of the Indians was marked by horrible bloodshed and devastation. Their course was practically unchecked, and they reached the northern agency, at length, thus attaining the object of their expedition.

"It was the Indian's nature to be cruel, and many of the conflicts between him and the Whites of the Plains were caused by the Whites' retaliatory measures for some atrocity born of Indian cruelty. On the other hand, as has already been hinted, many Indian cruelties arose from needless, petty cruelties and indignities, inflicted upon the latter by the Whites and afterwards avenged. These relations of hostility existed between the Indians and all classes of Whites on the Plains, excepting,

BETTER CLASS OF FULL-BLOOD PLAINS INDIANS OF
THIRTY YEARS AGO

possibly, the cowboy. He and the Indian had little to do with each other, therefore they had few encounters.

"It is often asked — since the United States had so much trouble with her western Indians, why has Canada had no trouble with hers? There are several good reasons. First, Canada, from the start, had a better method of dealing with the Indians. She was firm with them, and never deviated in the least from this course. They were awed by the Canadian police, and it is a well-known fact that this mounted police really protected Canada's frontier. Whiskey peddlers, as well as fugitive criminals, knew this, and knew how firm and just these police were, and the Indians entertained the same feeling toward them. Second, the Canadian Government always strictly kept its word with the Indians and never broke its agreements with them. It invited and warranted their confidence. Moreover, the Indians claimed no land over in Canada, as they did in the United States, and their best reason for keeping peace with the former when at war with the latter, was that they might have a refuge at hand, to which to fly in times of need. When they crossed the Canadian line, they knew they were safe from hostile pursuit. It was a healthy country, well watered by clear, cold streams; mountainous, where Indians could easily hide when hard pressed. It had plenty of game to sustain them, and beautiful, warm valleys, full of nutritious grasses and plenty of wood, where they could winter comfortably and feel in safety and at home. In summer it was an equally ideal place to live. It was also a place where they found a ready market for stolen horses and sold them to advantage. One may ask why they could not have selected Texas for like purposes. Well, for just the opposite reasons from those which led them to select Canada. Texas was much more unhealthy; they had always been at war with Texas, and besides, it was a glorious country upon which to forage. There they raided the frontier and not only got all the stock they wanted, but many other things that were useful to them.

"One should consider the natural propensities of the American Indian, and be convinced that he was better off in his original state than at the present time, with all the so-called advantages civilization has brought him. This was especially true of the Plains Indian. By nature he was a nomad, a warrior, a hunter, living in the open air. Under conditions favoring this nature, he was a healthy, hardy, happy individual, like any product of natural growth; under the absolute reversal from this to conditions imposed upon him by civilization, he became diseased, debilitated, and inferior; as might be expected from any unnatural growth."

## THE PLAINS INDIANS OF TO-DAY

Desiring to present a contrast between the past and present, in all its details, I wrote to numbers of missionaries among Indians, selecting those who had served for a long time. One of the missionaries on a large reservation where are located thousands of Sioux, answered me at length, and I present some of his recommendations. He speaks Sioux fluently. I have taken the liberty of changing a few expressions. His suggestions are brief, but contain much sound common sense. His letter was written in 1909, and some of the reforms he advocates have been inaugurated, but they have not been made general. This worthy missionary presents an accurate picture of conditions among the larger bands of Plains Indians (with some exceptions) at the present time. These Indians were entirely self-supporting forty years ago, and for their present deplorable condition, we, rather than they, are responsible.

"What strikes one most of all is the great poverty of these people. The majority suffer very much from hunger, because they do not know how to make a living. But they could make a good living for themselves, we believe, if they would but plant a couple of acres, say one acre corn, one acre potatoes. However, most of them will never do so unless they are held down to it. It is useless to treat with them as with white adults. They are nothing but grown-up children, not knowing what they want, and above all not knowing what is good for them. For this reason we ought to have more farmers who would see to it that these things are done.

"The Indian is a great traveller. Sometimes he does so for work, most generally for pleasure. Of what use is it to go to the railroad and work there for a few weeks, come back with little, find all his hay devoured by other people's stock, his own cattle and horses scattered over the country, and several head missing?

\*　　\*　　\*　　\*　　\*　　\*

"They should be supplied with seed in time; plenty but not many kinds, with the distinct understanding that they must pay for it before the next issue of money, or else it will be taken out of that. If they learn how to grow potatoes, corn and pumpkins or turnips, they have enough to start with. They ought to learn how to grind this corn and make corn-bread. If they raise corn, they could easily keep chickens, pigs, milk cows, and have butter and eggs and cheese, just what the consumptive needs. Of course it may be necessary before the crops are matured to issue rations until the harvest time comes, *i. e.*, for a year or two. After that they ought to have enough provisions to last them the year around. Indians ought to have facilities for buying pigs and chickens at ordinary market prices. In fact, they ought to be able to buy all their groceries at market prices.

\*    \*    \*    \*    \*    \*

"Another hindrance is the habit of visiting. Some go away for months at a time on a visit. Horses, cattle, and all are left to themselves or the wolves. When some one is sick, even if only a baby, work is quit, relatives have to come from miles and miles, etc. Sometimes they will go off to the Crows, Arapahoes, etc., and get a present of horses. Chances are that the Crows will be back here next year getting another present.

"A third hindrance is — to my mind — the method of work adopted here. (My intention is not to criticise but to offer a suggestion.) The Indians have to leave their homes and work on the roads for $1.25 per day. Consequently, they cannot look after their places nor take care of anything else. In the long run it is a loss. One head of stock lost at home, means one month's wages gone. Why could the Indians not make their money at home? Let them do the work that has been suggested, to cultivate their fields, to plant, etc.; have the District farmers control them and make payment for work done. Many of the thoughts above are the sentiments of the better class of Indians, so you may be sure there will be little opposition on their part to putting these, or similar plans, into operation.

"A fourth hindrance is the fact that so many go away to Buffalo Bill shows, etc., leaving wife, children and everything behind. When such an Indian gets back, some one else is liable to have his wife and cattle — not mentioning bad habits and shameful diseases he sometimes brings back.

\*    \*    \*    \*    \*    \*

"But it is the old people that ought to arouse the sympathy of us all. They lie around in the utmost filth and neglect, eating old scraps, or swill; starving and freezing in spite of the fact that they draw rations. If they get help from anyone, it is devoured by the neighbors, and the poor old people have little benefit from it.

"The children's lot is a hard one, too. If they live at home, they have to go through the rain, mud, cold, etc., to get to the day school. In many cases, the family must camp near the day-school. Then they have to neglect their own home entirely.

"At present, the prevailing idea seems to be that the best way to do with the Indian now is to throw him upon his own resources. If the plan outlined above or something similar were carried out for a few years, one could do so. To do so at present would mean, I think, a slaughter, a

massacre.  Let a death come in his family and he may give away his last
hoof.  He may barter away every thing for a jug of whiskey.     *   *   *   *
He is no match for the white man, especially when the latter is accompanied by what the Sioux call "Holy Water," and therefore it would be
nothing but murder to mix up the Indians with Whites too rapidly on
this reservation.

"The civilizing of the Indians is a slow process.  When some change
is going to be made it ought to be announced long ahead, and then the red
man can prepare for it.  Otherwise he is simply carried off his feet, dazed,
doesn't know where to go, or what to do.  It is all right to say, let those
who do not want to work starve, but what about the innocent family,
what about his 'sponging' on the others as they call it?  One Indian cannot
refuse another anything (especially as they are all relations) without being
ostracized.

"I note what you say about tuberculosis, and must say that the
opposite ought to be true, but it is not, for many reasons, most of which
are mentioned above.  Were it not for their careless and dirty habits,
their lack of food and proper care, they ought to be the strongest race on
the face of the earth.  By proper treatment many cases could be cured.
As it is they all die.  Two physicians cannot tend to everybody on so large
a reservation and with their limited means.

*     *     *     *     *     *

"These are a few things that I thought I should mention in order to
fully answer your questions.  By doing so, I did not in the least mean to
criticise anyone in the Service, for I know that much has been tried and
done in the past.  Still I believe with the other missionaries, that the
Indians can be saved if we try the methods suggested above or similar ones."

# CHAPTER XXXI.  THE INDIANS OF CALIFORNIA

No scientist has devoted more time and study to the California Indians than Dr. A. L. Kroeber.  In his description of California tribes and stocks, published in the Handbook of American Indians, he states that the California natives are rather shorter than the majority of those in eastern North America, and in the south, they are unusually dark.  The astonishing characteristic of California Indians is their diversified languages.  There are twenty-one distinct linguistic families.  The larger stocks such as the Athapascan, Shoshonean and Yuman have forced their way into the State, whereas the great majority are small bands and may be considered purely Californian.

While pottery was practically unknown, textile arts (particularly basket-making) were very highly developed.  "Houses were often made of grass, tule, or brush, or of bark, sometimes covered with earth.  Only in the northwest part of the State were small houses of planks in use.  In this region, as well as on the Santa Barbara islands, wooden canoes were also made, but over the greater part of the State a raft of tules was the only means of navigation.  Agriculture was nowhere practised.  Deer and small game were hunted, and there was considerable fishing; but the bulk of the food was vegetable.  The main reliance was placed on numerous varieties of acorns, and next to these, on seeds, especially of grasses and herbs.  Roots and berries were less used.*

"Both totemism and a true gentile organization were totally lacking in all parts of the State.  The mythology of the Californians was characterized by unusually well-developed and consistent creation myths, and by the complete lack not only of migration but of ancestor traditions.  Their ceremonies were numerous and elaborate as compared with the prevailing simplicity of life, but they lacked almost totally the rigid ritualism and extensive symbolism that pervade the ceremonies of most of America.  One set of ceremonies was usually connected with a secret religious society; another, often spectacular, was held in remembrance of the dead."

We are concerned in this book with the condition of the California Indians the past sixty years.  Without an exception on the American continent, there is no area in which the native population has so suddenly and generally diminished.  The confiscation of the mission properties by the Mexican Government, followed by the great influx of gold-hunters, adventurers and ranchmen from 1849-1860, are responsible for the de-

---

* Handbook of American Indians, page 191, Vol I.

plorable condition in which these Indians found themselves about 1880. Prior to the influx of the Forty-niners, the Indians had been self-supporting (although the action of the Mexican government came near bringing about their destruction). California people themselves took little interest in the wretched condition of the aboriginal inhabitants and it was not until the United States Board of Indian Commissioners and the Indian Rights Association became active and sent commissions or individuals to California, that reforms were inaugurated. Honorable Albert K. Smiley, a citizen of California (and founder of the Lake Mohonk Conference) was especially active in this humanitarian work. A Mr. Painter was sent out by the Indian Rights Association in 1885. Painter made a thorough investigation and laid formal complaint, with the backing of the Mohonk Conference, before the President of the United States. The usual delays occurred. The President referred the matter to the Attorney General, who in turn referred it to the Secretary of the Interior. The Indian Rights Association now assumed responsibility, and Mr. Herbert Welsh, Secretary of that organization, sent his check for $3,300 to be held while the case of the Indians was pending before the court.*

The wrongs of the Indians were made public at Lake Mohonk by various speakers, and through the country generally by Mrs. H. H. Jackson. The case of the mission Indians, sustained by these various organizations and individuals, was heard in the courts and resulted in victory for the Indians of California.

During the '90's the Indians were further evicted and became exceedingly destitute. Many died of starvation. The Indians seemed utterly unable to protect themselves and miners and ranchmen alike took every advantage of them. As an illustration of the situation in California as compared with that in the Black Hills, South Dakota, I will here relate a story told me at Deadwood in 1889.

A miner, who had spent some ten years in California, came to the Black Hills about 1875, when gold was discovered. He wore on his watch-chain, as a fob, two Indian teeth. In a Deadwood dance hall he informed some convivial companions, that on one occasion he took a California Indian by the hair and struck him in the mouth with his six-shooter, knocking out several teeth. Two of these he had a jeweler drill and wire to his watch-chain, as souvenirs. An old trapper, who happened to be present, suggested that the miner procure one or two Sioux teeth, as they might be different from "Digger teeth", and would add to his collection. Out in the foothills in the course of a few days, the miner met a Sioux

---

* Eighteenth Annual Report of the Board of Indian Commissioners, 1886, page 46.

Indian, seized him and undertook to treat him as he had the poor California native.  Instead of teeth, as a souvenir he received a knife-thrust between the ribs and was lucky to escape with his life.

While interest in the California Indians seemed to lag, Charles F. Lummis, Esq., a citizen of the State, and editor of a prominent western publication, *The Land of Sunshine*, began a campaign in the early 90's on behalf of the various tribes and bands, most of whom had been evicted from their ancient homes.  I present a brief bibliography of Mr. Lummis' articles at the conclusion of this chapter, as they sum up in a masterly fashion the wrongs of the Indian, and the efforts of good citizens to right them.  In all my reading, I have seen no stronger, more direct and interesting appeals than these made by Mr. Lummis in his journal (now published under the title, *Out West*.)

The National Indian Association through its Northern California Branch became active; there was formed the California Indian Association of which C. E. Kelsey, Esq., a prominent California attorney, was elected Secretary.  This organization cooperated with the others and the Board of Indian Commissioners and should be credited with the salvation of the remaining few thousand California aborigines from pauperism.

Mr. Kelsey cooperated with Mr. Lummis and really represented the people of California.  At last Congress was forced to act, the Indian Office instituted reforms (which it should have inaugurated more than twenty years ago) and satisfactory results were obtained.

Mr. Kelsey at my request kindly prepared for me a summary of the California Indians and the work of rescue as projected by friends, and carried to perfection through his intelligent and unselfish labors.  He has also written me a long letter and I take the liberty of appending in the form of footnotes a number of extracts from his letter, in addition to the article.

### MR. KELSEY'S BRIEF HISTORY OF THE CALIFORNIA INDIANS

The aboriginal population of California was large, possibly equal to that of all the rest of the United States.  Powers, in his "Indians of California," 1877, a work which has been liberally quoted by about everyone who has since written of the California Indians, estimates the number at 750,000.  Barbour and Wozencraft, who traveled over the State in 1851 as members of the California Indian Commission, estimated the native population to be between 200,000 and 300,000.  C. Hart Merriam[*] estimates the numbers at the beginning of the nineteenth century at

---

[*] American Anthropology, page 599, volume VII.

LINGUISTIC STOCKS IN CALIFORNIA
From Handbook of American Indians

260,000. Dr. Kroeber estimates the number at not less than 150,000. The figures of the Bureau of Indian Affairs for 1913 shows a little less than 20,000, being slightly larger than the U. S. census for 1910. This decrease is certainly extraordinary, being nearly 90% of the most conservative estimate of former population, and nearly all taking place within the memories of persons now living. The causes are variously given as war, famine, whiskey, disease, etc., and all doubtless played their parts in the decrease. Dr. Merriam states the causes as follows:

"The principal cause of the appallingly great and rapid decrease in the Indians of California is not the number directly slain by the Whites, or the number directly killed by whiskey or disease, but a much more subtle and dreadful thing: it is the gradual but progressive and resistless confiscation of their lands and homes, in consequence of which they are forced to seek refuge in remote and barren localities, often far from water, usually with an impoverished supply of food, and not infrequently, in places where the winter climate is too severe for their enfeebled constitutions. Victims of the aggressive selfishness of the Whites, outcasts in the land of their fathers, outraged in their most sacred institutions, weakened in body, broken in spirit, and fully conscious of the hopelessness of their condition, must we wonder that the wail for the dead is often heard in their camps?"

The Special Investigating Agent, appointed under the Act of March 3, 1905, states it as largely due to the "progressive absorption by the white race of the Indians' every means of existence."* During the famines to which all Indian bands were subject after the American occupation, the old people and especially the children would die.

After California was fully American, the National Government at Washington, sent out a Commission of distinguished citizens, as it has done many times in other parts of the country, to make treaties with the California Indians. This commission consisted of the Honorable George W. Barbour, Honorable Redick McKee and Honorable O. M. Wozencraft. They traveled about with a military escort and made treaties with all Indians west of the Sierra Nevada, about 90% of all in the State at that time. Two treaties were made by the whole Commission. They then separated, each member taking a different part of the State. Four treaties were made by Redick McKee, four by George W. Barbour and eight by O. M. Wozencraft. John C. Fremont, E. D. Keyes, George Stoneman, and others afterward well known, signed as witnesses to some of these eighteen treaties. The treaties were much alike and were all

* Report of C. E. Kelsey, Special Agent, March 21, 1906.

definite and simple. In each treaty the Indians accepted the sovereignty of the United States, agreed to keep the peace with Whites and with other Indians, ceded to the United States their title to their lands and agreed to accept reservations, duly laid out by metes and bounds in the treaties. On its part the United States reserved for Indian use forever the specified reservations and agreed to pay for the lands ceded by the Indians, in goods, not cash. When these treaties went to Washington, they were accompanied by a statement calling attention to the extraordinary cheapness of the lands acquired and congratulating themselves and the country upon the fact that the Indians were too unsophisticated to demand annuities or money. The goods promised consisted of thousands of beeves, thousands of sacks of flour, thousands of blankets, suits of clothes, dresses, tools, work animals, cloth, iron, steel, etc., worth about $1,000,000 at that time. Teachers, schools, blacksmiths, farmers, etc., were also promised on a large scale. The reservations promised aggregate more than seven and a half million acres of land. The eighteen treaties were signed by 422 chiefs representing 186 tribes, or bands. Some of the reservations were laid out in the mining districts and there was much opposition to the treaties among the miners. At that time, 1851-'52, Indian treaties were submitted to the Senate of the United States for ratification. These eighteen California treaties were duly brought before the Senate and were not ratified. Nothing further was heard about them until, fifty-two years later, they were discovered in the secret archives of the Senate, the injunction of secrecy removed and the treaties published. The Government of the United States seems never to have made any attempt to make any other or further treaties. The Government nevertheless has taken the land and the reservations, as well, and every other benefit to be derived from the eighteen treaties, but has not on its part paid the price agreed or carried out any other engagement then made. It would seem that if the Government received the benefits of the treaties, it should pay the price agreed, whether the treaties were ratified or not, and that the Government should have taken some steps to acquire the Indian right of occupancy, a right which has not been legally terminated to this day. The failure of the treaties and the ensuing period of inaction by the National Government, were disastrous to the Indians of California. Not a foot of land remained which they could call their own. There was no source of aboriginal food supply which might not be appropriated by some white man any day, and most of the country was soon appropriated for mines or cattle or agriculture. The Indians were forced into a hand-to-mouth existence, interspersed with periods of famine, during which the rising generation perished. A great variety of diseases, previously unknown, were introduced among the Indians, against which they had no inherited immunity. Diseases which among white people are considered of little consequence, such as whooping-cough, measles, etc., are fatal to Indians, especially during periods of scarcity. The more virulent diseases such as smallpox, tuberculosis, etc., also took their toll from the Indian camps, and whiskey claimed its thousands of victims.

In any other part of the United States, the failure of the treaties would doubtless have resulted in a general Indian war. This was not possible in California. The extraordinary number of Indian dialects (over 135 are now known), belonging to some twenty diverse and antagonistic racial stocks, was enough in itself, to have prevented anything like united action. Within a year or so California was occupied by from 100,000 to 200,000 active, vigorous, masterful men, armed with the best weapons of the day. The Indians could not have mustered 30,000 warriors in the mining districts and possibly not in all California, and they were armed with bows and arrows and clubs.* The Indian cause was hopeless from the start. Nevertheless, there ensued a period of near war, with occasional clashes between Indians and Whites, which was fully as disastrous to the Indians as an open campaign would have been. The encounters are referred to, locally, as "battles", of which quite a large number are recorded. The Indians were usually surrounded and shot down by posses of miners and citizens, in retaliation of some aggression by the Indians, or some alleged aggression. Some Indian bands are known to have been "wiped out" because their room was wanted by cattle men or settlers. No action by the Federal Government for the protection of the Indians is recorded. In one case the difficulties resulted in actual border warfare. The Hupa Indians, goaded into action by the influx of settlers into their valley, went on the warpath, during the sixties. They were joined by their neighbors, the Yurocs, or Lower Klamaths, and a sharp frontier war ensued for a couple of years. The Government finally bought out the squatters, restored the land to the Indians and gave the Hupas and Yurocs definite reservations. A similar trouble arose at Round Valley in the eighties, but war was averted by one of those compromises well known in the West, under which the Indians received one-quarter of their own land and the settlers received three-quarters.

Reports published from time to time at Washington show that the Indian Office was not wholly without knowledge of Indian conditions in

---

* The Federal census for 1850 showed a population of 92,597 Indians; State Census of 1852, 255,122 Indians, 31,266 being "domesticated."

California, but little was attempted and less accomplished for Indian relief. Several reservations were established, or attempted to be established by Executive order. One was invalidated by the Courts, which held the land to be within a Mexican land grant. One was raided and seized by settlers, who had sufficient political influence to hold the land and secure the cancellation of the Executive order. One was laid out with fine timber included and another was desired by cattlemen and sufficient influence was concentrated upon Congress to secure their "opening to settlement". Only one small reservation of that period remains to this day, and this one, Tule River, was diminished in size more than half, without the knowledge or consent of the Indians. The few items appearing in the Indian Office reports, or in reports to the Board of Indian Commissioners, were rather more optimistic than the situation warranted, for the officers making those reports were at the same time giving an account of their own stewardship and doubtless mentioned as many favorable things as they could. The fact that favorable items were so few is eloquent of the conditions then existing. Dr. C. Hart Merriam estimates that the California Indians were decreasing at an average rate of 7,000 per annum*, and this must have been under conditions involving an appalling amount of misery and suffering. It was well understood that the California Indians were "fading away" rapidly, yet it seems to have occurred to no one to look into the matter and see why the Indians were decreasing in numbers or what the physical steps were by which the Indians were being faded. Commissioner Wozencraft, in the early fifties, published an appeal to the people of California, but it met with no particular response. The process of ejecting Indians from the ownership or possession of anything considered of value to any white man went on without check, and the number of Indians who perished diminished each year, simply because there were fewer Indians left to die. It was hardly to be expected that the members of this savage race could at once readjust themselves to the fierce civilization under which they had been submerged so suddenly, and only a few Indians were able to do so. Nor could it be expected, doubtless, that the new white population, so largely from the Middle West, with 200 years' traditions of Indian fighting behind them, should show any particular consideration for Indians who were unable to fight. The attitude of the great majority of white citizens was apathetic, rather than hostile, and the more active minority were allowed their will with the Indians. For years no local church seems to have made any efforts on behalf of Indians, and though there were not wanting distinguished instances where individuals braved

---

* American Anthropologist, page 603, Vol. VII, No. 4.

local public opinion by standing out for the rights of Indians, the effect upon the times was small. The attitude of the Californians is reflected by the provisions of their early codes in regard to Indians. See Act of the Legislature of California approved April 22, 1850, Ch. 408, section 3650 et seq. of the California Code of that day. Indians were placed under justices of the peace. Originally an Indian could not sue or be sued, but this was altered in 1855. Cruel treatment of Indian minors was punishable by a fine of $10. Any Indian who had fallen into the clutches of the law upon a finable offense, had his labor sold to the highest bidder, until his fine was worked out, the purchaser giving a bond for the fine.* Any Indian could upon the complaint of any citizen, be haled into a justice court, adjudged an "able-bodied Indian vagrant" and his labor sold to the highest bidder for four months.† These laws were never enforced very oppressively and had become a dead letter long before they were finally repealed in 1883. Nor were State laws the only ones of which Indians might complain. After the American occupation, for some forty years, there was no practical way in which an Indian could in California acquire title to land from the public domain. The Indian was not a citizen and could not select land under the homestead or other land acts. He was not an alien and could not be naturalized as a citizen. There was no law under which a California Indian could become a citizen, until the passage of the general allotment Act in 1887.‡ The Indian homestead Acts of 1875 and 1883 were of little value, as the technical requirements were too onerous, no one was designated to see that Indians were assisted and few Indians ever heard of the Acts. Under the general allotment Act and subsequent to 1891, some 1800 Indian allotments were made in California. This allotting was done by Special Agents sent from Washington, who were unfamiliar with local conditions, hence water rights, soil qualities, timber, etc., were not looked after, and at least two-thirds of these allotments were of little or no value to the Indian allottees. About 1400 of the 1800 allotments were made in the five northeastern counties of the State and in these counties the few allotments that were inhabitable have proved of great value to the Indians. In the remainder of the State there was little land unappropriated and the allotment laws brought no relief to the larger number of Indians.§

---

* Sec. 3662.   † Sec. 3668.   ‡ Act of Feb. 28, 1887 (24 Statutes at Large, page 388).

§ In thirteen cases I found the land the Indians were occupying, that is, the more valuable little valleys, was outside of the reservation as laid out and in six of these cases the land occupied was not only unpatented and unprotected, but the land patented to the Indians was barren rocks, utterly worthless. In one case the reservation patented was six miles away from the land selected for the Indians in an entirely different township. In most cases the boundaries were not marked at all and the adjoining owners moved the lines over onto the Indians.

The period of war, near war and oppression lasted rather less than twenty years and was succeeded by a period of eviction of somewhat longer duration. At first, when a white man filed on a tract of land and summarily ejected any Indians he might find living there, the Indians could move on to some adjoining tract, where the opportunities for starvation were equally good. But as time went on, land became much scarcer and fewer land owners were willing to allow Indians to occupy their ranches even in small part. The evictions continued and as those recently evicted could find no unoccupied tract to live on, they began to crowd into other settlements, which had not yet been summoned to move. The result was that in many parts of the State, the Indians gradually concentrated in small settlements, locally known as rancherias, where they lived upon the sufferance of some kindly-disposed land owner. A change in ownership of the land usually meant eviction for the Indians. In these rancherias the conditions were unspeakable, both as to sanitation and morals. The Indians felt they were in their last ditch and that there was nothing for them to look forward to but extinction. The Indians were surrounded by civilization, but not of it. They came in contact chiefly with the vices of civilization and the vicious white element. Forty years after the American occupation three-fourths of the California Indians had still to learn what a missionary might be and nine-tenths of them were still heathen. The priest and the Levite had passed by on the other side, and the good Samaritan had been unavoidably detained in Jerusalem.

The first general awakening as to conditions among the Indians of California came with the publication of Helen Hunt Jackson's "Century of Dishonor" and "Ramona", in the eighties, and by 1890 Congress had passed an act for the relief of the Indians of Southern California. This was much needed. The Smiley Commission appointed under this Act increased the number of small reservations in Southern California from about seventeen to thirty-four and enlarged most of those formerly in existence. They were able to give a fixed indefeasible title and these Indians were thenceforward secure in their homes. The Smiley Commission was not given funds sufficient to develop water upon the tracts reserved, a most important matter, for the Indians had been crowded into the mountains and on to barren tracts, which no white man at that time wanted. The Southern California Indians had to wait some fifteen to twenty years longer before an attempt was made to put their lands into habitable shape, where they could live with some approach to comfort. The Indians of Northern and Central California, numbering more than three-fourths of those in the State, received no benefit from the awakening as to Southern

California. Their necessities were fully as great and they were as fully deserving, but interest in the California Indians died away largely before anything was accomplished north of Tehachipi. Two things did follow, first sending some allotting agents to Northern California, where they did some good, though they largely failed to live up to their opportunities, and second, a branch of the National Indian Association was established in Northern California and mission and school work was begun among the Indians. The policy of this Association has been to establish a school or a mission and when it is in good working order to turn it over to some church or society that will agree to carry on the work. Then the Association establishes another mission in the same manner. Some twenty missions and schools, reaching about 12,000 Indians, have been established in California, directly or indirectly through the efforts of the National Indian Association or of its Northern California branch. For some eight or ten years after the founding of the Northern California branch in 1894, their efforts were largely confined to the establishment of missions and schools among the Indians and to relieving such cases of distress as came to their knowledge. There were considerable difficulties. No church or other organization could afford to take over or begin work unless there was some fixity of tenure for the Indians. Where the Indians were subject to eviction at any time, as the majority were, no one could afford to begin work, for their work might be dissipated any day and the Indians scattered. Hence, for the first few years the efforts were confined to those places where Indians held land in some form.

The second awakening began about 1903, when the Northern California Indian Association, or as it is often called, the California Indian Association, began its campaign for the relief of the homeless Indians of California, then supposed to number about 8,000 souls. Every avenue of assistance proposed seemed to lead back to the land question. Without some security of tenure it seemed impossible to accomplish any lasting improvement in Indian conditions, and inasmuch as the landless condition of the Indians was due to the acts and omissions of the National Government, the Indian Association appealed to the Congress of the United States for relief, in so far as land was necessary. The Association did not ask for reservations, believing that more Indian reservations in California would be detrimental to all concerned. They did not ask that the Indians be given farms, or that they should be made rich; merely that they be given small allotments of land, where they would be secure. The California Indians have always been self-sustaining. That is, they have received no aid from the Government or from anyone else. They have often been below the starvation line and usually not far above it, but such as their living was, it was their own.  Most of the California Indians have in some measure adjusted themselves to the industrial life about them and perform whatever labor they can get.  The Indian Association planned not to interfere in any manner with their independence, or with their industrial position.  Above all things they did not wish the Indians pauperized.  Also, the Indian Association did not wish the Indians concentrated.  Where too many Indians are concentrated in one place, there is not sufficient work and the Indians themselves have their own reasons for remaining within their ancestral districts, which we may call superstitious or sentimental.  The old racial antagonism between the antagonistic racial stocks also renders it inadvisable to concentrate.  The Indian Association therefore proposed that in places where no land for allotment could be secured from the public domain, small tracts should be purchased, in the immediate neighborhood of the Indians, where they have friends and employers.*

The Indian Association then, 1904, began a vigorous campaign in California, largely educational, for the purpose of securing from Congress the land necessary as a basis for further work on behalf of the California Indians.  In this effort nearly all of the societies working for the benefit of Indians joined.  In Southern California matters had been nearing a crisis, with the Indians there, owing to lack of water on most reservations, indefinite boundaries, etc., and they were also asking for relief.  The Sequoya League, of which Charles F. Lummis, Esq., was the leading spirit, was the most active body in Southern California.  In 1905 Congress directed an investigation of the whole Indian situation in California, and C. E. Kelsey, General Secretary of the Northern California Indian Association, was selected to make the investigation.  The report of this investigation was published by the Indian Office March 21, 1906.  Congress soon made an appropriation of $100,000 for the relief of the California Indians and $50,000 was further appropriated two years later.  Some further sums were also given for fencing, surveying and other such items.  The plan presented by the Indian Association met favor with the Board of Indian

---

*When Kelsey took charge he found on no reservation was there an adequate supply of water for irrigation and on most of them none at all.  This in a country where irrigation is absolutely life.  On no reservation was there any attempt made to protect the water supply, and land which controlled the water was carefully left out of the reservations in most cases.  I think the surveyors must have done so knowingly.  This meant fifteen or twenty years' slow starvation for the Indians, and greatly increased difficulties later when we tried to correct things.  I presume I have spent one-third of my time during the last ten years in fighting for things for the Southern California Indians, which ought to have been settled twenty years before.

Commissioners and the Commissioner of Indian Affairs and was adopted almost *in toto*. Mr. Kelsey was appointed to have charge of purchasing and allotting such lands as were required and served until the appropriations were exhausted. The need for water upon the Southern California reservations was met chiefly from direct appropriations for the Irrigation Service and a large share of this work is already completed. The vexing boundary questions in Southern California have all been settled and some considerable additions made to the reservations from the public domain and from purchase. In Northern California the work of getting all Indians on their own small fraction of land is not quite so far along, but is nearing completion. When, in 1903, the Northern California Indian Association began its movement to secure land for the landless Indians of California, the land situation of the California Indians was estimated about as follows:

| | |
|---|---:|
| On reservations, So. Calif. | 3,500 |
| On reservations, No. Calif. | 1,700 |
| On allotments, So. Calif. | 250 |
| On allotments, No. Calif. | 2,800 |
| On land owned by churches, societies, etc., and by themselves | 1,100 |
| Estimated to be landless | 8,000 |
| | 17,350 |

It was estimated that about 2,000 could be given homes from the public domain. The above estimates proved inadequate in some respects. There were some 2,000 more Indians in the State than had been estimated and fewer Indians had land of their own than was supposed. Still as it proved possible to take care of 4,200 from the public domain and within the National Forests, the number from whom land must be purchased was not increased.

Congress has recently appropriated $10,000 more for the purchase of land for these Indians, but this will not be enough to take care of one-half of those remaining. When this appropriation shall have been used, nearly 10,000 of the California Indians will have been given homes. The others should be provided for immediately. It should be understood that all this has been done without the establishment of reservations or agencies and with practically no expense for maintenance. In comparison with the magnitude of the work, the expense has been small and it must be conceded that the debt which the Government owes the California Indians is by no means extinguished.

The present land situation (1914) in California is about as follows:

On reservations, No. Calif............................ 1,944
On reservations, So. Calif............................ 3,416
On allotments, No. Calif. (Old)...................... 2,800
On allotments, So. Calif. (Old)......................  250
On allotments, No. Calif. (New)......................  400
On allotments, So. Calif. (New)......................  238
On National Forests................................. 3,000
On newly purchased lands............................ 4,800
Allotments arranged for.............................  600
On land owned by Indians............................  300
On land owned by churches, societies, etc............  250
Not yet taken care of............................... 1,841
                                                    ——————
                                                    19,839

The awakening in regard to the California Indians was by no means confined to land.  The Indian Association has been working upon public sentiment from the first.  After the land purchases were under way, the Association began efforts to secure schools and school privileges and to urge religious and other organizations to take up various phases of Indian work.  The Indian Office established some eight day schools and increased the capacity of others.  Also an increased number of field matrons were appointed.  In 1904 it was estimated that only 1000 Indian children of school age in Northern California were in any kind of a school, out of 2800.  By 1914 it is estimated that less than 1000 were not in school.  The increase in school attendance is largely in the public schools of the State. Racial prejudice against Indians in California in the earlier days was intense and the idea of allowing an Indian child in school was considered preposterous.  As the Indians decreased in numbers all fear of them passed away, and in time a kindlier feeling arose.  For many years this racial prejudice prevented the greater number of Indians from getting an adequate amount of work.  With increased population and the increased development of California came an increased demand for labor with a diminished prejudice against Indians.  The industrial position of the Indians has therefore improved.  In some parts of the State the Indians are fairly well employed at fair pay.  In others there is little work for anyone and in these portions of the State Indians have to go many miles for a little work.  They cut wood, put up hay, cultivate and pick hops, pick grapes and other fruit and do all kinds of odd jobs.  As their employment is still largely seasonal, it is not wholly satisfactory.  One excellent thing about the more recent revival of interest in the California Indians is that it is largely in California itself.

In 1907 there were five Protestant missions to the Indians of Northern California and two or three Roman Catholic missions. By 1914 the Protestant missions have increased to seventeen, with twenty missionaries. The Catholic work has also been extended. There are now missionaries in the field for about 14,000 of the California Indians and quite a number of local churches have interested themselves in the Indians in their own neighborhoods. The number of converts probably does not exceed 4,000.

In California a considerable number of Indians, some 3,600, were found living within the National Forests, of whom some 600 had allotments made before the forests were established. Further legislation was necessary before the 3,000 could be given their own homes. This was accomplished in 1910. (36 Stat. L. 855)

The California Indian, often termed "Digger", has been considerably maligned. Statements are not wanting that the California Indians were of deficient mentality, little above the brutes and about the lowest of all human beings. Such statements are entitled to no credence. Kroeber, Barrett, Goddard, Merriam, Powers, Lummis, and all writers having actual acquaintance with the California Indians, place them as equal to any of the other American tribes. Teachers in the California Indian schools say that the California Indian children are as intelligent and capable as any Indians they have ever taught. Nearly one thousand Indian children are in the public schools of California and their scholarship is in no wise inferior to that of the white children of the same age, though it must be admitted that few Indian children attend after adolescence. A few of those in better financial circumstances have graduated from high schools with honors. Employers of Indian labor, without exception, pronounce them honest, reliable and capable. They can be trusted to work alone, which cannot be done with Oriental labor or floating Whites. Conviction of an Indian for theft is almost unheard of. Statistics gathered in 1909 showed twenty-eight Indians in the prisons of California for crimes of violence, mostly committed when under the influence of liquor, and not one Indian for theft or robbery or crimes against property. This is remarkable when we consider the straits under which the Indians are often placed.

Present conditions look favorable for the California Indians. In Southern California the most harassing troubles have been settled, and water is being supplied wherever possible. Southern California is overschooled. The Government schools have a capacity for about 1200 pupils and there are about 800 Indian children of school age in that district. In Northern California seven-eighths of the Indians have been supplied with minute amounts of land. The California white people seem aroused to the need for other forms of assistance and it seems unlikely that matters will ever revert to former conditions. The new appropriation will take care of a part of the Indians still homeless. More has been accomplished in this "spurt" than all others put together. This may be attributed to the fact that the external influences lasted longer. That is, an outsider from the Indian Association was in charge of the work for some eight years. The last one hundred years tend to show that the Indian Office has not within itself the power to initiate any movement for the relief of Indians. The spirit that compels redress has not resided in the Indian Office. The Indian Office has received at all times sufficient reports from the field and may be presumed to have had knowledge of conditions at all times and yet every movement for relief has come from the outside, from individuals, or more often from associations who have compelled an unwilling bureau to act, or, often an unwilling Congress to act. This is doubtless always the case with bureaucracy. I am inclined to think this results largely from the manner of organization. As it is, the authority to decide questions lies with persons who seldom or never see the field and are without personal knowledge of that they are doing. The men who know the field have no power and the men who have the power do not know the field.

Bureaucracy has one curious result and I am inclined to think more so in the Indian Service than in others. The employees seem to lose all power of initiative and all sense of individuality. They soon learn to resent any but routine work. This is probably why the reports of conditions in California and elsewhere have fallen into deaf pigeonholes.

My Brother's Keeper.— *Charles F. Lummis*, 1899. Land of Sunshine. Vol. XI, pp. 139, 207, 263, 333.

My Brother's Keeper.— *Charles F. Lummis*, 1900. Land of Sunshine. Vol. XII, pp. 28, 90.

The Story of Cyrus Hawk.— *C. J. Crandall*, 1900. Land of Sunshine. Vol. XII, pp. 352.

The Pity of It.— *Bertha S. Wilkins*, 1900. Land of Sunshine. Vol. XII, pp. 244.

The Sequoya League.— *Charles F. Lummis*, 1903. Out West. Vol. XVIII, pp. 81, 213, 355.

Turning a New Leaf. The Warner Ranch Indians Out West, 1903. Vol. XVIII, pp. 441; Out West, Part II, Vol. XVIII, pp. 589.

The Sequoya League.— *Charles F. Lummis*, 1903. Out West. Vol. XVIII, pp. 477, 625.

Bullying the "Quaker Indians."— *Charles F. Lummis*, 1903. Out West. Vol. XVIII, pp. 669.

The Sequoya League.— *Charles F. Lummis*, 1903. Out West. Vol. XVIII, pp. 743.

Reports of the Board of Indian Commissioners, and Interior Department, 1871-1908, for full descriptions of investigations, etc.

# CHAPTER XXXII.  A STATISTICAL TABLE.  PREPARED BY MEN AND WOMEN IN THE FIELD

The past forty years we have had statistics on Indian advancement in the Secretary of the Interior and Indian Office reports.  Until late years, these were not detailed, but presented in condensed form the opinions of Agents, Superintendents and employees.

In 1908 the United States Board of Indian Commissioners published a table containing answers to twenty-six questions.  The information is valuable and was of service to the Government in handling Indian problems.  I do not reproduce the table here for the reason that excellent though it was, it omits protection of property, and vital statistics.  Under my chapter devoted to health I have discussed, in a general way, the health of the Indians, but have not presented tables for the reason that I do not wish this book to become too statistical in character.

Feeling that none of the statistical and other reports submitted by Superintendents, Special Agents, Inspectors — or even the Honorable Commissioner himself — emphasized the phase of the situation which in my eyes seemed the most important, I have prepared a table of my own.

Two general questions might be asked every man and woman in the Indian Service, every educated Indian, and every person living in, or near, Indian communities.  These are:

*First.*  "Is the Indian citizen treated as the white citizen, or is he discriminated against?"

*Second.*  "Has his moral, physical, financial and general well being increased or diminished, the past twenty years?"

On these two very pertinent and important questions hang the entire future of the American Red Race.

After some thought, I decided to obtain opinions from those who knew at first hand how our wards were progressing.  The information I desired must cover all of the United States, where Indians now live.  Naturally, it was confined to the region west of the Mississippi, with the exception of tracts in Wisconsin and Michigan.

The excellent table prepared by Commissioner Sells in his report of 1913 is based upon statistics sent in by Superintendents, teachers and physicians.  Of necessity, it could not include statements or opinions of missionaries and other observers.  It presents the views of employees in the Department.

After deliberation, a series of fourteen questions were prepared and addressed to upward of 300 men and women representing every reservation, Indian community, or school. Nearly half of these replied, and on pages 345 to 358 I have presented their comments grouped under these various questions. I have tried to make the questions sufficiently elastic to cover every phase of the subject. Specific requests applied to one section of the country, might be out of place in another. For instance, a series of questions concerning the Navaho, might not be answered intelligently if applied to the Ojibwa of Wisconsin.

In studying the table of statistics, one observes that the answers indicate a wide difference of opinion. This is quite natural. As an illustration; at Pine Ridge, Major Brennan — a competent Superintendent, who has been in charge of the fighting Sioux for many years — thinks that there is less sickness and more progress than formerly; whereas a prominent missionary takes the opposite view. Another missionary offers a compromise as between Major Brennan's view, and the opinion of his worthy co-laborer. This difference does not reflect on the report of Major Brennan, but is an honest difference of opinion. Missionaries and their assistants go about among the Indians of a certain part of the reservation more than does the Agent, who is engrossed in many official duties.

Not a few of the answers are lengthy, and extremely interesting. Were it possible, all of them should be reproduced in this chapter.

A number of answers were received promptly, others have come to hand a few at a time, the past four months. Others are still arriving. It must be remembered that these people are all earnest workers, whether employed by the Government or benevolent organizations — hence the delays. Beyond question, many will reach me too late to be included in the table. There is also a class of excessively timid persons, who seem to think that to answer the questions, may involve them in controversy, or cast reflection on the Interior Department. It is quite surprising that so many correspondents should take this view.

The differences of opinion in nowise affect the table as a whole. On a large reservation, the Indians in one section may be rather backward. For instance, there will be more sickness at Pine Point, White Earth reservation, than about White Earth agency. Hence, the priest at Pine Point would report a worse condition among his Indians than the Agent at White Earth. In the great Indian area of eastern Oklahoma, near the schools conditions are satisfactory, whereas back in the hills, there is much suffering and distress. Also in Oklahoma, near the towns will live Indians who drink and gamble. Therefore, if such facts are taken into consideration,

From "*Indian Blankets and Their Makers*"
by George Wharton James,
A. C. McClurg & Co., Publishers.

OLD BAYETA SADDLE BLANKET

many of the apparent discrepancies in my table will be readily understood by readers. Upwards of a hundred of my correspondents have been very frank, and many of their recommendations and suggestions are purposely omitted for the reason that to incorporate them would seem like criticizing the present administration. This is not my purpose, as has been frequently pointed out in this book. All I desire to do is to present facts, and include sensible remedies suggested by correspondents on the ground.

If we average up the entire table and allow for the progress in the sections wherein are located schools; where Superintendents, through efficient farmers and teachers, have brought about advance of Indians, we will find that in many parts of the country there is a distinct advance. In other portions of the United States the natives are either at a standstill, or have retrograded. The best showing is in the Navaho country, where good work has been done by all the Superintendents and missionaries, by Rev. Johnson, and by the Agent at Shiprock, Mr. W. T. Shelton — where now the desert blossoms like the rose. The general policy as carried out by Major Peter Parquette, Superintendent of the Navaho, and his able assistants, has been to let them alone and permit them to work out their own salvation under a slight supervision. As the Navaho are today the largest body of Indians speaking the same language, and chiefly full-bloods, in this country, the Navaho statistics are sufficiently strong in the point of progress to appreciably raise the entire tone of Indians in the United States. This should be a lesson not lost on our Congress. While this is true and other communities, such as Tulalip Agency, Washington, show a marked gain, the general tone of Indian communities as to advance in the arts, health, etc., is not satisfactory. The table clearly indicates this. We must take into account two important factors in studying the reports of my correspondents. First, the Superintendents, very naturally, wish to present their wards in as creditable a manner as possible. They do not exaggerate, for they are all honest and competent observers. But they rather minimize the sad side of the story. The teachers, missionaries, priests, and the doctors rather lean toward a pessimistic view of conditions.

In our final analysis we find that a majority of the correspondents realize the difficulties under which the Indians labor, being discriminated against in their respective communities. That is, that although we claim citizenship for the Indians, all the facts point to the conclusion that the citizenship is not effective. While we claim to care for the health of the Indians, we have an insufficient number of doctors and hospitals. While we build many irrigation plants, prepare model farms, etc., we do not provide the Indians with sufficient seed, stock, implements, wagons, etc., whereby they may become self-supporting. Most important of all, where we have given the Indians deeds to their property, the majority of them lose the property. It is not pertinent in the table of statistics to enter into the question whether the Indian or the white man is at fault in this respect. The bald facts are to the effect that Indians lose their property.

The statistics indicate that education is advancing, and allotting of lands has far advanced. In education alone, the Indians certainly have advanced to a marked degree. Practically all Indians under fifty (save those referred to on page 27) have had some schooling.

For various reasons the names of the correspondents are omitted, although their original communications are preserved in my files. In various chapters throughout the book, I have incorporated partial or complete statements from these same correspondents. In the table, the answers to the questions have been presented in a few words. Many of the sentences are actual quotations, but others present in condensed form the opinions of the writers. Many correspondents have devoted an entire page to answering one question. Frequently, after answering the questions, the correspondent has written several pages in order to present his views concerning the Indian problem. Others have selected such questions as appeared to them to be of primary importance, and have answered these at considerable length. A majority of the correspondents realize that the protection of the Indian's property, the safeguarding of his health, and the relation between the two races constitute the essentials of the Indian problem, and that all other considerations are secondary.

# TABLE OF STATISTICS

| Correspondent | Is there more tuberculosis and trachoma among your Indians now than ten years ago? | Are children discharged from the schools because of diseases, properly treated at home? | Have many children the past ten years, been dismissed from the schools? | In your opinion, has there been a high percentage of deaths among the children, suffering from tuberculosis, sent from the schools to their homes the past ten years? | Are the Indians holding their allotments, or are the white people procuring the same? | Is the general condition of the Indians as a body more satisfactory than ten years ago? |
|---|---|---|---|---|---|---|
| **ALASKA** | | | | | | |
| No. 1 Nulato | Tuberculosis not very much increased, but ten times as much trachoma. | Not generally, but occasionally, seldom properly treated at home. | Very few, if any. | No. | Indians ready to sell regardless of consequences. | Rather less so. |
| No. 2 St. Michaels | No. | Not one. | Not one. | ......... | No white men here. | Much better. |
| No. 3 | Yes. | No. | Yes. | Uncertain. | None here. | No. |
| **ARIZONA** | | | | | | |
| No. 1 Ft. Defiance | Less tuberculosis and trachoma. | No. (No diseases treated properly at home). | Few, government regulation. | Yes. | Holding their allotments. | Yes, much better. |
| No. 2 Parker | Records do not show it. | No. | Eight, in last three years. | Yes. | Keeping their allotments. | Decidedly so. |
| No. 3 Phoenix | Increased, I think. | ......... | | | | |
| No. 4 Sacaton | No reliable statistics. | Not generally. | Not able to state. | Do not know | No allotments made. | Need water to improve. |
| No. 5 St. Michaels | No. | No diseases treated at home. | Few; tuberculosis cases. | Yes. | Holding allotments. | Yes. |
| No. 6 Tucson | Cannot answer. | Yes and No. | Very few. | Cannot answer. | Holding their allotments. | Cannot answer. |
| No. 7 ......... | There is. | Tuberculosis, discharged. Trachoma, treated in schools. | Many. | Yes. | Allotments held by the Government. | It is. |

| Correspondent | Is there more tuberculosis and trachoma among your Indians now than ten years ago? | Are children discharged from the schools because of diseases, properly treated at home? | Have many children the past ten years, been dismissed from the schools? | In your opinion, has there been a high percentage of deaths among the children, suffering from tuberculosis, sent from the schools to their homes the past ten years? | Are the Indians holding their allotments, or are the white people procuring the same? | Is the general condition of the Indians as a body more satisfactory than ten years ago? |
|---|---|---|---|---|---|---|
| CALIFORNIA | | | | | | |
| No. 1 Banning | No. | Yes, sent home to die. | Not many. | There has not. | No allotments. | Decidedly better. |
| No. 2 Campo | No. | No proper treatment at home. | One case on account of sickness. | No children sent home. | No allotments. | Fifty per cent better. |
| No. 3 Covelo | No. | No. No treatment at home. | Comparatively few. | Only healthy children enrolled. | No allotment held by white men. | More farming, morals very little improved. |
| No. 4 El Cujon | No. | No. | No. | No. | No allotments. | Yes. |
| No. 5 Greenville | I think not. | No. | Probably about twenty. | Yes. | Few allotments sold to best interest of Indian. | Yes. |
| No. 6 Likely | Yes, much more. | No. | No. | No. | Holding them. | No, much worse. |
| No. 7 Pala | There is much more than five years ago. | | Percentage very small. | All sent home have died (seven). | Holding them by law. | Much better. |
| No. 8 Ukiah | Not to my knowledge. | | ................ | ................ | ................ | ................ |
| No. 9 Yuma Yuma | No. | No. | ................ | No. | Holding them. | No. |
| No. 10 N. California | I would say not so prevalent. | By law, must be sent home. Necessary in few cases. | Not many. | No. | Just received allotments. | Yes, decidedly. |
| COLORADO | | | | | | |
| No. 1 Navaho Springs | No data. | No treatment at home. | No data. | Yes. | No allotments. | Yes. |
| No. DAKOTA | | | | | | |
| No. 1 Elbowoods | We have looked into the condition more, that is all, I think. | No. | No tuberculosis or trachoma cases admitted. | Yes. | Holding most of them. | Yes. |
| No. 2 Elbowoods | Yes, I believe there is. | | None of late. | Yes, from non-reservation schools. | Indian holds land. | Yes. |
| No. 3 Ft. Yates | Less frequent now. | No. | Few. | About 2%. | Holding them. | No. |
| No. 4 Standing Rock | Greatly increased. | Not sent home soon enough. | ................ | ................ | Holding them. | ................ |

| | | | | | | |
|---|---|---|---|---|---|---|
| **So. DAKOTA** | | | | | | |
| No. 1 Cheyenne | I think so, at least more of it is known. | I think not. | Not a great many. | No. | Some are, others want to sell. | No. |
| No. 2 Crow Creek | I do not think so. | No. | ............ | Percentage high. | Cannot dispose of lands. | No. |
| No. 3 Flandreau | More satisfactory. | | | ............ | Two-thirds of land now in hands of white people. | ............ |
| No. 4 Greenwood | About the same. | No treatment at home. | Not many. | No. | Very few sales. | In some respects yes. |
| No. 5 McLaughlin | Yes. | Only when case is hopeless. | Yes. | Very high. | Some sell. | Not much. |
| No. 6 Mission | Both very bad. | In some cases. | Yes. | High. | Holding allotments. | Yes and No. |
| No. 7 Oahe | I think not. | Not as a rule. | | Yes. | In most cases. | Yes. |
| No. 8 Pine Ridge | No. | Few given proper care. | Twenty-three from non-res'n schools, none from reservat'n. | One hundred percent from enteric tuber's, none from other tuber. | Holding allotments. | Much better. |
| No. 9 Pine Ridge | So it seems to me. | ............ | Few. | Per cent. not so high | Very slow sale. | Poorer. |
| No. 10 Rosebud | Less. | Not allowed to attend. | Few. | ............ | Holding own, but selling heirship lands. | Better. |
| No. 11 Rosebud Ag. | Not so much. | Yes. | None except for infectious diseases. | No. | Indians want to sell. | Yes. |
| No. 12 Sisseton | No. | No. | Sick children, because of lack of room. | Not a high percent. | Forty percent holding own. | Some improvement. |
| No. 13 Sisseton | No. | Some are. | Scarcely any. | Two percent. | Whites, as soon as they can. | Yes, great improvement. |
| No. 14 Sisseton | Probably less tuberculosis, more trachoma. | No. | Diseased ones not taken. | Yes. | Not allowed to sell. | No. |
| No. 15 St. Francis | Tuberculosis same, Trachoma better. | ............ | Not so very many. | No data. | | Yes, in some respects. |
| **IDAHO** | | | | | | |
| No. 1 Fort Hall | Yes. | No. | Aver. 31 per year. | Almost 100%. | None sold yet. | I think so. |
| No. 2 Ft. Lapwai | I think there is more. | No. | Yes, but taken to hospital. | Do not know. | Whites are buying heirship lands. | Yes. |
| No. 3 Lapwai | Less, it has been stated. | Examined before admitted. | Few. | Many deaths. | Largest percent held by Indians. | Better. |
| No. 4 Slickpoo | Yes, more tuberculosis. | Yes, for contagious diseases. | Yes. | Yes. | Whites buying from half-breeds. | I think not. |
| **IOWA** | | | | | | |
| No. 1 Toledo | Not on the increase. | They are not. | No data. | No. | Unallotted. | Yes. |

| Correspondent | Is there more tuberculosis and trachoma among your Indians now than ten years ago? | Are children discharged from the schools because of diseases, properly treated at home? | Have many children the past ten years, been dismissed from the schools? | In your opinion, has there been a high percentage of deaths among the children, suffering from tuberculosis, sent from the schools to their homes the past ten years? | Are the Indians holding their allotments, or are the white people procuring the same? | Is the general condition of the Indians as a body more satisfactory than ten years ago? |
|---|---|---|---|---|---|---|
| **KANSAS** | | | | | | |
| No. 1 Baxter Springs | Yes, among some families. | No. | No. | No. | Yes, until restriction is removed. | Yes. |
| No. 2 Powhattan | No. | Not well cared for at home. | Comparatively few. | Yes. | Majority are. | Yes, except for morals |
| **MINNESOTA** | | | | | | |
| No. 1 Winnebago | No,—not so much. | No. | None from our school. | Not from our school. | White people rent or buy fast. | No. |
| No. 2 Beaulieu | More tuberculosis, less trachoma. | None. | ............. | ............. | Only 15% will hold allotments in 6 years. | No. |
| No. 3 Cass Lake | I should judge so. | No. | Not many, they are examined before admitted. | Percentage high | Whites get all they can. | No. |
| No. 4 Cloquet | Not more than ten years ago. | Very few. | Few. | Thirty percent. | Holding their allotments. | No. |
| **MONTANA** | | | | | | |
| No. 1 Browning | No. | In many cases. | No data. | High percent. | No allotments made. | Yes. |
| No. 2 Crow Ag'cy | No. | Not a great many. | No. | High percent. | Sell patents in fee and heirship lands. | Yes, decidedly. |
| No. 3 Poplar | Tuberculosis same, more trachoma. | ............. | About ten a year. | Percentage is above the average. | Indians just received them. | Far better. |
| No. 4 Jocko | No. | No | No boarding-school. | No. | Full-bloods are, the others sell. | Yes. |
| No. 5 Lame Deer | Yes, more. | Not properly treated at home. | Not many. | High percent. | No allotments. | Yes |
| No. 6 Lodge Grass | No. | No. | Two in ten years. | No, the reverse is true. | Prefer to sell when they can. | Yes, decidedly. |
| No. 7 St. Ignatius | At least as much. | Tuberculosis cases sent home, trachoma treated at home. | Twenty-five in ten years. | Very high percent. | Holding them. | No. |
| No. 8 Wolf Point | I do not think so. | No. | No. | No. | Holding allotments. | Yes, much. |

348)

| Location | | | | | | |
|---|---|---|---|---|---|---|
| **NEBRASKA** | | | | | | |
| No. 1 Santee | Less tuberculosis but possibly more trachoma. | Very few. | No. | Very high percent. | Holding them fairly well. | Yes. |
| No. 2 Santee | I think not. More notice is made of it. | ............ | Cannot say. | Cannot say. | Many pass into white hands. | Yes. |
| **NEVADA** | | | | | | |
| No. 1 Nixon | No. | No. | Four. | No. | No allotments made. | Yes, very much. |
| No. 2 Schurz | Yes. | No. | Twenty to thirty. | Yes. | Holding allotments | Yes. |
| **NEW MEXICO** | | | | | | |
| No. 1 Albuquerque | Apparently there is more. | No. | Yes. | Yes. | Holding allotments. | Yes, slowly. |
| No. 2 Gallup | I do not think so. | No. | No record. | No. | Holding allotments. | Yes. |
| **OKLAHOMA** | | | | | | |
| No. 1 Anadarko | Probably more is known. | Not as a rule. | Do not know of many. | Yes. | Some Indians sell. | Yes. |
| No. 2 Anadarko | About the same. | No. | No, not very many. | Yes. | Those who can, sell. | Yes. |
| No. 3 Anadarko | On the increase. | Not as a rule. | Ninety-six not admitted, 25 dismissed from 1300 this year. | No. | Dispose of them whenever they can. | Yes. |
| No. 4 Atoka | I think so. | No. | Do not know. | Yes. | Whites getting many. | No. |
| No. 5 Bacone | No data. | No. | ............ | Yes. | Whites getting many. | ............ |
| No. 6 Carnegie | Less tuberculosis, trachoma same. | ............ | Not many. | Yes. | Whites getting many. | No. |
| No. 7 Checotah | Yes. | No. | A good number. | Yes. | All unrestricted are sold. | No. |
| No. 8 Darlington | Less tuberculosis, trachoma unknown ten years ago. | Not here. | Yes. | Very high, but reducing. | Both are true. | Yes. |
| No. 9 Durant | Considerably less. | Are not admitted. | ............ | ............ | Selling as fast as they can. | Yes. |
| No. 10 Durant | No increase. | No. | No. | Nearly all die. | Whites getting them. | Indian says, no. I say, yes and no. |
| No. 11 Eufaula | Not increasing. | No. | Six this year. | Not high. | Whites try to. | Yes. |
| No. 12 Hobart | No. | Yes and no. | No. | ............ | Holding allotments. | Yes. |
| No. 13 Holdenville | There is. | No. | I do not know. | ............ | They sell all they can. | Yes. |
| No. 14 Hugo | More. | Discharged for out-door exercise. | Not many. | ............ | Holding allotments. | Indian not satisfied |
| No. 15 Hugo | Less tuberculosis, trachoma same. | Very few. | Do not know. | High percentage. | Few Indians hold all their allotments. | Yes. |

| Correspondent | Is there more tuberculosis and trachoma among your Indians now than ten years ago? | Are children discharged from the schools because of diseases, properly treated at home? | Have many children the past ten years, been dismissed from the schools? | In your opinion, has there been a high percentage of deaths among the children, suffering from tuberculosis, sent from the schools to their homes the past ten years? | Are the Indians holding their allotments, or are the white people procuring the same? | Is the general condition of the Indians as a body more satisfactory than ten years ago? |
|---|---|---|---|---|---|---|
| **OKLAHOMA (cont.)** | | | | | | |
| No. 16 Lawton | Less tuberculosis, more trachoma. | Cared for in the schools. | Very few. | High percentage. | Very few sell their lands. | Yes. |
| No. 17 Mountain View | Less tuberculosis, more trachoma. | Not treated at home. | A good many, I think. | No. | Holding them. | Yes. |
| No. 18 Muskogee | More satisfactory conditions. | .......... | .......... | .......... | .......... | Yes. |
| No. 19 Pawhuska | Less tuberculosis, more trachoma. | .......... | None. | No. | Whites buying all they can. | No. Decidedly. |
| No. 20 Pawhuska | No, I think not. | In most cases, no. | I think not. | Nearly all have died. | Very few sales made. | Yes. |
| No. 21 Sapulpa | Tuberculosis more, trachoma common 10 years ago. | Not treated at home. | Not as many as should have been. | Yes. | Whites hold large per cent. | Yes. |
| No. 22 Shawnee | We think not. | One or two cases. | Very few. | Three fatal cases. | Holding allotments. | Marked improvement. |
| No. 23 Watanga | Less tuberculosis. | Not given proper care. | Allowed to go home if diseased. | .......... | Little demand for land | Better. |
| No. 24 White Eagle | I do not think so. | Not as a rule. | Very small percent. | Very low. | Nearly all holding lands. | Better. |
| No. 25 Wyandotte | I do not think so. | Few. | Three. | One has died, there has not been. | Whites hold a little less than one-half. | Better. |
| **OREGON** | | | | | | |
| No. 1 Klamath | About the same. | Not given proper treatment. | Yes. | Yes. | Sales just beginning. | Yes. |
| No. 2 Pendleton | More tuberculosis | Few. | .......... | .......... | Full-bloods hold, mixed-bloods sell. | .......... |
| No. 3 Roseburg | No data. | No. | No record. | .......... | .......... | Yes. |
| No. 4 Warm Spring | More trachoma. | | | Yes. | Holding them. | Yes. |
| **UTAH** | | | | | | |
| No. 1 Salt Lake City | No data. | | | | | .......... |
| **NEW YORK** | | | | | | |
| No. 1 Gowanda | No. | No. | No. | No. | Holding them. | Yes. |

(350)

| Agency | | | | | | |
|---|---|---|---|---|---|---|
| **WASHINGTON** | | | | | | |
| No. 1 Bellingham | No. | Yes. | Five. | All die. | Indians hold lands. | Yes. |
| No. 2 Bellingham | No. | Never treated properly at home. | A good many. | ........ | Whites getting lands. | Yes. |
| No. 3 Marysville | ........ | ........ | ........ | | ........ | Naturally better on account of selling land. |
| No. 4 Neah Bay | More tuberculosis, less trachoma. | Yes. | Do not know. | No. | Sold lands off reservation only. | Yes. |
| No. 5 No. Yakima | Perhaps not. | Not treated properly at home. | Cannot say. | ........ | Whites swindle lands. | Yes, but losing lands. |
| No. 6 Nespelem | More prevalent, I think. | Not as a rule. | Cannot tell. | No. | Not over 10% have passed into white hands. | Yes. |
| No. 7 St. Mary's | No. | Never properly treated at home. | Quite a few. | Some have. | Just now. | Worse on account of whiskey which they get all the time. |
| No. 8 Takoma | More tuberculosis, less trachoma. | We discharge only when very sick, and take charge of them. | Twenty from our school. | Seven died. | Only few hold lands after reservation is opened. | Yes. |
| No. 9 Tulalip | No. | Occasionally. | Five percent or less. | Yes. | Whites encroaching. | Generally, yes. |
| No. 10 Wheeler | I think there is more. | No. | Taken to government hospital. | Do not know. | White people buying heirship lands. | Yes. |
| **WISCONSIN** | | | | | | |
| No. 1 Adanah | No. | ........ | No. | No. | Cannot sell. | Yes. |
| No. 2 Ashland | No record of, ten years ago. Plenty now. | No, children not cared for at home. | Some. | Yes. | Indians holding them. | Hardly. |
| No. 3 Bayfield | I think not. | They get better treatment at the schools. | ........ | ........ | Whites not getting much. | Yes. |
| No. 4 Carter | There is some here. | No school at Agency. | No dismissals. | Cannot answer. | Indians hold no allotments. | Conditions improved since Agency was established. |
| No. 5 Kesbena | No. | Yes. | Thirty, but some have been transferred. | No. | Yes, whites buy when they can. | No. |
| No. 6 Kesbena | No. | Yes, or not admitted. | No record. | No. | Large number at Stockridge have. Menominees not allotted. | Very much so. |
| No. 7 Tomah | I think there is more. | No. | About fifteen. | No. | Indians holding them. | More satisfactory. |

(351)

| Correspondent | Is immorality, in your opinion, due to the presence of low whites, or because of the Indian himself? | Which of the two classes are in the better condition, the mixed-blood or full-blood Indian? | Are the white people crowding your Indians and taking advantage of them? | Do the Indians who are trained near their homes do better than Indians who are educated at a distance and return? | Is the population increasing or decreasing? | Are white men marrying Indian women in order to secure property? | Is the Government properly protecting the Indians? |
|---|---|---|---|---|---|---|---|
| **ALASKA** | | | | | | | |
| No. 1 Nolato | Both, former about five times as much as latter. | Not much difference. | Yes, to some extent, but Indian retaliates. | There is no difference. | Slightly decreasing. | No. | Bureau of Education, yes; laws very bad. |
| No. 2 St. Michaels | Low whites | .............. | | Better, (Yes). | Slightly increasing. | .............. | .............. |
| No. 3 .......... | Low whites. | Both in poor shape. | Not much. | .............. | Decreasing. | .............. | Not enough protecting. |
| **ARIZONA** | | | | | | | |
| No. 1 Ft. Defiance | Indian himself. | Mixed-bloods. | A little off the reservation. | Yes. | Slightly increasing. | No. | No. |
| No. 2 Parker | Due to old customs. | Few mixed-bloods same condition. | They are not. | Yes | Decreasing among the full-bloods. | No. | It is. |
| No. 3 Phoenix | .............. | .............. | .............. | | | | .............. |
| No. 4 Sacaton | Cases due to Indian. | Few mixed-bloods, these not impr'v'd | Yes, in regard to water. | Yes. | Slight increase, I think. | No. | Yes, but hampered by law and politics |
| No. 5 St. Michaels | Due to Indian, because of customs. | Mixed-bloods, only a few, however | Yes, off the reservation. | Yes. | Slightly increasing | No. | No. |
| No. 6 Tucson | To Indians. | Very few mixed-bloods. | Among the Papagos but not the Pimas. | I think so. | Increasing. | No. | Not as regards land and water |
| No. 7 .......... | Low whites. | No mixed bloods. | Yes, if possible. | Most assuredly. | Increasing. | Law forbids inter-marriages. | No. |
| **CALIFORNIA** | | | | | | | |
| No. 1 Banning | Little immorality. | Mixed-bloods. | No. | About same. | Just holding its own. | No. | Yes. |
| No. 2 Campo | Indian himself. | Few mixed-bloods, these are better. | No. | About same. | Slowly decreasing. | No. | Yes. |
| No. 3 Covelo | Both. | Mixed-bloods. | Not crowding, but taking advantage of necessities. | Yes. | About same. | Only reprobates. | Yes. |

| Location | | | | | | | |
|---|---|---|---|---|---|---|---|
| **CALIFORNIA (cont.)** | | | | | | | |
| No. 4 El Cujon | Very few cases. | ............ | No. | Few of them. | Increasing. | No. | Yes. |
| No. 5 Greenville | To both. | The mixed-bloods. | To no great extent. | No. | Holding its own. | No. | Yes. |
| No. 6 Likely | Low whites. | Full-bloods. | No. | Yes. | Decreasing. | No. | No. |
| No. 7 Pala | Little immorality. | Very few full-bloods here. | No. | Yes, much better. | Very slight increase. | No. | Yes, all it can. |
| No. 8 Ukiah | Indian himself. | | | Yes. | Same. | ............ | No. |
| No. 9 Yuma, Yuma | | Very few mixed-bloods here. | No. | Same. | | No. | Yes. |
| No. 10 N. California | Low whites. | Full-bloods. | No. | ............ | Seems to be on the increase now. | No. | Government has done very little. |
| **COLORADO** | | | | | | | |
| No. 1 Navaho Springs | No whites here. | No mixed-bloods here. | No. | Yes. | Increasing three percent per year. | No. | Yes. |
| **No. DAKOTA** | | | | | | | |
| No. 1 Elbowoods | Indian himself. | No difference. | No not much. | No difference noted. | Slightly increasing. | No. | More energy needed. |
| No. 2 Elbowoods | Indian himself | Full bloods. | No. | Yes. | Decreasing. | Law forbids it. | Yes. |
| No. 3 Ft. Yates | Low whites and mixed-bloods. | Mixed-bloods financially. | No. | Home training seems best. | Increasing. | Very seldom. | Intentions good, officials bad. |
| No. 4 Standing Rock | To Government, because Indian cannot marry until eighteen. | Full-bloods. | Yes. | Yes. | Increasing. | No. | No. |
| **So. DAKOTA** | | | | | | | |
| No. 1 Cheyenne | Both. | Mixed-bloods. | Yes. | Yes. | Holding its own. | Yes. | ............ |
| No. 2 Crow Creek | Indian nature (himself). | Mixed-bloods. | No. | Little difference. | Vacillating. | No. | Yes |
| No. 3 Flandreau | ............ | Mixed-bloods a little. | No. | ............ | ............ | No. | What is necessary. |
| No. 4 Greenwood | Both. | Mixed-bloods. | Yes. | Yes. | Increasing. | No. | Yes. |
| No. 5 McLaughlin | Both. | Mixed, materially, otherwise full-blood. | Only a large cattle company. | Yes. | Slight increase. | Very few. | No, in many respects. |
| No. 6 Mission | Low whites. | Same. | Often. | Yes. | ............ | Not often. | Failure. |
| No. 7 Oahe | Low whites. | Not much difference. | Not to any extent. | Yes. | Increasing. | Not to any extent. | Yes. |
| No. 8 Pine Ridge | Indian (Mixed-blood). | Mixed-blood. | No. | Yes. | Increasing. | Some. | Yes. |

| Correspondent | Is immorality, in your opinion, due to the presence of low whites, or because of the Indian himself? | Which of the two classes are in the better condition, the mixed-blood or full-blood Indian? | Are the white people crowding your Indians and taking advantage of them? | Do the Indians who are trained near their homes do better than Indians who are educated at a distance and return? | Is the population increasing or decreasing? | Are white men marrying Indian women in order to secure property? | Is the Government properly protecting the Indians? |
|---|---|---|---|---|---|---|---|
| So. Dakota (cont.) | | | | | | | |
| No. 9 Pine Ridge | Low whites. | Mixed-blood. | No. | Yes. | Mixed-bloods increasing, full-bloods decreasing. | Some. | .......... |
| No. 10 Rosebud | Both. | Both in some respects. | No. | Yes. | Increasing 1%. | Some. | In some ways. |
| No. 11 Rosebud Ag. | Indian himself. | Mixed-blood. | Not much. | Yes. | 4500 to 5490. | ......... | Yes. |
| No. 12 Sisseton | Indian himself. | Hard to say, full-blood in health. | Yes, when they can. | Cannot tell. | Increasing slowly. | Few. | Indians say no. |
| No. 13 Sisseton | Low whites. | Little difference. | Some try to. | Yes. | Increasing. | Some cases. | Indians are citizens. |
| No. 13 Sisseton | Indian mostly. | Little difference. | When they can. | Little difference. | Mixed-bloods increasing, full-bloods decreasing. | Not now, few cases. | To some extent. |
| No. 15 St. Francis | ............ | Mixed-blood. | Some. | Yes. | Slight increase. | ......... | Dealt honestly with them. |
| Idaho | | | | | | | |
| No. 1 Ft. Hall | Indian on sex, Low whites on liquor. | Not much difference. | No but would like to. | Yes. | Decreasing. | Not many. | Yes. |
| No. 2 Ft. Lapwai | Low whites. | Full-bloods. | Yes. | Yes. | Don't know. | Rarely. | Yes and No. |
| No. 3 Lapwai | Indian customs. | Mixed-bloods. | Not generally. | Yes. | Increase slightly. | No. | Yes, here. |
| No. 4 Slickpoo | Both. | Mixed-bloods little better. | Yes, as much as they can. | Much better. | Decreasing. | A few. | Not as regards morality and religion. |
| Iowa | | | | | | | |
| No. 1 Toledo | They keep aloof from whites. Indians themselves. | No noticeable difference. | Whites encourage them, but few prey on them. No. | ............ | Increasing slowly. | No. | .......... |
| Kansas | | | | | | | |
| No. 1 Baxter Springs | Indian himself. | Mixed-bloods. | When they get a chance. | Yes. | Decreasing. | No. | Yes. |
| No. 2 Powhattan | Indian himself. | Mixed-bloods, except morally. | Yes. | No. | Increasing some. | No. (Some Indians marry low white women.) | Yes, could be improved. |

| Location | | | | | | |
|---|---|---|---|---|---|---|
| **MINNESOTA** | | | | | | |
| No. 1 Winnebago | Low whites. | Not much difference. | Yes, to a great extent. | Stationary. | Not much now. | Indians dissatisfied. |
| No. 2 Beaulieu | Low whites. | ............ | ............ | ............ | 75% increase. | ............ |
| No. 3 Cass Lake | White man 90%. | Full-blood. | Yes. | Full-blood decreasing, Mixed-blood increasing. | ............ | Government ineffective. |
| No. 4 Cloquet | Low whites. | Mixed-blood financially; full-blood morally. | No. | Full-blood decreasing, mixed-bloods on the increase. | Yes, but not many. | Yes. |
| **MONTANA** | | | | | | |
| No. 1 Browning | Low whites. | Mixed-blood as a rule. | No whites here. | Increasing for two years. | Few. | Yes. |
| No. 2 Crow Ag. | Indian nature. | Full-blood, but little difference. | No. | Slowly decreasing. | Two, but do not know the incentive. | Yes, all possible. |
| No. 3 Poplar | Early low whites. | Mixed-blood. | Few whites here. | Increasing, Indian blood. | Few cases. | Yes. |
| No. 4 Jocko | Indian himself. | Mixed-blood. | Some trying to. | Increasing slightly. | Not to any extent. | Yes, all it can. |
| No. 5 Lame Deer | What little there is, is due to Indian. | Both the same. | No. | Standstill. | Three marriages to whites in eight years. | Yes. |
| No. 6 Lodge Grass | Low whites helped. | ............ | No. | Slight increase. | Very few whites marry Indians. | Yes, but system wrong. |
| No. 7 St. Ignatius | Low whites. | Mixed-bloods materially, full-bloods morally. | Trying to. | Full-bloods decreasing, but the population increasing. | Yes. | To some extent. |
| No. 8 Wolf Point | Both. | Full-bloods. | No. | Increasing. | No. | Trying to. |
| **NEBRASKA** | | | | | | |
| No. 1 Santee | Indian himself. | Mixed-bloods. | No, not to any extent. | Standstill. | No. | Yes. |
| No. 2 Santee | Both. | Full-bloods generally. | Yes, when they can. | Increasing. | No. | Not in some cases. |
| **NEVADA** | | | | | | |
| No. 1 Nixon | No whites here. | Full-bloods. | No. | Increasing. | No. | Yes. |
| No. 2 Schurz | Both. | Full-bloods. | Not on the reservation. | Decreasing. | No. | Yes, on reservation. |

| Correspondent | Is immorality, in your opinion, due to the presence of low whites, or because of the Indian himself? | Which of the two classes are in the better condition, the mixed-blood or full-blood Indian? | Are the white people crowding your Indians and taking advantage of them? | Do the Indians who are trained near their homes do better than Indians who are educated at a distance and return? | Is the population increasing or decreasing? | Are white men marrying Indian women in order to secure property? | Is the Government properly protecting the Indians? |
|---|---|---|---|---|---|---|---|
| NEW MEXICO | | | | | | | |
| No. 1 Albuquerque | Indian himself. | Mixed-bloods. | A certain class does. | No. | Increasing. | No. | Yes. |
| No. 2 Gallup | Indian himself. | No mixed-bloods. | No. | No. | Standstill. | No. | Yes. |
| OKLAHOMA | | | | | | | |
| No. 1 Anadarko | Both. | Same. | Some whites are. | Same. | Increasing. | In a few cases. | Yes and No. |
| No. 2 Anadarko | Largely to low whites. | Same. | Yes, when they can. | Yes, as a rule. | Increasing slightly. | Not to any extent. | ............ |
| No. 3 Anadarko | Indian himself. | Full-bloods. | No. | Yes. | Increasing. | A few. | Everything it can do. |
| No. 4 Atoka | To low whites. | Mixed-bloods. | Yes. | No. | Full-bloods decreasing. | Not much now. | No. |
| No. 5 Bacone | Both, mostly to whites. | ............ | Very much. | Yes. | ............ | Yes. | Partially so. |
| No. 6 Carnegie | Low whites. | Mixed-bloods. | Yes. | Yes. | Increasing. | Some, few. | No. |
| No. 7 Checotah | Low whites. | Mixed-bloods. | Yes. | No difference. | Full-bloods decreasing. | Not now. | Trying to. |
| No. 8 Darlington | Low whites. | Full-bloods, exceptions favor mixed. | No. | Cannot say. | Increasing slightly. | Not here. | Not doing all it can, or should. |
| No. 9 Durant | Both. | Mixed-bloods. | Many try to. | No. | Full-bloods decreasing, mixed increasing. | Not as much now. | Doing a great deal. |
| No. 10 Durant | Low whites. | Mixed-bloods. | Yes. | No difference. | Decreasing. | Yes, low whites are. | Do not think so. |
| No. 11 Eufaula | Early low whites, now Indian. | Mixed-bloods. | Yes. | ............ | Full bloods decreasing. | Yes. | It is now. |
| No. 12 Hobart | Both. | ............ | When they can. | Yes. | Increasing. | ............ | As far as Indian will let it. |
| No. 13 Holdenville | Low whites. | Mixed-bloods. | Yes. | I don't know. | Decreasing. | Not now. | No. |
| No. 14 Hugo | Both. | Mixed-bloods. | When they can. | Same. | Decreasing. | Yes. | Government does not understand. |
| No. 15 Hugo | Low whites. | Mixed-bloods. | Yes. | Yes. | Decreasing. | Not as much now. | Yes, but it makes mistakes. |

| | | | | | | |
|---|---|---|---|---|---|---|
| **OKLAHOMA (cont.)** | | | | | | |
| No. 16 Lawton | Low whites. | Little difference. | A certain class do. | Yes. | Increasing 15% in ten years. | A few have. | Yes. |
| No. 17 Mountain View | Both. | No difference. | Many do. | No difference. | Increase. | No. | As well as Indian lets it. |
| No. 18 Muskogee | Indian himself. | Mixed-bloods. | Yes. | No. | .......... | Not as a rule. | Making a conscientious effort. |
| No. 19 Pawhuska | Low whites. | Full-bloods. | Yes. | Yes. | Full-bloods decreasing, population increasing. | Nearly every time. | All it can. |
| No. 20 Pawhuska | Low whites and colored people. | Mixed-bloods. | Yes. | Yes. | Increasing. | Yes. | As far as possible |
| No. 21 Sapulpa | Both. | Full-bloods. | Yes. | Not if those trained away are well advanced. | .......... | Yes. | .......... |
| No. 22 Shawnee | Both. | Mixed-bloods. | Some try to. | Young children do. | Increasing. | .......... | Doing efficient work. |
| No. 23 Watanga | Early whites. | Same. | Some try to. | No difference. | Mixed-bloods increased. Full-bloods, standstill. | Two cases in 15 years. | All it can. |
| No. 24 White Eagle | Both. | Same. | They cannot. | Yes. | Increase. | No. | Yes, but needs changes. |
| No. 25 Wyandotte | Low whites. | Same. | All they can. | No difference. | Slight increase. | Not markedly true. | All it can. |
| **OREGON** | | | | | | |
| No. 1 Klamath | Indian himself. | Mixed-blood. | No. | I think so. | Standstill. | Not yet. | I think so. |
| No. 2 Pendleton | .......... | .......... | .......... | .......... | Full-blood decreasing, mixed-blood increasing. | No. | Yes. |
| No. 3 Roseburg | Both. | Mixed-blood. | Yes. | Yes. | .......... | Yes. | Yes. |
| No. 4 Warm Sp. | Indian (no whites here.) | Same. | Some do. | No. | Decreasing. | No. | Yes. |
| **UTAH** | | | | | | |
| No. 1 Salt Lake City | .......... | | | | | | .......... |
| **WASHINGTON** | | | | | | |
| No. 1 Bellingham | No low whites here. | Same. | They cannot. | Yes. | Increasing. | None. | Yes, could be improved. |
| No. 2 Bellingham | Low whites. | Same. | No, except gamblers. | I think so. | Standstill. | They try. | Yes, but need police. |
| No. 3 Marysville | .......... | Materially the mixed-bloods. Morally the full-bloods. | Few. | .......... | Slowly decreasing. | Very few. | Yes, at least theoretically. |

| Correspondent | Is immorality, in your opinion, due to the presence of low whites, or because of the Indian himself? | Which of the two classes are in the better condition, the mixed-blood or full-blood Indian? | Are the white people crowding your Indians and taking advantage of them? | Do the Indians who are trained near their homes do better than Indians who are educated at a distance and return? | Is the population increasing or decreasing? | Are white men marrying Indian women in order to secure property? | Is the Government properly protecting the Indians? |
|---|---|---|---|---|---|---|---|
| WASHINGTON (Cont.) | | | | | | | |
| No. 4 Neah Bay | Indian nature. | All mixed-blood. | No, they assist them. | In my opinion, no. | Some tribes increase, others decrease. | No. | Yes. |
| No. 5 No. Yakima | Low whites and colored people. | Mixed-blood. | Yes, in every way possible. | Do not know. | Holding own. | Yes. | No. |
| No. 6 Nespelem | Low whites. | Mixed-blood. | Yes, in places. | Yes, as a rule. | Mixed-bloods increasing. Full-bloods decreasing. | Not very much. | Doing very well. |
| No. 7 St. Mary's | Whiskey | About the same. | No. | I think so. | About the same. | They try. | Yes. Lack of police is bad. |
| No. 8 Tacoma | .............. | Mixed, temporally; full-blood otherwise. | As soon as they can. | Little difference. | Increasing. | Hardly ever. | Only on the reservation. |
| No. 9 Tulalip | Both. | Mixed-blood. | When they can. | Yes. | Increasing slightly. | Not to any extent. | Not sure it has. |
| No. 10 Wheeler | Low whites. | Full-blood. | Yes. | Yes. | .............. | Rare. | Yes and no. |
| WISCONSIN | | | | | | | |
| No. 1 Adanah | Low whites. | All mixed-bloods. | No. | Yes. | Standing still. | Now and then. | Too much red tape. |
| No. 2 Ashland | Both. | Mixed-bloods. | No. | Yes. | Decreasing. | No. | Yes. |
| No. 3 Bayfield | Low whites mostly. | Full-bloods, morally. Mixed financially and intellectually. | Treated as whites. | About same. | Full-bloods decreasing. Population increasing. | Occasionally | Yes. |
| No. 4 Carter | Very little immorality. | Only full-bloods. | To a small degree. | None have gone away. | Increasing. | No inter-marriages | Done a great deal. |
| No. 5 Kesbena | Both. | Mixed-bloods. | No whites here. | Yes. | Small increase. | No. | .............. |
| No. 6 Kesbena | Both. | Full-bloods. | Traders, outside, do. | Same. | Increasing. | Not yet. | Here it is. |
| No. 7 Tomah | Only to whites when they sell liquor. | What few mixed-breeds we have are better. | Not here. | Yes, perhaps. | Increased a little. | Indians have no property. | Yes. Mistakes are made. |
| NEW YORK | | | | | | | |
| No. 1 Gowanda | Indian himself. | No full-bloods. | Only hotels and saloons. | No. | .............. | No. | Not in some cases. |

(358)

# CHAPTER XXXIII. FARMING AND STOCK–RAISING
## INDIAN FAIRS

Commissioner Sells has made the "gospel of work" the chief aim of his administration. That is, he has emphasized and encouraged farming and stock-raising. Before quoting from the Commissioner's reports and circulars on this subject, it should not be taken amiss if the statement is made that during the administrations of Commissioners Morgan and Jones, this important feature of Indian education was not sufficiently emphasized. Many of the central, northern and mountain Indians took naturally to stock-raising. With the care of the horse, they were familiar. It was but a step from horse-raising to cattle-raising, as has been illustrated in the case of the Sioux (page 309). Truly, a number of tribes possessed more cattle a generation ago than at the present time.

From information received, I take it that under the administrations of Messrs. Leupp and Valentine, a serious effort was made to encourage farming and stock-raising, on a larger scale. While this new movement may have been inaugurated by either Mr. Leupp or Mr. Valentine, when Mr. Abbott became acting Commissioner, he encouraged and expanded efforts in this direction. Orders were issued to Superintendents, giving greater discretion in supervising individual Indian moneys; the leasing policy was simplified and self-supporting Indians permitted to lease their surplus lands and to a greater extent handle their own funds; a higher standard with larger salary was established for the Indian Service farmer, who was expected to do house to house work among the Indians under his supervision, giving practical advice and securing definite results in the way of increased production from Indian land; active cooperation between the Bureaus of Plant and Animal Industry of the Department of Agriculture was promoted; the Civil Service Commission provided tests for farmers intended to secure men with more experience and practical equipment, and the United States was divided into four Civil Service districts in order that eligible farmers might be secured for that part of the Indian country where their farming experience had been obtained. The possibilities of the working out of this policy in all its phases was demonstrated particularly on the Winnebago reservation in Nebraska, where in three years while Albert H. Kneale was Superintendent, this tribe of Indians was practically transformed into one of the most sober and industrious groups of Indians to be found on any allotted Indian reservation in the United States. From 3000 acres of Indian-farmed land, in the first year, under the new program, which gave the Superintendent freedom to act without discouraging delays in Washington, there were 12,000 acres farmed by Indians at the end of three years, and so many of the Indians had moved to their allotments that the Dutch Reformed Church had to build a new church and locate an additional missionary out in the heart of the reservation in order to reach its Indian adherents.

With the advent of Mr. Sells, as has been stated, the Department realized that if the Indian is to be saved, much more should be done than the mere issuance of instructions to Superintendents. Assistant Commissioner, Edgar B. Meritt has, the past few years, been very active in advocating reimbursable appropriations for Indians in order that they might purchase live stock and farming implements to improve their large areas of agricultural lands.

Mr. Sells' official instructions, under date of September 2, 1914, to all Superintendents are as follows:—

"I am not satisfied that we are making the greatest use of our school farms. They usually consist of large tracts of fertile land capable of raising every crop that the climate in which the school is located will permit. In some cases these farms are well irrigated.

"In every case the schools have been or can be furnished with all the equipment necessary to till their farms to the fullest extent, and they can be furnished with stock with which to make a substantial showing in stock-raising.

"The agricultural training of the boy pupils in our schools furnishes ample opportunity for intensive farming. If this training is to be of real value and be effective in accomplishing its purpose, the farming operations should be financially successful and at the same time conducted in accordance with modern methods.

"I am convinced that there is a large field for improvement in the handling of these farms, and I want every field officer who has charge of such a farm to see that its management is of such a nature as will insure its development to the highest degree of productiveness, practical usefulness and object lesson.

"The constantly increasing demands on the various appropriations for the Indian Service make it necessary not only to exercise the most careful economy consistent with the end sought, but at the same time to see that every resource in connection with Indian education and industry is developed to the highest obtainable degree.

"See that employees in charge of your farms are men capable of rendering proper and efficient service, carefully determine the suitable crops for the particular soil of the tillable land of your farm, giving the best attention to the raising and use of these crops.

"Our farms should grow corn, oats, wheat, and raise alfalfa, clover, timothy, etc. You should raise all the potatoes and other vegetables consumed. We should not be satisfied with raising feed for the school livestock, but we should raise everything the farm, garden and orchard will produce.

"I want you to raise livestock to the fullest of your capacity; raise colts from the school mares; let your calves grow into beef for your school. Grow a good herd of hogs to follow the cattle that you feed and use the waste from the table at the school. Make your dairy amply large and of such kind that there will be plenty of milk, cream and butter. Feed the skim-milk to the hogs and grow your pork meat. Where practicable cure your own bacon and ham, make your own sausage and dry and corn your own beef."

There is more, but this will indicate the earnest effort of the Commissioner to improve conditions.

In recent years, Indian fairs have become very popular, and are held on most reservations, or at schools. The old "Wild West" feature has been eliminated. At Red Lake, Minn., September 19th, 1914, the Ojibwa fair was attended by 2000 persons. The published account in the *New York World* stated: —

"Exhibits of grain grown by the Indians included specimens of oats, barley and wheat that would average twenty-five bushels to the acre, and yellow dent corn fully matured.

"What was perhaps next in importance was the stock display, which included blooded animals, the registered Holstein and Durham cattle being most numerous. The judging of the stock was done by Supt. C. G. Selvig, of the Crookston School.

"There was also a fine display of vegetables and fruit, all of which were raised by the Indians. The exhibits included cantaloupes and sugar-sweet watermelons. There were also crab apples and displays of other apples and fruits.

"The women and girls had exhibits of bread, pies, cakes, jellies, preserves, pickles, and other dainties. But probably the most artistic and beautiful display ever seen at a county fair was found in the display of beaded work. These exhibits not only were done neatly, but the beaded designs and colorings were gorgeous. The exhibit included among other things head dress, sacques, moccasins, dresses, belts, hat bands, banners, buckskin leggings, and jackets. All were new, having been made by the Chippewas the past year for display at the fair.

LEUPP HALL—STUDENTS' DINING ROOM

Domestic Science, Bakery, Domestic Art, etc., Chilocco Indian School, Oklahoma

"There was no disorder nor intoxication."

Commissioner Sells seized upon the fair proposition as a means of extending industry.  A portion of his sensible address to Superintendents is:—

"You should now be arranging for your Indian fair, and I desire to impress upon you my idea of the purpose and possibilities of these exhibitions.

"I want these fairs so conducted as to open to the Indians the vision of the industrial achievements to which they should aspire.  I want them to be an inspiration in arousing in the Indian a clear appreciation of the great opportunity before him for real industrial advancement.

"The ownership of land always has been and always must be the principal basis of man's wealth.  A wise development of the vast natural resources of the Indian reservations has tremendous possibilities.  The Indian's rich agricultural lands, his vast areas of grass land, his great forests and his practically untouched mineral resources should be so utilized as to become a powerful instrument for his civilization.

"I hold it to be an economic and social crime, in this age and under modern conditions, to permit thousands of acres of fertile lands belonging to the Indians and capable of great industrial development to lie in unproductive idleness.

"With keen appreciation of these conditions Congress in the current appropriation bill has made available for the Indians over $600,000 as a reimbursable fund, and $250,000 additional for general and specific industrial use, all for the purchase of stock and farm equipment, as well as about $800,000 of the funds of the Confederated Bands of Utes for the civilization and support of those Indians.

"I feel that a serious obligation rests upon me and upon every employee of the Indian Service to see that no effort is spared to make the most of the great opportunity which the Indian's property and the action of Congress now presents to the Indian.  It is my duty to require that every supervising officer, every Superintendent, every farmer, every stockman, and in fact every employee of the Indian Service meets this obligation in full measure.

"The political conditions of the world will make the next few years a period of great prosperity for the American farmer.  Let us see that the Indian with his broad acres is in truth an American farmer and that he properly participates in this unusual opportunity.

"I desire that our Indian fairs this year be made the opening of an intelligent and determined campaign for the industrial advancement of the Indian. Let this year's fair mark the start of the Indian along the road, the purpose of which is self-support and independence — hereafter let your fair each year be a milestone fixing the stages of the Indian's progress toward that goal.

"It is the primary duty of all Superintendents to understand the Indians under their charge, to study the resources of the reservation for which they are responsible, its climate, the character of its land, the type of cattle owned by the Indians, their horses, their sheep and their other stock.          *     *     *     *     *

INDIANS RECEIVING INSTRUCTION IN PLUMBING.  HASKELL INSTITUTE, KANSAS

"Former widespread negligence and mismanagement in the cultivation of the soil, the breeding of stock, and the handling of grazing land is no excuse for the continuance of such conditions, and they will not be permitted to exist on an Indian reservation during my administration.

"Be continually at the fair yourself with your farmers and all of your industrial employees.

"Let the exhibits emphasize in an impressive manner the difference between inferior and high-grade agricultural products, and let them demonstrate in no uncertain way that greater profit results from raising the best and the most of everything produced on the farm or ranch. Encourage the Indian to take the progressive view. This should not be difficult where he has before him a clear object lesson such as is emphasized by placing his horses, cattle and sheep, his corn, oats, wheat, alfalfa and forage on exhibition in legitimate rivalry with those of his neighbor at the Indian fair.

"The improvement of stock should be aggressively advocated and impressed upon the mind of every Indian farmer and stock-raiser. He should be brought to understand that the thousands of well-bred bulls,

NAVAHO SUMMER HOGAN
From G. W. James' "Indian Blankets and their Makers"

stallions and rams were purchased during the last few months to do away with the evils of lack of sufficient and well-bred male stock and the in-breeding almost universal in the past. He should understand that in order to secure the best results the male stock must not only be improved but that the old and worse than useless male animals which have heretofore been so destructive to the Indian's success as a stock-raiser must be disposed of."

\*     \*     \*     \*     \*

The Carlisle school farms this summer were quite prosperous, as were farms at all the educational centers. *The Carlisle Arrow* of September 4th, says:—

### THE FIRST FARM

"The forty-eight cows and the six head of young cattle are in fine condition, as are also 70 hogs, averaging 125 pounds; 30 shoats, averaging 30 pounds; 22 small pigs, and 12 brood sows.

"The average amount of milk produced during the summer months was eighty gallons a day, and butter, eighty pounds a week.

"There is material for hundreds of tons of ensilage."

\*     \*     \*     \*     \*

### THE SECOND FARM

"The wheat and oats were unusually good and the yield was abundant. There are thirty acres of fine potatoes. The large flocks of turkeys and chickens are thriving. The number of eggs gathered have kept the hospital well supplied throughout the summer."

\*     \*     \*     \*     \*

"The school garden crop exceeds, in quantity of production, any on record. The farms also have yielded abundantly, making this a record-breaking year for Carlisle in the fruition of agricultural products."

\*     \*     \*     \*     \*

The Indian fairs, now so popular on many reservations, will play no small part in solving the Indian problem. It does not matter which one of the Commissioners inaugurated this most excellent incentive to work and progress. Whoever was responsible for it, hit upon a most happy expedient. Manifestly, the Indians should be encouraged to continue these fairs and to engage in honest competition. Everyone will heartily approve of the scheme to abandon, or curtail, the "Wild West" feature — of which we have had entirely too much the past thirty years.

A few years ago, Indian farms, formerly under cultivation, had grown up to bushes in Minnesota and Oklahoma. If the plans of the Indian Office, as outlined above, are carried to a successful termination, most of these tracts will again come under cultivation. The Indian will feel encouraged to labor, especially so since the fruits of his toil will accrue to him rather than to the white man. The reimbursable appropriations and the encouragement of industry are two of the most hopeful signs of Indian progress.

## CHAPTER XXXIV.  FOUR IMPORTANT BOOKS

As I write this page there lie before me four important Indian books, and I would that every reader possessed them in his library, for the very good reason that all of them treat of the Indian of today.  Two of them are strictly historical, and the other two sufficiently accurate to be included in that category.

These books are: Helen Hunt Jackson's "Century of Dishonor," published in 1886; Seth K. Humphrey's "The Indian Dispossessed," published in 1906; Honorable Francis E. Leupp's "The Indian and His Problem," published in 1910; and Honorable James McLaughlin's "My Friend the Indian," 1910.

The authors of these books are all familiar with the Indian problem and Indian conditions, but approach the subject from somewhat different points of view.

Honorable F. E. Leupp was for years Commissioner of Indian Affairs. Major McLaughlin has served in the Indian Service forty-two years, and was on the frontier among the Sioux prior to that time.  Helen Hunt Jackson was a noble woman who became interested, first in the Mission Indians of California, and afterwards in all Indians of the United States. She wrote her "Century of Dishonor" and lived to see its influence spread throughout the English-speaking world.  A number of editions were published.  S. K. Humphrey, Esq., a Bostonian, who has long been a staunch friend of Indians, presents in his book the legal point of view of the breaking of treaties and agreements, and the despoilation of the following tribes: — Mission Indians, Poncas, Nez Perces, Umatillas, etc.  Each of these authors treats of the modern Indian, and I desire to call attention in my plea for him, to the testimony of these competent witnesses — "Lest we forget."

Major McLaughlin has been United States Indian Inspector during more years than any other man in the inspection corps.  He visited all the reservations in the United States, and he understands the Indian.

Beginning with the early days on the Plains, he relates his personal experiences, and gives sound advice in the handling of Indian affairs.  From all I can gather from reading accounts of, or talking with frontiersmen, who fought against Indians; officers of our troops in Indian wars; former Indian Agents; and after study of Government and Missionary reports, I think McLaughlin is correct when he says concerning the Indians of forty years ago —

"And they were a very different body of men, physically, from the Indians of today. They wore an air of sturdy independence. They were equipped according to their natural requirements. Their minds were generally attuned to magnificent ideas of time and distance. They abhorred the limitations that the white man accepts as affecting his dwelling-place. They were foes to be reckoned with, or they might be converted into friends worth the having. It is a matter of profound regret that the Indian of that day could not have been advanced to his present knowledge of, and capacity for, civilized pursuits without being subjected to the debasing and degenerating physical and moral conditions that were inseparable from the process of transmutation."

Major McLaughlin is perfectly correct in his chapter "Give the Red Man His Portion" when he states that the enormous sums of money, tribal and individual, now held by the United States should be divided among them. Otherwise, the swarm of shyster lawyers, feasting on Indian claims, will continue to increase. Congress should act immediately and provide for the division of this money, even though some of the Indians squander it. So long as fully $48,848,744 remains in the United States Treasury, just so long will we have this continual fight with "claim attorneys", and the Indians will not work pending the distribution of this great wealth. The Scriptural quotation which was somewhat changed by one of the speakers at the Lake Mohonk Conference last year, expresses this view most admirably —"Where the Indian money lies, there will the grafters be gathered together."

At the time of this writing Major McLaughlin is still a valued employee of the United States Indian Service. Undoubtedly he could have written a great deal stronger than he did. Reading between the lines of his book, I take it that the Major now realizes that the chief reason for the almost utter failure of our Indian policy is because of lack of proper protection of Indian property rights and health, and further, that the citizenship we handed the Indian, and of which our orators in Congress and in benevolent organizations had so much to say, has proved a hollow mockery and a sham.

I am not aware that Mr. Humphrey lays claim to legal training, but his book presents in a masterly fashion, exactly what has been done to the Indians who have accepted the pledged word of our civilized country. It is not a sentimental book, but a carefully prepared narrative drawn from official documents, and should have had an effect on our Congress and Interior Department long ago.

In the first chapter of "The Indian and His Problem", Mr. Leupp pays the Indian a merited tribute and sets forth his independence, his many virtues and his character. He emphasizes a trait of the oldtime Indian not generally understood — his honesty.

"Old, experienced traders among the Indians have repeatedly informed me that they had lost less money on long-standing Indian accounts, aggregating large sums, than in their comparatively small dealings with the white people in their neighborhoods. One successful trader among the Sioux who, in the early nineties, lent some $30,000 to the Indians near him in anticipation of a payment they were soon to receive, said afterward: 'I did not lose more than $150 on the whole transaction, and that I lost from a half-breed who did not live on the reservation.' The same testimony is borne on all sides, and the universal comment is that, until they were taught how to cheat in a trade, very few of them ever thought of doing so. I have seen Indians at a Government pay-table, after receiving their annuities, walk up to the Agent or some employee with so many dollars held out in their palms, to repay a loan which the creditor had forgotten all about. These instances, I ought to add, were observed among Indians of a pretty backward class, who were acting simply in obedience to their natural impulses."

Mr. Leupp states frankly in his preface: —

"The Indian problem has now reached a stage where its solution is almost wholly a matter of administration."

Because he served in various Indian capacities for almost twenty-five years with organizations as well as Commissioner of Indian Affairs, and as in that latter office it was his duty and privilege to regard the subject in its broad aspect, an extended review of his book is entirely proper.

Under Chapter II, "What Happened to the Indian," he discusses what we all know, the end of the "buffalo days", and the beginning of the ration system. He maintains that this encouraged idleness. Along with the ration and reservations systems sprang up the educational plan for the benefit of Indians. At first there were few government schools, and many denominational. The Government increased its appropriations to support these sectarian schools until in 1870 it was $100,000, and later the amounts were much larger. This brought about an unfortunate and unnecessary dispute between the denominations, the Protestant and the Catholic. Hard feelings were engendered, and instead of working together in amity to Christianize and educate the Indians, all these worthy people were engaged in a dispute as to who should receive the most money from the United States Treasury! We may imagine the feelings and

A FULL-BLOOD SIOUX GIRL, 1888

opinions of the brighter Indians as they viewed this unchristian and uncharitable dispute. The Government had to withdraw support from all denominational schools and as a result many closed their doors while others struggled along. Comparing the Government school system and the denominational, Leupp says: —

"In dimensions, in scholastic scope, and in material equipment, the Government school system as it stands today is an enormous advance on the old mission school system; but in real accomplishment as proportioned to outlay it does not begin to equal the latter, and in vital energy it must always be lacking. The reason for these differences is not far to seek. At the base of everything lies the fact that, except in magnificence, no governmental enterprise can compare with the same thing in private hands. The Government's methods are ponderous, as must always be the movements of so gigantic a machine. Its expenditures are from money belonging to the public, and therefore demand a more elaborate arrangement of checks and balances and final accounting than expenditures made from the funds of voluntary contributors. In spite of the now universal application of civil service rules, the whole business is under political control in the sense that the appropriations and the laws governing their use must be obtained from Congress, and that the school system is only a branch of one of the executive departments. This circumstance, while not necessitating the intrusion of partisan considerations into the settlement of any vexed question, does militate against the highest efficiency, because it requires that a great deal of ground shall be traversed two, three or a dozen times on the way to a clearly visible conclusion, involves harassing delays and temporary discouragements, calls for tedious consultations over petty details which one mind could dispose of more satisfactorily, and keeps the administrative staff always in a state of preparation to repel gratuitous interference."

Of the four books, the one that appeals to me most of all is that written by Helen Hunt Jackson. Bishop Whipple, long a friend of the Indian, wrote the preface to the edition of 1880. Page 7 is worthy of preservation.

"All this while Canada has had no Indian wars. Our Government has expended for the Indians a hundred dollars to their one. They recognize, as we do, that the Indian has a possessory right to the soil. They purchase this right, as we do, by treaty; but their treaties are made with *the Indian subjects* of Her Majesty. They set apart a *permanent* reservation for them; they seldom remove Indians; they select Agents of high character, who receive their appointments for life; they make fewer promises, but they fulfil them; they give the Indians Christian missions, which have the hearty support of Christian people, and all their efforts are toward self-help and civilization.  An incident will illustrate the two systems.  The officer of the United States Army who was sent to receive Alaska from the Russian Government stopped in British Columbia.  Governor Douglas had heard that an Indian had been murdered by another Indian.  He visited the Indian tribe; he explained to them that the murdered man was a subject of Her Majesty; he demanded the culprit.  The murderer was surrendered, was tried, was found guilty, and was hanged.  On reaching Alaska the officer happened to enter the Greek church, and saw on the altar a beautiful copy of the Gospels in a costly binding studded with jewels.  He called upon the Greek bishop, and said, 'Your Grace, I called to say you had better remove that copy of the Gospels from the church, for it may be stolen.'  The bishop replied, 'Why should I remove it?  It was the gift of the mother of the Emperor, and has lain on the altar seventy years.'  The officer blushed, and said, 'There is no law in the Indian country, and I was afraid it might be stolen.'  The bishop said, 'The book is in God's house, and it is His book, and I shall not take it away.'  The book remained.  The country became ours, and the next day the Gospel was stolen."

Mrs. Jackson takes up in detail the despoiling of the Indians even more thoroughly than Mr. Humphrey.  She treats of the Delawares, Cheyennes, Nez Perces, Sioux, Poncas, Winnebagoes, Cherokees, California Indians, etc.  She devotes a gruesome chapter to the massacre of Indians by white people  She devotes an appendix of 171 pages (small type), to a narration of outrages perpetrated by white people on Indians, broken treaties, and outrageous treatment of Indians by Whites.  The appendix includes a spirited correspondence with Secretary of the Interior, Hon. Carl Schurz.  There are also several letters to the *Rocky Mountain News*, a Denver paper, edited by Mr. W. N. Byers.  The letters were written in 1880.  Schurz was Secretary, it should be remembered, when the famous Ponca case occurred.  A tribe of Indians had been forcibly taken from their homes.  Through friends in Boston and Philadelphia, who had their case brought before the courts and were sustained in their contentions, these Poncas were returned to their reservation.  As to the Byers correspondence, the citizens of Denver had attacked and killed a large number of Indian men, women and children located in a village on Sand Creek, some distance from the mining camps.  Mrs. Jackson clearly has the better of both arguments.

It is unfortunate that the present condition of some of the Indian bands does not arouse the same interest as did the case of the Poncas.

The Chippewas of Minnesota suffered far greater wrongs than fell to the lot of the Poncas, and yet there has been no outburst of righteous indignation because of what happened to them.

In 1871, near Camp Grant, Arizona Territory, there were a number of Apaches encamped under the jurisdiction of the United States authorities and these Indians did not wish to join Geronimo and others in their raids in the Southwest and Old Mexico. By the 11th of March, 1871, there were over 300 Indians assembled near the camp. They had brought in, in a short time, more than 300,000 pounds of hay which the officer in command purchased. In view of the hostility of Geronimo and his band, that the Apaches should desire peace, and be willing to work, seemed incomprehensible in the Southwest. The frontier element — always hostile to Indians — resented their presence. The Indians continued to come in and presently there were 510 in the camp.

The 30th of April, these Indians were attacked by a large force of white men from Tucson, Arizona. The gentleman who furnished Mrs. Jackson with the information was C. B. Brierley, Acting Assistant Surgeon, United States Army. Mrs. Jackson presents Surgeon Brierley's report in detail. We need not present particulars, save to say that a large number of the Indians were surprised and killed while in camp and that the white people of Tucson, not satisfied with killing the men, mutilated the dead bodies of women and children.

A Mr. J. H. Lyman of Northampton, Mass., was a pioneer in Arizona in 1840 and 1841. He made a report to the Board of Indian Commissioners in 1871 which explains the hostility in later years of the Apaches toward the white people, as to how one Johnson agreed with the Governor of Senora to procure Indian scalps at an ounce of gold each. Johnson killed large numbers of women and children — and a few warriors. Mrs. Jackson reprints most of his report.

Mrs. Jackson's book, as I have previously stated, created a profound impression in this country and in England. None of the hundreds of facts and incidents contained in her "Century of Dishonor" were ever successfully denied. Many of the recommendations offered by her are sound and could be applied with profit at the present time, although thirty years have elapsed since she laid down her pen.

Mr. Humphrey may be said to have carried her work down to present times (1906), although there is much to our discredit since he wrote.

As to the irrigation problems, he says: —

"Whether he were the defenceless beginner of the Northwest, or the skilful agriculturalist of the Southwest desert with ancient systems of irrigation, the Indian was never regarded as a man. The forceful settler dispossessed the irrigating Indian with even less than usual formality because his highly-cultivated lands were the more valuable,— either by driving him into the desert and pre-empting his land, or by diverting his water, thus making his land a desert. Typical of these Indians were the four thousand Pimas of Arizona. They had practised agriculture by irrigation along the Gila River for more than three centuries. In the language of the early records, 'they are farmers and live wholly by tilling the soil, and in the earlier days of the American history of the territory

SEMINOLE INDIAN HOUSES AND CYCLONE CELLAR.   WEWOKA, OKLAHOMA, 1913

they were the chief support of both the civil and military elements of this section of the country.'

"In 1886 the Whites began to divert the waters of the Gila River. A suit in the federal court was talked of to maintain the clear rights of the Indians, but never pressed. No district attorney who would prosecute such a case against voting white men could expect to live politically. Within seven years the Pimas were reduced from independence to the humiliation of calling for rations, while the white settlers used the Indians' water undisturbed.

" 'Enough has been written about the need of water for the starving Indians to fill a volume,' wrote the discouraged Agent, after ten years. 'It has been urgently presented to your honorable office time and again, and yet the need of water is just as great and the supply no greater.' So the years went on. In 1900 came the cry from the desert, 'This water, their one resource, their very life, has been taken from them, and they are, perforce, lapsing into indolence, misery, and vice.' Thirty thousand dollars was appropriated for more rations.

"Finally, after eighteen years, the suit to recover the Indians' rights received its final quietus. The district attorney reported in 1904: 'There is no doubt but that the case could be taken up and prosecuted to a favorable ending, but . . *it would be impossible for the court to enforce its decree,* and the expense of prosecuting such suit would cost between twenty and thirty thousand dollars.'

"This Government long ago lost the right to say that it *could not* enforce a federal law against less than a thousand of its agricultural citizens. Its officials *would not* disturb the political balance of Arizona."

As to the opposing forces — the uplift, and its antithesis — he writes:—

"But there is another side to this picture. During all these years of trouble, the Indian was faithfully attended by a great Unselfishness, always striving to re-establish him, to educate and enlighten him. The Government met with no opposition in administering this portion of its trust, and the workers were granted its most generous and intelligent support; for the high ideals of the people have always been the Government's inspiration, even though it be often led to action by a selfish few.

"It is not within the scope of this book to recount the great good that has come to the Indian through this branch of the Indian Service, save to make full acknowledgment here of its greatness. It has done much more than attend the Indian's education. Many a tribe, and many individual Indians have had saved to them tracts of *good land*, upon which they have worked their way toward civilization. Indeed, had it not been for the constant presence of these among the Indians who labored for their good, little good land would have been left to any Indians.

"These are the two great influences which have shaped the Indian's destiny; one, steadily hewing away the foundation — his land; the other, faithfully moulding the superstructure — his education; both generously supported by a vote-seeking Congress.

"Where the first has failed, the Indian is coming into full citizenship through agriculture, education, and Christian teaching. Where both have succeeded in their opposing efforts, we find the Indian figuratively, and often literally, on the rocks; educated, saved, and forlorn,— amiable, but aimless, in his arrested development.  He has missed the fundamental lesson of mankind."

Mr. Humphrey's conclusions may here be reproduced in part.

"When we hear of dark injustice among the natives of Africa, or in Russia's Siberian wastes, we turn in horror from the oppressed to vent indignation upon the oppressor.  But when the tale of our own Poor Lo is told, we lift our eyes to Heaven — not being so well able to see ourselves

INDIANS' COMMERCIAL DEPARTMENT, HASKELL INSTITUTE

as to see others — and murmur, reverently, ''Tis the Survival of the Fittest!'  Those who think lightly are wont to exclaim impatiently, that the Indian's story is a closed book.  It is — nearly so; but the book of history is never closed except by those who think lightly.  *  *  *  *  *

"Bishop Whipple of Minnesota, who gave the best part of his life to the Indian cause, declared, after recounting the acts of broken faith which led up to the great Sioux massacre of 1863, 'I submit to every man the question whether the time has not come for a nation to hear the cry of wrong, if not for the sake of the heathen, for the sake of the memory of our friends whose bones are bleaching on our prairies.' This bookful of wrongs, and volumes more, have been perpetrated since. \* \* \* \*

"Col. Richard I. Dodge, after thirty-three years on the Plains as Indian fighter, displays in his 'A Living Issue,' this same confiding hope: 'It is too much to expect any one of these (politicians) to risk the loss of votes and thus jeopardize his future career for a miserable savage. Politicians will do nothing unless forced to it by the great, brave, honest, human heart of the American people. To that I appeal! To the press; to the pulpit; to every voter in the land; to every lover of mankind. For the honor of our common country; for the sake of suffering humanity; force your representative to meet this issue'." \* \* \* \* \*

"Thirty years ago a Commissioner of Indian Affairs delivered himself of a fervent opinion which should become classic. The miserable story of the California Indians had dragged itself through twenty-five years; every measure of relief had been blocked in Congress by the interested few — the Vociferous Few in the Indian country. 'This class of Indians,' concludes the Commissioner, 'seems forcibly to illustrate the truth that no man has a place or a fair chance to exist under the Government of the United States who has not a part in it.' A more illuminating commentary on the Indian's unhappy status in the land of the Free can hardly be written in one sentence. The Indian's story does not argue that the Indian should have been at any time given the protection of the franchise; but it *does* argue that in a loose-jointed republic where national legislation is at the beck and call of every little coterie of irresponsible voters, the Indian has been subjected to more devilish variations of human caprice than if he were at the mercy of an openly oppressive, but more consistent and centralized style of government. There is no despotism more whimsically cruel than that of men unused to power, who suddenly find themselves in absolute control of a people whose one vital interest — an advantageous foothold on *good land* — is in continual conflict with their own chief desire — the possession of that same good land."

I have reprinted from these books for a definite purpose. All four authors had practical experience with Indian affairs; all knew their subjects — not one was visionary. Our historians and public officials have denied none of the statements contained in these books. Since the abuses continue, and we have forgotten the lessons of the past, it now remains for us to change our Indian policy — to do so absolutely. We have been repeatedly warned, we cannot escape our responsibility.

# CHAPTER XXXV.  OFFICIAL VIEWS OF INDIAN
## CONDITIONS

Commissioner Sells very kindly instructed a number of his Supervisors and Superintendents to reply to my fourteen questions covering the present condition of our Indians.  The questions need not be repeated as they are given in the table, Chapter XXXII.

These replies present the administration point of view, and I herewith append such of the answers as are already not repetitions.  Those that do not convey special information are omitted.

Honorable H. B. Peairs, Supervisor of Schools, Washington, D.C., writes: —

VI.  "From extended observations during the past five years, I am confident that there has been very marked progress and that the general condition of the Indians is very much better than it was ten years ago. I had the opportunity of doing one full year's work in the field in 1897, during which time I traveled in all sections of the country and visited more than one-half of the reservations and schools.  The past four years have given me an opportunity to visit practically all of the reservations and schools, and I unhesitatingly say that there is a marked improvement."

VIII.  "The mixed-blood.  They are an English-speaking people, more intelligent and more capable in every way, considering the average mixed-blood.  Their homes are far superior and they are more ambitious to improve conditions.  The fact that they are unwilling to remain as they are in many instances results in their being somewhat troublesome, but this only emphasizes a desire for better conditions."

XIII.  "I believe the Government is making a conscientious effort to protect the Indian in all of his interests, both property and human.  Undoubtedly there are instances where, through bad legislation, weak administration, or both, great injustice has been done.  There is great difference of opinion as to what is best to do in many instances for the Indians.  What might be considered by some to be an injustice, might be considered by others as being the best possible thing for the Indian. For instance, some oppose very positively the taxation of Indian lands of any class.  Personally, I believe that all productive inherited Indian lands should be taxed in order that funds might become available for the support of local institutions, such as public schools, and for the proper maintenance of public roads, bridges, etc.  On the other hand, there are those who believe that there should be greater freedom in the matter of issuing patents in fee for allotted lands and to the allottee. Personally, I believe that the original allottee should not be permitted to dispose of his allotment and thus be without a permanent home. In instances it might be well to permit the allottee to sell a portion of his allotment, the receipts therefrom to be used in improving the remaining portion.

"I give these illustrations simply to show that differences of opinion with reference to what is best for the Indian and what is not best, may give color to the answer to the seventh question."

Honorable John B. Brown, Supervisor of Education, Muskogee, Oklahoma, says:—

VII. "The morality of the Indians in the Five Civilized Tribes is believed to be as good as the average of their community, which is reasonably high, except possibly in some full-blood communities where living conditions are not conducive to the best moral status."

X. "The opinion on this subject is divided. I have made careful inquiry at every Agency visited, both within and adjoining the Five Civilized Tribes. I believe that more depends upon the home conditions and efficiency of Government employees on the reservation than any other one point except the individual peculiarities of the young Indian in question. Given the same quality of manhood in the Indian under consideration, and the same efficiency on the part of officials in charge of the reservation, I have not been able to detect any marked change in favor of either the reservation or non-reservation system of education."

VIII. "My judgment is that under the more recent practices of our Department, the Indians are being as fully protected as it is practicable to do; that is, that every reasonable effort is honestly being put forth for such protection."

Honorable O. H. Lipps (at the time Mr. Lipps wrote he was in charge of Coeur D'Alene, Flathead and other Indians in the northwest.) Briefly summed up, his opinion is to the effect that the full-bloods are in the best condition; that white people are taking advantage of the Flatheads, but not of other Indians in his region. Few white men marry full-blood Indian women, but white men marry mixed-bloods for their property.

XIII. "I believe the Indian Department is doing all in its power to protect the Indians' property; more could be done to protect his health."

Mrs. Elsie E. Newton is one of the Supervisors in charge of health of the Indians. She has served for many years in the Indian Office, and is one of the most competent employees. I quote at considerable length from her letter.

VI. "I cannot answer this with precision as my knowledge of the Indian country, except in one or two localities, is less than ten years old.

"It can be said, however, that even in five years there has been a great change in the environment of the Indian, with few exceptions. The Whites have settled pretty well in and around him and have diffused ideas which in time he is bound to adopt in more or less degree. I speak of matters of dress, food, shelter, etc. The superficial aspect of his life is changing. In like manner, his attitude toward law, morals, etc., are being modified. It appears that he is going through that period of transition, forgetting the old code of life, or at least not regarding it, and yet not dominated by the new. This transition period is always one of distinct loss both in moral force, and achievement. From this point of view, he is not as well off today as he was ten years ago, but until he has passed through the critical period, it is unfair to make comparison by years merely."

VII. "Immorality is a relative term. Certain Indian tribes had moral codes under which they lived and lived acceptably, or morally. Those codes differed and the difference in them marks the diversity of the general condition of those tribes today. Thus we find the Crows deteriorating while the Northern Cheyennes, living practically next door, are still good stock. The sexual morality of the former is low compared to that of the latter.

"Few Indians practice monogamy after the Anglo-Saxon ideal — one partner only, and one partner for life. Divorces are common and frequent; even so, one finds few prostitutes among the best tribes, and promiscuity is not common. Even in the lower tribes where promiscuity is common, the prostitute is not. Such tribes have still the remnants of phallicism in their ceremonies.

"The state of morals is not due so much to the presence of low Whites, generally speaking, as it is to the fact mentioned above, that the tribal authority has become loosened, their own social restraints have disappeared, and there is no definite code, or its enforcement succeeding. The Federal law has never covered the ground on reservations where it retained jurisdiction and where the Indians are citizen allottees, the State does not exert itself to exercise control; local judicial machinery is reluctant to punish infractions of the law, partly because the community concerns itself very little with offences of the kind among Indians themselves, and partly because of the expense involved in prosecutions, in which Indians bear no share by taxation.

"As regards that morality which is designated honesty, I hardly believe that the word of an Indian today is as good, man for man, as in the previous generation. Traders would be more competent to give testimony on this point, because in their business they have learned whom to trust and whom to suspect.

IX. 'The white man is more likely than not to take advantage of an Indian where his own advantage is concerned. This is due as much to the innate pushing quality of the Whites, as the corresponding retiring quality of the Indian. It is frequently a racial rather than a moral matter. It is often a matter of mere competition between Whites. For instance, I once had a conversation with a bank official in an Indian country, where banks were discounting Indian notes at an impossible usurious rate. The man was highly respected in the community, well regarded for honesty, a church worker, and in my own opinion a good, typical American. We discussed the matter reasonably, and he concluded by saying, 'I suppose this sort of thing seems unpardonable to you,' and when I acquiesced, he continued, 'We look at it about this way,— if we do not get the Indian's money, some one else will.' The Indian makes no resistance to such treatment, partly through inability, partly through inambition.

XIII. "In general, it is; in some instances it is too paternalistic; in others, it is sometimes crowded to an issue contrary to distinctly good Indian policy by interests which bear upon general public policy. In other words, the Indian interest must frequently be sacrificed for general and broader interest.

"I might say that the Government is protecting the Indian, and protecting him well, but the public is not. If the public would be more just, the Government might exert less paternalism, with great advantage to the individual Indian.

"It should be added that often the Indian stands in the attitude of finding Government protection irksome, just as a child often feels toward parental authority. As one Government official aptly said, 'It is hard to protect the Indian when he doesn't want to be protected'."

Honorable Horace G. Wilson, Supervisor of Indians, Rosebud, Oregon, replies to the questions rather briefly. He believes that the general condition of the Indians is better than ten years ago; that the Indian is naturally immoral, but his wickedness increases through contact with low Whites; that the mixed-bloods are in the best condition; white people are taking advantage of the Indians; Indians should be educated near at home; white men are marrying Indian women to secure property. Finally, that the Government is protecting the Indians.

Honorable Charles F. Peirce, Superintendent of the Flandreau school, South Dakota, says he has in charge a large number of pupils each year.

He considers the condition more satisfactory than ten years ago; that the moral condition of Flandreau Indians compares favorably with that of white people in the surrounding community under same conditions; that there is little drunkenness; that the observance of marriage relat ons is as good as among white people; that most of the Indians are full-bloods; that the mixed-bloods are more industrious.

"The Flandreau Indians have been citizens of the State of South Dakota, voting and otherwise taking part in municipal affairs for twenty years, and while the Government is nominally holding jurisdiction over

CLASS IN DOMESTIC ART, HASKELL INDIAN SCHOOL, KANSAS

them, they need but very little protection, and that is being exercised by the Government as necessity demands."

Honorable Frank A. Thackery is Superintendent of the Pima Indian School, Sacaton, Arizona. As to the prevalence of trachoma and tuberculosis ten years ago as compared with the present, he cannot give much information. He admits that there is a high percentage of deaths from tuberculosis, and recommends inexpensive hospital camps.

VI. "Speaking for the Pimas alone, the matter of their water rights is the principal factor to be considered in connection with their advancement in the past ten years, as upon their right to the water of the Gila River rests their sole opportunity for industrial independence. The Pimas are victims of circumstances beyond their control in so far as the irrigation problem is concerned and the Indian Office is now taking very active steps to protect the rights of these Indians wherever the encroaching whites have jeopardized them.

VII. "The Pima Indians have a high standard of morality for a primitive people, but I believe such deviations as occur are due to the Indian's own nature, which is, after all, human nature, and as liable to err as his white brother, whose example we will all agree leaves much to be desired if set up as the standard to which other races should aspire."

IX. "Yes, in so far as appropriating river water to which the Pimas have a prior right.

X. "Again speaking of the Pimas only, I believe the peculiar climatic conditions here make it desirable that the boys and girls shall receive their training in this locality. It is safe to say that 95% of the boys will be farmers, and such training as they receive along agricultural lines should correlate with their home conditions and this it is not likely to do if obtained in a locality where climatic conditions vary greatly from southern Arizona.

XIII. "I believe the administration is taking every possible step to safeguard the interests of the Indians within the limits allowed by the laws governing and the funds at its disposal, hampered as it is by the political intriguers who now, as always, seek to control the management of Indian Affairs for their personal benefit and gain. Your true reformer is first and always an extremist; to him a thing is either black or white, good or evil, a crime or a virtue. He knows no gradation of color, no perception of proportions, no knowledge of values. To him the world is made up of entirely unrelated antitheses, and all acts of which he does not himself approve are evil. It is easy for such a person to contend that the Indians have been imposed upon by those entrusted with the management of their affairs and to find evidence to support their contentions. But the broad-minded investigator will recognize the peculiar racial problems with which those interested in the Indians' advancement have had to deal, will give due consideration to the enormity of the task set them, will weigh carefully the intricacy of the machinery with which the workers have been forced to labor and will hesitate to judge adversely where superficial observation would appear to warrant such a judgment justifiable."

I regret that I could not produce these lengthy communications in full. But the quotations will give an idea of the Departmental point of view, and that the dangers are fully appreciated, and every effort made to overcome them.

## Past Commissioners' Views

Honorable T. J. Morgan, appointed Indian Commissioner in June, 1889, might be said to have crystalized the policy having as its chief aim, the allotting, and the educating of Indians. He was followed by Honorable D. M. Browning, who served for four years. Honorable W. A. Jones, appointed in May, 1897, served until December, 1904, when Mr. Leupp succeeded to the office. We may dismiss the careers of the Commissioners preceding Mr. Leupp, with a blanket statement that they did not foresee that a policy emphasizing allotting and educating, and minimizing protection, would bring about disastrous results. Mr. Leupp's administration felt the full force of the evil effects of policies inaugurated by his predecessors. We have already discussed Mr. Leupp's views, and further comment is unnecessary.

Coming down to Mr. Valentine's appointment, June, 1909, we find that Mr. Valentine recognized in the full sense the dangers confronting the Indian and strove to combat them. At the Lake Mohonk Conference, October, 1909, he delivered a splendid address entitled, "What the Public Should Know About the Indian Bureau." In this he admits that his inspection service has been weak and that much of the trouble is due to incomplete, or faulty reports. I have commended elsewhere in this book Mr. Valentine's health propaganda — for it is largely due to his efforts that Congress became aroused to the necessity of increased appropriations.

The acting Commissioner, Honorable F. H. Abbott, who served from September, 1912, to Mr. Sells' appointment in June, 1913, carried out the policies inaugurated by his former chief. Abbott opposed wholesale allotments hastily made, as in the past. He took a firm stand against the allotment schemes proposed for the Navaho Indians at the present time.

Mr. Sells' policy has been referred to at length on previous pages of this book. He was fortunate in his selection of Honorable E. B. Meritt as Assistant Commissioner, who entered the Bureau in 1910 as chief law officer. It was due to Mr. Meritt's efforts that the application of a railroad for the granting of a right of way for the construction of a line through the San Carlos Indian Reservation, Arizona, was prevented. His work on behalf of the Yakima Indians, in protecting their water rights, was especially effective. He has delivered a number of addresses at Lake Mohonk, setting forth the aims of the Department under the present administration, and cooperates with the Indian Rights Association in its excellent work.

The inspection service is now under a new chief, Honorable E. B. Linnen. As a practical field-man of wide experience, he has selected a corps of competent men. Investigations are now carried on in a thorough manner, and incompetent persons removed, and not simply transferred, as in former times.

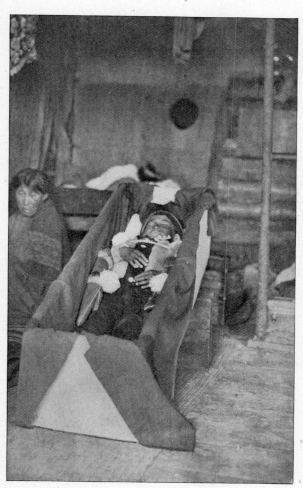

MOURNING THE DEAD

Photographed by Rev. Julius Jette, S. J., in a cabin at Nulato, Alaska, April. 1913

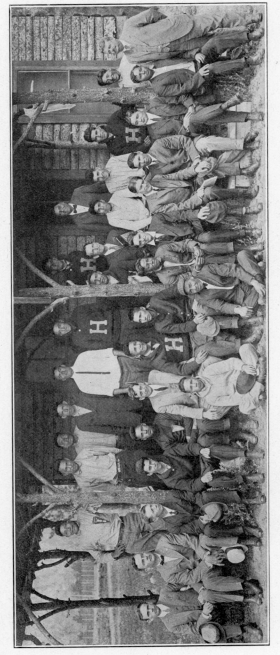

CONFERENCE OF INDIAN Y. M. C. A. STUDENTS AT DENVER, COLORADO

# CHAPTER XXXVI. RECOMMENDATIONS AND SUGGESTIONS FROM FIELD WORKERS

Of the many correspondents who aided in the preparation of the table of statistics, there were large numbers who made most excellent recommendations. I have selected some thirty of these and herewith present them in order that they may be preserved. The writers are all persons of experience in Indian affairs. It will be observed that in many details, they do not agree, and yet they suggest, for the most part, sensible reforms. Practically every one of the entire correspondents had no criticisms to offer of the intentions of the Government, or Indian Office officials. A few criticized local officials with whom they came in contact. The following recommendations are not offered in controversial spirit, nor as a reflection on our able men at Washington. They are presented as the result of years of experience on the part of unselfish men and women, whose only aim is to see the Indian saved out of his troubles; simple justice meted out to him, and that he should take his place in American life as a real citizen.

"I never did in my private opinion approve of the allotment plan and never will. I am in favor of the old Roman style of civilizing; give the race or nation, for themselves, a large enough tract of land, facility for commercial opportunity, let them wrestle with their fate, pay a small tribute to the crown; if fit they will survive.

"Time will show the merits and demerits of the allotment system. The condition of the reservations was much better before this plan was inaugurated. Those who have tried to civilize any race or nation within twenty-four hours, figuratively speaking, have invariably failed. All history will support this statement."

Correspondent, Beaulieu, Minn.

"I believe the Government made a serious mistake in allowing the Indians to sell their land. They could be much helped by the leasing of their lands, but when the lands are gone there is no further help."

Correspondent, Greenwood, So. Dakota

"They have better homes than they had ten years ago, have better clothing and more to eat. They have advanced too in farming. But their lands are going, dead claims are sold often before the Indian owner is buried.

Their lands rent better now, bringing more money to them than they did ten years ago.

"I think our Government is doing all it can do for the Indians' interest. And I think it has been for several years trying harder and harder each year to do its full duty by these people. The restrictions on their lands, their perfect system of schools, their vigilance to keep whiskey from them, their eagerness to protect them; all these things go to show that the heart of the Government has a soft spot for the Indian and it will be a sad day for the Indian when the Government turns him loose."

Correspondent, Hugo, Oklahoma

"The Government should do more to secure justice for citizen Indians in the local courts. Conditions are very bad."

Correspondent, Santee, Nebraska

"Too much red tape."

Correspondent, Odanah, Wisconsin

"If the U. S. Government laws, protecting the Indians, could be only enforced, the Indians would be well protected."

Correspondent, Beaulieu, Minn.

"The best protection to the Indians would be the giving to each man the portion of goods and lands that belong to him as an individual, or to his family, and then for a very brief period exercise an elder brotherly control of his affairs, rather by way of suggestion. This is my opinion as to the Indians in this region at the present time."

Correspondent, Rosebud, S. Dakota

"When I came here, over eighteen years ago, many lived on their farms, miles away from town, wore citizens' clothes, talked English, were industrious in a way. When they were allotted, they were allowed to have Indian villages and in consequence they left their farms, flocked together, returned to the blanket, Osage language, old customs, etc. In northeastern Oklahoma, where they were allotted, they were forced to live on their allotments and became industrious.

"In conclusion, I would say turn the Indians loose entirely, place them on a par with the Whites, as soon as possible, and that should be very soon."

Correspondent, Pawhuska, Okla.

"The Government is doing something in the way of intellectual and industrial training of the young, but fails to stir up an ambition to carry these things into life; the Government has established a hospital for the sick, and has several physicians who are paid for caring for the sick; yet disease and death are on the increase; the Government recognizes the Indians as wards, and says that no liquor shall be sold to them, yet will sell a license to a man that he may open a saloon on a reservation. The saloons may not sell liquor to Indians, yet drunken Indians are as common as dandelions on a lawn. I need not say more. The Government is too big; it is ineffective. The whole problem should be put into the hands of a Commission made up of men with hearts that are something more than pumping-stations, and who are experts in this matter. I say this without any criticism of individuals but of the system as a whole. We must get the Indian problem out of politics; we must give the Commission power to act within certain limits.

"Had we had men of heart and of vision, what might not have been done for the Indians on the White Earth Reservation? A study of the Indian would have revealed him as a social creature; of choice he lived in a settlement surrounded by his friends. This would have suggested the gathering of Indians into villages rather than scattering them upon allotments of land without any knowledge of, or taste for farming. In these villages might have been built houses on one-acre tracts for 150 families, and there might have been provided a school, hospital, store, etc. The school would be a day-school, and the children left in the homes of their parents. Two field matrons could visit every home at least once each week, and from time to time gather the women for instructions in care of the home, care of children, etc. The physician could easily look after the sick."

Correspondent, Cass Lake, Minnesota

"In the town of Yerington, Nevada, having a white population of 682 (last census), there are at least fifteen places where liquor is sold. Yerington is situated in Mason's valley about twenty-five miles from the reservation, and is surrounded by a farming section and in the outlying hills are many mining prospectors and a few mines in operation. Occasionally a stranded prospector drifts into the town, and readily learns that the easiest way to get another 'grubstake' is to bootleg whiskey to Indians, and so there is considerable of this work done. Also, in the town of Yerington are many places where 'yen-chee' is sold, and a good per cent. of these Indians are opium users.

"Since the Agent took charge of the agency in June he has made some regulations restricting the Indians from leaving their land (allotments) at any and all seasons, by requiring each Indian to get a pass from the office before leaving the reservation, and this regulation has cut down the revenue of some of these towns, so much so that an attorney of low caliber and an ex-judge made and circulated a petition among both Indians and Whites, requesting an investigation of the Agent's disciplining the Indians be made, which was supplemented by a request that he be removed. Their charges were heard by an officer at Yerington and the testimony submitted in a way that was more amusing than many theatrical comedies; one of the witnesses even turned to the attorney and asked what it was he told him to say! The smell of whiskey on the attorney and some of the witnesses was very noticeable.

"The so-called Medicine Men are, I think, the greatest hindrance among the tribal evils that the Paiute Indians have to conquer; when they are 'doctoring' a sick person and are convinced that the patient is going to die, they accuse some progressive Indian of being a 'witch' and claim the sickness is due to a spell cast over them by the 'witch'.

"I think it would be better if the Indian children were not forced to go to school at such a very early age (five to six years). The change from a free life at home to a strict routine school life is hard, especially at such a tender age. I do not doubt that in a number of cases it weakens the constitution and makes them far more susceptible to tuberculosis.

"I also am convinced it would be far more to the benefit of the Indians if a great percentage of the money which is yearly spent in large non-reservation schools, would be used on the reservation in order to develop more water and to improve more land, so that every Indian could get enough agricultural land, so as to make it possible for him to make a living on his farm. A part of said money could even be spent to assist him in fencing his land, procuring farm implements and the like. With such a start and well-meaning officers, who, when necessary, even would strictly insist that all cultivate their lands properly, most of the Indians would, within a few years, become self-supporting and also support their children. These children, as they grow up, in turn should be made to assist their parents in their home duties.

"Reservation day-schools, as a rule, should suffice also for the Indian children. In these they could surely receive such an education as is necessary for an honest and happy living. Most of the white children in country districts have no better opportunity.

Correspondent, Phoenix, Arizona

(*Formerly lived at Yerington, Nev.*)

"Competent Indians should be given control of their business; full-bloods or near full-bloods educated by the retention of coal royalties, or schools maintained by direct Congressional action. Oklahoma needs schools for Indians more than it needs Federal buildings or battleships."

Correspondent, Muskogee, Oklahoma

"The general tendency of the Government to take away the safe-guards over the Indians' property and person, while of course in line with the generally agreed plan for ultimate citizenship is proving very destructive at the present stage of advancement. It is the general rule that Indians given patents in fee sell their holdings and waste the proceeds either in riotous living or foolish investments or manipulations of their affairs. Such procedure cripples the coming generation more than the present one.

"The Government is further at a disadvantage in having to educate a politician about every three years to take charge of the Indian Bureau. An experienced field man should always be in this position.

"The attempt to put Indians in public schools while finally desirable and necessary is at present a failure in most places and should be pushed with the greatest care, meantime supporting Indian schools until such time as the Indian is in shape to attend public schools of a type better than we have now.

"The theory of administration is sound if it were followed up by experienced men, who were content to follow a policy already promulgated instead of hunting for new ideas to be called their own."

Correspondent, Sisseton, South Dakota

"Continually giving things gratis does not make them appreciate what is being done for them, but rather makes them inert and destroys all ambition. It looks rather strange to see yearly thousands of dollars spent in educating these poor children of the desert in distant and magnificent schools. Thousands of well-to-do white parents could not even think of giving their children such a change.

"Sooner or later the taxpayers of the United States will object to having their hard-earned money thus spent. And, if by that time the Indians have not learned to help themselves, depend on themselves, and make a living for themselves, and support their children, then their future will be hopeless."

Correspondent, Phoenix, Arizona

"The building of homes would suggest the necessity for material which the forests would furnish in abundance. Study of the men would suggest the necessity of regular employment as a proper discipline leading to civilization. Mills should have been established and the men set to work turning the forests into lumber as fast as it was needed for lumber, and a sufficient over-plus to pay the men for their work, and all other expense of operation.

"The warming of the homes and other buildings would suggest the necessity of fuel; the barbaric improvidence of the Indian would be overcome by setting a time when every able-bodied man must go to the woods and gather a year's supply of fuel for his home, as well as for all the public institutions.

"The need of clothing, blankets, etc., and the peculiar abilities of the Indian women as evidenced in their beadwork, rush mats, and grass baskets, together with the wide acres of grazing lands, would suggest the raising of sheep and the establishment of mills for the manufacture of woolens.

"The need of foods would suggest the establishment of one or more large farms, where, under proper supervision, men would learn to till the soil, care for stock, handle machinery, etc.

"The Indian does not need charity, but he must be trained to use the powers he possesses. I would do away with all annuities and substitute work and wages therefor. I would not make personal allotments of land except to Indians who had learned to farm, and then only on the homestead plan requiring them to live on the land and make certain improvements before they secured title. Except for supervisors and experts, I would have all the work on the reservation done by Indians, nor would I permit a white man to hold title to an acre of land."

Correspondent, Cass Lake, Minnesota

"There is for instance the question of honesty and justice. Fifteen years ago the majority of the Osages were honest, truthful, just, paid their debts. The U. S. Government told them: you can deal with licensed traders and must pay them; dealers that are not licensed you must not pay. They trade with both kinds for convenience sake and otherwise; after a while when money is short, they refuse to pay the unlicensed dealer, and become dishonest and unjust.

"Of the Osages, nineteen years ago, all the full-bloods were poor, and very glad to get a piece of beef when sick. The first year after allotment they let the renter bring them their share of the grain, but the second year they went after their share themselves and improved their opportunity so that some Osages loaned money to others not only this year but ten years ago. The money is the greatest misfortune to the Osages and I say often it is a curse to them. They have a large trust fund in Washington and an apparently unlimited supply of oil and gas and also other minerals "

Correspondent, Pawhuska, Oklahoma

CREEK MAN AND WOMAN CUTTING WOOD. SYLVIAN, OKLAHOMA, 1913

"In some ways the Indians are improving but not so surely and rapidly as ten years ago. The encouraging of the old native dances which is simply heathen worship; the enacting of war scenes to please the Whites, is fast putting him back of what he was ten years ago. The full-blood Indians are the most law-abiding in most cases. The white people always take advantage of the Indian. The Government is not properly protecting the Indian. Largely the local politicians run reservation affairs."

Correspondent, Standing Rock, No. Dakota

"I think more could be done here in the way of nursing. There is no trained nurse among these Indians, no field matron. The people are ignorant in the matter of knowing how to care for young children, and in matters of cleanliness and ventilation."

Correspondent, Greenwood, So. Dakota

"Government farmers who *farm*, and a doctor — I will not say more capable — but one who takes an interest in his work and his people, and who at least visits the sick, are among the needs of these people."

Correspondent, Pala, California

"The Indian courts are incompetent and unjust. The boarding-schools should be nonsectarian. There should be more day-schools to promote the home life. If the Indians are wards, they should be protected in the courts. For instance, two years ago a young girl whose father had just left her a nice property, was sued for breach of promise by a mixed-blood. Ignorant, she did not appear in court. She was not defended by the Indian Agent. Many of her fine horses were sold at low prices and the mixed-blood received $1,000. This case was reviewed by the Department of Justice in Washington but never righted. They recognized evidences of fraud, but the time limit had elapsed. There should be a good lawyer as legal clerk at each agency. There should be much smaller districts, and more and better farmers in charge of them, who would by example encourage the Indians to farm their land, milk cows and raise stock. Notwithstanding the large issues of stock, the Indians have few more cattle and horses than twenty-seven years ago when I first came out here. With a railway station within ten miles of nearly every Indian on this reservation, very little is raised to ship out, either stock or grain."

Correspondent, McLaughlin, So. Dakota

"The Indians, largely, are holding their lands. Immorality is due to several causes; first and greatest I blame the Government for insisting upon Indians obtaining licenses to marry. Many of them are a hundred miles from the agency. The old custom of early marriages was best for them. But now unless they are past eighteen years of age they cannot get a license. Any authorized minister should be allowed to marry them without a license. The boys and girls are kept in school too long. If forced at all to be sent to school after they are sixteen, it should be optional with the students and parents.

Correspondent, Standing Rock Reservation, North Dakota

"A commission of ten or twelve men announce that they will be here on a certain date to make payments to certain Indians. These Indians are notified to come. They travel, some of them, 100 miles. On arriving there they find, perhaps, that they have come too soon or too late. This means a wait of several days at heavy expense. I have known instances where the amount drawn was less than the expenses. We have wondered why the Indian could not receive his payment just as the old soldier gets his pension, but it is claimed that he would not get the check — so many would be on the watch for it.

"When it is announced that the payment party is to be at a certain place, this proclaims to every grafter in the land that he had better be there. He *is* there.

"I have known the whiskey Indians use to contain poison. The full-blood Indian leaves the payment party with little money. This may be a rather broad statement, but I think I can prove it. The country is full of people, supposedly the Indian's friends. If I wanted to find one this afternoon, I would at once go to the grafter's office, and there be sure to locate him."

Correspondent, Durant, Oklahoma

"Within this jurisdiction the Indians have leased the railroad sections of five townships to retain control of a portion of the range they need, but the Whites have leased many more townships and some of them are trying to keep the Indians out of the townships leased, or to confine them to their allotments. Such conditions are unbearable; allotments are valuable mainly as a foothold to control the surrounding range. One hundred and sixty acres in that part of the country will support no more than about ten sheep. Recently a man from Chama leased *all* the Santa Fe railroad lands in San Juan country, excepting a half-township which a Navaho had leased, and brought in about 30,000 head of sheep.

"Why should a dozen stockmen and politicians have control of the range to the detriment and ultimate destruction of the 2,200 Navahos in that part of the country?

"Again: Why should a dozen sheepmen be permitted to supplant a hundred or thousand Navahos supported through the sheep industry?

"Those who are educated at a distance and return — and they all return sooner or later — are dissatisfied. With a few exceptions they are adverse to taking up stock-raising and farming *in earnest*; they clamor for positions in Indian trading stores and for Government positions, which are too few to 'go around.' If the main school of the tribe, the one at Fort Defiance, were well equipped as a trade school, much good would accrue to the tribe; in fact, I consider this a prime necessity for the advancement of the tribe."

Correspondent, St. Michaels, Arizona

ALASKAN INDIAN CHILDREN; NULATO, ALASKA
Two have trachoma, four are normal. Photographed, 1914

"Years ago the Indian chief and headmen kept strict order among the people, punished the guilty by fines or imprisonment, kept all Indian doctors from the place and fined them as much as fifty dollars if caught on the reservation. After a while the Government abolished the ruling of the chief and headmen by appointing paid Indian judges. If the guilty were fined they hardly ever paid their fines, if put in jail they managed by some way or other to escape, and many years ago the jail was destroyed by fire and no attempt has ever been made by the Agent to rebuild it. For the last year or two the judges have been dismissed so that now there seems to be no more law or authority on the reservation.

"In conclusion, in this my 80th year of age, I hope never to see the day when the Indian reservation will be thrown open to white settlers. Such a step would be a sure extermination of the Indians, who would soon be tricked out of their little holdings by bad Whites and sent to die on the beach of Puget Sound. The Indian race is doomed to disappear. Let us at least allow them to die a natural death and give them a decent funeral."

Correspondent, Bellingham, Washington

"The Indians' land is without water and worthless. Whites have taken all the water. The law is such the Indians can not hunt. Many of them suffer for food."

Correspondent, Likely, California

"The Government should stop paying the Chippewa money, now and then. Give them all that belongs to them — allotments, houses, and no money. The more they get, the less they exert themselves. They are lazier today than twenty years ago."

Correspondent, Cloquet, Minnesota

"With respect to the full-blood Indian here, it is to be said to his great credit that he has no desire to receive a patent in fee to his land, and the full-bloods are holding on to their original allotments, and inherited land, with a spirit which is truly commendable. Little land is offered for sale belonging to the full-blood, and there is a well-fixed determination among the full-bloods to hold on to their land. As the land here is so valuable and as they know they can receive a good figure if the land is sold, and knowing too of the great pressure brought to bear upon an Indian by white men who desire to purchase their land, I say again that the Indian full-blood here is to be congratulated upon his determination that he will not sell the land which the Government has allotted to him and his family."

Correspondent, Pendleton, Oregon

**BAY-BAH-DWUN-GAY-AUSH, AGE 87**

Photographed in 1914

This old blind medicine man was possessed of a remarkable memory and knew the family
history of some hundreds of Ojibwa. He was the chief witness for the Government
in establishing blood relationship   (*See pages 95 and 399*)

# CHAPTER XXXVII. THE COMMUNISTIC LIFE. INDIAN MEN AND WOMEN OF PROMINENCE. MORALITY

There was much of the old Indian life, beyond the Mississippi, in the years preceding 1880, that was picturesque if not beautiful. Contrary to popular belief, the Indians were not continually at war. Certain organizations of young men among some bands did make warfare their chief aim of life until reaching middle age. But the average Indian at home was just as different from the Indian on the warpath, as are our troops in action, the opposite of the same men as citizens. Entirely too much emphasis has been placed upon the Indian as a warrior.

The communistic life was in vogue in many places west of the Mississippi between 1850 and 1878. The communistic sentiment, evinced in nearly every village and clan-group, was so different from our life to-day, that I find myself compelled to illustrate it through the following incident.

The old blind medicine man of the Otter-tail Pillagers, Bay-bah-dwun-gay-aush, was found by me helpless, living in a wretched shack on the edge of a swamp at Pine Point, Minnesota. He had been swindled out of his property. Commissioner Valentine, on my recommendation, kindly issued orders that old Bay-bah-dwun-gay-aush and his friend, the aged May-cud-day-wub, be rationed every Wednesday as long as they lived. Out of gratitude, the old man gave me the original birch-bark roll of the Mid-di-we-win, or Grand Medicine Society. He was the roll-keeper. In 1909, when received, the roll was 102 years old. It contains five degrees, which have been translated, but the old shaman requested that publication be deferred until his death. I desire to present in abridged form the fourth, or the Beaver degree, illustrating that phase of Indian character to which I have referred. In a general way, the sentiment is expressed as follows: —

The beavers live together in harmony. They occupy one village. They do not take advantage of each other as do white people. They share everything in common. They strike the water at night, and thus signal to each other when danger is near. Their storehouses of food are open to all. They help each other, build the dams together, care for the young and support the old. Thus we Ojibwa should live as do the beavers and as did our grandfathers, who learned this from the beaver clan.

The contrast between this beautiful sentiment and that obtaining in most Indian communities today is very marked. With the passing away of the communistic life, and the adoption of the more selfish point of view of the white man, Indian character was not greatly improved.

The begging dance, quite common two or three generations ago, survives here and there in spite of efforts of the Government and the missionaries to extinguish it. This same begging, or gift dance, has been persistently misunderstood. Originally, a Sioux, Pawnee, Cheyenne, or other Indian, who assembled his friends together and distributed in addition to food, even his blankets and ponies, became a famous man. He had done a good thing. His act was prompted by generosity, and a love of his fellowman. The Agent and missionary, however, told him that one should not give gifts, but on the contrary he must accumulate and hoard. All of this was very confusing to the Indians of the transition period. The older Indians (*page 324*) cannot refuse their friends food, and such as still continue in the faith of their fathers feed those less fortunate than themselves, although by so doing they deprive themselves of food.

The absolute change from these communistic ideas, from the general brotherhood of the red man, to the more practical (if not sordid) views of the white man, had a curious effect on many of the Indians. The sharper Indians soon observed that among the white people there were rich and poor. The missionary, unselfishly laboring to uplift the aborigines, was very poor in this world's goods. Yet he was self-sustaining and endeavored to persuade the Indians to become so. Both the Government teacher and the missionary impressed upon the aborigine ideas of thrift. Soon after allotments were issued, and the Indians received same, appeared other white men — bankers, real estate men and merchants. All of these secured Indian land or timber, and thus became well-to-do or rich. A certain class of half-educated Indians shrewdly observing that although the missionary pleaded, and the Agent and lawyer of the Great Father talked and blustered much, one hard, cold fact stood out indisputably: the missionary waxed poor, the Indian poorer, but the man in the frontier town waxed rich. It was incomprehensible to the old Indian, who clung to communistic ideals, but perfectly clear to the educated Indian. The latter realized that certain white men did not practice what the good missionary preached. To such, the word *theft* sounded very much the same as *thrift*. So the Indian — in many cases — drifted into evil ways, and like the white man of the frontier town, he scorned the old communistic life of his father, and to his ear there appeared practically no difference between the two words I have mentioned: thrift and theft.

## INDIAN MEN AND WOMEN

Of those representing the olden days, there were a large number who achieved more or less prominence. I am very sorry that space forbids a consideration of their careers in this book. I present a partial list of their names, and if readers will consult the *Handbook of American Indians*, short biographical sketches of most of these will be found. The negro has produced far fewer great men than the Indian, yet the negro has always vastly outnumbered the former. During forty years there has been practically no discrimination against the black man save in the South. His educational advantages in the North have been many, and his opportunities multitudinous. Slavery retarded him in a sense, yet slavery taught him enforced industry — which the Indian has never had. We would therefore, expect a larger proportion of prominent negro men and women.

Omitting those previously mentioned in this book, we have: American Horse, Oglala Sioux; Big Mouth, Brulé Sioux; Black Beaver, Delaware; Black Kettle, Cheyenne; Bloody Knife, Arikara; Chas. Curtis, Kaw; Chas. D. Carter, Chickasaw; George Copway, Chippewa; Francisco, Yuma; Gall, Sioux; John Grass, Sioux; Hollow-horn Bear, Brulé Sioux; Peter Jones, Missisauga; Kanakuk, Kickapoo; Kamaiakan, Yakima; Keokuk, Sauk; Kicking Bird, Kiowa; Kintpuash (Capt. Jack), Modoc; Leschi, Nisqualli; Little Crow, Sioux; Little Raven, Arapaho; Little Thunder, Brulé Sioux; Little Wound, Sioux; Lone Wolf, Kiowa; Mahtoiowa (Whirling Bear), Brulé Sioux; Many Horses, Piegan; Joel B. Mayes, Cherokee; Nagonub, Chippewa; Nakaidoklini, Apache; Namequa, Sauk; Nana, Apache; Napeshneeduta, Sioux; Nawah, Apache; Albert Negahnquet, Potawatomie; Ojibwa, Ojibwa; Oronhyatekha, Mohawk; John Otherday, Sioux; Ouray, Ute; Eli Samuel Parker, Seneca; Quana Parker, Comanche; Peter Perkins Pitchlynn, Choctaw; Pizhiki (Buffalo), Chippewa; Simon Pokagon, Potawatomi; Pleasant Porter, Creek; Alexander Lawrence Posey, Creek; John W. Quinney, Stockbridge; Rain-in-the-Face, Sioux; Red Horn, Piegan; Red Iron Band, Sioux; Gabriel Renville, Sioux; Roman Nose, Cheyenne; John Ross, Cherokee; Sassaba, Chippewa; Satanta, Kiowa; Scarface Charlie, Modoc; Schonchin, Modoc; John Sunday, Chippewa; Souligny, Menominee; Standing Bear, Ponca; Tamaha, Sioux; Tendoy, Bannock; Solimon Twostars, Sioux; Wabanaquot (White Cloud), Chippewa; James D. Wafford, Cherokee; Wamditanka (Great War Eagle), Sioux; Wapasha, Sioux; Washakie, Shoshoni; Eleazar Williams, Iroquois; Winema (Woman Chief), Modoc; Wopohwats, Cheyenne; Allen Wright, Choctaw; Yellow Thunder, Winnebago.

Doctor Charles A. Eastman — than whom there is no more competent judge of the Plains Indians of 1850-1890 — has informed me that next to Red Cloud and Sitting Bull, he considers Spotted Tail and Crazy Horse (Sioux) two of the greatest Indians of modern times.

In addition to the Indians, both educated and not, whose names have been presented in this Indian History, there occur two who were particularly prominent in helping their own people.

Bright Eyes (Susette La Flesche) was born in Nebraska about 1850. She was educated at a mission school on the Omaha reservation, and later at a private school in Elizabeth, N. J. In 1877-78 the Ponca were forcibly removed to Indian Territory from their home on Niobrara reservation, South Dakota. In order to bring Indian removals before the public, Standing Bear, accompanied by Susette La Flesche and her brother, visited the principal cities of the United States, where her appeals for humanity toward her race aroused the interest of thousands. As a result, a request was urged on the Government that there be no more removals of tribes, and this request has been respected, when practicable. She was very active with her pen until her death in 1902. She was considered one of the brightest Indian women of modern times.

Sarah Winnemucca, a Paiute, was born in Nevada in 1844. She became interpreter to Government officials, and served General O. O. Howard as scout in the Bannock War of 1877, when no Indian man would penetrate the country occupied by the hostiles. She lectured in the East in the eighties, and wrote a book on the Piaute's wrongs. She died in 1891, after a remarkable career.

A score of others might be included as worthy of a place in an Indian biography.

Mr. Leupp in his book stated that people were continually asking him this question: "Will the Indians produce a Booker T. Washington?"

It is quite possible for the Indians to produce a national character. There is a splendid work to be done by such a person. For more than a century we have labored in educating Indians, yet we have not produced a single great man or woman. Do not misunderstand me. I mean a truly great Indian, one of the stamp of Tecumseh, Chief Joseph, Red Cloud, Sacagawea, or Sequoya. The latter was trained and educated fifty years before we devoted any attention to Indian progress, and his alphabet, his attainments, and his reputation are due to his own efforts rather than to us. What woman have we of the fame of Sacagawea, the poor Shoshoni, who guided Lewis and Clark to the Pacific ocean? Not one. Excepting Clara Barton, the noble Civil War nurse, and a few other American women,

*The Last Outpost*

we have no person, even among white women, who underwent such dangers and privations, or stood forth more clearly as a brave and heroic character than this same Sacagawea. We have produced a great many noble Indians, men and women, prominent, but not to be considered truly great.

One may not misrepresent, if one claims that the Indian great men and women are of the past. There will not arise a Booker Washington, unless some strong, able Indian champions the cause of his people in the large sense. There are a number of young, bright Indians, chief among whom is Mr. Henry Roe-Cloud, and one or two others. But most of the educated Indians are concerned with other than Indian matters. None of them may be said to have entered the public arena as a dominant figure. If an educated Indian should give up his entire time to working for his people, as Doctor Grenfell works for the fishermen of Labrador, he would become famous. It has always been a surprise to me that the educated Indians have not seen this opportunity and availed themselves of it. Hundreds of the educated Indians are teachers, ministers, or Government employees. All of them are, as everybody knows, upright and able. But there is a vast difference between a position held by these excellent gentlemen, and a position that might be held by one of their own in standing as a true sponser for the Red Race in America, and in an intelligent and forceful manner presenting the needs and aims of his race. Such a man should present an uncompromising front against graft and incompetency. A mediocre man could not attain to this position, but given the opportunity, there is no reason under the sun why some educated Indian should not go down into history as a truly great man.

It is quite incomprehensible that so many of our educated Indians are timid. All of them realize the dreadful situation of many of their brothers in the West. A few have referred, in a more or less guarded fashion, to the wrongs of Indians. Dr. Eastman is especially frank upon this subject — as is Dr. Montezuma. Admitting so much, it remains to be said that not one has come before the American public as a stern, able, uncompromising fighter for the rights of his race.

The Indians need a national character. The moment that an Indian of exceptional ability, presence and strength appears on the platform, and through the press, becomes the champion of his race, the American people will rally to his support. But if such an Indian is chiefly concerned in furthering the interests of some society, or missionary organization, or of a single tribe of Indians; and if he presents mere denunciations and does not suggest proper remedies, he will achieve no great success.

The Society of American Indians is doing a good work, but in my humble opinion, it might accomplish far greater results if in addition to its advocacy of new laws, the division of Indian money, etc., its powerful organization began a fight through the medium of some selected champion, for the full protection of Indian rights and an effective, and not a paper citizenship.

LARGE INDIAN HOUSE, FORT BERTHOLD RESERVATION. FAMILY OF SIX

## Indian Morality

On page 380, Mrs. Elsie E. Newton stated that morality was a relative term, or depended on one's point of view. This is entirely true. The oldtime Indians were not immoral, although some of them were unmoral. Immorality came with the white man. There was an abundance of cruelty among Indians, and I have alluded to it elsewhere. Many Indians would not do things which we consider proper, or at least do not forbid in our moral code. As against this, some Indian customs are considered by us to be immoral. Drinking, while practiced in Mexico and among Apaches, and in some Southwest tribes, was practically unknown throughout the rest of the United States prior to the landing of our respected ancestors on the shores of Virginia, New York, and Massachusetts. The black drink of the Creeks was ceremonial, and not indulged in as an intoxicant. I have referred elsewhere to plural marriages. These do not seem to have been considered by the Indians any more immoral than they were by the patri-archs of the Old Testament. Indians usually supported their wives, even after separation. The modern method of easy divorce, followed by the usual suit for alimony, is reserved to polite white society. I once heard a worthy gentleman lamenting plural marriages among the Navaho. An educated Indian happened to be present, and he mentioned the names of two prominent white persons (to be found in *Who's Who in America*). Both occupy high positions, and one has had six wives and the other five husbands. The educated Indian ventured to remark to the worthy "up-lifter" that a careful search of the Navaho reservation would fail to produce (even among the so-called pagans) two polygamists equal to these repre-sentatives of the white man's civilization!

I have never seen a really immoral dance among Indians. I have heard many addresses at various public gatherings in which the immorality of the Indians during these dances was denounced. Although witnessing thirty or forty dances on different reservations, all the performers I observed were properly dressed. Even in the Sioux Omaha dance, the men wore quite as much as do college students during a track meet. In the squaw dance, in which both sexes take part, the partners do not even hold each other. Yet, a minister once denounced me for taking part in so innocent a pastime. The very next evening the white employees on that reservation gave a dance, all of us attended, and I had the pleasure of dancing with the reverend gentleman's daughter. He saw nothing wrong in the waltz or two-step in which partners hold each other — and there is no harm in such dances. Yet he objected to the squaw dance in which the participants scarcely look at their partners. I mention this merely to indicate how inconsistent many people are with reference to Indian dances. I am informed that some of the educated Indians now take part in the maxixe and the fox-trot. If the reverend gentleman, to whom I have referred, was scandalized in observing a squaw-dance, what must be his feelings when he observes educated young men and women lapsing into the paganism of Paris and New York!

The Government's taboo of the begging dance, and the curtailment of the ordinary Indian dances, leave no amusements in which the older Indians may participate. Consequently, they are quite likely to gamble and engage in far more harmful pastimes. Ordinary dances should be permitted, and the gift dance regulated.

ACADEMIC BUILDING

TEACHERS QUARTERS

ADMINISTRATION BUILDING

SUPERINTENDENT'S RESIDENCE

CARLISLE INDIAN SCHOOL

# CHAPTER XXXVIII.  TWO STORIES.  UNWISE PURCHASES

Some one should write a book devoted to stories of Indian heroism, the fulfilment of promises and kindred subjects.  There is much material of this character available on many of our reservations.  I do not mean folk-lore, or traditions, but stories of actual happenings, most of which are quite unknown to the average white citizen.

During the White Earth investigation in Minnesota, I frequently joined a group of Indians and through interpreters, Mr. John Lufkins, or Mrs. Rose Ellis, persuaded the old men and women to relate some of their experiences.  The first story, that of Ojibwa, was told by a man bearing the same name as the tribe.  He was a famous warrior, noted for his bravery in action against the Sioux.  His friend, No-de-na-qua-um (the Temperance Chief), also a famous warrior, had been shot through the right lung, and proudly exhibited to us the scars in his chest and back.

The story of Ojibwa is presented as taken down at the time, without explanations or additions, being a literal translation.

## Ojibwa's Story

"When I was young, long ago, there were three Sioux who went into a home and assaulted a white woman, near Fort Snelling.  The white woman screamed, and her husband ran up, took one of the three guns left outside the door by the Indians, shot one of the Indians, and the other two killed the white man.  During this summer the soldiers tried to get the two Sioux who did this and could not find them.

"About a year afterwards, while at war, I killed a Sioux myself, and about the middle of the winter when we were camping at Little Rock Lake we heard that the soldiers were coming.  The soldiers came and sent for Hole-in-the-Day, who was head chief.  After he had been with them a little while the soldiers sent for me.  I went over and found them eating dinner.  As soon as I was there, they told me to eat, which I did.  The Captain sat near me.  The Captain said, 'Did you kill the Sioux?' and I replied, 'I am the man.'  Then he asked me how I killed him, and I said I used my gun.

"He said, 'What did you put in your gun?'  I told him, 'I put in powder and bullet.  Then I shot him and scalped him.'

"Then the Captain said, 'I am sent to come after you.'  I said, 'I will go along with you.'  He said, 'Have you made up your mind fully to go along with me?'  I again said, 'Yes.'

"Hole-in-the-Day then stood up and said, 'You cannot take him until I give my consent. I will bring him myself after the ice goes out.'

"The Captain said, 'You are a chief and you can bring him down when convenient.' The Captain shook hands with me and said to Hole-in-the-Day, 'Bring your son down to the fort in the spring.' Hole-in-the-Day told our hunters not to go out but to go to Fort Snelling, and about forty of us went down there in canoes. When we got near there, we sent a letter by the interpreter saying we would arrive about noon the next day. When we arrived at the landing a soldier tried to shove our canoes back. Hole-in-the-Day jumped out and kept the soldier from hurting us and sent word to the General that we were there. Then some officers came down and Hole-in-the-Day tore all my clothes off, leaving me naked. Hole-in-the-Day made himself naked and painted himself red. We walked up the hill together, the Ojibwa back of us. We were led to the flagpole. The General came out and shook hands with us. Hole-in-the-Day said to the General, 'I am here. I am Hole-in-the-Day. I promised you I would be here at this time and bring my son. I am giving my son to you. If you want to hang him, hang him; if you wish to punish him, do so; if you care to place him in the guardhouse, put him there. I give him to you.'

"I did not speak.

"'Just a minute, Hole-in-the-Day,' said the General. 'I'll wait until the Sioux arrive and you tell me then the same words in their presence.' Then the Sioux came. The General was in the center and 400 Sioux back of him, with head men scattered in front. Then the General said,' Hole-in-the-Day, speak.' And my chief repeated the same words he had said before. Then the General spoke to the Sioux: 'Hole-in-the-Day is head chief here today and he has given me his son to punish as I see fit and I shall do so accordingly.'

"After the General said this, the Sioux head man said, 'Turn this man over to us and we will punish him as we see fit.' The General said, 'No; he was given me to be punished.'

"Then the soldiers came up and put handcuffs on me while all the Indians looked on. The soldiers took me to the guardhouse and put me inside. They let me look through a small window and see what was going on.

"The Sioux would speak and then Hole-in-the-Day would answer, and they kept at it all day long. About evening I saw the soldiers with two Sioux on whom they had fastened balls and chains, and they led them to the guardhouse. The guards unlocked my door and brought me down to where the two Sioux were. We were put in the same room and guarded there. Then the guard took me back upstairs. Then I saw the Sioux march out of the fort and the Ojibwa stayed.

"After the Sioux were out of sight my guard came, unlocked my door, took off the handcuffs and hung them on the wall and brought me out. He took me to the General and when I got there the General was laughing and held out his arm and shook hands with me.

"The General patted me on the shoulder and said, 'Thank you, thank you. You have helped me capture the men I wanted.' He said, 'If ever you get in trouble my authority will protect you.' He wrote a paper and sent me to a store nearby where I was clothed  Then I returned to the General, who had me shown about the fort, and we camped all day and were guarded by soldiers so the Sioux would not bother us. Next day a steamer arrived. We saw the Sioux prisoners march down and get on the steamer and go away.

"After some time we went home and reached our country safely, being guarded part way by the soldiers."

## The Story of Mah-een-gonce

Mah-een-gonce, or Little Wolf, was a rather small Ojibwa Indian about fifty years of age. He was an inmate of the Indian boarding-house at White Earth, Minnesota, in 1909. I observed that this Indian had lost both legs at the knee, and walked about with great difficulty. On Sundays, he arrayed himself in his best garments and strapped to his knees two cork legs, on the feet of which he wore laced shoes. He managed to walk fairly well when he had on what he called his "white man's legs". I asked him how he happened to lose his feet and he told me a remarkable story of his own suffering, and sacrifice on the part of his grandfather.

"When I was twelve years old, I happened to be in camp with my parents near Crow-wing, Minnesota. At this place there were four large wigwams in which lived thirty or more Indians. One of the head men called us together and made announcement that he would move the camp to a place called Hackensack. Some of the Indians did not wish to go there, as it was snowing heavily and we were comfortably located. But Say-kash-e-gay, the head man, started in one direction with the main party, and my mother, grandmother, grandfather and myself went in another direction. Grandfather said that game was very scarce and food short in the Hackensack region, and that he thought he could take us to a small lake where we would be able to pass the winter without suffering.

"You must know that this was the winter of the great blizzard in northern Minnesota, when some people died, many suffered, and much stock of the white people froze to death.

"As we walked along, my grandmother said she did not feel well. It grew exceedingly cold and the wind blew very hard. We traveled along slowly, each helping the other through the drifting snow. We came to a little creek, and my grandfather said, 'Let us stop here'. Near this creek, my grandmother sank down exhausted. Grandfather broke dry wood and made a large fire. We put grandmother by the fire and she lay down while the rest of us moved about to warm ourselves. During the night grandmother died and grandfather carried her over the side of a big rock and placed her there. We passed a hard night; it was bitterly cold and the wind howled through the trees. Grandfather said the evil spirits in the pines were laughing at us. In the morning I felt pains in my feet and spoke to my grandfather and said, 'Grandpa, my feet hurt very much. There is something the matter with them.' He built up a big fire and helped me to remove my leggings and we warmed them by the fire, but I could not keep my feet near the heat, because of the pain I suffered.

"We had eaten the last of our food the previous evening. It continued to snow and was so cold that the limbs of the trees snapped with loud noises. My mother died of the cold about noon. After she died, we changed our position to the side of a sheltered hill and grandpa built another fire. All that afternoon and night it continued to snow. Grandfather lay down about dark near the fire, and he lay partly doubled up with his face toward the fire, and his back away from it. He put me inside the hollow his body formed, so that the fire warmed me, and his body protected my back from the cold. I felt that I was freezing. Grandfather could not keep up the fire, for he began to get stiff and he told me to throw on the wood. He held me close to him all night and said, now and then, 'Are you warm?'

"The snow continued to bank up all of the next day. Grandpa could not move about, but I managed to get wood enough to keep the fire burning. The third day we were too weak to travel. Then the sun came out, it was a beautiful day, and we heard a bell ringing in the distance.

"Grandpa said, 'That must be the bell of the Mission church. We can hear it because the air is still and cold.'

"After a long silence, grandfather said, 'My son, I cannot live. Try to get up and save your life.'

"I replied, 'No, I will not leave you. I will die with you.'

"'No,' commanded my grandfather, 'you must go. You must not stay here. You are too young to die.' And he gave me his papers, for he was a chief and had papers from Washington and a medal, and other things. I shook hands with him and told him goodbye, and started in the direction of the bell. I cut two sticks for canes to help hold me up, as my legs were like wood. I was very weak and hungry. Grandfather raised his body a little — he was half sitting up, raising himself with his hands — when I looked back at him, he looked at me and then put his head down. I went along slowly for some time. I heard some one singing. Then I thought that people were calling me. About noon I was weak and sleepy and could not go on. My legs were heavy, like logs. But it had become much warmer, so I cut down some small bushes, made a bed and lay down, very tired. While lying there my grandfather seemed to come and stand by me, and I said to him, 'Are you going along?' and he replied, 'Yes, yes, don't lie here. Get up and exert yourself like a man.'

"When I woke up it was morning and I was very stiff and cold. I had to roll over and get my feet and legs down a hill in order to stand up. I cut two more canes with which to hold me up. I struggled on most of that day and in the afternoon reached some cabins of my people. They carried me in and gave me soup and afterwards some meat chopped fine. Then my legs began to hurt me. They rubbed them with snow but that did no good. Oh, what pain I suffered! In a few days my feet began to decay, and they took me to a doctor, and he cut off both my legs. For many months afterwards I suffered tortures and wished to die.

"A few weeks later, the people went out and found my grandfather dead by the ashes of our little fire. They also recovered the bodies of my grandmother and my mother. If grandfather had not held me next to the fire, and protected me with his own body that long, cold night, I, too, would today be in the Land of the Spirits."

## Unwise Purchases

The educated Indians should take a more positive stand in the matter of protecting their more unfortunate brethren. Far be it from me to cast reflections on these persons, but truth compels the statement that a number who should have been foremost in safeguarding the interests of ignorant aborigines availed themselves of close association with their fellowmen to secure property. At White Earth, of the thirty-seven men and women mentioned in the Government affidavits as securing lands, at least a dozen were educated Indians. This sad fact impressed Inspector Linnen and myself,

PARADE GROUND AND BUILDINGS IN DISTANCE

CARLISLE INDIAN SCHOOL—THE CAMPUS

and we often talked regarding it. The temptation on the part of some educated Indians is to follow the example set by white men. Let me present an illustration. In Oklahoma I met Joe B——. He informed me that forty acres of land were enough for any Indian. I said, "Joe, how many acres do you own?" "Oh, about 2,000." Joe was red, as to color, but he had the heart of the white man.

Years ago the Department of Justice began an investigation of land cases in the State of Oklahoma. Honorable A. N. Frost acted as Special Assistant to the Attorney General. Mr. Frost was asked to resign from his office a short time ago. He delivered a stirring address at the Lake Mohonk Conference this year. In this address (of which I present a part) Mr. Frost referred to the 30,000 Oklahoma land suits before the Department of Justice. According to his published statement, Senator Owen is concerned in 154 of these suits. I present excerpts from Mr. Frost's remarks herewith.

*Lake Mohonk Conference, Wednesday evening, October 14, 1914*

\* \* \* \* \* \*

"Immediately subsequent to the removal of the restrictions act of 1908 a veritable Saturnalia of deed-taking from the unrestricted allottees was carried on by the hungry land-buyers, white, red, and black. The man who has secured a prior deed from the now unrestricted allottee had the best chance to secure a new one, and he did so in thousands of cases. Many such had been secured by Senator Owen of Oklahoma, or by his agents for him. There are today pending in these bills 154 so-called cases against him for recovery of Indian lands, most of them involving restricted allottees and many now unrestricted.

\* \* \* \* \* \*

"Under the law a deed taken in pursuance of an illegal contract is as void as the illegal contract is; in the absence of a new and completely valid consideration. If the prior deed was invalid, if it was a violation of the restrictions against alienation imposed by an act of Congress and therefore totally and completely void, and if that subsequent deed was in pursuance and in furtherance of that invalid contract, then it is my firm belief that the second deed is as totally and absolutely invalid as the first. Involved in this proposition is necessarily the question of adequacy of consideration. Using the Owen unrestricted cases again solely as an illustration, I do not know whether an adequate consideration was paid or not, though an attempt was made to secure from him the necessary information to determine it, without success. If such was paid, of course, in his, as in all other cases, no further action ought to be taken by the Government. I presented this proposition of law to the Court; the Court said, that may be so, you may be right in the principle of law which you have stated, but the Government itself, the allottee being unrestricted, is without any power to bring a suit on his behalf to have that second deed cancelled. I urged upon the Department an authorization to appeal from the decision of the Court for the reason that a remedy left to the volition of the incompetent allottee is no remedy at all. Up to the time of my ceasing to be connected with the work in Oklahoma, no appeal had been authorized. I do not know why.

\*    \*    \*    \*    \*    \*

"A word in conclusion. It seems evident that there has been of late, upon the part of the Washington departments dealing with Indian affairs, a susceptibility to political influence in connection with Indian matters. I want to lift my voice in emphatic protest against the introduction of the spoils system into Indian activities. As an illustration: Mr. Mott, than whom there was no more faithful servant of the Indian people, and who has accomplished wonders in their behalf in the matter of minors' estates, was removed; he was replaced by Judge Allen as counsel for the Creek tribe of Indians. At the time, there were in the litigation I conducted some sixty odd cases to cancel deeds taken by him personally, or by a company in which he was interested, from members of the Creek tribe of which he was appointed counsel. Mr. Owen, the United States Senator, as I have said before, is involved in some 154 cases, covering full-blood and mixed-blood lands, taken from the Cherokee people. In charge of the litigation has been placed an official commonly reputed to be a personal appointee of Senator Owen, the United States attorney who was at one time himself a defendant in the suits. I do not mean by this to imply that any one, or all of these gentlemen, have not or will not accomplish much good for these people, but I do wish to contend most emphatically for the utmost singleness of purpose and freedom from all possible entanglements which might even unconsciously warp judgment in the men selected to deal with these and all Indian matters. I cite these illustrations, not for the purpose of striking at anybody in high places. It is farthest from my thoughts and I sincerely wish for them all the highest degree of success in their efforts in behalf of the Indian. What I have said with reference to them is true to an all too great degree among many other men of prominence in Oklahoma. I wish to repeat that there should be selected in connection with the litigation, in connection with all Indian affairs in the State of Oklahoma, men absolutely free from all suspicion of influence, of any kind, in order that their efforts and their work may be devoted, singly and solely, to that which will benefit the Indian allottee; and in this connection I want to say, too, that no man ever had associated with him in public work a more loyal, efficient and devoted set of men than it has been my privilege to have had in the years of my activity in Indian matters in Oklahoma. I am not among those who decry the people of the State of Oklahoma as a whole; I have lived among that people for a period of six years; I have learned to love and respect them, and to admire their enterprise and spirit of progress amid necessarily adverse circumstances, not a little of which was caused by the work I was engaged in, necessary as I believe it was.

"Arouse the citizenship of Oklahoma as you would the citizens of the State of New York or of my own State of Massachusetts, and you will find that it is composed of the same class and type of men, ready to respond at once to the call of duty to suppress wrong.

"That there exists the other class is beyond question, just as it exists elsewhere. The existence of the conditions which called forth the litigation is proof of this; but, mark you, since the institution of these suits, and as a consequence thereof, because of the work of the Commissioner to the Five Civilized Tribes and the Superintendent of Indian Affairs in the administration of their offices and in connection with these suits, a much better feeling has existed among the citizens of Oklahoma, and today you will find that except among such as have heretofore taken widespread and universally of these lands and are therefore interested personally, there are many who deprecate the wrongs as much as you or I.

"Another wrong impression I want to attempt to correct. In consequence of the litigation and other causes among them, too much generality in the discussion of these matters, statements have been made that titles in eastern Oklahoma are unsafe. Based upon my years of experience in connection with this work, necessitating the reviewing of more titles probably than ordinarily falls to the lot of any one man, I confidently make the assertion that nowhere in the United States can there be found any better titles than those in eastern Oklahoma once they have been properly acquired."

AN OJIBWA WOMAN DYING OF CONSUMPTION

After hearing her story, I drew an affidavit containing her testimony, to the effect
that she was swindled out of $20,000 worth of property, and left to die in poverty.
Unable to sit up, she requested that I take her hand and affix her
thumb print to the paper. The photograph was taken in
a room where the light was very poor, and
it has been necessary to redraw it.
March 1909, Pine Point, Minn.

# CHAPTER XXXIX. GENERAL COMMENTS AND SUGGESTIONS

There are some general observations which I desire to make prior to my conclusions. Any one of these might be expanded into an entire chapter, but since that is impracticable, it is necessary in the following pages to refer to a number of subjects both related and unrelated.

An illuminating comment as to affairs on the Great Plains between 1850 and 1880 is found in the Mormon records of their great migration from the East to Salt Lake City. There is no authentic narrative indicating a serious clash between these Mormons and the thousands of Indians whom they encountered. After their location in Salt Lake City and vicinity they preserved friendly relations with the Indians. Brigham Young made a statement, embodying the above facts, to Honorable J. V. Farwell, one of the original members of the Board of Indian Commissioners, in 1869.

People interested in Indians would do well to consult the early reports of the Board of Indian Commissioners. The first one was written in 1869 and published in 1870. Contrary to general belief, the Five Civilized Tribes, living in what was then Indian Territory, were working, building houses, fencing lands, and progressing. In other sections of the country as well there was progress to be noted. We do not need to confine our observations to the Apache country, Oklahoma or California in order to prove that the disinclination of many Indians to work, was entirely due to the fact that the Indian was suddenly removed from savagery and placed in civilization. Practically all Indians were self-supporting, prior to white domination. Otherwise, they would have soon died of starvation. The deterioration of the Indian was caused not entirely by removal of the means of livelihood (lands, game, irrigation, etc.,) but because of unwise, not to say foolish and incompetent, handling of Indian affairs. Washington is not so much to blame as is the entire country. Let us consider a specific instance at some length. Mr. John H. Seger went among the Cheyenne Indians in 1872. From Darlington, Oklahoma, he ran a stage to Fort Elliot, Texas, 160 miles. In 1884 the cattle men leased all the Cheyenne and Arapaho reservation west of the South Canadian River. They paid $100,000 per year, cash rent. As these Indians were drawing blankets, rations and clothing from the Government, so large a sum of money nearly ruined them. Captain J. M. Lee was appointed Agent, and after two years the Government cancelled the leasing privilege. These Indians, who formerly raised corn and hauled freight (thus earning money in addition to their free sustenance) complained, and desired to continue the leasing privilege in order that they might loaf.  Captain Lee concluded that Mr. Seger was the only man able to persuade the Indians to return to their former mode of life.  Seger was given to understand that if he learned the language, and gave up his life to the care of this band of Indians, he would be continued in the Service.  He moved the Indians sixty miles to the Washita River and founded what is known as Seger's Colony.  The story of his work among these Indians and the many difficulties he overcame makes very interesting reading.  Seger established a school and later the place was known as Seger township.  Indians soon constructed twenty-eight houses.  He labored for more than twelve years, persuaded a missionary organization to establish a mission and the last year he was in charge the net profits of the industries carried on at his school amounted to $6,993.  The story of his removal and the subsequent purchase of much of the Indians' land would be a repetition of what has occurred elsewhere in this country.  I never could understand why competent men are not retained.  Frequent removals, or changes in Washington, are of less moment, but in Indian communities much is lost and very little gained when a faithful employee, who has perfected himself in a study of his people, is removed from office and some stranger placed in his stead.

Several thousand Indians owning farms protect themselves and hold their own against white people.  They do this notwithstanding changes of men or of laws.  Such need no protection, and I have said little concerning them in this book.  I would that all Indians were so satisfactorily placed in our body politic.  As an illustration of this class of Indians, I present the following incident.

When travelling with Major Brennan across Pine Ridge reservation, I observed on the cabin of an educated Indian, who wished to protect his allotment, a large board sign which read as follows:

NOTICE

NO TRESPASSING WILL BE ALLOWED

ON MY ALLOTMENT UNDER PENALTY

OF THE LAW

———

JOHN T. BEAR

There have been a number of references in this book to Canada. Mr. Duncan C. Scott, who holds that office in Canada corresponding to our Commissioner of Indian Affairs, attended the Lake Mohonk Conference this year.  He showed us a few thin pamphlets — all the regulations, laws, statements, methods of procedure, etc., necessary in the management of Canadian Indian affairs. With us we employ skilled lawyers to fathom the intent of our legislators. They must needs delve into thousands of pages of conflicting laws, rules and statutes. And after one set of attorneys have presented their views, the mass of legal rulings is so enormous and complicated that other attorneys assigned the same task usually arrive at exactly opposite conclusions from those presented by the first corps!

Mr. Scott also informed us that when a white man marries an Indian woman in Canada, he has no part in tribal or individual property. The Government issues no deeds to the Indians, but they live on their farms

MEDAL PRESENTED BY PRESIDENT GRANT TO CHIEF RED CLOUD IN 1871

Secured from Mrs. Red Cloud and Jack Red Cloud for the Trustees of Phillips Academy, Andover, Mass., in 1909, by W. K. Moorehead. Solid silver. Full size.

as do ours. All incentive to graft is removed. The simple, effective Canadian management of Indian affairs, compared with our ponderous, complicated and ignorant handling of the same class of people in this country, points a very strong moral.

Of those who have done much on behalf of the Indian, I neglected to emphasize the work of Honorable James M. Graham, Congressman from Illinois, and Honorable Henry George, Jr., of New York.

These two gentlemen served on the Congressional Committee referred to in Chapters IV-VIII. There were other members on this same Committee, who did good work, but I believe Messrs. Graham and George were the only two who attended all of the sessions. Omitting the members of Congress already mentioned in the book, those who have been especially active in protecting Indians are Honorable Senators LaFollette, Townsend, Ashurst, Lane, Page and Gronna; and Honorable Congressmen Konop, Church, Campbell, McGuire, Miller, Lenroot, Murdock and Stevens (Nebraska).

I have tried to indicate in a number of places in this book why so many of our Indian tribes are practically at a standstill, so far as progress along lines of civilization is concerned. Put into one concrete statement, the reason for the unsatisfactory condition of many of our Indians is due to the following:— First, we have hurried them into citizenship before they were qualified to assume full responsibility. Second, many of the farms and tracts improved by Indians, after much labor, have been taken away.

Certain of the missions were very successful, and numbers of them are so at the present day. The famous Riggs family of missionaries among the Sioux, succeeded in building up communities of Christian Indians and promoting thrift and industry. Rev. Gilfillan's missions in Minnesota, and the Catholic mission near Pine Ridge are illustrations of what can be done with Indians when one has secured their confidence. So long as there is no change in management, and the Indians are not hurried, much progress on their part is sure to result. But, unfortunately, as has been indicated, we have no more than persuaded a band of Indians to become progressive than we destroy all incentive to further progress. This was done in the case of the Pima and Papago, in addition to other tribes frequently mentioned. Indians develop farms and become self-supporting only to see the result of their labor swept away. Beyond question, we have hurried the Indian, and forced allotments and citizenship upon him far too rapidly. We should have moved slowly, as they do in Canada, and avoid the dreadful scandals and the increase of disease and pauperism. The Indians are more or less confused by our numerous rulings, changes of officials, etc. An Indian said to me in Minnesota: "We used to live in the open air and were healthy. You told us to live in houses. We became sick. Now you tell us to again live in the open air. The white man has many minds."

The old method of gradual extension of civilizing influences was generally successful. And, in all sections of the country where such a plan is followed, the Indians are doing quite well. Indians can be led, or persuaded, far more satisfactorily than driven. The Navaho have never been driven, but were permitted to slowly, yet satisfactorily, progress along certain lines. An educated Indian once summed up to me our general policy with reference to the average Indian in Oklahoma:— "You put a few words of English in his mouth, a coat on his back, thrust a deed to valuable property in his hands, and send him out among shrewder white men, expecting him to hold his own."

Even the wildest Indians might have been led along the path to civilization had we approached the subject in the proper manner. Setting aside temporarily my rule not to refer to affairs prior to 1850, permit me to indicate what Rev. Zeisberger and Rev. Heckewelder accomplished in the Ohio wilderness before the American Revolution. They established missions on the Muskingum River and conducted these successfully, in spite of the fact that all the Ohio and Indiana Indians were at war with the settlers of Kentucky, Virginia and Pennsylvania. These men dealt with, and worked among, a class of Indians as hostile as many of those in the West. At the time the missions were destroyed by one Williamson and other white murderers, the chapels, houses, fenced fields, and other evidences of civilization were in advance of that exhibited in any white community lying between central Pennsylvania and the Spanish missions. The reason for the success of the Moravian mission lay in this fact: that the missionaries were permitted to labor unhampered in a remote section of the country, there were no white people near, no demoralizing influences. They did not force industry upon the natives suddenly, but by a slow and persistent policy of training and education, brought about the desired result. With us, in these modern days, in far too many places, we have not only exhibited undue haste in preparing our Indians for citizenship, but we have shown a general incompetence in managing their affairs.

There is yet another and equally important reason so many of our Indians are discouraged, or backward, or indolent. Most nations, or tribes of men, learn the lessons of life in the hard school of adversity. The Indian had his school of adversity, but the curriculum was totally different from that observed in any other institution of similar character. He had, on the one hand what Mr. Humphrey has called "the great Unselfishness" (*page 375*), and on the other the exact opposite of "the great Unselfishness." The "great Selfishness" destroyed the Indian — nothing else. The Indian found it exceedingly difficult to adapt himself to the new conditions. Through education, he was able to fathom the inconsistencies of the white man's teachings and practices. Being human, he refused to develop his property, if by so doing he merely fattened the pocketbook of some covetous white man. His vast tribal estates furnished him with moneys at stated occasions, and, relying too much upon these, he drifted into indolent habits. The unlettered aborigine, as well as the educated Indian, observed that we were continually concerned with the Indian rather than with white people responsible for the Indians' condition. This to them was inexplicable. The illustration presented me on this score by a certain educated Indian presents the thought quite forcibly. "Suppose a ranchman owned a large tract of land on which grazed some thousands of sheep. Around his ranch ranged hundreds of coyotes. The wolves frequently destroy the sheep. The ranchman is continually changing the sheep from one pasture to another, in order to avoid the wolves. He devotes all his energies to the sheep, instead of destroying the wolves."

Consider the whiskey problem, about which so much has been printed. There are laws and regulations sufficient to control this evil. Yet everyone seems concerned in preventing Indians from drinking whiskey, or arresting drunken Indians. So long as the State authorities do not enforce the laws against white men who introduce whiskey, it will be impossible to prevent Indians from drinking. Equally applicable are the laws against theft from Indians. In spite of all our investigations, few white men are ever sent to the penitentiary for swindling Indians. As in the case of whiskey, there are ample laws for the protection of Indian property and the punishment of grafters, yet they are seldom enforced. Honorable William H. Taft, ex-President of the United States, has in his public addresses frequently called attention to our lax enforcement of laws and our apparent disrespect of the courts, as compared with the high regard in which the English hold their legal machinery, and the impartial manner in which they administer justice.

All these things, in their ensemble, discourage the average Indian, just as they would affect the average white man. Prison sentences, instead of small fines, would put an end to graft and drunkenness, and would have a far-reaching effect in raising the Indian to a real citizenship. We have tried moral suasion and it has failed absolutely. Let us now employ force against the guilty.

# CHAPTER XL. CONCLUSIONS

In studying Indians, the scientist deals with facts. The historian is a scientist in that he records facts; the sociologists and persons interested in political economy and government, draw conclusions from facts. Manifestly, we should formulate our Indian policy upon scientific principles. We should be governed solely and absolutely by facts and past experiences. Yet, although our Government in all other branches of its great Service profits by human experience in our own country and elsewhere, in our handling of the Indian, it is safe to affirm that we have not heeded the lessons of the past.

The Indian policy the past two or three years has appreciably changed for the better. If the reforms instituted by Honorable Cato Sells can be carried out as planned, we shall conserve much of the Indian property that remains. The Indians still possess vast estates, and with economy and protection, there is sufficient land to care for all of them, save on a few reservations. In Oklahoma and Minnesota it will be necessary to either buy farms, or permit Indians to continue as paupers, or move them to Montana, Idaho or Nevada. The great Navaho tract, including a portion of the Public Domain, is now crowded. There can be no further increase of Navaho population in the present area. Either the Indians must have more land, or suffer. Omitting all other reservations and Indian areas, and classifying them as satisfactory (although some of them are not) the situation confronting us today may be bluntly stated as follows: — You can take no more land away from the Indians, unless you desire to make of them paupers. You cannot expect them to hold their own with the white people, unless you change their status from a paper citizenship to a real citizenship. Making of them citizens, without the ordinary protection enjoyed by other Americans, produces instead of citizens, paupers. The detailed evidence of this has been presented in previous chapters.

We all admit that we owe the Indian much. Nobody denies that we have done the individual Indian a service, through our education and civilizing influences. Why, then, is it that there is not more land under cultivation today than in 1871? Because of the conflicting rulings and laws, the breaking of treaties, the cancelling of agreements entered into by States, and, finally, the taking of individual farms. This has discouraged the average Indian.

Far be it from me to be disloyal to my own Government, but I express the firm conviction that our particular form of government is such that administration of Indian Affairs is rendered extremely difficult. Put plainly (if not bluntly), our form of government is not conducive to satisfactory management or supervision of a dependent people. The reason, as every thinking man and woman knows, is because we make the high office of Indian Affairs a political appointment. The Commissioner no more than learns his duties, and becomes competent and efficient, than he is removed and another installed in his place. Since 1834 there have been thirty-one Commissioners, and the average tenure of office is a trifle over two and one-half years. The same is true of Indian Superintendents — formerly called Agents. I never could understand why they changed the name, for the Superintendent is still an Agent. I am perfectly willing to accept the shrewd Indian's definition —"It is the same man, only he wears a different coat."

The frequent changes in the office of Commissioner has not worked to the advantage of the Indians. Since 1907 we have had three Commissioners and an acting Commissioner — F. E. Leupp, R. G. Valentine, F. H. Abbott, and Cato Sells. All of these men have been energetic and intelligent, as were their predecessors, but they have been removed, or they resigned under political pressure; and as a result those who are fighting for the Indians' rights must go over the same old story, again and again, submit and resubmit the same evidence as one appointee succeeds another. This is even true of the Honorable Secretary of the Interior himself. As an illustration, I would cite the case of French-Canadians of northern Minnesota.

After the White Earth investigation, we begged Secretary Garfield to strike from the White Earth rolls the French-Canadian element — headed by one Gus H. Beaulieu. It was contended that those persons had come down from Canada and settled themselves on the Ojibwa, and were a continual source of trouble. Enough evidence was presented to make our position impregnable. Secretary Garfield hesitated to act, and passed the matter to his successor, Mr. Ballinger, who in turn transferred it to Mr. Fisher, and it is now before Secretary Lane. If the Honorable Secretary, Mr. Garfield, had acted in the first place heroically and promptly, he would have placed the burden of proof on the shoulders of the French-Canadian element (where it properly belonged), and several pages of unpleasant American Indian history would not have been written.

Be these things as they may, they exist, and until our Congress appoints a national and paid commission to take over the entire Indian body and their property — so long as the Indian, and the Indian Office, remain political footballs, just so long will the games continue played in the old way, with no new rules, and since coaching from the side-lines is permitted, the strongest and the most brutal teams will win.

The freest and most varied opinions regarding Indian affairs are expressed at the Lake Mohonk Conferences. I have referred to them elsewhere, but I desire to repeat that at the conferences, where hundreds of missionaries, philanthropists, sociologists, Government employees and others assemble, we obtain the facts, hear recommendations, and debate on the policy concerning our wards.

The addresses delivered at these remarkable gatherings carry great weight throughout the country, for the reason that those who address the audiences have made extended observations in various parts of the field. A summary of these many opinions delivered during the past five years, indicates one general trend of thought. And that is that the end of the tribal system among the Indians is not so much at hand, as already accomplished. It requires no prophetic vision to observe the setting of the Indians' sun. All agree to this general proposition. The many scientists of our research institutions, both large and small, are energetically seeking out what little remains of tribal and aboriginal customs and beliefs. They know that in a few years it will be too late to make scientific researches among Indians. They employ patient search and much discrimination to here and there discover a smouldering ember of the ancient council fire. And, I think, it requires further energy and patience on the part of the ethnologists to fan the feeble ember until it bursts forth into flame!

The Government employee is pushing his educational problem, persuading most of the Indians to work, and improving the daily life of these people. The doctors and the field matrons use their best endeavor to establish sanitary measures, and proper home life. The great Indian schools are discharging hundreds of competent graduates; the Congressmen are removing restrictions, according citizenship, selling surplus lands, and doing all that they can to hasten the end of the Indian as a dependent body. And last of all, comes the undesirable class — the grafter and the bootlegger — one taking away the Indian property in many sections of our country, and the other debauching all Indians who have not the moral stamina to resist. The good people, and the majority, are uplifting, saving and preparing the Indian for citizenship. Working together, they are acting in the best interests of that great and new movement, known as "Social Service." Fighting against them is the undesirable element — that class responsible for the pauperizing of the Indians of Oklahoma, Minnesota, California and elsewhere. I have pointed out in previous chapters of this book both the good and the evil. The real workers —

MISS KATE BARNARD, OF OKLAHOMA.  See pages 137, 150, and 170
She is waging battle for the protection of Indian minors and orphans.

whether in the Government Service, employed by missions, members of philanthropic organizations, state officials, or private citizens — are doing their part. We may criticize some of their rulings or methods of procedure, for we all make mistakes, and no man or woman engaged in the real work of the world can avoid error. Frequently we make enemies — particularly so if we stand up for the rights of the Indian. But while this is true, the general trend is in favor of just treatment of the Indian, and the great object in view is his absorption into the body politic.

Whether this shall be accomplished depends entirely upon the relative strength between those who build up, and those who destroy. The issue is between the grafter and bootlegger, and the respectable citizen. The great Navaho is as yet unspoiled. The Sioux, the Apache, the Crow and others are doing very well. If we permit foolish or unwise legislation to dominate in the region inhabited by the tribes I have named, we shall destroy the best of that which is left, even as we have destroyed in Oklahoma and Minnesota. I have clearly pointed out the high character of the Ojibwa and the Five Civilized Tribes forty years ago as compared with the present, and that the responsibility for this decline rests with us, rather than with the Indians themselves, or the Indian Office.

Since 1834, we have gone on in a well-meaning but stupid and blundering way. We have persuaded scores of bands to take the white man's road, and by foolish legislation, wars, the crowding by Whites, etc., destroyed their original confidence in us. As if these were not sufficient, in the great State of Oklahoma, where one-third of the entire Indian body is located, we have had brought before us through reports of Commissions and individuals and a cloud of witnesses, the result of our policy. In spite of this, we have recently deliberately removed, or forced to resign, some of the persons most competent and longest in the Service in that State — Messrs. Mott, Gresham, Frost, Kelsey and Wright. What was the real reason? Did the great majority of citizens of Oklahoma — the law-abiding and upright — desire that faithful servants, who understood their duties, should be forced out? No! Because a relatively small number of oil, coal, land, timber and stock men wished to become rich. Public sentiment through the newspapers has been influenced, persons who were not interested in politics have been accused of the very thing which dominated their accusers. Politics is at the bottom of it all.

The agitation in Oklahoma, begun by the small coterie referred to, and, at the insistence of interested persons and newspapers, and not prevented by Congressmen from that State, has resulted in the present removal from office of the men best able to protect the Indians. Does all of this indicate that the Commissioner, Mr. Sells, will not protect the Indians? By no means. As I have said, he and his able assistant, Mr. Meritt, and all the officials are honorable and upright men. But they cannot stand against the wishes of Congress. The Congressmen are all honest and upright in their intentions — although two or three of them are on record as dealing in Indian lands — but they are compelled to act in accordance with the desires of their constituents. Witness the statement that the candidates for office, with very few exceptions, ran on the platform that all restrictions were to be removed and federal safeguards withdrawn (*pages 139 and 144.*)

The Commissioner, although he may prepare a method of procedure for the Judges handling Indian cases in the Probate Court (as Mr. Sells has done), is really powerless, if Congress decides to remove the few remaining safeguards in Oklahoma, or to divide up any other reservation. All Commissioners have said practically the same thing: that they stood back of the Indian, protected his rights, were in favor of progress and education, etc., etc. Statements embodying this sentiment are found in every public address of the various Commissioners during thirty years.

The Commissioner may spend years in upbuilding industry among a certain band of Indians. The moment the reservation is thrown open to settlement, most of the Indians are speedily dispossessed. If he desires to protect the water rights of the Pimas and the white people living along the Gila River w sh the water, all the Inspector's reports, and all the Commissioner's speeches, and all the Agent's protests, are in vain. The Congressmen from any of the affected districts must agree with their constituents, else they will be defeated at the next election. There are many exceptions, such as Honorable W. N. Murray of Oklahoma, Honorable Charles H. Burke of South Dakota, Honorable James M. Graham and others, who have, in spite of popular clamor, stood for the rights of the Indians.

The lack of true publicity in Indian Affairs, is also a factor working powerfully against the Indian. Between 1900 and 1909 we were given the impression that the Indian generally in the United States was in splendid condition. This had a very evil effect, in that there was no public agitation outside of the Indian Rights and the California Indian Associations for protection. The very best thing that ever happened to the Indian was the making public of dreadful conditions in California, Minnesota, Arizona, and Oklahoma.

This aroused both the officials and Congress. Victor Locke, Chief of the Choctaws, said regarding the Oklahoma exposé: —"The very day after Commissioner Moorehead's report was made public, I saw one of the county judges in the Choctaw country going from a printing-office with 750 printed notices to guardians with respect to settlement with their Indian wards."

If we had such publicity applied to every reservation, while it would be unpleasant, the taxpayers of the United States would soon realize that, unless our policy is radically changed, they will be called upon to support a vast number of homeless paupers. Beyond question, either the nation, or the respective States, will soon assume this burden. I desire to go on record as making this prophecy.

As a concrete illustration of how those high in authority have misled the public, I desire to state that Honorable James S. Sherman, Vice-President of the United States, and for some years Chairman of the House Committee on Indian Affairs, in a public address before the Lake Mohonk Conference in October, 1911, stated that the United States Government had kept all its treaties and obligations with the Indians. Respect for the high office he occupied, prevented anyone replying to this amazing and preposterous utterance. The audience was composed of 400 or more persons of prominence, and Mr. Sherman's address was reported in many newspapers, with the result that the average reader naturally concluded that those who were seeking to better the condition of the Indians were sentimentalists, and that the Government had done its full duty. If the Committee of which he was chairman took that view, we have the explanation of many of the evils of the past fifteen years. For every agreement or promise, faithfully kept by the Government, I can cite a score which the authorities either ignored or made no effort to fulfill.

"The treaties with the Indians have been gathered and published in a single volume. It may be said with confidence, that leaving out the merely formal ratifications of existing friendly relations, there is not one treaty that was negotiated in good faith by the United States."

As the final proofs of this chapter were struck, the announcement came from Washington to the effect that the Honorable Secretary of the Interior intended to grant the Indians more freedom. In Mr. Lane's report, just issued, he takes the position that as many of our Indians are intelligent, the Government should hasten the day of removal of restrictions, or withdrawal of supervision over individual Indians.

A careful study of the field, indicates that somewhere between one-third and one-half of our Indians might be immediately merged into the body politic. As against this statement, the evidence is indisputable that the remaining two-thirds (or one-half) if made free, in the full sense that term implies, will be in the same condition as the Indians of California,

CHIEF PEO-PEO-TOLEKT.  NEZ PERCE WARRIOR.  CHIEF JOSEPH'S WAR, 1877
Photographed and copyrighted by L. V. McWhorter, 1911

Minnesota, and Oklahoma. If all of our Indians were made free, and permitted to progress as the Cherokees did, prior to their removal west of the Mississippi, and until about the year 1900 in the State of Oklahoma, the Secretary's plan would succeed. But so long as the white people discriminate against Indian citizens, and the citizenship of the Indian is different from that enjoyed by ourselves, the setting free of all our Indians at this time will end in certain disaster.

## Two Plans for Indian Administration Reform

On page 26 I have referred to the great and efficient machinery of the United States Indian Office. This tremendous institution is composed of many and complicated parts, and they run smoothly. Frequently certain parts are replaced. But is this great machine operated in the best interests of the Indian and of the public? The brain responsible for the guidance, or management of this plant, and the officers in charge of its various Departments desire to produce a finished product of real value to the world. How can they do so when they must needs change their operation often, not in the real interests of a finished product, but because of political expediency?

It seems to me there are two, and only two ways, by which we may solve satisfactorily the Indian problem. Granted that a proper man is secured to occupy the position of Commissioner of Indian Affairs, that man should remain in office ten or fifteen years. England seldom makes mistakes in her management of a dependent people. When a good man is found, he is continued in office until he understands his people thoroughly. With us the reverse is true. The Commissioner of Indian Affairs has no real advisory body with whom to consult, except the committees in Congress. Naturally, more or less politics creep into the Office through such arrangement. Thirty years ago the United States Board of Indian Commissioners consulted and advised with the Commissioner of Indian Affairs. There is no reason why such a sensible arrangement is not carried into effect today. If the Board stood between the Commissioner and the Congressional Committees, a Commissioner would not be forced to accept decisions which he believed were inimical to the best interests of the Indians. Assuming that the Commissioner was continued in office ten or fifteen years, and that the Board frequently met with him, unwise legislative acts would not be common — as at present.

While the first suggestion has its merits, it seems to me that the plan proposed in the Lake Mohonk platform October, 1913, presents the most practical solution of the Indian problem.  One of the speakers advocated a paid National Commission to take the place of the Commissioner of Indian Affairs and the Board of Indian Commissioners.  In view of the fact that the welfare of 330,000 human beings and $1,200,000,000 worth of property are involved, he proposed the National Commission idea. This has caused considerable discussion.  Some critics contended that nine were too many, that the Commission should be composed of seven. Others thought that five would be sufficient.  Honorable Senator Joe Robinson of Arkansas, last winter, having heard of the Mohonk platform, introduced a bill appointing a Commission of three.  Mr. Sells and Mr. Meritt were to be two of the Commissioners, and some one else would be selected as third member.  This would not solve the problem, since such a commission would be political — although the members were all personally above criticism.

The Board of Indian Commissioners, serving in honorary capacity, cannot devote sufficient time for investigation of conditions on the reservations, and in Indian communities.  Its members are all exceedingly busy men.  They have given much time, in spite of their other callings, to the work, as I have indicated in previous pages.

The Commissioner himself, able though he be, in my humble opinion is beset by political considerations — which is no fault of his own.

A high Commission in charge of our Philippine affairs with the work differentiated, and responsibilities placed upon each Commissioner, has resulted in a development of the Islands which has attracted the attention of the world during the brief period since the Spanish War.  A similar commission of men of recognized qualifications, is entirely practicable in Indian affairs.

The Mohonk recommendation is absolutely sound.  The seven men would divide the work between them, one having charge of education, another of health, a third of citizenship, a fourth irrigation, a fifth finance — and so on through the list.  Having assumed control, the office of Commissioner and that of the honorary Board would be abolished.  The hearings of this Commission would be open, quarterly reports would be published, and its findings made public.  Its first duty would be to compile a roll, based on ethnological lines, of the full-blood and mixed-blood Indians. All competent educated Indians could be immediately eliminated from Government supervision.  They would thus become citizens and cease to be included in the Indian body.  The property of every ignorant full-blood, minor child, or incompetent would be restricted for twenty-five years, thus enabling all Indians to have reached adult age.

The Fading Sunset

We owe it to the American Indian that the Commission idea be carried into effect. Politics would not interfere with the Commission, for the reason that its public hearings would be reported in the papers, the good citizens, as well as the undesirable class, would either attend the hearings or familiarize themselves with the quarterly reports. Thus a general steal would be impossible. A single Commissioner cannot make all of his business public, and much that he does never reaches the light of publicity. In fact, I believe that because the Commissioner cannot take the public into his confidence, abuses are bound to occur. Often it remains for the Indian Rights Association, or other organizations, to appeal to the public and do that which the Indian Office should establish without outside influence. There would be far less incentive to dishonesty, were covetous white men compelled to deal with a Commission instead of an individual. The publication of the Board's hearings and findings would have a deterrent effect on certain men who otherwise appeal to Senators or Congressmen.

I have often contrasted the work of Dr. W. T. Grenfell in Labrador with that of organizations laboring among our Indians. We are not responsible for the condition of the fishermen in Labrador, and they are numerically but a fraction as compared with our total Indian population. Yet Dr. Grenfell, through his lectures and publications has aroused such an interest in this country that he can collect for his Labrador work a sum far greater than that expended in support of six Indian missions. People are interested in him and his work because of the appeal he makes. The Labrador fishermen suffer no wrongs compared with our Indians, and their condition is far better than that of the average aborigine. Similar publicity given to Indian affairs through the reports and hearings of a National Commission, would arouse the American people, and a brighter day for the Indian would certainly dawn.

No matter what is said, the Commissioner must fight alone and single-handed with the members of Congress. His is a great responsibility. Both Mr. Leupp and Mr. Valentine, in conversations with me, have admitted that the chief difficulty in handling the Indian problem is found in the word "politics". The Commissioner is dependent on Congress for his appropriations. He may be sustained or opposed by members of Congress, and the public will remain in ignorance. He may not appeal save to the Secretary of the Interior. He must keep in mind the wishes of his political party. He will not admit political pressure when in office, but after leaving the Service, he may tell his story of trouble with politicians, as Mr. Leupp has in his book. Mr. Valentine could enlighten us further on "The Indian Office in Politics", did he care to speak. A paid National Commission would be dominated by *no* political party. Ten years' service would enable it to become entirely familiar with the needs of the Indians, whereas the average Commissioner, serving less than three years, barely becomes acquainted with the problem when he is succeeded by a new appointee.

I recommend to the earnest consideration of the American people the Commission idea, as the only means of salvation of the American Indian. It will be said by critics that many of the tribes are making satisfactory progress and need no Commission; that the present organization of the Indian Office is sufficient. This is partly true, but a study of the table of statistics, and reference to the testimony submitted in this book, establishes the sad fact, that the majority of the Indians must lose unless we make a radical change in our policy. It is useless to blind our eyes to hard facts; and these are that we develop a certain area after painstaking labor, and then through unwise acts (or legislation) we destroy the very tracts we have improved.

The Indian must ultimately be merged into the body politic, as has been affirmed. But in bringing about this deseratum, it is not necessary to crush all happiness out of his life. For fifty years the Indian has followed a devious and uncertain trail, in the fond hope that he might reach his journey's end. If men and women, who through unintentional ignorance have given no heed to the welfare of our red Americans, will interest their Representatives in Congress, and also help to crystallize public opinion against further harmful legislation, it is quite possible that the National Commission plan may be carried into effect. After many years of study of the subject, I firmly believe that the welfare of the Indian depends upon the creation of such a Commission as has been indicated — one composed *not* of those interested in political parties, but on the contrary of competent men who understand Indians and their needs, of men who are willing to devote the best years of their lives to transforming the rough, uncertain trail along which the Indian has toiled, into a broad highway, upon which the Red Man may safely travel to his ultimate destination—the civilized community. And having reached the end of his journey, the Indian will live henceforth peacefully, and enjoy to the full the blessings of liberty, equality and justice.

# INDEX

# 440                    INDEX